Business and Human Rights in Southeast Asia

Business and human rights has emerged as a distinct field within the corporate governance movement. The endorsement by the United Nations Human Rights Council of a new set of Guiding Principles for Business and Human Rights in 2011 reinforces the State's duty to protect against human rights abuses by third parties, including business; the corporate responsibility to respect human rights; and greater access by victims to effective remedy, both judicial and non-judicial.

This book draws on the UN Guiding Principles and recent national plans of action to provide an overview of relevant developments within the ASEAN region. Bridging theory and practice, the editors have positioned this book at the intersection of human rights risk and its regulation. Chapter authors discuss the implications of key case-studies undertaken across the region and various sectors, with a particular focus on extractive industries, the environment and infrastructure projects. Topics covered include: due diligence and the role of audits; businesses' responsibilities to women and children; and the mitigation of human rights risks in the region's emerging markets. The book sheds light on how stakeholders currently approach business and human rights, and explores how the role of ASEAN States, and that of the institution itself, may be strengthened. In doing so, the book identifies critical challenges and opportunities that lie ahead for the region in relation to business and human rights.

This book will be of excellent use and interest to scholars, practitioners and students of human rights, business and company law, international law and corporate governance.

Mahdev Mohan is Assistant Professor of Law at the Singapore Management University, where he directs the Asian Business and Rule of Law initiative. He is also an Advocate and Solicitor of the Singapore Supreme Court, Executive Director of the Singapore Society of International Law and an Associate Member of Temple Garden Chambers in London.

Cynthia Morel is Special Advisor to the Asian Business and Rule of Law initiative at the Singapore Management University and a member of the advisory group to the Human Rights Committee of the Law Society of England and Wales. She additionally serves as a legal consultant on matters relating to land, governance and equality.

Routledge Research in Human Rights Law

Available titles in this series include:

The Right to Development in International Law
The case of Pakistan
Khurshid Iqbal

Global Health and Human Rights
Legal and philosophical perspectives
John Harrington and Maria Stuttaford

The Right to Religious Freedom in International Law
Between group rights and individual rights
Anat Scolnicov

Emerging Areas of Human Rights in the 21st Century
The role of the Universal Declaration of Human Rights
Marco Odello and Sofia Cavandoli

The Human Right to Water and its Application in the Occupied Palestinian Territories
Amanda Cahill

International Human Rights Law and Domestic Violence
The effectiveness of international human rights law
Ronagh McQuigg

Human Rights in the Asia-Pacific Region
Towards institution building
Hitoshi Nasu and Ben Saul

Human Rights Monitoring Mechanisms of the Council of Europe
Gauthier de Beco

The Positive Obligations of the State under the European Convention of Human Rights
Dimitris Xenos

Vindicating Socio-Economic Rights
International standards and comparative experiences
Paul O'Connell

The EU as a 'Global Player' in Human Rights?
Jan Wetzel

Regulating Corporate Human Rights Violations
Humanizing business
Surya Deva

The UN Committee on Economic, Social and Cultural Rights
The law, process and practice
Marco Odello and Francesco Seatzu

Business and Human Rights in Southeast Asia

Risk and the Regulatory Turn

Edited by Mahdev Mohan and Cynthia Morel

Routledge
Taylor & Francis Group

LONDON AND NEW YORK

First published 2015
by Routledge
2 Park Square, Milton Park, Abingdon, Oxon, OX14 4RN

and by Routledge
711 Third Avenue, New York, NY 10017

Routledge is an imprint of the Taylor & Francis Group, an informa business

British Library Cataloguing in Publication Data
A catalogue record for this book is available from the British Library

Library of Congress Cataloguing in Publication data
  Business and human rights in Southeast Asia : risk and the regulatory turn / edited by Mahdev Mohan, Cynthia Morel.
    pages   cm – (Routledge research in human rights law)
  Includes index.
  1. Human rights–Southeast Asia.   2. Social responsibility of business–Southeast Asia.   3. International business enterprises–Law and legislation–Southeast Asia.   4. Corporate governance–Law and legislation–Southeast Asia.   5. United Nations Human Rights Council.   I. Mohan, Mahdev, editor of compilation.   II. Morel, Cynthia, editor of compilation.
  KNC572.B87   2014
  342.5908′5–dc23
  2014014885

ISBN: 978-0-415-70745-9 (hbk)
ISBN: 978-1-315-86764-9 (ebk)

Typeset in Baskerville
by Out of House Publishing

To:
Vinita.

To:
Madeleine & Zoë.

Contents

Contributors

Editors and chapter authors

Mahdev Mohan is Assistant Professor of Law and directs the Asian Business and Rule of Law initiative at the Singapore Management University. A former Fulbright scholar, Mahdev's research and writing in the fields of international law and conflict resolution have been awarded Stanford University's Carl Mason Franklin Jr Prize for International Law and the Richard S. Goldsmith Research Grant for International Conflict and Negotiation. He has a background in commercial and international dispute resolution, and is an Associate Member of Temple Garden Chambers' public international law practice. He is also the Executive Director of the Society of International Law (Singapore). Mahdev is the editor of the *Journal of East Asia and International Law* and writes on international law, investment arbitration and human rights in Asia. Mahdev represents genocide victims before the UN-backed Khmer Rouge Tribunal. He is a member of the Africa/Asia coalition that has been commissioned by the United Nations Working Group on Business and Human Rights to assist with crafting a structured template for use by business, government and civil society.

Cynthia Morel has been an adviser to the Asian Business and Rule of Law initiative at the Singapore Management University since 2011. In that capacity, she has contributed to submissions to various bodies, including the UN Working Group on Human Rights and Transnational Corporations. She additionally helped conceptualize and coordinate SMU's first Summer Institute on Business and Human Rights in 2012, an initiative which informed this publication. Cynthia has concurrently served as a consultant to ASEAN-based and international non-governmental organizations on matters relating to large-scale land acquisitions, community stakeholder engagement and advocacy strategies for rights-based development. Prior to moving to Asia, Cynthia established Minority Rights Group International's strategic litigation programme in 2002. In her capacity as founding legal officer, and later as senior legal adviser, she spearheaded landmark cases before the European Court of Human Rights and the African Commission on Human and Peoples' Rights. She has also litigated on behalf of the Open Society Justice Initiative.

Editorial assistants

Lisa Farrah Ho and **Kexian Ng** are research assistant and researcher, respectively, with the Asian Business and Rule of Law initiative at the Singapore Management University.

Other chapter authors

Philip Cook is the founder and current Executive Director of the International Institute for Child Rights and Development (IICRD). Since 1991, Philip has overseen the Institute's growth as a leader in developmental approaches to systems supporting youth and children's rights in the context of human development, good governance and human security across diverse cultures and situational contexts. During this time, the Institute has been working in partnership with a cross section of UN agencies (e.g. UNICEF, UNESCO, WHO, UNDP), governments (e.g. Canada, South Africa, Malawi, Philippines, Russia, Cuba, Thailand, Myanmar, Cambodia, Indonesia, Mexico, Colombia, Venezuela, Brazil, East Timor, Jordan, Egypt), government aid agencies, various international non-governmental organizations, foundations and the private sector, as well as with children, youth and families. These partnerships have resulted in successful interventions at the local, national and regional levels in relation to early childhood protection, children affected by HIV/AIDS, children affected by natural disasters, children affected by migration and trafficking and indigenous child protection.

Kathryn Dovey has been working within the field of business and human rights issues for almost a decade. From 2009 to 2014 she was a Director of the Global Business Initiative on Human Rights, a business-led programme focused on implementing the United Nations Guiding Principles on business and human rights within companies. Prior to this, she worked as part of the Secretariat of the Business Leaders Initiative on Human Rights. Kathryn has also been involved in several projects designed to draw attention to gender issues within the business and human rights movement. To date, Kathryn has provided business and human rights expertise in a variety of countries, including Brazil, China, Colombia, Egypt, Ghana, India, Jordan, Liberia, Myanmar, Russia and the United Arab Emirates. She holds an LLM from McGill University, Montreal, and an LLB/Maitrise from King's College London and Paris I Panthéon-Sorbonne.

Mark Hodge has been working in the field of sustainability and corporate responsibility since 1999. In recent years, his work on business and human rights has been focused on engaging with companies, civil society and governments in emerging and developing markets. Mark has undertaken field visits, assessments and training about human rights and business in a range of countries, including Colombia, Vietnam, Thailand, Bangladesh, Malaysia, the UAE, South Korea and multiple locations within India.

James Kallman is President Director of Moores Rowland Mazars Indonesia. As an emerging markets veteran, it is almost 30 years since James first made his home in Asia. Observations during that time have increasingly led him to realize the need to incorporate respect for human rights into business culture. James played an instrumental role in the development of the Moores Rowland Mazars proprietary human rights audit methodology. Moreover, based on experience gained from the use of this methodology, he has also been involved in a joint project with Shift to develop a pair of complementary international and widely accepted standards for auditing companies based on the UN Guiding Principles for Business and Human Rights. In November 2013, James was awarded the President's Achievement Award from Association of Chartered Certified Accountants (ACCA) – an award bestowed on individuals who exemplify ACCA's core values of accountability, diversity, innovation, integrity and opportunity, and granted in recognition of outstanding contributions to the development of the accountancy and finance profession.

Deanna Kemp is Deputy Director of Industry Engagement and Community Relations. As Principal Research Fellow at the Centre for Social Responsibility in Mining (CSRM), The University of Queensland, Deanna leads an international programme of work and research focused on the social dimensions of mining. Deanna engages with industry, government, civil-society groups and mine-affected communities through applied research, advisory work and education. Prior to joining CSRM, she held senior positions in the mining industry. She has also collaborated with non-government organizations on industry-related campaigns and capacity-building programmes. Deanna has published widely on topics such as company–community conflict, community development, grievance mechanisms and community relations in mining as a professional field of practice.

Daniel King works as a legal adviser to environmental and human rights public-interest lawyers in the six Mekong River countries (Cambodia, China, Lao PDR, Myanmar, Thailand and Vietnam). Before this, Daniel worked as a legal adviser to Cambodian lawyers representing urban, rural and indigenous communities fighting for their land rights. He has experience with international legal advocacy and community engagement. Daniel has also worked as a lawyer in the environment and planning jurisdiction in Australia, representing both corporate and public-interest clients. Daniel holds a Bachelor of Social Sciences and Bachelor of Laws from Sydney University and is completing a Masters of Public and International Law at Melbourne University. He is admitted to legal practice in New South Wales, Australia.

Delphia Lim was the project leader of a regional baseline study by the Human Rights Resource Centre in ASEAN on the role played by ASEAN States in protecting against business-related human rights abuses. She has also conducted research and policy analysis regarding ASEAN's business and human rights challenges with the Asian Business and Rule of Law Initiative at the Singapore

Management University and the Institute for Human Rights and Business. Delphia has law degrees from the National University of Singapore and Harvard Law School, and has practised commercial litigation as an advocate and solicitor of the Supreme Court of Singapore. She is presently a staff attorney with Accountability Counsel, a non-profit organization specializing in non-judicial grievance mechanisms for development projects.

Geetanjali Mukherjee was the senior research coordinator and author of the Lao PDR country report for the baseline study on business and human rights by the Human Rights Resource Centre in ASEAN. She has also conducted research on sustainability, business and human rights and transitional justice in South and Southeast Asia at the Asian Business and Rule of Law initiative at the Singapore Management University. Geetanjali holds a degree in law from the University of Warwick, UK, and a Masters in Public Policy from Cornell University. She received the Everett Public Service Fellowship in 2008 to work with the Asia Division, Human Rights Watch, on post-conflict transition issues in Nepal, Sri Lanka and Bangladesh.

Kerri-Ann O'Neill is Aviva's Head of Corporate Responsibility, Communications and Engagement (Asia), based in Singapore. Kerri-Ann is also co-lead for Aviva's Human Rights Practice within the Corporate Responsibility function alongside her colleague Joanne Goddard, responsible for strengthening the integration, embedding and communication of human rights within the insurance division. Aviva is an international insurer offering life and general insurance and asset management to over 32 million customers in 17 countries, 8 of which are in Asia. Kerri-Ann has recently spearheaded Aviva's work to support street-connected children's rights in Asia, leading to innovative collaborations across the region involving government, the Office for the High Commission of Human Rights, business, non-government organizations and academia, as well as street-connected children themselves.

John Owen is an Honorary Senior Fellow at the Centre for Social Responsibility in Mining, University of Queensland. His current academic interests focus largely on the problem of social knowledge and professional integration in the resources sector. Recent research projects have seen this interest applied to the planning, implementation and evaluation of involuntary resettlement programmes throughout the Asia Pacific region.

Bobbie Sta. Maria is the Southeast Asia Researcher and Representative of the Business and Human Rights Resource Centre, currently based in Myanmar. She previously served as Southeast Asia Legal Coordinator of EarthRights International, working from their Thailand office. In that role, she worked with advocates from the Mekong region to seek redress for corporate human rights and environmental abuses, and to engage regional mechanisms in an effort to promote the rule of law. Prior to working with EarthRights, Bobbie worked at Saligan (Alternative Legal Assistance Center) in the Philippines. Her work involved litigating land rights, environmental rights and domestic violence cases, advocating for agrarian reform and gender policy laws, and training paralegals in rural areas. Bobbie is a member of the Philippine Bar, and has a Bachelor of Laws from the University of the Philippines and a Masters of Human Rights and Democratisation from the University of Sydney.

Vani Sathisan is an International Legal Adviser to the International Commission of Jurists and works on matters relating to business and human rights in Myanmar. As a former Research Associate at the Asian Business and Rule of Law initiative at the Singapore Management University, she has undertaken research on responsible investment relating to land acquisitions and extractive industries in Southeast Asia, and has assisted with direct impact litigation before the UN-backed Khmer Rouge Tribunal.

Puvan Selvanathan is a member of the United Nations Working Group on the issue of human rights and transnational corporations and other business enterprises. He currently leads the development of new business principles for sustainable agriculture at the UN Global Compact and was formerly Chief Sustainability Officer to the Sime Darby Group, the world's largest producer of sustainable palm oil. He is also an adviser to the Asian Business and Rule of Law initiative at the Singapore Management University.

Bindu Sharma serves as the Asia-Pacific Policy Director at the International Centre for Missing and Exploited Children (ICMEC), based in Singapore. She leads the ICMEC programme in the region, establishing international relationships and partnerships, creating awareness and developing programme strategies for combating child sexual exploitation and abuse. Bindu is concurrently a Researcher at the Lien Centre for Social Innovation at Singapore Management University, authoring an upcoming study on the Asian Context of Corporate Social Responsibility. She is also on the Advisory Council of the International Centre for Not-for-Profit Law (ICNL), USA. Bindu holds Master of Arts degrees in Public Policy and International Development from the Sanford School of Public Policy, Duke University, USA.

Thomas Thomas is the CEO of the ASEAN CSR Network, a coalition of corporate social responsibility (CSR) networks in ASEAN. Thomas is also an Honorary Professor of CSR with the Nottingham University Business School, UK; a member of the UN Economic and Social Commission for Asia Pacific's Business Advisory Council; and the leader of the ASEAN Intergovernmental Commission on Human Rights study team on CSR in ASEAN. Thomas was the founding Executive Director of the Singapore Compact for CSR, the national CSR society in Singapore and co-chaired the National Tripartite Initiative for CSR that formed the Singapore Compact. He was the Singapore focal point for UN Global Compact. He was also involved in developing the ISO 26000 international guidance standard on social responsibility. Thomas has been active with trade unions, cooperatives, the consumer movement and social enterprises. He was also a Nominated Member of Parliament in Singapore.

Salil Tripathi is Director of Emerging Issues at the Institute for Human Rights and Business, where he has worked in Myanmar on issues such as land, conflict, information technology and mega-sporting events. Earlier at Amnesty International, he undertook research in Nigeria and Bosnia-Herzegovina and developed Amnesty's work on corruption, corporate complicity, privatization and sanctions. He also participated in negotiations that created the Kimberley Process Certification Scheme and the Voluntary Principles for Security and Human Rights. Later, at International Alert, he assessed conflict impact in Colombia and was part of the research team that developed the Red Flags initiative. He is on corporate citizenship panels at GE and Exxon, an adviser to the Global Business Initiative on Human Rights and the Asian Business and Rule of Law initiative at the Singapore Management University, and has been a non-resident visiting fellow at the Harvard Kennedy School. Salil graduated with a Master's in business administration from the Tuck School at Dartmouth College in the United States.

Christopher L. Yeomans is an international development consultant of conflict transformation, child protection and child development, working in a variety of programme management and evaluation capacities, with 18 years' experience across four continents. He has extensive experience in conflict resolution services, published research/diagnostics and analysis, public/private sector community and environmental mediation, capacity development and process facilitation. As the Programs Director for the International Institute for Child Rights and Development (IICRD), he has managed and been responsible for monitoring and evaluation of field staff and project results for multi-year, multi-million dollar programmes globally. Christopher has taught as associate faculty at Royal Roads University's (RRU) School for Peace and Conflict and for its joint IICRD/RRU Child Protection in Development Programme.

Foreword

The adoption of the UN Guiding Principles on Business and Human Rights in 2011 was a significant development in the recognition of the need to regulate the activities of corporations that abuse human rights. However, the application and implementation of this and other developments in the area has too often been seen solely through the lens of transnational corporations domiciled in Western European and North American industrialized states or by observing those states' actions in relation to the activities of transnational corporations operating in developing states. Yet if these developments are to be effective globally, it is essential that a much broader view is taken.

This book brings a strong and clear vision of the position in Southeast Asia on business and human rights. It considers the prospect of a 'regulatory turn', a development that is noteworthy and one that is conditioned and mediated by Southeast Asia's context, and that holds lessons for other regions, especially in the global South. A strength of this book is in its breadth of coverage combined with its depth of understanding. The authors' expertise ranges across the social sciences, business and law, including social and public policy, international development, business management, political science, human rights and public and international law. Their experiences include management of corporations, leading non-governmental organizations, diplomatic, parliamentary and academic careers, work in international organizations and close engagement with both communities and corporations.

Indeed, it is this depth of understanding of the position on the ground in the region that is evident in this book. Specific examples are given, a diversity of situations described and analysed, detailed examination of some human rights provided and the relevant case law considered. This is accomplished in the context of their awareness of the complexities and diversities of the situation in Southeast Asian states, corporations and communities. They show the need to consider risk and regulation, expectations and practices, laws and implementation, institutions and communities, litigation and consultation, and intentions and finances, as well as the differences between corporate social responsibility and human rights, between laws, policies and practices, and between international, regional and national regulations. It is very clear from this analysis that for business and human rights developments to be effectively implemented in Southeast Asia, much further active engagement by governments, institutions, courts, corporations, public and private sectors, civil society, communities and individuals is required.

The combination of these chapters, so well brought together by the editors of the book, provides a map of the Southeast Asian region in relation to business and human rights. This map is multi-layered and intricate, with the contours of the activity on the ground indicated in a way that is accessible and informative.

This book does much to offer new insights, and to advance understanding and action, in this important area.

Professor Robert McCorquodale
Director, British Institute of International and Comparative Law

Preface and acknowledgements

This book draws from conferences, meetings, multi-stakeholder forums and courses held in America, Europe and Asia under the auspices of or in collaboration with the Asian Business & Rule of Law Initiative at the Singapore Management University (SMU) since the initiative's inception in 2010. In particular, a summer institute held in Singapore in 2012 underscored the paucity of systematic academic analysis available at the intersection of corporate regulatory responsibility and human rights in Southeast Asia.

We also noted the absence of a suitable book to guide our teaching. This book aims to be a scholarly yet accessible source for academics, students and professionals. It examines a wide range of issues of contemporary relevance to the emerging discipline of business and human rights and is organized around our conceptual frame, 'the regulatory turn'.

As the discipline of business and human rights does not always focus on law alone, and one of our aims is to help legal scholars and lawyers engage with inter-disciplinary scholarship, this book has a policy-relevant aim as well. The book hopes to complement the ASEAN Inter-Governmental Commission on Human Rights' (AICHR) inaugural thematic study on Corporate Social Responsibility and Human Rights, recently published in June 2014. AICHR's commitment to this thematic area as the region embraces economic integration provides a window to the contours of the regulatory turn.

This book looks within and without, as chapters have been penned by regional experts, such as the leader of the AICHR study, as well as by thought-leaders from London-based think-tanks. We are thankful to the Human Rights Resource Centre for ASEAN, led by Marzuki Darusman and David Cohen, AICHR's Rafendi Djamin and Richard Magnus, and former ASEAN Secretary-General Ong Keng Yong for their unflinching commitment to stimulating dialogue, disseminating best practices and developing databases for the improvement of business and human rights standards across the region.

In the process, we hope that this book will inform initiatives by national, regional and international commissions and bodies, including the United Nations Working Group on Transnational Business and Human Rights (UNWG), which has commissioned a coalition, including SMU, to contribute to a structured template for national action plans in Asia and Africa. We also hope that responsible businesses will refer to this book in assessing and responding to human rights risks in their operating contexts.

We are enormously indebted to Robert McCorquodale, Makarim Wibisono, Puvan Selvanathan, Sumi Dhanarajan, Donna Guest, Vicky Bowman and the 2013 Academic Fellows of the Rockefeller Foundation's Bellagio Center and others who have had faith in the importance of this book and who have variously authored the foreword and afterword, or have provided important feedback on certain chapters.

Special thanks are due to the SMU Law's faculty, researchers and students; and Santa Clara Law School's Singapore Programme, particularly Vinita Bali and Michael Flynn, for their insights. SMU's Centre for Cross-Border Commercial Law in Asia and its Sim Kee Boon Institute for Financial Economics provided support and assistance in bringing this book to completion, including by making it possible to engage our indispensable researchers Lisa Farrah Ho and Kexian Ng. The book benefited immensely from their diligent assistance. We are also grateful to Mark Sapwell and the editorial team at Taylor & Francis for painstakingly editing and improving the book, and to Sue Browning for her copy-edit.

Finally, we hope this book shows that there is an epistemic community of scholars and experts in, and working on issues relevant to, Southeast Asia in the discipline of business and human rights. Their expertise will be crucial for understanding the discipline in years to come.

Mahdev Mohan and Cynthia Morel
Singapore

Introduction

Mahdev Mohan and Cynthia Morel

In June 2011, the United Nations Human Rights Council (UNHRC) passed a historic resolution welcoming and endorsing the Guiding Principles on Business and Human Rights (GPs).[1] The GPs comprise thirty-one principles, each with commentary elaborating its meaning and implications for law, policy and practice. The GPs are designed to 'operationalize' the 2008 *Protect, Respect and Remedy* Framework for Business and Human Rights (Framework),[2] and were the culmination of a series of carefully considered multi-stakeholder processes involving representatives of states, businesses and civil society.[3]

The GPs have had a significant impact. International standards, including the United Nations Global Compact's Ten Principles, the Organisation for Economic Co-operation and Development (OECD) Guidelines for Multinational Enterprises,[4] and the International Finance Corporation (IFC)'s Performance Standards on Environmental and Social Sustainability,[5] have been updated to reflect aspects of the GPs. Elements of the GPs have been or are being acted upon

[1] Report of the Special Representative of the Secretary-General on the issue of human rights and transnational corporations and other business enterprises, John Ruggie, *Guiding Principles on Business and Human Rights: Implementing the United Nations 'Protect, Respect and Remedy' Framework*, UNHRC, 17th Sess, UN Doc A/HRC/17/31 (2011).

[2] Report of the Special Representative of the Secretary-General on the issues of human rights and transnational corporations and other business enterprises, John Ruggie, *Protect, Respect and Remedy: A Framework for Business and Human Rights*, UNHRC, 8th Sess, UN Doc A/HRC/8/5 (7 April 2008).

[3] John G. Ruggie, *Just Business: Multinational Corporations and Human Rights* (Norton Global Ethics Series, 2013). The UNGPs have been described as an example of polycentric governance. See Larry Cata Backer, 'On the Evolution of the United Nations', "Protect-Respect-Remedy" Project: The State, the Corporation and Human Rights in a Global Governance Context', (2011) 9 *Santa Clara Journal of International Law* 37.

[4] Organisation for Economic Co-operation and Development, *OECD Guidelines for Multinational Enterprises* (OECD Publishing, revised edn, 2011), p. 3 ('OECD Guidelines').

[5] International Finance Corporation's Performance Standards on Environmental and Social Sustainability, 1 January 2012.

by individual governments through domestic legislation and national action plans, or in the form of discrete legal and policy measures.[6]

In the words of Professor John Ruggie, the former United Nations Special Representative to the Secretary-General on Business and Human Rights, 'the Council's resolution establishes the (GPs) as the authoritative global reference point for business and human rights'.[7] Additionally, the UNHRC, through resolution A/HRC/17/4, established a working group consisting of five experts from across the world. The working group on the issue of human rights and transnational corporations and other business enterprises (Working Group) is tasked with the promotion and implementation of the GPs.

'New territory'

The resolution also envisions an annual multi-stakeholder forum to address challenges encountered while implementing the GPs. Put simply, the Working Group's mandate is translating the GPs from paper into practice. At the first annual Forum on Business and Human Rights in 2012 in Geneva, Dr Puvan Selvanathan, a co-author of one of the chapters of this book, in his capacity as then Working Group Chairperson, stated that 'going forward, the Working Group aims to include regional consultations as part of the Forum process and encourage participants to show the courage that is needed to take the [GPs] into new territory'.[8] Since 2011, the Singapore Management University's Asian Business and Rule of Law initiative has organized and conducted multi-site applied research projects, academic and executive education courses; and held regular dialogues with relevant UN bodies and specialized agencies to strengthen engagement towards the effective and comprehensive dissemination and implementation of the GPs in Southeast Asia (SEA).

We agree with Dr Selvanathan and believe that the time is ripe for entering 'new territory' in SEA, but would add that the GPs' legacy in the region depends on their context-sensitive application. There are significant concerns that the move towards integration and sustainable development in the Association of Southeast Asian Nations (ASEAN) will be undermined. There are fears that these countries with rapidly developing extractive industries will fall prey to the 'resource curse', i.e. the paradox that countries with an abundance of natural resources tend to have

---

[6]   John G. Ruggie, *A UN Business and Human Rights Treaty?*, Harvard Kennedy School, An Issues Brief by John G. Ruggie, 28 January 2014. The GPs have been globally received and applied in various forms in this regard 'by the European Union (for example, through its new corporate social responsibility policy and mandatory non-financial reporting requirements); the International Finance Corporation (through its new sustainability framework and some performance standards); ASEAN (where the Intergovernmental Commission on Human Rights is drawing on the GPs in its own work); the African Union (in relation to the Africa Mining Vision); the International Organization for Standardization (ISO 26000); and the Equator Principles Banks (covering three–fourths of all international project financing)', http://business-humanrights.org/media/documents/ruggie-on-un-business-human-rights-treaty-jan-2014.pdf, accessed 8 May 2014.

[7]   *Guiding Principles on Business and Human Rights: Implementing the United Nations 'Protect, Respect and Remedy' Framework*, A/HRC/17/31.

[8]   A/HRC/FBHR/2012/4, p. 23.

less economic growth than countries without these natural resources.[9] However, there is a paucity of systematic interdisciplinary research and analysis needed to properly inform and support risk-management initiatives in the region.

For such implementation to take place in SEA, there needs to be a keen appreciation of unique regional developments and trends that are informed by scholarly research and sustained action to embed the GPs. Importantly, we believe that, to bridge theory and praxis, the *practice* of business and human rights, which lies at the core of the Working Group's overarching desire to implement the GPs, must be rooted in a responsive *academic* inquiry that permits a regulatory analysis of a region that is in flux.

Constructing a map

When it comes to charting a course in 'new territory', a map is essential. Our academic inquiry is rooted in the discipline of regulation. In regulation, space and interactions between business, government and other stakeholders are key constituents of regulatory dynamics. This concept of 'regulatory space' was first posited by Hancher and Moran,[10] and has been more recently developed by Vibert.[11] This book provides a map that will help to orientate those encountering SEA's regulatory space for the first time and who wish to implement the GPs. The map's topography of regulatory space in SEA in the field of business and human rights is also charted by reference to the related concept or 'risk management', which is inherent in the GPs.

This interplay between regulation and risk is explained by Professor Ortwin Renn: 'the term "risk" is often associated with the possibility that an undesirable state of reality (adverse effects) may occur as a result of natural events and human activities. Risk therefore is a descriptive and normative concept and … and carries the implicit message to reduce undesirable effects through appropriate modification of the causes, or less desirable, mitigation of the consequences'.[12]

The map we draw is structured around three pillars of the GPs and the attendant facets of regulation. The GPs refer to a State duty to protect human rights from abuses by non-State actors, including businesses; a corporate responsibility to respect rights, which suggests that business enterprises should adopt a human rights policy and engage in human rights due diligence in order to avoid causing or contributing to adverse human rights impacts; and the importance of access to remedy for victims, including through both judicial and non-judicial, State-based and non-State-based mechanisms.

---

[9] *The Guardian*, 'Cambodia's Oil Must Not Be the Slippery Slope to Corruption and Catastrophe', (21 June 2011); 'Revenues from Oil, Gas and Mining Must Benefit All Cambodians, New Coalition Urges', Cambodians for Resource Revenue Transparency press release, (12 June 2009); *The Economist*, 'Cambodia's Oil Resources: Blessing or Curse?', (26 February 2009).

[10] L. Hancher and M. Moran (eds), *Capitalism, Culture and Economic Regulation* (Oxford: Oxford University Press, 1989).

[11] Frank Vibert, *Regulation in an Age of Austerity: Reframing International Regulatory Principles*, LSE Global Governance Papers, 2011.

[12] O. Renn, 'Three Decades of Risk Research: Accomplishments and New Challenges', (1998), *Journal of Risk Research*, 1: 49–71.

Whereas the State duty to protect rights may reflect existing international invest-ment and human rights law, the responsibility of business enterprises to respect rights is, by contrast, rooted in societal expectations of business which are 'distinct from issues of legal liability and enforcement, which remain defined largely by national law provisions in the relevant jurisdiction'.[13] Ecuador and South Africa has boldly proposed the negotiation of a legally binding treaty on business and human rights, focused upon 'providing appropriate protection, justice and remedy', but this has not yielded the desired result at the time of writing. Nor it is clear that such a treaty would enjoy widespread and consistent acceptance by states.[14] This book nonetheless reveals that, while there has been broad acknowledgement of the GPs across SEA, the potential legal status of the principles that they enshrine is inter-preted in a variety of ways by scholars, policy-makers and practitioners.

International conventions and legal instruments will likely play a role in the continued evolution of the business and human rights regime, but to be successful they should be 'carefully constructed precision tools', addressed to specific govern-ance gaps that other means are not reaching.[15] We therefore find that a conven-tional *legal* analysis of the role and application of the GPs in SEA, as perhaps may be the case in other parts of the Global South, may be premature or inappropriate in the absence of regional and international instruments or tribunals for compli-ance and enforcement. The GPs are not an international convention as yet, and so there is no possibility of states legally binding themselves. Indeed, the GPs make clear that they do not create new international law obligations; the State duty to protect, for example, is explicitly said to reflect (rather than codify) existing obliga-tions of states under international human rights law.[16]

The research and conclusions canvassed in this book reveal that there is a strik-ing need for greater compliance, enforcement and good governance, rather than more stringent laws in the statute books. The relevant question to ask is not *where* the quantitative evidence of the GPs' uniform and efficient application is in the region. The liminal question appears to be *how* the GPs can be harmonized with

---

[13] UNGPs, at 'Commentary to Principle 11' and 'Commentary to Principle 12'. UNHRC, 26th Sess, UN Doc A/HRC/26/L.22 (24 June 2014). This resolution directs the UNHRC to establish an inter-governmental working group with the mandate to "elaborate an international legally binding instrument to regulate, in international human rights law, the activities of" business. However, there are pitfalls. According to Professor Ruggie,"from the vantage of victims, an all-encompassing business and human rights treaty negotiation is not only a bad idea; it is a profound deception". See John G. Ruggie, International Legalization in Business and Human Rights, Harvard Kennedy School, 11 June 2014, p. 6.

[14] See, for example, Ruggie, n. 6.

[15] John G. Ruggie, 'Business and Human Rights: The Evolving International Agenda', (2007), 101 *American Journal of International Law* 819.

[16] UNGPs, see note 7, at 'General Principles' and 'Commentary to Principle 1'. Some argue that the state duty to protect is often too narrowly construed in the UNGPs. International Commission of Jurists (ICJ), Needs and Options for a New International Instrument in the Field of Business and Human Rights, June 2014, p. 46. Similarly, it may be argued that the state duty to protect is too broadly stated in the UNGPs. The United Kingdom, for example, objected to the suggestion that international law imposes a general state duty to protect against abuses by non-state actors, or that such a duty is gener-ally agreed to exist as a matter of customary international law. See http://www.business-humanrights.org/media/documents/uk-comments-guiding-principles-2011.pdf, accessed 8 April 2014.

applicable regional standards and *when* they may be deployed to guide national and regional policies and practices that are designed to achieve sustainable development for states, businesses and, not least, the peoples of SEA.[17] Put differently, this decentred account of regulation asks how and when to combine different mechanisms of regulatory policy, risk management and accountability and to understand their interaction in SEA.

To begin to answer this question, this book draws together contributions from a range of disciplinary perspectives from law and the social sciences. The contributors are leading scholars and practitioners in these fields. As we shall explain, each of the book's four sections fleshes out our broad inquiry. Throughout this book, the reception of the GPs in SEA may be measured by references to, and interpretations of, the UNGPs by UN human rights treaty bodies, the universal periodic review process, UN special procedures mandates, regional human rights treaty bodies and other similar sources of international law. The overall taxonomy is intended to provide a descriptive sense of the breadth and scope in approaches to regulation in the context of the GPs.

Chapter overview

Part I of the book demonstrates that, while countries in SEA have not attained a uniform singularity of purpose in their reception of the GPs, ASEAN has taken strides towards adopting common human rights standards. Efforts are underway in laying the groundwork for an institutional framework to facilitate free flow of information based on each country's national laws and regulations; preventing and combating corruption; and cooperation to strengthen the rule of law, judiciary systems and legal infrastructure and good governance. In 2009, ASEAN Member States designed a 'road map', which envisions the creation of a 'rules-based Community of shared values and norms' built on three pillars – namely, an ASEAN Political-Security Community, the ASEAN Economic Community and the ASEAN Socio-Cultural Community, each with its own blueprint and infrastructure for implementation and integration. It is widely reported that the establishment of the ASEAN Economic Community (AEC) in 2015 will be an important source of growth for Southeast Asia, as it will help boost intra-regional investment and exports.

Thomas Thomas underscores these developments in Chapter 1, drawing on his experience as lead researcher for the ASEAN Intergovernmental Commission

---

[17] Evidence of such trends in the Cambodian context are outlined in Surya P. Subedi, *Report of the Special Rapporteur on the Situation of Human Rights in Cambodia: a Human Rights Analysis of Economic and Other Land Concessions in Cambodia* (11 October 2012), UN Doc A/HRC/21/63/Add.1/Rev.1, paragraph 97. The Filipino context, which is underpinned by multiple laws, rules and standards, also reveals serious challenges to implementation – challenges that are partly rooted in conflicting provisions. Similar issues arise in Indonesia, where overlapping and sometimes conflicting powers between the central, provincial and local governments translate into further conflict and lack of legal certainty for communities, companies and government officials alike at the local level. See also Study Team on Business & Human Rights of the ASEAN Intergovernmental Commission on Human Rights (AICHR), Baseline Study on the Nexus Between Corporate Social Responsibility & Human Rights: An Overview of Policies & Practices in ASEAN (13 June 2014).

on Human Rights' baseline study on the state of corporate social responsibility (CSR) in the ASEAN region. His case-study of non-financial disclosure by companies listed on the Thai and Singapore stock exchanges is noteworthy. He observes that the number of companies that have published and filed sustainability reports according to the Global Reporting Initiative (GRI) framework has doubled since 2011. Beyond these figures, his deeper question relates to the effectiveness of CSR reporting, and whether businesses domiciled in Asia are willing to acknowledge that their responsibilities with regard to human rights are no longer limited to the realm of CSR misconstrued as philanthropy. Significantly, the GPs require companies to respect human rights law; they do not permit companies to confine themselves to only those issues with which they feel comfortable.

Delphia Lim and Geetanjali Mukherjee note in Chapter 2 that ASEAN is alive to the environmental and social impact of business operations in the region. It has taken cognizance of international developments in business and human rights, leading to a degree of influence over developments across ASEAN States. They note that Indonesia in particular has, in a novel step, made CSR a wide-ranging and mandatory statutory obligation for domestic and foreign companies. Moreover, the Philippines' Revised Code of Corporate Governance, which is binding on specified types of corporations, imposes a duty to establish and maintain an alternative, non-judicial dispute resolution system for disputes within the corporation. Nevertheless, they also note that there remains a gap between the adequacy of these laws on paper and their implementation. Several of these laws remain ineffective in practice.

Kathryn Dovey's Chapter 3 explores the importance of including a gender perspective in the field of business and human rights in SEA, especially in the light of the recent ASEAN Declaration on the Elimination of Violence against Women and Elimination of Violence against Children. Examples are given throughout this chapter that relate both to SEA and to business operations globally. Specific attention is paid to female migrant workers in Malaysia, Cambodia and Thailand. Dovey notes that the premium these countries place on building export-oriented economies and attracting foreign direct investment has led to the creation of poorly regulated special economic zones, which have negative impacts for women.

In Chapter 4, Philip Cook, Bindu Sharma and Chris Yeomans carefully consider the recent General Comment on Children's Rights and Business developed by the UN Committee on the Rights of the Child (CRC), and the regional challenges in supporting children's rights in the context of ASEAN's imperative for economic integration. They note that the CRC's Concluding Observations in its review of Cambodia's national report criticized the Cambodian government's lack of a regulatory framework for multinational companies working in Cambodia. Similarly, a Concluding Observation was made to the government of Thailand, encouraging improved monitoring on the sale of children, trafficking of children and exploitative child labour practices. Finally, the chapter authors consider what role the GPs can play in protecting child rights in the context of information and communication technologies and social media.

Part II of the book provides thematic and sectoral case-studies across the region and continues to interrogate the regulatory space between State and corporate individual actors, as well as ways for State and corporate actors to manage risk and be accountable for the impact of their activities on human rights.

Daniel King's Chapter 5 critically assesses the obligations of Thai banks, which have become key financiers in the Mekong Sub-region, as Thailand moves many of its large infrastructure projects to neighbouring countries with limited institutional and regulatory frameworks, such as Myanmar and Lao PDR. He considers the case-study of the Thai banks that finance the Xayaburi dam project in Lao PDR – the first of eleven dams proposed along the Mekong River.

Regardless of reports of the project's potentially grave transboundary social, health or environmental impacts, and in the absence of consultation with affected communities in Thailand, King notes that Lao PDR and Thailand are moving ahead with the project. Thai banks have also agreed to finance the project, contrary to international banking standards such as the Equator Principles, which are a credit-risk-management framework for determining, assessing and managing environmental and social risk in project finance transactions.

By contrast, in Chapter 6, Puvan Selvanathan and Vani Sathisan note that Singapore's newly announced transboundary haze pollution bill, which has extra-territorial effect, will go some way towards holding errant companies responsible for causing or contributing to haze pollution in Singapore. Further, they write that extra-legal measures such as the Principles and Criteria of the Roundtable for Sustainable Palm Oil (RSPO) codify norms and practices that are well accepted among industry actors as being pertinent in the production of sustainable palm oil.

Mahdev Mohan's Chapter 7 notes that the prudent use of resources can help developing nations in ASEAN overcome poverty, but the combination of conflict, corruption and corporate complicity in human rights abuses has contributed to significant business-related harm. This chapter looks specifically at Cambodia, Laos, Myanmar and Vietnam – commonly referred to as the 'CLMV' States within the ASEAN region. Known for weak governance, these nations face grave challenges in relation to ensuring corporate responsibility. Mohan also considers the prospect of transnational litigation. While the US Supreme Court's *Kiobel* decision has increased challenges in accessing judicial remedies in the USA under the Alien Tort Statute (ATS), he analyses the ongoing *Song Mao* case in the UK, which originated from Cambodia, and argues that, going forward, the causes of action for such transnational litigation do not have to be rooted in ATS conceptions, but may be based on garden-variety torts and should be commenced in the courts of any state with a connection to the parties. Finally, the chapter notes that the GPs may also be domestically incorporated into national or regional development and action plans consistent with the UN's post-2015 development agenda.

Part III of the book critically assesses the steps a company should take in furtherance of its due diligence policies and obligations. In other words, these are the steps that a company may take, and that the State may encourage or require it to take, to become aware of, prevent and mitigate adverse potential and/or actual human rights risks and impacts.

Salil Tripathi and Mark Hodge's Chapter 8 addresses the challenges faced by foreign investors in carrying out effective human rights due diligence in the uncertain, ambiguous and complex context(s) of Myanmar. Both Daw Aung San Suu Kyi and President Thein Sein have called for ethical and responsible investment. Drawing on real-life interactions with multinational corporations, experts and stakeholders, the chapter considers the pragmatic problem-solving process needed to give effect to these calls. Investors seeking entry into Myanmar will have to carefully select who they partner with. Like other companies that have done business in Myanmar, they run the risk of allegations of complicity if they associate with businesses with close relationships to members of the former military government – or others whose names appear on sanctions lists – as they face credible allegations of human rights abuses. In particular, Tripathi and Hodge analyse the Myitsone dam project, which was suspended due to public pressure and lack of adequate social and environmental impact assessments by the company.

Few companies based in SEA have systems in place enabling them to say with confidence that they respect human rights. In Chapter 9, James Kallman writes about the challenges of carrying out comprehensive human rights audits 'in instances where management's conviction of the advantages of human rights compliance clashes with the perception of grizzled veterans on the shop floor who do not see why they should suddenly have to change the way they may have been doing things for years or even decades'. Based on audits that he has been a part of, he recommends internal auditing standards, policies and practices that companies should adopt to address adverse human rights impacts.

In Chapter 10, Kerri-Ann O'Neill considers the scale and influence of the financial services sector and how it relates to human rights in connection with project finance, investment, supply chains and labour practices. The sector is positioned, according to one report, to support or undermine respect for human rights – '(a)s most financial institutions have clients and investments in a wide range of sectors, the finance sector's exposure to human rights risks is potentially broader than any other sector'. She underscores the potential for the sector to comply with voluntary principles such as the UN Principles of Responsible Investment and related initiatives by the UN Global Compact, and to do good through community engagement programmes. But she asks if this is the full picture, given that the interplay between human rights and several aspects of financial services, such as hedge funds, brokerage houses, insurance, derivatives, private equity and variable income investments, have proved difficult to analyse. Strikingly, as O'Neill notes, Panama, a Latin American country of just 3.8 million people, in contrast to SEA's half a billion, has nine financial services companies listed on the latest UN Global Compact's list of responsible businesses participants compared to SEA's six.

Part IV of the book examines the nature and scope of access to adequate accountability and judicial and non-judicial redress in SEA where people are harmed by business operations. After all, any application of the GPs should produce concrete and tangible improvements in the lives of affected individuals and communities in the region.

Bobbie Sta. Maria's Chapter 11 analyses unprecedented judicial decisions delivered by the Philippines courts based on new rules of procedure for environmental cases. Under these rules, a special writ of *kalikasan* can be filed to seek injunctive relief when an unlawful act or omission involves environmental damage that prejudices the life, health or the property of inhabitants in two or more Philippines cities. In 2011, such a writ was granted by the Philippines Supreme Court in favour of residents of Marinduque Province affected by the 1996 tailings disaster in a mine then operated by Placer Dome (now Barrick Gold). The Court directed the company to restore and rehabilitate the environment; a remedy that affected residents had been seeking for fifteen years. Sta. Maria argues that the *Placer Dome* case highlights the value of the new Rules in holding corporations accountable for their misconduct. She asks if this value is diluted by the fact that enforcement remains in the hands of government agencies that may not be prepared to embrace the Court's progressive environmental decisions.

Providing access to remedy where business-related human rights abuses do occur is easier said than done.

In Chapter 12, Deanna Kemp and John Owen note that there is a stark gap in knowledge as to how community grievances are handled beyond 'standard public responses issued by legal counsel or media representatives about specific claims (by mining-affected communities), case studies in glossy company-produced reports, or abstract CSR policies that typically have no bearing on particular claims'. To address this gap, they present a study undertaken at an anonymous large-scale mine in SEA that has attempted to establish a non-judicial, project-level grievance mechanism aligned with the GPs and the third pillar of the Framework, in a context where State protection of political rights is problematic. The chapter highlights the challenges associated with attempting to break old patterns and establish new pathways for responding to community grievances and the importance of considering the socio-political context. Drawing on interviews with forty local-level stakeholders, including company personnel, government authorities and community representatives, the chapter examines contestation in mining and community relations, questions the causes and consequences of mining-related conflict, and seeks to meet the challenge of building a rights-compatible grievance mechanism.

Cynthia Morel's Chapter 13 completes the book by exploring the nexus between the right to development (RTD) and the right to an effective remedy in the context of business and human rights in SEA. Morel notes that despite criticisms levelled against the newly adopted ASEAN Human Rights Declaration (AHRD), the inclusion of RTD within its provisions reflects the region's potential for creative approaches to existing challenges and to 'meet equitably the developmental and environmental needs of present and future generations'. Morel sees RTD as a right of process and outcome to identify means of rendering effective remedy to communities facing development-based evictions. She notes that traditional compensation schemes may serve no practical purpose in SEA as they often extend only to those with formal legal title, and many indigenous or tribal peoples and ethnic minorities, such as the Karen ethnic group in Thailand, are considered ineligible for resettlement. She underlines the importance of the *Endorois* decision by the African Commission on Human and Peoples' Rights, which granted the affected pastoralist community rights of ownership in relation to the land on the basis that it would enable it '(to) engage with the State and third parties as active stakeholders rather than as passive beneficiaries'.

Conclusion

Despite ASEAN's impressive institutions, reforms and growth, if human rights risks continue to be wilfully ignored – and if states and businesses fail to institute risk and impact assessments of their operations in such areas – the stability that currently supports investor confidence and economic progress in SEA may be short-lived. No empirical assessment is available of the overall reception or efficacy of the GPs in SEA. Nonetheless, the value of the GPs must be measured not only in terms of their ability to avert or mitigate such risks, but, perhaps even more importantly, by the way in which they mutually reinforce existing or emergent regulatory norms in ASEAN, a regional bloc that aims to achieve parity of rules and regulations across the ten countries through economic integration by 2015.

This book suggests that rules can serve as a tool to address governance gaps, but should be understood in their proper context. The GPs must therefore be interpreted and augmented by continued engagement with regional stock exchange regulators, State-owned enterprises, sovereign wealth funds, financial institutions and other leading public and private sector entities so that the GPs can be firmly embedded into SEA's corporate psyche. The national or international laws that states enact or sign up to are only as strong as the ability of their subjects (including corporations) to begin self-regulation and face external regulation.

The GPs' recognition of the distinct yet complementary roles that states and businesses must play further highlights their relevance for addressing the scale and complexity of the challenges facing ASEAN and its counterparts across the globe. There is an increased pluralism of actors involved and implicated in this process, which reflects a general trend towards a hybrid or decentred account of risk and regulation.

As this book hopefully demonstrates, the legitimacy and utility of the GPs in promoting and protecting human rights comes into sharp relief when viewed through the lens of risk and regulation. An emerging player on the world stage, SEA is poised to take the lead in forging the way forward if it is understood that compliance can be secured 'by a complex array of interdependent and overlapping mechanisms rather than through a vertical hierarchy in which top-down state centered mechanisms and institutions legitimate the activities of regulatory actors'.[18]

---

[18]   B. Morgan and K. Yeung, *An Introduction to Law and Regulation* (Cambridge University Press, Law in Context series, 2007), p. 11.

Part I

1 Whither corporate social responsibility and the UN Guiding Principles on business and human rights in ASEAN?

Thomas Thomas

Introduction

The Association of Southeast Asian Nations (ASEAN) has made tremendous progress in the field of corporate social responsibility (CSR) and human rights. The ASEAN Intergovernmental Commission on Human Rights (AICHR) was established in 2009 as a consultative body of the regional bloc. The ASEAN Human Rights Declaration (AHRD) was subsequently adopted in November 2012.[1] The Declaration underscores ASEAN's commitment to ensuring that the implementation of the AHRD occurs in accordance with its commitment to the Charter of the United Nations, the Universal Declaration of Human Rights, the Vienna Declaration and Programme of Action, and other international human rights instruments to which ASEAN Member States are party.

CSR also constitutes a strategic objective under the ASEAN Socio-Cultural Community Blueprint (ASCC Blueprint). Under the ASCC Blueprint, CSR is said to contribute towards sustainable socio-economic development in ASEAN Member States. The ASCC Blueprint recommends that ASEAN undertake several steps.

First, a model public policy on CSR should be developed specifically for ASEAN Member States' reference. A possible model to emulate is the ISO 26000, a voluntary international standard that provides guidance on social responsibility.[2] The ISO 26000 has several commendable features: it clarifies what social responsibility involves,[3] translates principles into concrete actions that organizations of all types and sizes can undertake, and lists several socially responsible best practices. It

---

[1] ASEAN Human Rights Declaration adopted on 18 November 2012 at the 21st ASEAN Summit in Phnom Penh, Cambodia.

[2] See generally, 'ISO 26000: Social Responsibility', http://www.iso.org/iso/home/standards/iso26000.htm, accessed 27 March 2014.

[3] The ISO 26000 defines CSR as 'social responsibility of an organization for the impacts of its decisions and activities on society and the environment, through transparent and ethical behaviour that contributes to sustainable development, including health and welfare of society; takes into account the expectations of stakeholders; is in compliance with applicable law and consistent with international norms of behaviour; and is integrated throughout the organization and practiced in its relationships'. See Section 2.18 of the ISO 26000 Online Browsing Platform, https://www.iso.org/obp/ui/#iso:std:iso:26000:ed-1:v1:en, accessed 27 March 2014.

also emphasizes the importance of acting in an ethical, transparent manner that contributes to societal health and welfare. International organizations such as the International Labour Organization (ILO), the UN Global Compact (UNGC), and the Organisation for Economic Co-operation and Development (OECD) were major stakeholders in the drafting process, ensuring that global standards were captured in the ISO 26000's seven key principles. The standards were likewise developed with significant input from emerging economies – a factor that only serves to increase their legitimacy and practical application within the ASEAN context.[4] On this basis, a working document reflecting these aspects was developed by the ASEAN CSR Network.[5]

Second, the ASCC Blueprint recommends that ASEAN engages the private sector to support the CSR-related activities of sectorial bodies and the ASEAN Foundation. The ASEAN CSR Network is a major CSR initiative of the ASEAN Foundation. It was launched by the ASEAN Foundation on 11 January 2011[6] and aims to incorporate CSR into businesses' agendas, as well as to contribute towards sustainable socio-economic development in ASEAN Member States. As a regional network, it provides opportunities for exchange of information between stakeholders, platforms for discussing and addressing regional issues and concerns, and, occasionally, representation for the business community to the ASEAN body and other inter-governmental agencies or think-tanks on relevant policy issues concerning CSR. It also functions as a centralized repository of ASEAN knowledge on CSR, primarily in the form of case-studies and research on the practice of CSR within ASEAN. Capacity-building is another of its core activities, through formal teaching and training approaches. While the ASEAN CSR Network's range of activity has contributed much to the practice of CSR in Southeast Asia thus far, progress has neither been uniform nor consistent across countries. Increased support and commitment from the private sector would undoubtedly help to rectify this, to the benefit of both business and society.

Third, the ASCC Blueprint recommends that ASEAN encourages the adoption and implementation of international standards on social responsibility. AICHR is currently undertaking a baseline study on CSR and human rights in ASEAN. Its aims include, but are not limited to, ascertaining State practice in facilitating or encouraging CSR, including businesses' respect for human rights in all ASEAN Member States; highlighting the CSR practices of businesses based and/or operating in the ASEAN region as they relate to human rights; identifying judicial

---

[4] Of the 99 countries involved in developing the ISO 26000, 69 were developing nations. See ISO Secretary-General's perspectives on ISO 26000 (2010–09–11) – ISO (11 September 2010), http://www.iso.org/iso/home/news_index/news_archive/news.htm?refid=Ref1564, accessed 27 March 2014.

[5] See http://www.asean-csr-network.org/c/news-a-resources/csr-policy-statement, accessed 27 March 2014.

[6] For an overview of the events leading to the ASEAN CSR Network's formation, see 'ASEAN CSR: A Network of CSR Practitioners in ASEAN', http://www.aseanfoundation.org/csr, accessed 27 March 2014. For information on the ASEAN CSR Network and its activities, see generally, 'ASEAN CSR Network', http://www.asean-csr-network.org/c, accessed 27 March 2014.

and non-judicial mechanisms which provide those impacted by business-related human rights harm in the region with access to effective remedy, as well as any barriers to such access; and formulating initial recommendations relevant to the region as a whole, including such further work as would be necessary to develop a common framework to accelerate the promotion of CSR and human rights in the region.[7]

The explicit recognition of the close link between CSR, respect for human rights, and the adoption of an approach that references international frameworks such as the UN Guiding Principles, is particularly encouraging as it directly addresses some of the challenges identified thus far, such as lack of time and know-how, and a general perception that CSR is irrelevant to business and/or not a financially worthwhile undertaking.[8] AICHR will conduct an outcome workshop in June 2014 to present the findings of this thematic study on CSR and human rights.[9]

Fourth, the ASCC Blueprint recommends that ASEAN increases awareness of ensuring sustainable relations between commercial activities and the communities where they are located, particularly by supporting community-based development.

CSR requires organizations to identify their stakeholders and their expectations, and to meet these expectations. Mutual trust and confidence are expected outcomes, along with community involvement and development.

This chapter will consider how effective efforts have been in implementing the above ASEAN Blueprint recommendations. Specifically, the chapter seeks to address the following questions. With the wide variation of political, economic, and social development in the ASEAN region, what role can CSR play in achieving sustainable socio-economic development as envisioned by the UN since Rio + 20? Can CSR be an effective tool to promote human rights norms in the region? What are the challenges for the implementation of globally acceptable CSR and human rights in ASEAN, such as the UN Guiding Principles on Business and Human Rights (Guiding Principles)?[10]

Bearing these questions in mind – along with the fact that the responsibilities of businesses with regard to human rights are not limited to the realm of CSR alone – this chapter examines the avenues available for promoting and protecting human rights. It will also examine the state of human rights practice in ASEAN through the Guiding Principles and its associated *Protect, Respect and Remedy* Framework (Framework), and concludes with practical suggestions for bringing the human rights agenda forward.

---

[7] ASEAN Intergovernmental Commission on Human Rights, 'Terms of Reference: Baseline Study for Corporate Social Responsibility (CSR) and Human Rights in ASEAN', (21 April 2011), p. 2.

[8] These challenges were identified within the Singapore business community; nevertheless, they are clearly not unique to Singapore alone. See 'Baseline Study on Corporate Social Responsibility (CSR) on Singapore 2012', (25 July 2012).

[9] AICHR Press Release, '14th Meeting of the ASEAN Intergovernmental Commission on Human Rights', (11 February, 2014), http://aichr.org/press-release/14th-meeting-of-the-asean-intergovernmental-commission-on-human-rights/#sthash.LA6yDm5A.dpuf, accessed 1 April 2014.

[10] John Ruggie, *Guiding Principles on Business and Human Rights: Implementing the United Nations 'Protect, Respect and Remedy' Framework* (21 March 2011) A/HRC/17/31.

Avenues available for promoting CSR and human rights in the ASEAN region

The current state of CSR in ASEAN is as follows.

1 **Uneven levels of awareness and understanding of international CSR norms and standards across all stakeholder groups (e.g. governments, businesses, and NGOs).**

There is significant divergence in the awareness, understanding, and implementation of CSR across countries in the region. Lax monitoring of compliance with regulatory requirements, the absence of grievance mechanisms, and widespread corruption stymie effective enforcement and undermine the rule of law in some of these countries. This diminishes the significance of legislation related to environmental, economic, and social performance standards. As a result, CSR has not had the desired effect in countries where reforms have been introduced.

For instance, Vietnam has a law that provides guidelines for implementing a 2006 law on providing legal-aid services in eight areas, including environmental law for poor people, policy-supported groups, and other marginalized groups.[11] Providing legal-aid services for poor and marginalized groups is intended to protect their rights and interests and to improve their legal knowledge. It also aims to avoid needless loss of business. Thus, legal aid plays an important role in raising people's awareness on the environment and eradicating poverty. However, statistics show that the number of environment-related cases are low and none have yet to be successful.[12]

Another example can be drawn from the Oxfam study of Unilever's labour practices in Vietnam, which found it wanting in terms of meeting living wage standards and the UN Guiding Principles. It was only after this study that Unilever took some positive steps to improve working conditions and provide access to an effective grievance procedure.[13]

Furthermore, Myanmar companies' general business conduct is noteworthy. Because Myanmar is a society where the success of a business is often determined by relationships, it is difficult for international organizations to identify local partners and establish long-term relationships.[14] As a result, there is little impetus for established businesses to engage in international CSR norms.

---

[11] Article 34 of Decree No. 7/CP dated 12/1/2007.

[12] UICN, 'Problems in enforcing environmental law and ensuring environmental rights for legal aid beneficiaries', (30 December 2012), http://www.iucn.org/news_homepage/news_by_date/?11857/2/Problems-in-enforcing-environmental-law-and-ensuring-environmental-rights-for-legal-aid-beneficiaries, accessed 28 March 2014.

[13] Tim Smedley, 'Unilever's Labour Practices in Vietnam Found Wanting by Oxfam Report', (*The Guardian* Sustainable Business Blog, 7 February 2013), http://www.theguardian.com/sustainable-business/blog/unilever-labour-practices-vietnam-oxfam-report, accessed 28 March 2014.

[14] Richard Welford and Miriam Zieger, *Responsible and Inclusive Business in Myanmar* (CSR Asia, 2013), p. 13.

2 **CSR is commonly understood to mean philanthropy, which is embedded in the region's cultural and religious norms.**

Philanthropy has grown considerably across the region, both in monetary terms, as well as in profile and approach. One reason may be the strong communitarian tradition present in nearly all Southeast Asian countries. Another may be the influence of the region's dominant religions. For instance, Buddhism emphasizes *dana*, which is translated as giving and charity.[15] Whichever is the case, the fact remains that corporate philanthropy has been increasing. Business tycoons and regional conglomerates have donated vast sums of money for public services, including education and religious institutions.

However, while philanthropy is not an undesirable outcome in itself, there is also a risk of companies using philanthropy to conceal or whitewash their misdeeds. There is also a risk that companies may be lulled into a false sense that they are adopting sustainable practices because of their philanthropic activities, despite these potentially falling short of international CSR practices.

Efforts are thus needed to modify existing practices, such that they conform with international CSR norms and standards.

3 **Economic considerations take precedence vis-à-vis environmental and social impact considerations.**

Despite the economic advancements across ASEAN, much of the region's population still lives below the poverty line.[16] Foreign direct investment is needed to create jobs, upgrade infrastructure, and build new industries – many of them export focused to capitalize on lower labour costs. The rise of Myanmar is a prime example. The need to balance economic development with responsible business practices has been emphasized several times by President Thein Sein. Nobel Laureate and Member of Parliament Daw Aung San Suu Kyi also spoke of the challenge of achieving economic growth and managing its social impact during her trip to Singapore in September 2013.

It is also important to recognize that, as the ASEAN Member States' primary preoccupations are economic growth and the establishment of an integrated economic community by 2015,[17] they are likely to overlook non-economic indicators when assessing investment and economic gain. Additionally, the most commonly accepted measure of a country's economic health, the Gross Domestic Product, only includes goods and services produced. In preferring this standard to assess progress, primacy is once again accorded to economic growth at the expense of considering the contribution of intangibles like trust and relations.

---

[15] Ibid., p. 1.

[16] Specifically, 21 per cent: see UN Economic and Social Commission for Asia and the Pacific, 'Statistical Yearbook for Asia and the Pacific 2011', http://www.unescap.org/stat/data/syb2011/I-People/Income-poverty-and-inequality.asp, accessed 28 March 2014.

[17] See generally, 'ASEAN Economic Community', http://www.asean.org/communities/asean-economic-community, accessed 28 March 2014.

Some key groups are beginning to take action

The situation is such that the social and environmental impact of economic development cannot be ignored. For instance, the Chinese Embassy in Yangon utilizes Facebook to communicate with civil-society organizations in Myanmar even though Facebook is banned in China.[18] This was precipitated by the strong reaction of local communities against projects of Chinese companies that had caused negative social and environmental impacts in Myanmar. Clearly, the social and environmental impacts of economic development need to be managed more effectively. To this end, some key groups are taking positive actions to promote responsible business conduct. These include stock exchanges, Global Compact local networks in Singapore, Malaysia, Indonesia and Vietnam, and business chambers and federations (some as part of the ASEAN CSR Network).

Stock exchanges

The Singapore Exchange (SGX), Bursa Malaysia (BM), and the Stock Exchange of Thailand (SET) encourage listed companies to implement and report on their CSR initiatives.[19] The SET established a Corporate Social Responsibility Institute, which promotes awareness and understanding in implementing and reporting CSR practices in line with international benchmarks.[20] However, this is still not as advanced as the Johannesburg Stock Exchange Socially Responsible Investment Index (SRI Index), which tracks companies' policies and reporting based on their performance across the triple bottom line (economic, environment, and social).[21] The SRI Index provides investors with the information to evaluate the performance of companies' sustainability practices. Encouragement by the stock exchanges is expected to push responsible business conduct through their supply chains. This will have a positive impact in mainstreaming CSR and sustainability practices.

The SGX has taken initiatives that encourage CSR reporting. In 2006, it launched a shariah-compliant index (the FTSE/SGX Shariah Index Series), which may be 'compared to a responsible investment index'.[22] This index specifies that eligible securities are those whose core activities are (or are related to), inter

18 *The New Times*, 18 May 2013.
19 Initiative for Responsible Investment at Harvard University, 'Global CSR Disclosure Requirements', http://hausercenter.org/iri/about/global-csr-disclosure-requirements, accessed 28 March 2014.
20 *SET News*: 'Thai Bourse Supports Thai Firms to Produce CSR Reports for Sustainability Disclosure', (5 April 2013).
21 Johannesburg Stock Exchange, 'Introduction to SRI Index', http://www.jse.co.za/About-Us/SRI/Introduction_to_SRI_Index.aspx, accessed 28 March 2014.
22 Cotty Vivant Marchiso Lauzeral, *Mandate of the Special Representative of the Secretary-General (SRSG) on the Issue of Human Rights and Transnational Corporations and other Business Enterprises*: Corporate Law Project (Singapore) (September 2009), http://www.business-humanrights.org/media/documents/ruggie/corporate-law-tools-reports-singapore-sep-2009.pdf, accessed 1 April 2014, pp. 4 and 10.

alia, banking or any other interest-related activity, alcohol, tobacco, gaming or arms manufacturing, as well as securities which comply with shariah-compliant financial ratios.[23] However, as this index focuses on shariah principles rather than CSR per se, it still falls short of forming a full CSR index.

Subsequently, in 2011, the SGX launched its voluntary guidelines for sustainability reporting. This set of guidelines has had an impact on Singapore businesses, according to a study on reporting currently being undertaken by the Singapore Compact for CSR.[24] Results indicate a rise in the number and scope of reports. For example, in 2011, only ten companies published sustainability reports according to the Global Reporting Initiative (GRI) framework. In 2013, it nearly doubled to nineteen. At the same time, the number of companies reporting material non-financial data grew from 79 to 160 of the 610 listed companies over the two years. Beyond these mere figures, a deeper question relates to the effectiveness of CSR reporting. Of the seventy-nine reports on sustainability in 2011, 83.5 per cent were integrated reports, i.e. a section contained within the company's annual report, and only the remaining 16.5 per cent were separate reports.[25] Whilst the form of the report in itself does not dictate the effectiveness of CSR reporting, it has been observed that companies that provided separate reports tend to provide more information on sustainability performance and practices than integrated reports.[26] Further, none of the reports had 'true online reporting', in that they were not tailored or interactive, were not targeted at individual stakeholder groups, did not incorporate reader feedback, and were not regularly updated.[27] These all suggest that CSR reporting in Singapore remains at a nascent stage.

A closer look at these seventy-nine reports on sustainability in 2011 demonstrates that the focus of reporting is often based on size and sectors of the companies. Large enterprises and small enterprises accounted for 60 per cent and 25 per cent of listed companies that practised sustainability reporting in 2011, although the former only accounted for just under 15 per cent of all listed companies.[28] This is not entirely surprising given that large companies are likely to face greater global scrutiny as well as greater public and media attention, thereby creating more impetus to engage in sustainable reporting.[29] Further, companies tended to place different weights on different components of sustainability reporting depending on the focus of their respective sectors. For instance, finance companies provided significantly more information than other sectors on corporate governance as this sector is heavily subject to regulations and investor scrutiny

23 FTSE, 'Ground Rules for the Management of the FTSE SGX Shariah Index Series', Version 1.2 (January 2014), http://www.ftse.com/Indices/FTSE_SGX_Shariah_Index_Series/Downloads/FTSE_SGX_Shariah_Index_Rules.pdf, accessed 1 April 2014, p. 6.
24 Singapore Compact for CSR, *Non-Financial Reporting Among Mainboard Listed Companies in Singapore: A View of the Sustainability Reporting Landscape in 2010–2011* (2011).
25 Ibid., p. 9.
26 Ibid., p. 9.
27 Ibid., p. 9.
28 Ibid., p. 7.
29 Ibid., p. 8.

on this issue.[30] Non-financial reporting remains a relatively new process for many other sectors. Industries whose operations are directly associated with the environment, such as agriculture, performed well in relation to communicating their environmental concerns.[31] However, labour-intensive industries, including construction, mining and quarrying, reported in more detail on labour practices rather than on environmental disclosure, even if their businesses have a direct and potentially adverse impact on the environment.[32]

Viewed holistically, this suggests that companies have not been encouraged by sustainability reporting to go above and beyond their ordinary reporting obligations. By and large, meaningful sustainability reporting has been limited to those components that directly impact their businesses. As such, whilst there is a mechanism which encourages sustainability reporting, the exercise itself is still in the nascent stages. It remains to be seen whether and how sustainability reporting will increase in Singapore. It is hoped that these reporting requirements will encourage positive changes in the practice of responsible business conduct, which must include respect for human rights.

Global Compact local networks in Singapore, Malaysia, Indonesia, Vietnam

The UNGC is the world's largest corporate citizenship initiative. Companies in Indonesia, Malaysia, Myanmar, Philippines, Singapore, Thailand, and Vietnam have committed to applying the UNGC's ten principles covering human rights, labour rights, environmental protection, and anti-corruption. More specifically, the UNGC asks companies to embrace, support, and enact, within their sphere of influence, a set of core values in the important areas of human rights, labour standards, the environment, and anti-corruption. Companies that sign up to the UNGC must submit annual Communications on Progress (COP) detailing how they are implementing the ten principles. Signatories that do not submit COPs are delisted.

Hence, the COP regime can, theoretically, help to secure high-level commitment from within the company to the ten principles. It can also serve to pressurize companies into re-examining their CSR policies and practices, with a view to constantly improving themselves. However, the translation of this commitment to the UNGC is limited in practice due to the fact that in Southeast Asia, only Indonesia, Malaysia, Singapore, and Vietnam have established Global Compact Local Networks (GCLNs). The reluctance to form GCLNs within the other signatory ASEAN States is disappointing, given that GCLNs function as national CSR 'pressure points'. Indeed, GCLNs play an important role, both independently and in partnership with relevant stakeholders, in promoting awareness and uptake of international CSR norms and standards, disseminating best practices

---

[30] Ibid., p. 12.
[31] Ibid., p. 13.
[32] Ibid., p. 14.

and guidelines, assisting with capacity-building and CSR advocacy, and coordinating with partner networks to work on regional and international projects. In light of this fact, efforts should be made to establish GCLNs in the remaining ASEAN Member States.

Business chambers and federations (some as part of the ASEAN CSR Network)

These organizations are important partners in promoting CSR in their respective countries. Those that are members of the ASEAN CSR Network (ACN) can take on the role of the GCLN in countries where no GCLNs exist. Beyond this, business chambers can also coordinate CSR-promoting initiatives with their members, as well as governments and other business associations with whom they have connections. Obtaining their members' commitment is particularly critical in ensuring the success of CSR promotion initiatives. This is particularly so where members are major multinational enterprises, as the latter's global presence confers them with the power to exert significant pressure down their supply chain to comply with the CSR agenda.

Wide variance in practice, both between and within countries

Responsible business practice varies between and within countries.[33] Family and State-owned enterprises dominate the region's business players. It may be believed that these companies face low public pressure for compliance with CSR. However, this argument may in fact have little force, as many family and State-owned companies are listed on stock exchanges, and hence are not necessarily able to completely disregard public disapprobation.

That aside, the main CSR practices vary in accordance with the particular country's priorities. Within countries, variations exist based on the company's size, capacity, ownership, and sector of operation. For instance, businesses in countries that are prone to natural disasters are expected to contribute towards relief work and in mitigating these disasters. Finally, as levels of poverty are high in middle and low-income countries, CSR has been mainly seen as philanthropy and charity, while CSR in high-income countries has focused on good governance, transparency, and accountability.

Special attention needed to reduce gap with Cambodia, Lao PDR, and Myanmar

Cambodia, Lao PDR, and Myanmar have the lowest per capita income in ASEAN. Yet they also represent the region's strongest possible growth potential.

---

[33] For a detailed analysis of the 'geographies' of corporate social responsibility, see Elsabet Garriga and Domènec Melé, 'Corporate Social Responsibility Theories: Mapping the Territory', (2004), *Journal of Business Ethics*, 53: 51–71.

If economic progress is not managed well, social unrest will likely arise. This is arguably already being manifested in community protests against investments from certain countries, labour unrest, and environmental degradation. Protests against Chinese investments in Myanmar and garment workers' strikes in Cambodia for better terms provide striking illustrations of such social unrest. Additionally, the fact that the protesting parties in both situations faced violent responses strongly suggests that CSR has yet to be wholly assimilated into the business culture of these countries. More work is therefore needed to build the capacity of CSR networks in Cambodia, Lao PDR, and Myanmar. Without a network, the task of promoting CSR is largely ad hoc and done, at times, by Western donors and international organizations. These countries are experiencing significant economic growth and the influx of investments underscore the urgent need to ensure that CSR is understood and implemented. Some areas of focus will include:

1   **Advocacy on CSR as more than philanthropy is needed**

As explained earlier, many companies interpret CSR as philanthropy alone – i.e. voluntary charity as opposed to mandatory obligations. This is undesirable because philanthropy can be used to conceal misdeeds, and it may not comply with 'thick' conceptions of CSR and human rights standards in other areas (e.g. environment, labour, governance). A 'thin' conception of CSR risks being defined and delineated by more established and wealthy companies that turn to it as a form of window-dressing. Notwithstanding that philanthropy may remain necessary in certain situations, companies should ensure they uphold robust corporate governance, labour relations, environment policies, and community engagement programmes to fulfil their CSR responsibilities. There is now agreement that CSR is not about making donations or contributing to charity. It is about how businesses operate and contribute positively in social and environmental stewardship while creating wealth. The fact that this position is embodied in many international initiatives, such as the ISO 26000 international standard on social responsibility, the ILO tripartite declaration, the OECD guidelines, and the UN Global Compact, indicates that the best way to address challenges in these areas is through responsible business.

2   **Low attention to critical issues like human rights and corruption**

There is low awareness of human rights as an element of CSR and the UN Guiding Principles. Although the State's duty to uphold and protect the rights of the citizen can be found in constitutions and national legislation, the responsibility of businesses to respect the rights of individuals is not well understood. Human rights should be made an explicit central element of CSR through State-led efforts at increasing awareness and understanding of the Guiding Principles, as well as the implementation of its Framework.

3   **CSR and risk management**

Global companies in Asia face a new reality that has changed the nature of risk and risk management: networked operations and global supply chains, empowered stakeholders, and increased dynamic tension among industry sectors. The emergence of these new forms of social risk cannot be effectively mitigated through traditional means. This need to bridge the gap between traditional risk-management methods and modern forms of social risk is illustrated by how palm oil companies had to react positively when, in 2010, Greenpeace targeted Nestlé for sourcing palm oil that was potentially destroying the orang-utan habitats. Palm oil companies in ASEAN became more aware of the issues and worked to address these concerns. The incident also highlights the power of social media in attracting sustained consumer scrutiny of, inter alia, supply chains.[34]

Nevertheless, this changing landscape provides opportunities for new companies to capitalize on value chains to produce products at competitive prices, whilst concurrently assisting vulnerable communities. Kool Kiwi Pure Milk (KKPM), a private Burmese company, constitutes one such example.[35] KKPM plans to produce pasteurized cow milk in Karen State, Myawaddy, Myanmar. KKPM estimates that it will be able to sell milk locally and in neighbouring states for a price that is 44 per cent lower than conventional pasteurized milk.[36] It will do this by capitalizing on an effective and efficient supply chain and will serve its milk through mobile and indoor dispensers maintaining optimal milk conditions, thereby saving on packaging costs.[37]

Concurrently, KKPM aims to target poor, rural communities. Apart from allowing people from these communities to consume milk and dairy products on a daily basis, KKPM aims to employ a veterinarian and agronomist to provide free advice to the local farmers and medicines for animals at wholesale price.[38] This, in turn, could potentially lead to income creation, increasing smallholders' dairy production techniques, as well as improved overall health and nutrition in these communities.[39]

4   **Growing interest, spurred by current events/problems**
  i   ***Climate change and its effects: typhoons, flooding, etc.***

The effects of climate change are transforming the way companies look at non-economic considerations, such as recycling and wastage, as well as the use of environmentally harmful raw materials. The car industry, for example, is turning to clean-emission cars and fuel-efficient technologies to spur customer interest in this area. Large, well-established companies are realizing that sustainable business models need to include

---

[34] Aileen Ionescu-Somers and Albrecht Enders, 'How Nestlé Dealt with a Social Media Campaign Against It', *Financial Times* (3 December 2012), http://www.ft.com/cms/s/0/90dbff8a-3aea-11e2-b3f0-0144feabdc0.html#axzz2tPNNFwbT, accessed 28 March 2014.
[35] Richard Welford and Miriam Zieger, *Responsible and Inclusive Business in Myanmar* (CSR Asia, 2013), p. 29. This story was shared by Cesar Russo, a shareholder and board member at KKPM to the members of CSR Asia on 19 February 2013 in Yangon.
[36] Ibid., p. 29.
[37] Ibid., p. 29.
[38] Ibid., p. 29.
[39] Ibid., p. 29.

climate change mitigation strategies and that a failure to do so may have an adverse impact on their brand.

ii   ***Large migrant work force in ASEAN***

Migrant labour abuse is a common concern among the labour-sending countries in the region. There is a particularly large migrant work force in Malaysia and Singapore. In most cases, labour laws protect nationals of the receiving country from liability for migrant labour abuse. At the same time, labour-sending countries, driven by the contribution of remittances to their economy, have accepted that some exploitation of their workers is acceptable. The lack of protection of these workers' rights and their access to remedies is an important issue, as it has the potential to cause social tensions and social unrest in receiving countries. Multi-stakeholder approaches are vital to making headway on this, and it is encouraging that migrant labour abuse is on the agenda of the AICHR. It is also covered in the ILO's Tripartite Declaration of Principles concerning Multinational Enterprises on Social Policy (MNE Declaration), and the OECD Guidelines for Multinational Enterprises provide practical guidance on migrant workers.

iii   ***Opening up of Myanmar***

The lifting of sanctions on Myanmar has opened up various new business opportunities for foreign and regional investors. The government has cautioned against excessive profit-seeking behaviour at the expense of the environment and well-being of local communities.[40] Nonetheless, the risk of a 'gold rush' into Myanmar remains. Myanmar's path to modernization will prove to be a litmus test of corporate maturity and responsibility and the government's commitment to the Guiding Principles and its Framework.

iv   ***Haze in/from Indonesia, Singapore, Malaysia***

The haze that affects Indonesia, Malaysia, and Singapore has adversely affected air quality. Its constant recurrence since the 1980s has eroded public confidence that this phenomenon would be tackled decisively.[41] The haze is caused by environmentally irresponsible land-clearance methods adopted by the palm oil and pulp-and-paper industries, among other actors.[42] This highlights the importance of sustainable agriculture and why companies need to utilize environmentally responsible land-clearance methods. That said, the haze has also demonstrated that customers are becoming more discerning and that they are increasingly

---

[40] Thomas Fuller, 'Democracy Leader Cautions Investors Against "Reckless Optimism" in Myanmar', *The New York Times* (1 June 2012).

[41] Abhrajit Gangopadhyay, 'Haze From Indonesia Thickens, Shrouds Parts of Malaysia', *The Wall Street Journal* (24 July 2013), http://online.wsj.com/news/articles/SB10001424127887324144304578623484141089730, accessed 8 March 2014.

[42] Yenni Kwok, 'The Southeast Asian Haze Is Back and Worse May Follow', *TIME*, http://world.time.com/2013/07/30/the-southeast-asian-haze-is-back-and-worse-may-follow/#ixzz2vLaolepF, accessed 8 March 2014.

willing to boycott products from companies that negligently contribute to the haze.[43] Encouraging consumer-side pressure may well prove the most effective and pragmatic means of penalizing negligent companies, as efforts to undertake transboundary legal action remain fraught with obstacles.[44]

v *Corruption scandals*

The spate of corruption scandals involving big businesses in the region has tainted the public perception of business within ASEAN countries. The recent arrest of the head of Indonesia's upstream oil and gas regulator SKKMigas is a sobering reminder that corruption is still pervasive and takes place at various levels of government and business.[45] Moving forward, businesses now have to look beyond profitability to gain the trust of the public and revamp the image of businesses.

vi *International organizations helping shape agenda based on international norms*

International organizations have an important role to play in shaping the CSR agenda within the region, based on international norms and standards. They will help to ensure that CSR standards across ASEAN follow international best practices, meet recognized standards on reporting and disclosure, and create a level playing field for benchmarking CSR regionally and internationally. International organizations such as the GRI, the OECD, the ISO and the UN Global Compact have an important role in this regard.

Businesses in ASEAN will likewise draw guidance from the latest GRI Sustainability Reporting Guidelines. These guidelines offer Reporting Principles, Standard Disclosures and an Implementation Manual for the preparation of sustainability reports by organizations, regardless of their size, sector, or location. The Guidelines also offer an international reference for all those interested in the disclosure of governance approach and of the environmental, social, and economic performance and impacts of organizations. The Guidelines are useful in the preparation of any type of document which requires such disclosure. The objective is to streamline the company's data on its sustainability impacts such that its reports are more focused, credible, and easier for stakeholders to navigate and

---

[43] A 2012 McKinsey survey found that 44 per cent of Chinese consumers were willing to pay more for more environmentally friendly products. China is one of the largest consumers of palm oil products worldwide.

[44] In February 2014, Singapore proposed draft legislation permitting it to exercise extra-territorial jurisdiction over private entities charged with or accused of causing or contributing to the haze. However, even the minister who proposed the Transboundary Haze Bill admitted that enforcing such a law outside Singapore's territory would encounter problems: 'More Riau Haze Arrests as Singapore Drafts Legislation', *The Jakarta Globe* (25 February 2014).

[45] Holman Fenwick Willan, 'Indonesia Oil and Gas – Time for (Another) Reformation', (October 2013), http://www.hfw.com/Indonesia-oil-and-gas-time-for-another-reformation-Oct-2013, accessed 8 March 2014.

comprehend.[46] This is expected to encourage sustainable reports to go beyond public relations tools to address real and relevant issues facing the business.

Finally, the OECD Guidelines for Multinational Enterprises is also expected to have a far-reaching impact on business conduct. It encompasses forty-four governments from all regions of the world, accounting for 85 per cent of all foreign direct investments. This will encourage the OECD-country businesses to observe these guidelines wherever they operate and affect the conduct of businesses that are part of their supply chain.

ASEAN community 2015: an opportunity

The ASEAN Community 2015 Blueprint constitutes a good opportunity to elevate discussions on CSR and the role of business in achieving ASEAN goals, not only in spurring economic growth but also in social and environmental sustainability.

As the most economically advanced country in the region, Singapore is best positioned to move forward ASEAN's social and environmental sustainability agenda. This agenda is especially relevant for ASEAN, as it is required to promote environmental protection and social justice through CSR under the ASCC Blueprint. Several laws and regulations in Singapore can contribute towards ensuring that businesses act in a socially and environmentally responsible manner. These include the Employment Act, which stipulates that employers must refrain from certain actions that violate the rights of employees, and the Environmental Protection and Management Act, which requires businesses to seek permission before occupying and using any scheduled premises. Recently, the Inter-Ministerial Committee on Suitability was formed, which aims to release a report to encourage industries to adopt long-term sustainable practices in the areas of resource management, pollution control, and quality of the physical environment.[47] The National Environment Agency has also issued codes of practice and provides for tax incentives for environmentally friendly investments.[48] With effective law enforcement and adjudication, Singapore's legal and regulatory framework can complement and support efforts to promote social and environmental sustainability in Singapore and ASEAN. The assumption of such a role has been highlighted by private sector entities, such as Cotty Vivant Marchisio and Lauzeral in its September 2009 report to Prof John Ruggie, the Special Representative of

---

[46] Global Reporting Initiative, *Main Features of the G4 Guidelines*, https://www.globalreporting.org/reporting/g4/Pages/default.aspx, accessed 8 March 2014.

[47] Cotty Vivant Marchiso Lauzeral, 'Mandate of the Special Representative of the Secretary-General (SRSG) on the Issue of Human Rights and Transnational Corporations and other Business Enterprises: Corporate Law Project (Singapore)', (September 2009), http://www.business-humanrights.org/media/documents/ruggie/corporate-law-tools-reports-singapore-sep-2009.pdf, accessed 8 March 2014, p. 20.

[48] Ibid.

the UN Secretary-General on the issue of human rights. The foreign law firm stated that:

> The government has so far taken a leading role to enhance the domestic level of corporate governance. As is usually the case in Singapore, this is done mainly through incentives and schemes. However, the opening up of the city-state to the world and the attractiveness of Singapore force the city-state to constantly improve its standards, including with respect to corporate social responsibility.[49]

The UN framework and guiding principles in ASEAN

ASEAN faces key challenges in promoting sustainable socio-economic development. These include, but are not limited to the following.

1 **Migrant workers**, with regard to their treatment, as well as impacts on their families. The issue of migrant workers, both between and within countries, is a key human rights-related issue in ASEAN. Business and governments have a key role to play in respecting the rights of these migrant workers and providing an environment in which their rights are protected.
2 **Land acquisition**, especially in the context of agriculture and industrialization. Land acquisition constitutes another problem facing the region, as many governments seek to develop land with little or no compensation for its indigenous inhabitants. The evictions of residents around Boeung Kak Lake and in the Borei Keila commune in Cambodia count as an example. The filling of the lake has caused significant social and environmental problems for the people living in proximity to its banks. Despite protests from civil-society groups and opposition from the local community, the development has continued and is nearing completion.[50]
3 **Women's and children's rights**, especially with regard to labour conditions. Serious forms of abuse of women's and children's rights still prevail in the region. This is particularly the case with respect to forced and child labour. For example, despite the current regulatory framework,[51] an estimated 3.2 million children were considered to be engaged in some form of child labour.[52]

---

[49] Ibid.
[50] Human Rights Now, *Human Rights Now, Fact Finding Report for Cambodia: In Cambodia, People are Deprived of Land* (June 2012), http://hrn.or.jp/eng/activity/HRN%20Cambodia%20Report%20on%20 Land%20Rights%202012.pdf, accessed 12 May 2014.
[51] The Philippines government ratified ILO Convention 189 on Domestic Workers and passed both the Domestic Workers Act and the Expanded Anti-Trafficking in Persons Act in 2012.
[52] Philippine Statistics Authority: National Statistics Office 'The Number of Working Children 5 to 17 Years Old Is Estimated At 5.5 Million (Preliminary Results of the 2011 Survey on Children)', (18 July 2012), http://www.census.gov.ph/content/number-working-children-5–17-years-old-esti-mated-55-million-preliminary-results-2011-survey, accessed 8 March 2014.

State of practice of CSR and human rights

The state of practice of CSR and human rights in the region is nascent, with some countries at a more advanced stage of CSR than others. The key challenges to the practice of CSR include the absence of legal or regulatory frameworks, a corporate culture that places a premium on CSR, and access to remedies in the event of a breach. The Guiding Principles are still a relatively new concept and governments as well as businesses have a considerable task ahead in implementing the *Protect, Respect and Remedy* Framework. The recognition of the State's duty to protect human rights alone in the constitutional instruments and laws of countries in the region is not enough, as focus on sustained economic growth and the prevalence of common development challenges will continue to give rise to challenges in the area of CSR and human rights.

The way forward

Promotion of international norms in ASEAN

The development of CSR practices in ASEAN should be consistently benchmarked against global best practices. The UNGC, the GRI, the ISO 26000, OECD Guidelines for Multinational Enterprises, and the ILO's Tripartite Declaration for Multinational Corporations, which are universally recognized sustainability frameworks, are proposed as a possible reference point. Equally, where relevant, additional reference should be made to sector-specific standards such as the International Finance Corporation's Sustainability Framework. Further consideration should be accorded to Harvard University's Sustainability Scorecard, which constitutes an innovative means of presenting sustainability performance in an accessible, target-specific format.

Capacity-building support needed

More capacity-building support is essential to establish the capability, knowledge, and implementation systems required to entrench the practice of CSR in the region. There is also a pressing need to build the capacities of national Global Compact networks in Cambodia, Lao PDR, and Myanmar. Capacity-building support in the form of skills training, workshops, and seminars would support the systems required to ensure that all the countries in the region can effectively embark on CSR projects and work with all the relevant stakeholders.

Research, documentation, and communications

Apart from capacity-building support, communication channels should also be established. To that end, CSR manuals could be disseminated to companies to guide their CSR strategies and programmes as well as their methods of reporting and communicating their performance on CSR indicators to the public. GCLNs could simultaneously function as a repository for these guidebooks and ensure that the information is aligned with the latest international norms.

Even as the private sector works on establishing CSR as the norm in business operations, we must remain cognizant of the public sector's role. Work that is done on CSR must ultimately be used as input to influence government-level policy development. This may have to take the form of an iterative process that builds on the inputs from various stakeholders to create a broader philosophy that reflects a holistic approach to CSR and, in turn, informs policy development at the national and regional levels.

Multi-stakeholder engagement

Checks and balances are necessary to ensure that growth and development take into account the expectations and needs of all stakeholders. Representing and articulating these expectations and aspirations will be an important role of civil-society organizations. The role of NGOs and trade unions cannot be understated. Since NGOs are often driven by issues the public considers to be worthy causes, and are independent from business interests and government influence, they enjoy high standing in terms of uncompromised moral and professional authority. Impartial information on controversial issues, from human rights violations to corruption, is more likely to be expected from an independent NGO than from a government agency or a business corporation, leaving NGOs in an ideal position to check the conduct of both businesses and governments to ensure that CSR is performed in a transparent, accountable manner.

Conclusion

ASEAN has made much progress over the last few years in promoting CSR and human rights. Compared to where we stood a decade ago, the progress is remarkable. But when it is compared to global standards, it is clear that much work remains to be done. ASEAN is building institutions to enable good and sustainable practices in CSR and human rights. We have access to standards, tools, and initiatives developed at the global level. The challenge for ASEAN is to adopt and adapt these standards, tools, and initiatives for the region. Varied though the individual Member States may be, we are nevertheless united in seeing the benefits of closer integration and having a stronger ASEAN community. The ASEAN CSR Network can play an important role in embedding responsible business conduct, CSR, and respect for human rights in the region. As the (former) UN High Commissioner for Human Rights Navi Pillay has said, 'other regions have shown how regional human rights systems can evolve and improve over time, and I am confident this will be the same for ASEAN'.[53]

53 'Pillay Encourages ASEAN to Ensure Human Rights Declaration Is Implemented in Accordance with International Obligations', UN Office of the High Commissioner for Human Rights (19 November 2012), http://www.ohchr.org/en/NewsEvents/Pages/DisplayNews. aspx?NewsID=12809andLangID=E, accessed 8 March 2014.

2 Business and human rights challenges in ASEAN

The role and modalities of the State

Delphia Lim and Geetanjali Mukherjee[1]

Introduction

Implementation of the United Nations Guiding Principles on Business and Human Rights (Guiding Principles) is gaining momentum. In 2011, the European Commission issued a communication to all Member States to formulate national plans of action to implement the Guiding Principles.[2] As of December 2012, more than two-thirds of Member States had done so or were in the process of doing so.[3] In March 2013, the UN Working Group on business and human rights called on all states to consider elaborating such action plans.[4] In September 2013, the United Kingdom became the first state publicly to issue its national action plan for implementing the Guiding Principles.[5]

The landscape is different in the ASEAN region. While the promotion of responsible business is on the policy agenda of ASEAN, the purpose is not explicitly to implement the Guiding Principles, and responses are less rigorous than those in the European Union. The 2010 deadline set out in the ASEAN Socio-Cultural Community (ASCC) Blueprint for the development of 'a model public policy on Corporate Social Responsibility or legal instrument for reference of ASEAN

---

[1] The authors were respectively involved as team leader / synthesis report author, and senior research coordinator / Lao country researcher in a region-wide research study, Human Rights Resource Centre (HRRC), *Business and Human Rights in ASEAN: A Baseline Study* (Jakarta: Human Rights Resource Centre, 2012). The country reports by individual country researchers in the said study were relied on as a valuable resource for identifying and understanding relevant laws and policies.

[2] Communication from the Commission to the European Parliament, the Council, the European Economic and Social Committee and the Committee of the Regions, *A Renewed EU Strategy 2011–2014 for Corporate Social Responsibility*, (25 October 2011), http://tinyurl.com/cdyhv8b, accessed 17 December 2013.

[3] UN Forum on Business and Human Rights, 'Keynote Address by European Union Special Representative for Human Rights, Stavros Lambrinidis', (4 December 2012), http://tinyurl.com/lj4a4yp, accessed 17 December 2013.

[4] Human Rights Council, *Report of the Working Group on the Issue of Human Rights and Transnational Corporations and Other Business Enterprises*, A/HRC/23/32 (14 March 2013), para. 71(f).

[5] UK Government Press Release, 'UK First to Launch Action Plan on Business and Human Rights', (4 September 2013), http://tinyurl.com/p32dutz, accessed 1 December 2013.

Member States' has long passed.[6] A thematic study on CSR and human rights undertaken in furtherance of the CSR objectives of the ASCC is still ongoing.[7] In September 2013, final recommendations for an ASEAN Action Plan for CSR were issued by representatives of government, the private sector and civil society; these do not appear to relate to individual State action, but instead actions, such as capacity-building, knowledge sharing and cross-border communication and cooperation among states.[8] In short, concerted national action appears distant.

Primarily, the goal of policy objectives, whether they involve the formulation of national action plans, or issue-specific or sectoral reforms, is the achievement of effective reforms to address adverse business-related human rights impacts in ASEAN. To that end, specific and concrete recommendations for action are needed.

This chapter focuses on the formulation of concrete policy recommendations and strategies for reform in ASEAN, keeping in mind the policy and regulatory contexts of ASEAN States. It does not, for the most part, address the implementation of said policies, except where fuller context is needed.

Part II of this chapter gives a detailed overview of the policy and regulatory contexts of five ASEAN States, namely, Indonesia, Laos, Myanmar, the Philippines, and Singapore, using individual country analyses.[9] Each country analysis canvasses the State's approach in relation to:

- the mitigation of the impacts of business activities and the State's economic development agenda, particularly on rural and indigenous peoples;[10]
- the use of the concept of corporate social responsibility (CSR);[11]
- the domestic applicability of international human rights law to business-related policies and activities.[12]

---

[6] ASEAN, *ASEAN Socio-Cultural Community Blueprint*, (2009), http://tinyurl.com/mwzr6ay. Notably, the said blueprint does not require or expressly encourage ASEAN Member States to take action; the model policy or legal instrument is purely for reference.

[7] AICHR, 'Press Release of the 11th Meeting of the ASEAN Intergovernmental Commission on Human Rights (AICHR)', (2 February 2013), http://tinyurl.com/mpz3ml5, accessed 2 March 2014.

[8] Singapore Compact, 'Regional Workshop on ASEAN Action Plan on CSR Proposes Recommendations to ASCC Council', (2013), http://tinyurl.com/mn9vc3g, accessed 17 December 2013.

[9] These five states were selected based on two considerations; the first and more important consideration was the need to ensure that the countries comprised a range of levels of socio-economic development; the second was the familiarity of the authors with these contexts and availability of information sources.

[10] This issue was identified as salient in view of how business and human rights challenges in developing countries are often closely related to the adverse impacts of the social changes brought by economic development.

[11] This issue was identified as salient in view of how CSR can be a regulatory tool to advance the business and human rights agenda, as well as its known currency in ASEAN, as seen from, for example, the establishment by ASEAN of the ASEAN CSR Network. (ASEAN CSR Network website, http://www.asean-csr-network.org/c, accessed 1 December 2013.

[12] This issue was identified in order to shed light on the prospects for rights-based strategies for policy reform.

Other distinctive policy and regulatory approaches are also highlighted where relevant, especially where they shed light on policy considerations that may compete with human rights protection. These vary from country to country.[13]

Finally, Part III sets out observations arising from the country analyses that are relevant to determining what policy or regulatory reform is needed, and strategic considerations to be taken into account when seeking to achieve reform in these ASEAN States.

Understanding ASEAN's policy and legal contexts

A.   *Indonesia*

Overview

In Indonesia, potential conflict arising from social change brought about by economic activities is a prominent concern that laws attempt to address. 'Traditional communities' and local cultural traditions are taken into account in legislation relating to business activities. Also, and as will be shown, Indonesia's investment law calls on businesses to maintain a 'harmonious' and 'balanced' relationship with society.

The State has used a strong hand when it comes to ensuring business revenue contributes to economic development. High-revenue businesses and industrial areas may be designated as 'national vital objects' and provided with police or military protection. Further, a range of companies, such as those in the natural resources industry, are compelled by law to contribute to community development.

Custom and tradition are legal counterweights to private sector development

Indonesia's laws formally recognize the land rights of 'traditional communities', and thus indigenous customs and traditions can be used as legal arguments for contesting private sector activities. These rights are embodied in the legal concept of *hak ulayat*, a communal right to land ownership or use.[14] 'Traditional communities' with *hak ulayat* are entitled to veto private sector investment projects and the building of plantations by businesses and persons on the land concerned, by withholding the grant of their land use rights.[15] Indonesia's deference to 'traditional communities' is more measured in other cases. *Hak ulayat* in relation to forests is confined to being a user right and not an ownership right, and is

---

[13]   Many of the highlights were identified from the methodical survey of the land, labour, environment, corporate governance, and CSR regulations of ASEAN States set out in the HRRC 'Baseline Study'.

[14]   P. Waagstein, 'Indonesia Report', in Human Rights Resource Centre, *Business and Human Rights in ASEAN: A Baseline Study* (Jakarta: Human Rights Resource Centre, 2012), p. 119, citing Law No. 41 on Forestry 1999, Article 67(1); Agrarian Law No. 5 1960, Article 5; Law No. 18 on Plantations 2004, Article 9(2).

[15]   Ibid., p. 119, citing Regulation of Ministry of Agrarian No. 5 on Guidelines of Dispute Settlement of Hak Ulayat 1999, Article 4; Law No. 18 on Plantations 2004, Article 9(2).

recognized only if such right is not contrary to the national interest.[16] Also, the land and property rights of 'traditional communities' cannot bar the acquisition of land in the public interest, although the law provides for consultations with affected local communities, customary leaders and clerics, and sets out a framework for the appraisal and negotiation of compensation.[17]

Hak ulayat rights can be desirable as a matter of socio-political values and needs, constituting brakes that halt or mitigate the adverse social ruptures of modernization that are often keenly felt by such communities. They could also be regarded by some as overly impeding modernization and development or even entrenching unjust customary hierarchies and power structures,[18] thereby contributing to conflict. The implementation of these rights and their effects in relation to development and social protection warrants further investigation.

With regard to investment activities generally, Indonesia's investment law obliges investors to respect the cultural traditions of the community around the location of their activities[19] and imposes administrative sanctions for failures to comply.[20]

Legislating for 'corporate social responsibility'

Indonesia has, in a novel step, made CSR a statutory obligation.[21] This obligation entails corporate contributions to community development and empowerment.[22]

---

[16] Law No. 25 of 2007 Concerning Investment, Article 67.

[17] Law No. 2 of 2012 Concerning Acquisition of Land for Development in the Public Interest, Articles 7(3), 19–21 and Part Four.

[18] It has been reported that '[t]here has also been a lot of co-optation of traditional elites both in Papua and West Kalimantan, where religious leaders or local customary leaders were bought out by the ruling party, by the Golkar elite', Sidney Jones, 'Causes of Conflict in Indonesia', Asia Society website, http://asiasociety.org/countries/conflicts/causes-conflict-indonesia, accessed 1 December 2013.

[19] Law No. 25 of 2007 Concerning Investment, Article 15(d).

[20] Law No. 25 of 2007 Concerning Investment, Article 34.

[21] Another country that has made corporate 'social responsibility' mandatory is India. India's Companies Bill requires companies with a net worth of at least US$90 million, turnover of US$180 million, or net profit of US$900,000 to spend 2% of profit after tax on social welfare: M. Hodge, *Two Elephants in the CSR Room: Time to Focus on Business Impacts and State Duties*, Institute for Human Rights and Business, (20 August 2013), http://www.ihrb.org/commentary/guest/two-elephants-in-the-indian-csr-room.html, accessed 30 August 2013.

[22] International Bar Association, 'Corporate social responsibility regulation in Indonesia', http://www.ibanet.org/Article/Detail.aspx?ArticleUid=103427a1-0313-4d6c-b7f7-c5deb0bedbb5, accessed 30 August 2013, citing Government Regulation No. 47 of 2012 Concerning Social and Environmental Responsibility of Limited Liability Companies; see n. 14, at p. 123, citing Law No. 4 of 2009 on Minerals and Coal Mining, Articles 71, 79, 96 and 107 (requiring extractive companies to implement community development by among other things, employing local workers and engaging local entrepreneurs), Article 6 of the 2011 Law of East Belitung Regency No. 13 on Corporate Social Responsibility 2011, Article 6 and Batam Law No. 2 on Corporate Social Responsibility 2012, Article 10. For limited liability companies, the corporate resources to be allocated to fulfilling this responsibility are to be appropriate and reasonable. This gives leeway for these companies to adjust their expenditures in accordance with their financial situations, and they are mandated to report their 'social responsibility' implementation in their budget: see n. 14, at p. 108, citing the elucidation

The obligation appears mandatory for domestic and foreign direct investors,[23] limited liability companies that manage, utilize or impact natural resources,[24] all mining companies,[25] and State-owned enterprises.[26] All other limited liability companies are not mandated to, but will be rewarded for fulfilling, their statutory 'social responsibility'.

Critics see such legislation as simply a means of shifting to the private sector a responsibility that should instead be borne by the State. It has also been argued that the additional burden imposed on corporations will ultimately result in negative economic and social impacts, such as weakened economic competitiveness and the downsizing of staff.[27] Further, there is the concern that the regulation's definition of 'corporate social responsibility', with its emphasis on corporate contributions, may divert attention from the adverse impacts of business operations and the State's duties to protect against these impacts.[28]

On the other hand, these CSR obligations can be an opportunity for more businesses to take effective steps to manage conflict risks. The community-development initiatives that businesses in natural resources industries are required to undertake are similar to existing risk-management strategies used in those industries.[29] This is especially pertinent given the communal tensions that often surround natural resources exploitation in Indonesia.[30]

Through these CSR laws, Indonesia has provided an institutional underpinning for the 'harmonious' and 'balanced' business–society relationship it desires.[31] But other relevant State institutions, such as local government, ministries and public security forces, may be supporting or impeding the realization

---

of Government Regulation No. 47 of 2012 Concerning Social and Environmental Responsibility of Limited Liability Companies, Article 5.

[23] Law No. 25 of 2007 Concerning Investment, Article 15(b). Article 34 of the said law provides for sanctions for non-compliance.

[24] See n. 22.

[25] See n. 14, at p. 129, citing Government Regulation No. 23 of 2010 Concerning the Implementation of Mineral and Coal Mining Business Activity. Mining companies are also required to have development and empowerment programmes.

[26] Law No. 19 of 2007 on the State-owned Enterprise and Regulation of the Ministry of State-owned Enterprise.

[27] See n. 14, at p. 122, citing Verdict of Constitutional Court on the Judicial Review of the Corporate Law, Article 74 Case no. 53/ PUU-VI/2008, 106. See also S. Gayo, 'Mandatory and Voluntary Corporate Social Responsibility Policy Debates in Indonesia', *ICIRD* (2012), p. 1.

[28] See n. 21.

[29] The International Petroleum Industry Environmental Conservation Association (IPIECA), an oil and gas industry association for environmental and social issues, has noted that '[a]chieving sustainable economic and social development is a key factor in resolving conflicts and improving lives of the people in the region. Companies recognize this and are contributing to national development efforts': IPIECA, *Guide To Operating in Areas of Conflict for the Oil and Gas Industry*, 2008 (citing case-studies).

[30] See n. 18.

[31] A company's 'social responsibility' is defined by the investment law as 'the responsibility adhered to any investment companies in creating harmonious, balance relationship in accordance with the environment, value, norms, and culture of local community': Elucidation of Law No. 25 of 2007 Concerning Investment, Article 15(b).

of this vision.[32] Risks of State capture and poorly designed and implemented community-development projects cannot be over-estimated.

Protecting high-revenue businesses regarded as 'national vital objects'

The State's emphasis on the importance of business income for the national interest is again seen in Indonesia's laws governing the provision of security by the State for 'national vital objects'.[33] Such businesses include those in the energy and natural resources sector that provide a significant income for the country.[34] These businesses can request the Indonesian police to provide security, and security may be provided depending on need and the extent of the threat faced.[35]

According to the Indonesian government, securing these 'national vital objects' helps maintain national growth.[36] There have been allegations, however, that Indonesia's security institutions, particularly the military, have committed human rights violations.[37] This raises the question of whether the prevailing protection of these 'national vital objects' is coming at too high a social cost.

---

[32] According to the World Bank Group's regulatory quality index, Indonesia is ranked in the 41.7th percentile of all countries in the world, with 0 being the lowest rank: World Bank Group, 'Worldwide Governance Indicators', http://info.worldbank.org/governance/wgi/index.asp, accessed 14 January 2014. (This indicator captures 'perceptions of the government to formulate and implement sound policies and regulations that permit and promote private sector development'.) According to the World Bank Group's rule of law index, Indonesia is ranked in the 30th percentile of all countries in the world, with 0 being the lowest rank: World Bank Group, 'Worldwide Governance Indicators'. (This indicator captures 'perceptions of the extent to which agents have confidence in and abide by the rules of society, and in particular the quality of contract enforcement, property rights, the police, and the courts, as well as the likelihood of crime and violence'.)

[33] The law defines these 'national vital objects' as covering 'any zone or location, building or installation, and business that carry the hopes of many, or are of national importance, or are a source of state revenue, or are characterized as of strategic importance': Lubis, Ganie, Surowidjojo, 'Presidential Decree on the Security of National Vital Objects', LGS Newsletters, 9 October 2004, http://www.lgsonline.com/pages/g/lgsimp370/node/lgs4a1d783104616, accessed 30 August 2013.

[34] See n. 14, at p. 131, citing the Presidential Decree No 63 on Security for National Vital Objects 2004 and the Ministerial Decree No. 2288/K/07/Mem/2008 on the Amendment of Ministerial Decree No. 1762/07/Mem/2007 on the Security Measure of National Vital Objects in Energy and Natural Resources Sector.

[35] The Indonesian police can, if required, ask the Indonesian military for assistance: see n. 14, at p. 131, citing the Presidential Decree No 63 on Security for National Vital Objects 2004 and the Ministerial Decree No. 2288/K/07/Mem/2008 on the Amendment of Ministerial Decree No. 1762/07/Mem/2007 on the Security Measure of National Vital Objects in Energy and Natural Resources Sector.

[36] *The President Post*, 'National Police Chief: Securing Vital Objects for People's Welfare', (30 August 2013), http://www.thepresidentpost.com/?p=32251, accessed 17 December 2013.

[37] For example, the operations of US mining firm Freeport McMoran in Papua, Indonesia, have been involved in violent workers' strikes and implicated in allegations of turning a blind eye to human rights abuses committed by the military it pays to provide security to its mine (K. Vaswani, 'US firm Freeport Struggles to Escape Its Past in Papua', *BBC News*, (9 August 2011), http://www.bbc.co.uk/news/world-asia-pacific-14417718, accessed 25 August 2013). As another example, ExxonMobil has been implicated in allegations that it abetted human rights violations by the Indonesian military in the ongoing separatist conflict in Aceh, Indonesia ('Exxon "Helped Torture in Indonesia"', *BBC News*, (22 June 2001), http://news.bbc.co.uk/2/hi/business/1401733.stm, accessed 25 August 2013).

Corporate governance: space for stakeholder interests

Stakeholder interests are incorporated in Indonesian law through corporate governance requirements. For example, CSR-related reporting is mandatory for public-listed companies; their annual reports in theory must include information on their whistle-blowing system for activities that may put the company or stakeholders at risk and disclose other pertinent information related to human rights issues.[38] The mandatory nature of this reporting obligation and the specificity given to its content may facilitate greater scrutiny by stakeholders of corporate practices and influence how companies include the numerous stakeholder interests in their policies and practices. Nevertheless, according to the ASEAN Corporate Governance Scorecard, Indonesia's ninety-seven largest public-listed companies[39] showed a wide variance in the extent to which they disclosed corporate responsibility policies and practices.[40]

The consideration of stakeholder interests by directors is formalized in law to varying degrees. Directors of State-owned enterprises are obliged under government regulations to take into consideration the interests of all stakeholders, including society as a whole, in making decisions and formulating policies.[41] Shareholders, members of the Board of Commissioners and Board of Directors of all corporations are encouraged, by the non-binding Code of Good Corporate Governance, to implement their business's 'responsibility to the communities and environment' by, among other things, having 'an awareness of the environmental and societal interests of the communities in which the company operates'.[42]

International human rights law applicable domestically to business-related policies and activities

It is unclear whether Indonesia practices monism or dualism, as Indonesia's implementation of treaties has been inconsistent. Under the 1999 Human Rights Law, all international human rights treaties 'accepted' by Indonesia appear to be rendered applicable domestically without the need for further implementing legislation.[43] There are also laws implementing specific international human rights treaties.[44] These provide a potential legal basis for the use of Indonesia's

---

[38]   These issues include workplace health and safety, gender perspectives in company policies, workplace opportunities, environmentally sustainable practices, contributions to social and community development, and consumer and product safety. (See n. 14, at p. 126, footnote 185.)

[39]   Based on market capitalization as of 30 June 2012.

[40]   ASEAN Capital Markets Forum and the Asian Development Bank, 'ASEAN Corporate Governance Scorecard, Country Reports and Assessments 2012–2013', May 2013, p. 14.

[41]   See n. 14, at p. 132, citing the Regulation of the Ministry of State-owned Enterprises No. PER.01/MBU/2011 Concerning the Implementation of Good Governance by State-owned Enterprises and noting that no sanctions for non-compliance are provided.

[42]   National Committee on Governance, 'Indonesia's Code of Good Corporate Governance', 2006, 2, 6, http://www.ecgi.org/codes/documents/indonesia_cg_2006_en.pdf, accessed 25 August 2013.

[43]   Law No. 39 on Human Rights 1999, Article 7(2).

[44]   E.g. the Elimination of Racial and Ethnic Discrimination (Law No. 40/2008), and Law No. 21 Year 1999 on the Ratification of ILO Convention No. 111 on Discrimination In Respect of Employment and Occupation.

international human rights obligations to constrain and compel State action relating to business activities.

These obligations have been used by the State as a basis for justifying government policies relating to business. For example, the Constitutional Court has upheld Indonesia's CSR legislation on the grounds that these laws advance the State's obligation to respect, protect and fulfil its citizens' economic, social, and cultural rights.[45] The minimum age limit (of 21 years) imposed by Indonesia on migrant domestic workers was also upheld on the grounds that it implemented the State's duty to protect its citizens from potential abuses.[46]

Indonesia also has a National Human Rights Commission, KOMNAS HAM, which is accredited by the International Coordinating Committee of National Institutions for the Promotion and Protection of Human Rights. It employs international human rights standards in investigating adverse business-related human rights abuses.

B.   Lao PDR

Overview

Lao PDR, one of the least developed countries in Southeast Asia, is advancing its development with investment projects that depend on the country's abundant natural resources. Despite being designated one of the highest risk countries for investment,[47] foreign investment in this country has increased sevenfold in the past few years.[48] The government is driven by its commitments under the ASEAN Free Trade Agreement and its desire to join the World Trade Organization (WTO) to undertake economic reforms.[49] Indeed, the desire to promote foreign investment and 'create favourable conditions for the injection of capital' is enshrined in the revised 2003 Constitution.

It is quite likely that this desire has overshadowed or, at the very least, created tensions in respect of human rights concerns. The government's approach to permitting investment projects has been problematic. Recognizing this, in 2007 the Prime Minister announced a moratorium on further land concessions, in order to review the policies and practices of government agencies in this area.[50]

---

[45]   See n. 14, at p. 105, citing Verdict of Constitutional Court on the Judicial Review of Article 74 of the Corporate Law, Case no. 53/ PUU-VI/2008.

[46]   Ibid., p. 106, citing Judicial Review of the 2004 Law No. 39 on Placement and Protection of Indonesian Migrant Workers Abroad, Constitutional Court Decision on Case No. 028–029/ PUU-IV/2006, 56–58 (decided in 11 April 2007).

[47]   World Bank, 'Ease of Doing Business in Laos', http://www.doingbusiness.org/data/exploreeconomies/lao-pdr, accessed 1 February 2013.

[48]   From US$110 million in 2003 to US$770 million in 2008. International Labour Organization (ILO), 'Report on the review of the ILO Country Programme: Lao PDR 2006–2009', ILO Regional Office for Asia and the Pacific, Bangkok, (2011), p. 8.

[49]   G. Mukherjee, *Lao PDR Report*, p. 150, citing Bertelsmann Stiftung, 'BTI 2012 – Laos Country Report', Gütersloh (2012), p. 3.

[50]   Cor H. Hanssen, 'Lao Land Concessions, Development for the People?', (paper presented at International Conference on Poverty Reduction and Forests: Tenure, Market and Policy

Additionally, in 2012 the State imposed further moratoriums on concessions for mining projects and rubber plantations, in an attempt to stop the loss of agricultural land and forests.[51] These moratoriums, which were taken in response to complaints over the impacts of development and investment projects, also indicate a reactive and rather haphazard approach to the administration of investment.

Given its current low level of development, it is foreseeable that the country's economic development will give rise to significant social upheaval. As explained earlier in relation to Indonesia, the grant of special legal rights to traditional communities can potentially mitigate these social ruptures. Such rights are not granted in Lao PDR. As a matter of policy, the State does not recognize the existence of any indigenous people and instead gives equal regard to all ethnic groups.[52] The social impacts of investment projects are mitigated and managed through requirements for environmental impact assessments and compensation and resettlement of affected communities by project owners.

As will be shown, Lao PDR's detailed legislation in the areas of natural resources and land allocation, written in consultation with international organizations,[53] is on its face commendable, and gives the impression of significant regulatory oversight. However, as the laws were not the result of internal change processes and are reportedly poorly implemented, it is arguable that they are more aspirational than reflective of the realities on the ground.

Other social and political particularities in Lao PDR should be noted. Industrial action in the form of work stoppages is prohibited, perhaps due to the ruling communist party's emphasis on social order. The country's fledgling legal sector is still developing,[54] and international human rights law has no formalized role. Additional challenges arise in the absence of a national human rights institution.

Reforms, Regional Community Forestry Training Center for Asia and Pacific, Bangkok, September 3–7, 2007).

[51] Asia Miner, 'Laos: 4 Year Moratorium on New Project Approvals', (July 2012), http://www.asiaminer.com/magazine/current-news/news-archive/148-july-2012/4448-laos-4-year-moratorium-on-new-project-approvals.html, accessed 17 June 2013. These moratoriums do not include projects that have already received approval but have not commenced operation.

[52] This reportedly reflects the government's intention to create unity among all Lao peoples: International Fund for Agricultural Development, *Country Technical Notes on Indigenous Peoples' Issues. Lao People's Democratic Republic*, (November 2012), p. 19.

[53] In 2001, the United Nations Development Programme instituted the International Law Project in Lao PDR, to strengthen capacity for negotiating, ratifying and monitoring international treaties, harmonizing the domestic legal framework in line with international instruments, and enhancing Lao's participation in the international legal system (UNDP, 'Linking National Legal Systems with the International Human Rights Framework: Lessons from the International Law Project in Lao PDR', UNDP, December 2012).

[54] The state is undertaking a 'Master Plan for Law Development to 2020' in partnership with the UNDP (UNDP, 'Support to the Implementation of the Legal Sector Master Plan', http://www.undp.org/content/lao_pdr/en/home/operations/projects/democratic_governance/Legal_Sector_Mnaster_Plan.html)

Environmental regulations that limit the primacy of development

Laws limit the primacy of development where the environment will be negatively impacted. The Environmental Protection Law stipulates that development projects and activities that have or will have the potential to affect the environment must submit an Environmental Impact Assessment (EIA) report for an Environment Compliance Certificate before commencing the project.[55] The implementing decree for this requirement, however, states that EIAs are required for large-scale projects 'which are complicated or create significant environmental and social impacts'.[56] The decree does not define what is considered 'significant', which leaves room for creative interpretation of which projects require mandatory EIAs.

EIAs are legislated to be comprehensive, covering not only environmental but also social impacts. They take into account all possible impacts of the proposed project on the environment and the people resident around the development site or otherwise affected by the project.[57] The relevant administrative authority must reject the EIA report, and accordingly withhold approval of the project's commencement, if the project would cause more negative than positive impacts.[58] However, some reports suggest that, in practice, EIAs are conducted without stringency,[59] failing to take into account crucial negative impacts on the environment.[60]

---

[55] See n. 50, at p. 164, citing Environmental Protection Law 1999, Article 8(3).

[56] Decree on Environmental Impact Assessment 2010 (EIA Decree), Article 2.

[57] The EIA is defined as 'studying, surveying, researching-analysing and estimating of possible positive and negative impacts on the environment and society, including short and long term impacts on health created by the investment projects … as well as offering appropriate alternatives, environmental management and monitoring plan, and social management and monitoring plan to prevent and mitigate possible impacts which are likely to happen during construction and operation of the investment projects' (EIA Decree, Article 3). These assessments must also be conducted with the participation of the local administration, mass organizations, and the population likely to be affected by the development project (Environmental Protection Law 1999, Article 8(5)).

[58] EIA Decree, Article 15(3).

[59] Earth Rights International, 'I Want To Eat Fish, I Cannot Eat Electricity: Public Participation in Mekong Basin Development', (2009), https://www.earthrights.org/publication/i-want-eat-fish-i-cannot-eat-electricity-public-participation-mekong-basin-development, accessed 20 August 2012.

[60] See n. 50, at p. 175. For instance, a pre-feasibility and environmental study conducted on the Ban Kum Hydropower project illustrated the negative impacts of the project, including the flooding of four villages and a large dip in the fisheries on the river, impacting the food security of populations dependent on that income. The report found that the EIA conducted previously was inadequate, leaving out the potential impacts on the villages' ecosystem (see n. 61, at p. 113.). Also see Ian G. Baird and Mark S. Flaherty, 'Mekong River Fish Conservation Zones in Southern Laos: Assessing Effectiveness Using Local Ecological Knowledge', (2005), *Environmental Management* 36: 440–441); Özgür Can and Sheldon Leader, 'Nam Theun 2 Hydroelectric Project: Memorandum Of Legal Issues In Relation To The Concession Agreement: An Analysis For Mekong Watch', Human Rights Centre, Essex University (2005).

Inclusion of public participation in development

Stakeholders have the right to participate and provide input in consultations at all stages of a development project.[61] In the case of business activities that have a significant impact on the environment, they have the right to participate in discussions on compensation, resettlement and restoration of the environment.[62] In respect of development projects, the details of the compensation must be publicly disseminated.[63] In respect of business activities with a significant impact on the environment, stakeholders have the right to receive information regarding the assessments conducted, the environmental and social impacts of the project and any benefits they will receive.[64] In practice, the right to public participation is not always implemented, and can lead to mistrust between the developers and the community.[65]

Mitigating development's adverse impacts through compensation, resettlement and restoration

In the event of negative impacts to the environment and community, the Decree on Compensation and Resettlement of Development Projects (Compensation Decree) provides for all affected persons to be compensated by the owners of the development project concerned,[66] and for details of projected resettlement costs to be included within the cost of the project in the budgeting process.[67] Project owners are obligated to carry out surveys and investigations to identify the affected communities and provide appropriate funds for relocation and income assistance.[68] Additionally, those who lose more than 20 per cent of their income-generating land or employment are entitled to additional income.[69] The regulations stipulate that damage to the environment caused while engaging in commercial activities must be mitigated and the environment restored under the guidance of the appropriate State authority.[70] Ideally, the amount of compensation would emerge from an EIA, which would investigate the extent of the negative effects to the community and environment. However, as EIAs are often conducted with a minimum of investigation, some

---

[61] Compensation and Resettlement of the Development Project 2005 (Compensation Decree), Article 12. This decree applies to 'all development projects including government and domestic or foreign private development projects that require acquisition of land or land use rights or rights to possess fixed or immovable assets, change in land use or restriction of the use of resources that affect the livelihood or income of the people' (Compensation Decree, Article 2).

[62] EIA Decree, Article 7.

[63] Compensation Decree, Article 12.

[64] EIA Decree, Article 7.

[65] For instance, an environmental study conducted on the Ban Kum Hydropower project reported that villagers were not consulted on dam projects but were informed of the location of the dam once the agreements were signed (see n. 61, at p. 124).

[66] Compensation Decree, Articles 5 and 6.

[67] Compensation Decree, Article 14.

[68] Compensation Decree, Article 4.

[69] Compensation Decree, Article 8.

[70] Environmental Protection Law 1999, Article 28.

significant negative impacts are overlooked by the assessments. Additionally, research has also suggested that the compensation agreed upon is not always paid.[71]

Ensuring trickle-down effects of development benefits

Laws impose obligations on businesses that seek to ensure that economic benefits to the country 'trickle down'. Investors have the obligation to 'introduce (a) social insurance and social security system for the workers in their enterprises … promote the employment of Lao labour; give the emphasis on labour skill development, upgrading of specialized skill and transfer of technology to Lao workers'.[72] Foreign business owners are required to give priority to recruiting Lao workers and training and upgrading their skills, as well as to 'address matters of social security, healthcare and safety of the employees'.[73] Employers have a direct obligation to train their labour force and build skills, using 1 per cent of the employees' salary or wages reserve fund to cover expenses.[74] Additionally, the Minerals Law makes it a requirement that investors contribute to community-development funds, with the intention that these funds be used to compensate the community and provide local benefits.[75]

Industrial action: tension between social order and human rights

Lao PDR's policies relating to worker protection give significant weight to the maintenance of social order. Its Labour Law prohibits work stoppages, including 'in the event of a dispute concerning the implementation of labour law and regulations and benefits'; persons involved in work stoppages and thus causing 'social disorder' may be punished.[76] Further, the State keeps a tight rein on trade unions. While trade unions are legal,[77] in practice, only trade unions under the control of the ruling communist party are allowed to operate.[78]

C.   *Myanmar*

Overview

Myanmar is determinedly writing its new development story. Among the key instruments recently enacted to realize Myanmar's development vision are laws relating to land, labour, foreign investment and special economic zones. The legal framework pertinent

---

[71]   For instance, those affected by the Nam Theun II project are reportedly still awaiting compensation (see n. 61, at p. 130).

[72]   Investment Promotion Law, Article 69(3).

[73]   Foreign Investment Promotion Law 2004, Article 13.

[74]   Law on Labour 2006, Article 10.

[75]   See n. 50, at p. 164, citing World Bank, 'Lao PDR: Government Partners with the Mining Sector to Support Local Communities', http://bit.ly/1fX6Rmh, accessed 29 January 2013.

[76]   Law on Labour 2006, Article 65.

[77]   Law on Labour 2006, Article 5.

[78]   See n. 50, at p. 162, citing Bertelsmann Stiftung, 'Laos Country Report', p. 12.

to responsible business is still being built. For example, legal procedures relating to the conduct of environmental impact assessments prior to approvals of investment projects and other activities, at the time of writing, are being drafted.[79]

The legal framework relevant to business activities may be described as one that is State-enabling – the State is enabled to be interventionist or hands-off in regulating business activities as it sees fit. As will be shown, rather than being a firm bulwark against the adverse human rights impacts of modernization, Myanmar's laws providing for social safeguards and protections also come with caveats that give the authorities wide discretion to grant exemptions from these safeguards to businesses, enabling the State to pursue, with few fetters, its vision of development.[80]

As most of Myanmar's population is agricultural[81] and comprised of ethnic groups accustomed to traditional living, the redistribution of land rights to investors and businesses for economic development poses significant human rights risks. As will be shown, laws provide protections in the form of procedures for raising objections and obtaining compensation; discontent and conflict resulting from the adverse social impacts of land redistribution are dealt with through provisions for negotiations by the State on behalf of landless farmers and the establishment of parliamentary institutions to which grievances may be brought.

With regard to the domestic applicability of international human rights law to business-related policies and activities, it is unknown whether there is a judicial doctrine governing the reception of international human rights law domestically. Although the State has established the Myanmar National Human Rights Commission, it may be overly optimistic to view this as evidence of the its willingness to address business-related activities and policies in terms of international human rights standards.[82]

---

[79] Environmental Conservation Law 2012, Article 7 envisages the formulation and implementation of a system for environmental impact assessments and social impact assessments. The Asian Development Bank's Core Environment Program is supporting the Myanmar government in establishing this system, among other environmental safeguards (ADB website, 'Environmental Impact Assessment Procedures Workshop', (26 July 2013), http://www.gms-eoc.org/events/stakeholders-consultation-workshop-on-environmental-impact-assessment-procedures-yangon-myanmar-, accessed 8 May 2014.

[80] The current government has formulated a development approach that is 'people-centred' and prioritizes fulfilling the basic needs of the people (Eleven Media, 'People-Centred Development Tops Government's Agenda', (11 August 2013), http://elevenmyanmar.com/politics/3031-people-centred-development-tops-government-s-agenda, accessed 17 December 2013).

[81] In 2012, Myanmar's agricultural population comprised 32.35 million of a total population of 48.72 million (Food and Agriculture Organization of the United Nations, *Myanmar Country Profile. Economic Indicators*, http://faostat.fao.org/CountryProfiles/Country_Profile/Direct.aspx?lang=enandarea=28).

[82] The Myanmar National Human Rights Commission regards its duties as involving human rights as articulated in Myanmar's Constitution, which is not necessarily compliant with international human rights law. According to a statement by the Commission, it 'was established in order to promote and protect the fundamental rights of the citizens of Myanmar enshrined in the Constitution as well as to interact with the United Nations and other international organizations. This is to enable the enhanced enjoyment of human rights and to contribute to the current democratization process both in form and essence', http://www.altsean.org/Research/Regime%20Watch/Judicial/HRCStatements/2012/HRC-270312.php, accessed 13 October 2013. Also, the Myanmar National

Wide State discretion to derogate from social safeguards

Under the Foreign Investment Law, foreign investment is restricted or prohibited where it might affect the traditional culture and customs of the national races within the country, affect public health, or cause environmental damage.[83] The Environmental Conservation Law imposes obligations on businesses to prevent environmental pollution and provides a legal foundation for the establishment of a system of environmental and social impact assessments.

However, the State is able to derogate from these protections. First, the Foreign Investment Law contains a wide caveat that restricted or prohibited investments may nevertheless be permitted by the government if it deems it 'in the interests of the Union and its citizens'.[84] Second, there is additional scope for the government to derogate from provisions in the Foreign Investment Law when entering into international investment agreements, as the Foreign Investment Law provides that where there is a conflict between provisions of that law and any international treaty and agreement adopted by Myanmar, the latter shall prevail.[85] Third, for both domestic and foreign investment, the 2012 Environmental Conservation Law similarly contains a broad clause allowing the government to exempt, among others, any private business from complying with its provisions 'for the interests of the Union and its people'.[86]

Wide State discretion in managing businesses' investment activities may not necessarily be detrimental to social protection. The policies that guide the exercise of this discretion and the existence of formal and informal checks are also relevant.

Social protections in land distribution: public participation and compensation

Myanmar is implementing a policy of redistributing land rights to maximize the productivity of land for economic growth.[87] Laws contain a number of social safeguards in the form of public participation and compensation that may address potential adverse impacts of this policy.

The law appears to give the 'public' the power to veto the grant of investment permits and land leases to foreign investors coming under the Foreign Investment Law, where their investment projects involve the transfer and

---

Human Rights Commission is not accredited by the International Coordinating Committee of National Institutions for the Promotion and Protection of Human Rights.

[83] Foreign Investment Law 2012, Article 4(a), (b) and (c).

[84] Foreign Investment Law 2012, Article 5.

[85] Foreign Investment Law 2012, Article 54.

[86] Environmental Conservation Law 2012, Article 36.

[87] For example, Article 20(b) of the 2012 Farmland Rules encourages the grant of farmland rights to businesses that are, among other things, able to implement the 'modern mechanized farmland system'. The policy objective of maximizing productivity is seen from Article 45 of the 2012 Vacant, Fallow and Virgin Land Management Rules, which requires that approved agricultural projects must be completed within the stipulated time, and Article 12(j) of the 2012 Farmland Law, which requires that the land rights-holder must continually put the land to use and not permit it to lie fallow.

clearing of 'houses, buildings, farm and garden lands, fruit trees and edible plants etc.'.[88] There is wide scope for defining who actually constitutes the 'public', and the term could be interpreted to require substantial public disapproval beyond the discontent of affected communities. The absence of any further qualifications to this veto power also means that the 'public' can veto projects for any reason at all. The broadness of this provision may give rise to problems in implementation.

The role given to public participation in other laws is, in contrast, more muted. Where persons or entities apply for agricultural land rights, and where the State undertakes land acquisitions, the governing laws provide procedures for the public to be notified of these developments and for interested parties to raise objections.[89] In addition, the 2013 Foreign Investment Rules require the Directorate of Investment and Company Admission (DICA) to consider the input of the local people and social organizations in the area where the proposed investment is to be located when deciding on whether to grant a foreign investment permit.[90] Whether the authority is required to obtain such comments proactively through holding consultations is not clear.

Finally, in the case of government land acquisitions, laws provide for the payment of compensation to land rights-holders.[91] Where a foreign investment project requires the resettlement of persons, the foreign investor is required to pay compensation and damages to the relevant property owners.[92]

Conflict management in development

Myanmar has adopted regulatory solutions that purportedly seek to manage conflict and mitigate the social unrest that economic development may bring. For example, situations where farmers are rendered landless may lead to resentment and social tensions.[93] Thus, where agricultural lands had been cultivated by farmers over a period of time without legal land rights, and are leased by the State to other persons or entities, the law provides for government-led negotiations to ensure that these landless farmers are 'not unfairly or unjustly dealt with'.[94]

---

[88] Union Government Notification No. 39 2011, Article 28 ('...In place that public not desirous to transfer and vacant, [the investor] shall not have the right to lease the land and invest').

[89] Vacant, Fallow and Virgin Land Management Rules 2012, rules 9(b), 11, 12 2012; Farmland Rules 2012, rules 6, 9–12; Land Acquisition Act 1894, Article 5A.

[90] Foreign Investment Rules 2013, Rule 14(a).

[91] Vacant, Fallow and Virgin Land Management Rules 2012, Rule 56, Farmland Law 2012, Article 26, Land Acquisition Act 1894, Article 11.

[92] Union Government Notification No. 39 2011, Article 28.

[93] For example, in August 2012, farmers forced off their lands and relocated to poor farming land, and given allegedly inadequate compensation, demonstrated in front of the investor company's premises in Yangon (H. W. Yee, 'Myanmar Report', in Human Rights Resource Centre, *Business and Human Rights in ASEAN: A Baseline Study* (Jakarta: Human Rights Resource Centre, 2012), p. 253).

[94] Vacant, Fallow and Virgin Land Management Rules 2012, rule 52(b).

A few institutions provide channels for grievances to be addressed, and constitute an additional layer to business regulation. The Parliamentary Commission on Land Confiscation Investigation was established to investigate land confiscation cases. While it has no mandate to decide on the merits of a case, it has strengthened regulation through publicizing findings and calling for action.[95] The Myanmar National Human Rights Commission and the Rule of Law and Stability Committee, a parliamentary body, were also recently established. They address business-related human rights abuses that are not confined to land confiscations and have only investigative rather than adjudicative powers.[96]

Limited mitigation of adverse impacts on indigenous and traditional ways of life

Like Lao PDR, Myanmar does not accord special rights to indigenous peoples and traditional communities. Myanmar instead gives equal regard to ethnic groups that are recognized as the country's 'national races'.[97] Communal and customary land rights are also not recognized by laws. Customs and traditions of the national races nevertheless do play a role to a small degree in relation to the admission of business activities. The State has the discretion to restrict or prohibit foreign investment where it can affect the traditional culture and customs of the national races within the country.[98]

'Corporate social responsibility': an undeveloped concept

The State has not developed the concept of CSR, although the concept does feature in some regulations, including brief references in the foreign investment laws. For instance, potential foreign investors are to include reference to their CSR programmes, if any, in their investment proposals,[99] and foreign investors 'shall carry out socially responsible investment in the interest of the Union and its people'.[100] The content of a corporation's social responsibility is, however, undefined in these regulations.

[95] For example, its findings include that certain cases of land confiscation were undertaken for the benefit of families of former military generals rather than the public interest. It encouraged the military to investigate these cases and take action accordingly. The military has reported that 4,000 acres of land were returned and 999,258 million kyats were given in compensation the same year (see n. 93, at pp. 267–268).

[96] See n. 93, at pp. 260–270.

[97] These are ethnic groups that made Myanmar their permanent home 'from a period anterior to 1185 BE, 1823 AD', including the majority Barma group (Burma Citizenship Law, Articles 3 and 4.) Not all ethnic groups are recognized as these 'national races'. A high-profile exclusion from those constituting 'national races' is that of a group of Muslims in Rakhine state, also known as the Rohingya.

[98] Foreign Investment Law 2012, Article 4(a).

[99] The investment proposal form to be submitted in order to obtain an MIC permit has a section relating to social impacts that is named 'corporate social responsibility programme', where a proposed investor is presumably to fill in details of any CSR programme it intends to implement in connection with the investment.

[100] Foreign Investment Rules 2013, Article 54(b).

D.   The Philippines

Overview

In the Philippines, laws seek to be a strong force protecting society from adverse business impacts. The State's duty to protect society is made explicit in the Philippines' Constitution and other laws, and businesses can potentially be held to constitutional and customary international human rights standards. As will be shown, statutory obligations on businesses that have the effect of preventing adverse human rights impacts are interventionist and expansive. Further, indigenous communities are accorded special legal rights, and the State has, in its laws, ceded control over development projects to these communities where their lands are involved.

Upholding the 'State duty to protect'

The State's duty to protect rights is made explicit in the laws of the Philippines. The Philippine Constitution expresses this in the arena of health, labour, and environmental rights. For example, it states that, '(t)he State shall protect and promote the right to health of the people'.[101] It likewise stipulates that: '(t)he State shall protect and advance the right of the people to a balanced and healthful ecology'.[102]

Significantly, the State's duty to protect has been invoked by the Supreme Court to justify impugning the conduct of at least one non-State entity. In *International School Alliance of Educators (ISAE)* v. *Quisumbing*, the Supreme Court held that ISAE's policy of giving expatriate teachers a higher pay than their local counterparts was discriminatory and hence invalid. The Supreme Court stated that:

> The Constitution enjoins the State to 'protect the rights of workers and pro-
> mote their welfare,' 'to afford labour full protection …' The State, therefore,
> has the right and duty to regulate the relations between labour and capital …
> Should (labour contracts) contain stipulations that are contrary to public pol-
> icy, courts will not hesitate to strike down these stipulations.

The State's duty to protect in the Philippines thus constitutes a potential legal basis for applying constitutional rights standards to the conduct of not only the State and its agents but also non-State actors.[103]

---

[101] Constitution of the Republic of the Philippines 1987, Article II, section 15.

[102] Constitution of the Republic of the Philippines 1987, Article II, section 16.

[103] Not all jurisdictions apply constitutional safeguards to non-State actors. In Malaysia, for example, constitutional safeguards deal only with contraventions of constitutional rights by the State or its agents. In *Beatrice A/P AT Fernandez* v. *Sistem Penerbangan Malaysia and Ors*, [2005] 3 MLJ 681, a case concerning the alleged wrongful dismissal of a pregnant flight stewardess by the national airline, the Court of Appeal held that a constitutional safeguard such as the right to equality dealt only with 'the contravention of individual rights by a public authority, that is, the state or any of its agencies', (para. 469).

Expansive corporate obligations

Corporate obligations are relatively expansive in the Philippines. To prevent child pornography, business such as Internet service providers, owners or operators of business establishments such as malls, photo developers, information technology professionals and banks have an obligation to report to the authorities when, in the course of their business, they have knowledge suggesting that child pornography has occurred.[104] Specified types of employers have statutory obligations to provide night workers with free health assessments and first-aid facilities.[105] Employers are statutorily obliged to prescribe procedures for the investigation of sexual harassment cases and consequent administrative sanctions, and create a committee on decorum to investigate cases of sexual harassment.[106] The Philippines' Revised Code of Corporate Governance, which is binding on specified types of corporations,[107] imposes a duty to establish and maintain an alternative dispute resolution system in the corporation for disputes within the corporation.[108] It is worth noting that the Labor Code requires its provisions and implementing rules and regulations to be construed in favour of labour in the event of doubt.[109]

Such regulatory intervention can buttress a robust understanding of CSR that views the costs incurred to, for example, undertake the requisite due diligence to prevent or avoid contributing to child pornography and sexual harassment, as a mainstream part of business operations. However, there are a number of potential downsides to prescribing specific due diligence measures. When implementing the

[104] I. Ramos, 'Philippines Report', in Human Rights Resource Centre, *Business and Human Rights in ASEAN: A Baseline Study* (Jakarta: Human Rights Resource Centre, 2012), p. 308, citing Anti-Child Pornography Act 2009, Republic Act No. 9775, §§9, 10, 11, 15(j), 15(k), 15(l).

[105] See n. 109, at p. 304, citing Republic Act No. 10151, §8 (an Act allowing the employment of night workers). The said legislation applies to 'all persons, who shall be employed or permitted or suffered to work at night, except those employed in agriculture, stock raising, fishing, maritime transport and inland navigation, during a period of not less than seven (7) consecutive hours, including the interval from midnight to five o'clock in the morning, to be determined by the Secretary of Labor and Employment, after consulting the workers' representatives/labor organizations and employers', (§154).

[106] See n. 104, at p. 331, citing Anti-Sexual Harassment Act 1995, Republic Act No. 7877, §§4 and 7. Implementation by businesses of the requirements for committees on decorum and investigation was, a decade after the enactment of the Anti-Sexual Harassment Act of 1995, reported to be poor (Immigration and Refugee Board of Canada: *The Protection Offered to Female Victims of Sexual Abuse* [PHL42572.E], (14 June 2004), http://www.ecoi.net/local_link/191377/294990_en.html, accessed 16 December 2013.)

[107] The Code applies only to 'registered corporations and to branches or subsidiaries of foreign corporations operating in the Philippines that (a) sell equity and/or debt securities to the public that are required to be registered with the [Securities and Exchange] Commission, or (b) have assets in excess of Fifty Million Pesos and at least two hundred (200) stockholders who own at least one hundred (100) shares each of equity securities, or (c) whose equity securities are listed on an Exchange; or (d) are grantees of secondary licenses from the Commission': see n. 109, at p. 331, citing SEC Memorandum Circular No. 6, Series of 2009, Revised Code of Corporate Governance.

[108] See n. 109, at p. 314, citing Revised Code of Corporate Governance, Articles 3(F)2(e) and 3(F)2(j).

[109] Labor Code, Presidential Decree No. 442, Article 4.

law is not feasible in practice, for example, because a business has fewer resources or incompatible internal processes, the law may consequently be disregarded by that business. Further, having specific prescriptions could narrow the space for effective alternatives to be employed.

Binding commitments to indigenous peoples: restraints on business activities and development

Indigenous communities have significant control over the acquisition of their land, at least in law. Ancestral domains and lands and indigenous peoples' rights of ownership over them, are recognized and protected by the Philippines' Indigenous Peoples Rights Act. Any relocation of indigenous people from their ancestral lands can only be done by the State's exercise of eminent domain, and requires their free and prior informed consent.[110] Where exploration of natural resources is to be conducted on their lands, they have the right to negotiate the terms and conditions of exploration to protect and conserve the environment in accordance with their customary laws.[111] Specific protection is further given regarding the transfer of these rights to others, such as private businesses. The transferor indigenous community has the right to redeem the rights transferred, before a certain time limit, where the agreement was made in circumstances that vitiate consent, or where the land or property rights are transferred for an 'unconscionable' consideration or price.[112] However, while the provisions of the Indigenous Peoples Rights Act are promising, their implementation has reportedly been 'disappointing', due, among other things, to the restrictive manner in which they have been interpreted and implemented by the courts and government agencies.[113] The unforeseen consequences of the said Act are also noteworthy. In 2012, controversy arose over the significant reduction of the area of protected forests due to the grant of titles to forests to indigenous peoples.[114]

A norm of participatory development

Stakeholder consultations are provided for in various laws governing business impacts on society. Indigenous communities have 'the right to an informed and intelligent participation in the formulation and implementation of any project, government or private, that will affect or impact upon the ancestral domains'.[115]

---

[110] Indigenous Peoples Rights Act 1997, Republic Act No. 8371, §7(c).

[111] Indigenous Peoples Rights Act of 1997, Republic Act No. 8371, §7(b).

[112] Indigenous Peoples Rights Act of 1997, Republic Act No. 8371, §8(b).

[113] Alternative Law Groups Inc. *et al*, *Submission to the Committee on the Elimination of all forms of Racial Discrimination, Shadow Report*, August 2009, 21 (a joint submission by 14 non-governmental organizations).

[114] Indigenous people granted title over otherwise protected forests are able to exercise ownership rights, including transferring and leasing the forests and felling trees (Norman Boradora, 'Drilon Seeks Review of Law on Indigenous People's Rights', *Philippine Daily Inquirer* (18 September 2012), http://tinyurl.com/kc666ao).

[115] Indigenous Peoples Rights Act of 1997, Republic Act No. 8371, §7(b).

Underprivileged or homeless citizens affected by proposed evictions or demolitions, including for government development projects that may be undertaken by the private sector, have the right to be consulted on the matter of their resettlement.[116] Similarly, public participation and disclosure of information is required in the conduct of environmental impact assessments.[117]

Domestic applicability of international human rights law

There is legal basis for international human rights law to be applied by the courts in reviewing business activities and the State's business-related policies. International human rights that are part of 'generally accepted principles of international law' form part of domestic law in the Philippines by virtue of §2, Article II of the Constitution. The Supreme Court, in identifying what these principles are, has had recourse to core international human rights instruments, such as the Universal Declaration of Human Rights.[118] Further, the State's constitutional duty to protect has been held to require courts to impugn practices of non-State entities that flout constitutional rights.[119] This decision can arguably be applied to business enterprises.

The establishment of the Philippines National Human Rights Commission has enabled adverse business-related impacts to be evaluated by international human rights standards.[120] Its cases have involved business-related human rights abuses, including adverse impacts of mining operations on indigenous peoples and the responsibility of local media in relation to child entertainers.[121]

E.   Singapore

Overview

In seeking to balance social protection with minimal impediment to the wheels of commerce, the State has, as will be shown, placed the balancing weight as near to the latter goal as possible, without, in its view, compromising on desired social protection. Underlying these policies is the fact that the people of this natural resource-scarce country are its only economic resource. Maintaining and advancing Singapore's strong position in the market is seen by the government as an imperative to ensure the nation's survival. Rights such as the freedom to strike, freedom of association and non-discrimination are recognized, but regarded as

---

[116] Urban Development and Housing Act of 1992, Republic Act No. 7279, §28.

[117] Department of Environment and Natural Resources Memorandum Circular, *Standardization of Requirements and Enhancement of Public Participation in the Streamlined Implementation of the Philippine EIS System* (29 July 2010), http://tinyurl.com/ms9xr9l.

[118] See *International School Alliance of Educators (ISAE)* v. *Quisumbing*.

[119] See *International School Alliance of Educators (ISAE)* v. *Quisumbing*.

[120] The Commission is a national human rights institution accredited by the International Coordinating Committee of National Institutions for the Promotion and Protection of Human Rights.

[121] See n. 109, at pp. 331–332.

derogable for the greater good of society, or as being malleable to Singapore's needs according to the prevailing context at the time.[122]

A non-adversarial workforce for a market-competitive nation

Labour-related laws and policies limit the availability of external adversarial legal avenues for employees and workers to express grievances. First, laws generally do not protect employees against discrimination by employers or potential employers, save for prohibiting dismissal of employees under the age of 62 on the grounds of age, and prohibiting the dismissal of non-managerial and non-executive female employees during maternity leave.[123] Neither are there equal opportunities laws. Besides the aforementioned laws and a common law action for wrongful termination, there do not appear to be available grounds to sue for workplace discrimination that does not result in dismissal or resignation. The government's position is that, while it 'does not entirely reject' workplace anti-discrimination legislation, such legislation will not change mindsets, and it hence prefers to use 'persuasion'.[124] According to the Tripartite Alliance for Fair Employment Practices (TAFEP),[125] '(a)nti-discrimination legislation could make our labour market more rigid and hence less competitive without achieving its aims'.[126] Instead, TAFEP relies on guidelines encouraging employers not to discriminate on grounds of race, religion, marital status, age, or gender in recruitment. Also, complaints regarding workplace discrimination may be submitted to TAFEP for oversight and mediation.

Second, the dominant labour union, the National Trade Unions Congress (NTUC), has largely kept in line with the government's 'no strike' policy.[127] In an interview with *Asiaweek*, former Singapore president Ong Teng Cheong noted that he had, during his time as head of NTUC, permitted one labour strike in 1986 without informing the government, upsetting State officials as a result. He said,

---

[122] For instance, the court in *Chee Soon Juan* v. *PP* [2003] 2 Sing. L.R.(R.) 445, discussing Article 14 of the Singapore Constitution on freedom of speech, assembly and association, noted that '[i]n any society, democratic or otherwise, freedom of speech is not an absolute right. Broader societal concerns such as public peace and order must be engaged in a balancing exercise with the enjoyment of this personal liberty': at [22].

[123] See Retirement Age Act.

[124] T. Y. Chuan, 'Government "Does not Entirely Reject" Workplace Anti-Discrimination Laws', *The Straits Times* (20 May 2013).

[125] TAFEP is a tripartite partnership between the government, NTUC and the Singapore National Employers Federation. Through TAFEP, government, labour unions and employers are seen to put forward, in a united manner, policies relating to fair employment practices.

[126] Tripartite Alliance for Fair Employment Practices, 'Frequently Asked Questions', http://www.tafep.sg/faqs.asp#A2, accessed 30 August 2013.

[127] With 60 affiliated trade unions, NTUC is a national labour union movement that has also been a close partner of the ruling political party. It has identified one of its achievements as its contribution to establishing a collective bargaining scheme that is 'collaborative and not confrontational': 'About NTUC', http://tinyurl.com/nqtusvd accessed 1 September 2013; 'History of NTUC', http://tinyurl.com/lg959wo, accessed 1 September 2013; 'Little by Little, Step by Step', http://tinyurl.com/kgu4qjy, accessed 30 August 2013.

'(i)f I were to inform the cabinet or the government they would probably stop me from going ahead with the strike'.[128] Singapore has since remained an almost strike-free country. A strike in 2012 by foreign bus drivers was the first strike in Singapore in almost twenty-five years.[129]

Third, State policies allow business autonomy in relation to personnel matters. The recruitment, promotion, internal transfer, retrenchment, dismissal, or reinstatement of an employee – including the assignment or allocation of duties or specific tasks to the person in question – cannot be the subject of demands made in collective bargaining.[130]

To determine whether reform is needed, a pertinent issue for investigation is whether relying on Singapore's model of tripartism and 'soft' regulation, in place of broader legal rights to bring suit or conduct labour strikes, creates a permissive environment for workplace abuse and discrimination.

Corporate social responsibility: embraced as a matter of market competitiveness

CSR has been a national initiative in Singapore for at least a decade. A National Tripartite Initiative on CSR was founded in 2004, and comprised government, business and national non-governmental institutions. This State-allied initiative went on to launch the Singapore Compact in 2005.

Business regulators have issued guidance to businesses that assert a prevailing robust understanding of 'corporate social responsibility', namely, not only consisting of philanthropy but of integrating concern for business impacts on society and observance of 'fundamental human rights' throughout businesses' everyday operations.[131] The guidebooks seek to make companies aware of prevalent CSR-related principles and tools, such as the UN Global Compact's principles, the ISO 26000, and the Global Reporting Initiative. They also set out norms and up-to-date best practices for embedding CSR in a company's operations. These State-led CSR initiatives are most likely to be primarily driven by a concern for market competitiveness. According to an official:

> (CSR is) of concern to Singapore due to our position as a hub for international businesses and the international expansion plans of local companies

[128] Asiaweek.com, 'I Had a Job to Do', (10 March 2000), http://www-cgi.cnn.com/ASIANOW/asiaweek/magazine/2000/0310/nat.singapore.ongiv.html, accessed 8 May 2014.

[129] That strike was regarded by the state to be illegal under a law governing strikes by workmen in essential services for breaching the requirement for 14 days' notice to be given, and resulted in the conviction and imprisonment of four for up to seven weeks. Their work permits were revoked by their employer, resulting in their repatriation ('Singapore Jails Bus Drivers for Inciting Strikes', *BBC News Asia* (25 February 2013), http://tinyurl.com/mt6oe2j; Royston Sim and Maria Almenoar, 'SMRT Bus Strike: 5th Driver to Be Charged, 29 to Be Repatriated', *The Straits Times* (1 December 2012), http://tinyurl.com/ln84bwh).

[130] Industrial Relations Act, Article 18.

[131] ACRA Guidebook for Directors 2011; Singapore Stock Exchange Guide for Sustainability Reporting.

and government linked companies. A lack of knowledge and management expertise in dealing with CSR issues may impede our development.[132]

Similarly, the Singapore Exchange's (SGX) intention to move to a 'comply or explain' basis for listed companies to report on their sustainability standards appears to be driven by the same concern for market competitiveness. According to SGX's chief executive, this move was undertaken in view of the fact that 'the world (is) moving forward' and embracing sustainability as integral to success; he also stated that SGX was concerned to maintain a 'competitive platform that can attract sustainable companies to the Singapore market'.[133] The State's approach to the promotion of CSR is hence a utilitarian one. Future State action in respect of CSR will likely be with a view to keeping up with CSR market trends. For as long as this philosophy of CSR prevails, Singapore is likely to be a keen follower, but not an initiator, of CSR trends.

Public consultations and participation in economic development

The public is given a role in shaping the allocation of land between economic uses and fulfilling the expectations of the citizenry for a good quality of life. The government has, as a matter of policy, conducted public consultations in relation to concept and master plans for the use of land nationwide, as well as for area-specific plans and development control guidelines; these have involved in-depth focus groups as well as online surveys, among other platforms.[134] However, as a matter of law, the State ultimately has the discretion to do as it sees fit in relation to these matters. The relevant legislation does not require the government to conduct public consultations on land use planning.[135] Further, Singapore's land acquisition legislation does not provide any procedure for objections to be made to the acquisition of land by the State; accordingly, the State is not required to take cognizance of objections and public opinion on land use planning and State land acquisitions.[136]

In respect of individual investment projects and business activities, laws do not reserve space for public participation.[137] Public consultations or consideration

---

[132] E. Tan, *The State of Play of CSR in Singapore* (Lien Centre for Social Innovation, Social Insight Research Series, July 2011), citing Lim Boon Heng, 'Keynote address by the NTUC Secretary-General, at the NTUC– DGB seminar on 'Global Challenges and Union Response', (11 January 2005).

[133] 'SGX To Get Stricter on Sustainability', *Business Times* (20 March 2013), http://tinyurl.com/o7bbdpp.

[134] Urban Redevelopment Authority, 'Designing Our City: Planning for a Sustainable Singapore', (May/June 2012), p. 5.

[135] See Planning Act (Cap. 232). A procedure for objections to be made to proposed master plans, which must be made public, is provided for by the Planning (Master Plan) Rules.

[136] Land Acquisition Act (Cap. 152).

[137] There are no special laws governing foreign or local investment in Singapore. Accordingly, business permits are governed by ordinary company laws, such as the Business Registration Act and the Companies Act, which, as with similar laws in other jurisdictions, do not require public consultations with affected persons or public notification.

of stakeholder opinion are also not required in the conduct of environmental and social impact assessments[138] or the grant of land for individual commercial projects.[139] Nevertheless, it is noteworthy that there do not appear to have been any allegations of human rights violations in the government's acquisition of land and the establishment of investment projects.

Limited domestic applicability of international human rights law

International human rights law has no legal force independently of domestic laws.[140] However, there is some scope for international human rights law to be applied domestically to assess business-related policies and activities. In this regard, Singapore's highest court has held that domestic law should 'as far as possible' be interpreted to be consistent with Singapore's international human rights obligations.[141] Notwithstanding the court's position, it remains that in the event of conflicting laws, domestic provisions, including domestic law incorporating treaty obligations, prevails.[142] Finally, Singapore does not have a national human rights institution to serve as an additional layer of domestic human rights-based regulation.

Observations

From the above analyses, a few observations can be derived. Together, they serve to shed light on the reforms needed to effectively address business-related human rights abuses in these countries.

First, for Indonesia, Lao PDR, Myanmar, and the Philippines, the developmental dimension must be squarely addressed in formulating any policy prescription. One reason is that there are apparent tensions to be resolved between economic developmental policies and human rights norms. For example, Indonesia's policy of maintaining national growth by drawing upon its police and military to provide

---

[138] The Environmental Protection and Management Act (Cap. 94A) gives the state the discretion to require the conduct of environmental impact assessments. There are no regulations prescribing procedures for the conduct of such assessments.

[139] Land Acquisition Act (Cap. 152). This legislation does provide a mechanism for appeals against compensation awarded for such acquisitions. The Singapore Land Authority Act (Cap. 301), which establishes the governmental authority in charge of land administration, requires the said authority to have regard to '(a)… efficiency and economy and to the social, industrial, commercial and economic needs of Singapore; and (b) as far as practicable, promote, develop and provide facilities or services that facilitate or are necessary for land planning, land infrastructure development and maintenance and the economic growth in Singapore'. While not expressly provided for in this statute, the Singapore Land Authority would most likely have the discretion to take into account public opinion and environmental and social impacts.

[140] International treaties that Singapore has ratified are not self-executory, i.e. they must first be transformed and incorporated into domestic law by an act of Parliament before they can have the force of law.

[141] *Yong Vui Kong* v. *PP* [2010] 3 S. L.R. 489, at [59].

[142] *Nguyen Tuong Van* v. *Public Prosecutor* [2004] SGCA 47 at [94].

security to industrial projects has reportedly incurred heavy social costs.[143] In turn, Myanmar's policy of redistributing land rights to maximize the productivity of land for economic growth is said to be detrimental to citizens' rights, due to its adverse impact on land tenure security.[144]

Second, quite apart from issue-specific policies, general business regulation policies may need to be addressed in proposing policy reform. This is the case in relation to Myanmar and Singapore. With regard to Myanmar, the State's general approach to business regulation across a variety of issues is to reserve for itself wide discretion, enabling it to be interventionist or hands-off in regulating businesses depending on the circumstances of each case. With regard to Singapore, its general policy, as previously discussed, is to minimize impediments to business freedom in the market to the extent possible, in order to ensure the small and resource-strapped country stays market-competitive. Whether the absence of legislation as a consequence of this policy is creating a permissive environment for business-related human rights abuses also merits investigation. In proposing any policy reform that requires these states to change or make exception to these policies, one may need to consider and address their underlying rationales.

Third, the effectiveness of laws and their implementation – as opposed to their adequacy in coverage – is often a priority issue in developing countries, such as in Lao PDR and the Philippines. As explained above, the breadth of protection afforded by certain laws in these countries is robust.[145] However, the laws in question are reportedly ineffective in practice.[146] Causes of the ineffectiveness should be investigated. In exploring this matter, it is important to consider not only failures in implementation but also concerns with regard to the suitability of the laws themselves, such as their operability, feasibility, and potential adverse impacts.[147]

Fourth, although the concept of CSR has the potential to be an effective regulatory tool for fostering corporate cultures respectful of human rights, proposals for using CSR in policy reform should be mindful that states tend to use CSR strategically. Indonesia and Singapore have, in their corporate governance regulatory guidance, defined CSR as going beyond philanthropy and covering the impacts of business operations.[148] At the same time, Indonesia has used CSR as normative justification for imposing statutory obligations on limited liability companies to

[143] See n. 37.

[144] Food Security Working Group's Land Core Group, *Legal Review of Recently Enacted Farmland Law and Vacant, Fallow and Virgin Lands Management Law*, (November 2012), at Chapter III, pp. 19–20.

[145] E.g. Laos' Environmental Protection Law 1999, Decree on Environmental Impact Assessment 2010, and Compensation and Resettlement of the Development Project 2005; the Philippines' Indigenous Peoples Rights Act of 1997, Republic Act No. 8371, and Department of Environment and Natural Resources, *Enhancement of Public Participation in the Philippine EIS System*.

[146] See e.g. footnotes 63, 64, 69.

[147] For example, the reported susceptibility of religious or local customary leaders in Indonesia to corruption throws into question whether the grant of communal land rights, the exercise of which is influenced by these traditional elites, is buttressing unjust and corrupt social structures (see Sidney Jones, 'Causes of Conflict in Indonesia', Asia Society website, http://asiasociety.org/causes-conflict-indonesia, accessed 8 May 2014).

[148] See n. 33, 138.

contribute to community development, thereby harnessing CSR for its development objectives. The business opposition arising in response to such CSR legislation could negate efforts to promote the 'enlightened' concept of CSR (i.e. one that addresses the impacts of business operations, not just philanthropy). With regard to Singapore, it has been argued that the State's promotion of CSR has been strategically used as a substitute for regulatory intervention.[149]

As concerns strategies for effecting needed policy reform, the respect accorded to international human rights norms is an important aspect of the domestic context to bear in mind, particularly as the business and human rights movement relies on international human rights norms to compel State action. Such reliance may face some resistance in Myanmar and Singapore. In this regard, the deontological nature of international human rights obligations, and their potential to override executive powers, do not sit well with Myanmar's concern to maintain wide and unfettered executive powers. It is telling that the Myanmar National Human Rights Commission regards its mandate as involving simply to 'interact with the United Nations and other international organizations', instead of upholding Myanmar's international human rights obligations.[150]

Further, arguments based on international human rights obligations are often a priori or non-empirical in nature. In contrast, in Singapore, it is the practical consequences of policies that primarily guide the State's business-related policy decisions, as opposed to purely ideological considerations, as evident from its utilitarian approach to workplace regulation and adoption of CSR. Hence, although the State may be receptive to human rights-based policy recommendations, its ultimate decision will likely be influenced more by utilitarian considerations than a priori and non-empirical human rights-based arguments. Such rights-based strategies may, however, find greater success in Indonesia and the Philippines. Among the ASEAN States canvassed, it is Indonesia that has permitted international human rights law to be domestically applicable to the largest extent, which could foster institutional norms that are receptive to international human rights-based policy-making. In the Philippines, the State has explicitly recognized that it has a duty to protect against the violation of constitutional rights by businesses, which suggests potential for a rights-based approach to policy-making. It should be emphasized that this chapter does not put forward any view as to which approach to policy-making, e.g. utilitarian or deontological, is better.

Conclusion

Although the language of human rights and business is being invoked more frequently in ASEAN, most states have not paid serious attention to promoting awareness, acceptance and implementation of the Guiding Principles. Despite this, in many states progress is being made to embed the notions of respect for, and the protection of, the rights of people in the areas of land, labour, and the

---

[149] See n. 132, at pp. 49, 51.
[150] See n. 86.

environment. Additionally, institutions such as National Human Rights Institutes are being created in some states to generally improve human rights norms and access to remedies.

While ASEAN lags behind the world in terms of trailblazing initiatives in the arena of business and human rights, there are many behind-the-scenes systems, both voluntary and compulsory, that are contributing to changing perspectives and creating gradual positive changes regarding business regulation. With the increased global focus on emerging markets in East and South Asia, there is increased opportunity in ASEAN for initiatives that increase economic competitiveness and sustainability of development, while improving the standards of human rights enjoyed by its people. It is hoped that sharing best practices and lessons learned will provide the necessary information resources to policy-makers in ASEAN to make these initiatives more mainstream and widespread.

3 Why gender matters for the business and human rights agenda in Southeast Asia

Kathryn Dovey

Introduction

The purpose of this chapter is to explore what it means to bring a gender perspective to the field of business and human rights. Initially, some common definitions are set out to clarify the terminology, followed by an exploration of gender in relation to the State duty to protect and the corporate responsibility to respect human rights. Examples are drawn upon throughout the chapter that relate both to the Southeast Asian context and to company operations globally. The overall intention is to underline that there is still an important dynamic to be explored in ensuring that corporate impacts on women and men are understood by both states and corporations.

Context

Challenges in the face of existing gender gaps

Gender equality is an important human rights issue because gender differences can be the basis upon which people are discriminated against, i.e. not granted the same rights or ability to enjoy rights. Globally, women fare less well than men when it comes to the gendered norms and roles in place for them.[1] For instance, today every country has 'gender gaps' which need to be closed – whether in relation to equal access to education, health care, economic opportunities or political participation.[2] The extent and prevalence of these gaps, of course, varies significantly from country to country. In 2012, the World Bank focused their World Development Report on Gender Equality and Development and noted certain global improvements, such as the closing of gender gaps in primary education, improvements in life expectancy and increased number of women in the labour force. The report notes, however, that the most egregious gender

---

[1] For the purposes of this chapter I will focus on women as opposed to women and girls, although globally similar challenges affect girls.

[2] R. Hausmann, L. Tyson, Y. Bekhouche and S. Zahidi, *The Global Gender Gap Report 2013*, (World Economic Forum, 2013), http://www3.weforum.org/docs/WEF_GenderGap_Report_2013.pdf, accessed 27 January 2014.

gaps still present include excess of deaths of women and girls in many low- and middle-income countries, disparities in girls' schooling in parts of South Asia and Sub-Saharan Africa, unequal access to economic opportunities and difference in voice within households and society.[3] The 2012–2013 UN Women Annual Report notes:

> Gender inequality, despite much progress, remains among the greatest challenges of our times. Fed by deeply embedded discrimination against women and girls, it is wrong and costly, whether it interrupts economic progress, undercuts peace or restricts the quality of leadership. Ending it should be foremost among global and national goals.[4]

Within the ten ASEAN Member States, there are significant differences with regards to gender equality. The World Economic Forum's Global Gender Gap report ranks nine of the ten Member States out of a total of 136 countries according to the four criteria of economic participation and opportunity, educational attainment, health and survival and political empowerment.[5] The Philippines is the only country from the ASEAN region to hold a place in the top ten of the global rankings, maintaining this position in all but one of the categories.[6] In contrast, the worst performing ASEAN Member State is Cambodia, which ranked at 104 in 2013, scoring poorly on educational attainment in particular, followed by political empowerment. Vietnam ranked at 73, falling six places from the 2012 index, which was attributed mainly to an increase in wage inequality.[7] Meanwhile, Brunei Darussalam dropped thirteen places to 88, scoring zero for the political empowerment category, which measures the number of women holding seats in parliament, as well as the number of women at ministerial level and the number of years with a female head of state.

   Taking a closer look at the economic participation and opportunity category (which measures female to male labour force participation; wage equality for similar work; female estimated earned income over male; the ratio of female legislators, senior officials and managers over male and, finally, female professional and technical workers over male), the rankings of the ASEAN Member States range from 8 for Lao PDR and 33 for Brunei Darussalam, through to 100 for Malaysia and 103 for Indonesia. It is worth noting that Lao PDR has scored significantly

[3] The World Bank, *World Development Report 2012* (2011), http://siteresources.worldbank.org/INTWDR2012/Resources/7778105–1299699968583/7786210–1315936222006/Complete-Report.pdf, accessed 27 January 2014.

[4] UN Women, *Annual Report 2012–2013* (2013), http://www.unwomen.org/~/media/Headquarters/Attachments/Sections/Library/Publications/2013/6/UNwomen-AnnualReport2012–2013-en%20pdf.pdf, accessed 27 January 2014.

[5] *The Global Gender Gap Report*, see n. 2. The 2013 ranking placed the nine ASEAN economies as follows: Philippines (5), Singapore (58), Lao PDR (60), Thailand (65), Vietnam (73), Brunei Darussalam (88), Indonesia (95), Malaysia (102) and Cambodia (104).

[6] The Philippines ranked 16th for economic participation and opportunity.

[7] *The Global Gender Gap Report*, see n. 2, p. 29.

well in this category, despite still having a high education gender gap to close.[8] Perhaps tellingly, the report attributes the high economic participation and opportunity score to the number of women in low-skilled work in the country.[9]

Since 2009, the Organisation for Economic Co-operation and Development (OECD) has measured social institutions that discriminate against women and influence gender roles and relations.[10] This index focuses on issues such as early marriage, inheritance, violence against women, missing women, son preference, access to land and access to credit. In 2012, the index examined eighty-six countries in total, including seven of the ten ASEAN economies. The results were as follows: Philippines (12), Cambodia (13), Thailand (25), Indonesia (32), Vietnam (43), Myanmar (44) and Lao PDR (49). The OECD and the World Economic Forum studies examine slightly different angles of the gender inequality debate, both of which are essential when considering the barriers that women still face in a variety of countries – including those of ASEAN.

The topic of gender equality is of utmost relevance for the business and human rights movement, since the gender inequalities set out above are a component of the social fabric within which companies are operating. If companies were to ignore the gender dynamics at play in any given situation, they would risk exacerbating existing inequalities and further isolating women or men in the process.

Terminology

What do we mean by gender?

For the purposes of this chapter, gender refers to the socially constructed roles, functions and responsibilities of women and men. In this sense, there are gendered expectations of both women and men, which vary from country to country, from community to community and over time. Whereas sex is understood as biologically determined, gender is a socially constructed phenomenon. By way of example, the gendered expectations of men in a given situation may be that work should come before parental responsibilities and, because of this, a father may struggle to obtain sufficient flexibility at work in order to care for his child. Conversely, the gendered expectation of women can be that care responsibilities will come first and therefore they may be overlooked for promotion in a work context.

Key terms

The terminology related to gender issues can be complex. In essence, when exploring the topic from the perspective of policy formulation, it is understood that any process that does not take into account existing inequalities and the potential impacts of the policy on women and men is said to be 'gender-blind'. 'Gender-sensitive' policies,

[8] Lao PDR ranks at 113 in relation to the latter category.
[9] *The Global Gender Gap Report*, see n. 2, p. 34.
[10] OECD, 'Social Institutions and Gender Index', http://www.oecd.org/social/poverty/theoecdsocialinstitutionsandgenderindex.htm, accessed 27 January 2014.

on the other hand, have taken those impacts into account. Such policies are sensitive to the ways in which women and men may experience the policy effects in different ways as a result of the societal norms in place. An additional grouping is defined as 'gender-responsive'. This indicates those policies that have not only considered impacts on women and men at the design stage but have also identified proactive steps that can be taken to increase equality.

By way of example, a 'gender-sensitive' strategy to compensate members of a community for loss of land due to a mining project would typically assess the different land ownership structures that are prevalent in the society in question, and thus the level of access that women and men may have to compensation as a result. Within Southeast Asia, rural land is mainly held communally or informally and the majority of titles are held by men. In the Philippines, for example, women represent 10 per cent of all landowners. In Malaysia the figure is between 12 and 13 per cent. Meanwhile, in Indonesia and Vietnam, it is less than 10 per cent.[11] In light of this reality, a 'gender-responsive' version of the same policy might have in place some proactive steps to ensure that women and men are directly employed or offered access to finance, depending on what is most needed. Finally, a gender-neutral policy would simply offer compensation to individuals with formal title to the land – whether male or female – and not take into account the limited land ownership by women. Such a policy, although neutral in its formulation, is not neutral in its impact since it would predominantly benefit male landowners.

A common rebuttal against the use of gender as a differentiator in the assessment of business impacts on human rights is – why gender and why not other distinguishing factors such as race, ethnicity, religion or disability? Or, why not other groups such as children, indigenous peoples or migrant workers? Clearly, a contextual sensitivity and appreciation for gender does not diminish the importance of protecting and respecting the rights of these other groups from business-related harm. In reality, states and companies alike need to be aware of characteristics and risks of vulnerability that may affect the rights-holders they interact with and potentially impact upon. As a differentiator, gender affects the entire spectrum of the globe, since communities will always be composed of women and men. Therefore, its prevalence is a compelling factor.

Factors that result in vulnerabilities and marginalization nevertheless also need to be considered. A female migrant worker, for instance, may be at greater risk of sexual exploitation than a local female employee. Alternatively, the multiple barriers that an indigenous woman may face in order to get her voice heard could be profoundly different from those experienced by an indigenous man. Such crossing and multiplication of characteristics is known as 'intersectionality' – a term which effectively recognizes the experiences of individuals who are subject to multiple

---

[11]   Food and Agriculture Organization of the United Nations. 'Gender and Land Rights Database', http://www.fao. org/gender/landrights/topic-selection/en, accessed 27 January 2014, and Asian Development Bank, 'Gender Equality and Food Security – Women's Empowerment as a Tool Against Hunger', (2013).

forms of discrimination. It is another layer to be considered when looking at the human rights impacts of business.[12]

What do we mean by women's human rights?

Although all individuals are equal under the Universal Declaration of Human Rights, certain areas of human rights that predominantly affect women did not receive necessary attention until relatively recently. Two key turning points in the women's human rights movement have included the creation of the Convention on the Elimination of All Forms of Discrimination Against Women (CEDAW), which was adopted in 1979 and has been ratified by 187 states at the time of writing, and the Beijing Declaration and Platform for Action, which came out of the Fourth World Conference on Women in Beijing, China, in 1995. It was at this conference that Hillary Clinton famously stated: 'human rights are women's rights and women's rights are human rights'.[13]

Sustained advocacy in relation to these standards over the past few decades has been underpinned by the call for a greater gendered understanding of how human rights issues affect women and men differently.[14] Accordingly, it sought to broaden the scope of the international human rights system, which until then, had focused narrowly on the protection of individuals against infringements of their rights by states. This was driven by the fact that many issues affecting women consist of harms at the hands of society or within the family structure – areas that had traditionally been considered the domain of the 'private sphere'. Bringing such concerns into the public sphere has been the overall aim over time. On this basis, issues such as reproductive rights, access to safe family planning, health care, sexual violence in conflict, domestic violence, as well as issues relating to inheritance and freedom of movement without male permission, have gradually been brought into central human rights discourse.[15]

Ultimately, the consideration of gender is not a stand-alone, separate process. Instead, it is a lens through which all human rights impacts should be examined. It is this reality that underlines the need for business and human rights policy-makers and practitioners to adopt a gender perspective. Any nascent area of human rights

---

[12]   K.W. Crenshaw, 'Mapping the Margins: Intersectionality, Identity Politics, and Violence Against Women of Color', in Alison Bailey and Chris Cuomo (eds), *The Feminist Philosophy Reader*. (New York: McGraw-Hill, 2008), pp. 279–309.

[13]   In 1995, the UNDP Fourth World Conference on Women in Beijing produced the Beijing Declaration and Platform for Action (BPFA), which highlighted twelve critical areas of concern including women and human rights.

[14]   C. Chinkin, S. Wright and H. Charlesworth, 'Feminist Approaches to International Law: Reflections from Another Century' and K. Engle, 'International Human Rights and Feminisms: When Discourses Keep Meeting', both in D. Buss and A. Manji (eds), *International Law – Modern Feminist Approaches* (Hart, 2005).

[15]   Nevertheless, some challenges remain, as seen recently during the Rio+20 conference, where references to women's sexual and reproductive rights were removed from the final agreed text, going back on previously agreed wording at the UN International Conference on Population and Development in Cairo in 1994.

that affects such a broad swathe of society, such a variety of economic models, such diversity of countries and cultures cannot do so in isolation from persistent inequalities that exist between women and men; inequalities that are sustained as a result of the gender norms and relations at play in countries where women in particular face legal, cultural, societal and religious discrimination. This chapter will now examine how gender has featured to date in the work of UN special procedures on business and human rights.

Gender and the UN

Gender and the UN special procedures

In 2007, the UN Human Rights Council adopted a Resolution which requested all special procedures to 'integrate a gender perspective into the implementation of their mandate including when examining the intersection of multiple forms of discrimination against women and to include in their reports information on and qualitative analysis of human rights of women and girls'.[16] The same Resolution also incorporates a gender perspective and women's rights issues into the Universal Periodic Review mechanism. This step by the Human Rights Council echoes a 2002 Resolution from the former UN Commission on Human Rights, which made the same request of mandate holders.[17] Several special procedure mandate holders have taken a specific gender focus to date, including the Special Rapporteur on adequate housing, the Special Rapporteur on the right to food, the Special Rapporteur on the right to education, the Special Rapporteur on the rights of indigenous peoples, the Special Rapporteur on the situation of human rights defenders and the Special Rapporteur on violence against women.

Gender in the UN Guiding Principles

In 2008, the aforementioned request to integrate a gender perspective was explicitly included in the resolution setting out the second phase of Professor John Ruggie's mandate as Special Representative on business and human rights.[18] The following year, a gender consultation was held, which identified the need for the mandate to explore such issues as women's role in the care economy, and particularly the long, unpaid hours that women tend to work as carers for children,

---

[16] UN Human Rights Council, UN HRC Res 6/30 (2007) UN Doc A/HRC/RES/6/30, Part Two of the Sixth Session, 10–14 December 2007, 'Integrating the Human Rights of Women Throughout the United Nations System', (14 December 2007).

[17] UN Commission on Human Rights, UNCHR Res 2002/50 E/CN.4/RES/2002/50, 58th Session, 18 March – 26 April 2002, 'Integrating the Human Rights of Women Throughout the United Nations System', (23 April 2002). The UN Commission on Human Rights was replaced by the UN Human Rights Council in 2006.

[18] UN Human Rights Council, UN HRC Res 8/7 A/HRC/RES/8/7 paragraph 4(d) called upon the Special Representative '(t)o integrate a gender perspective throughout his work and to give special attention to persons belonging to vulnerable groups, in particular children'.

the sick or the elderly.[19] This reality was further discussed in the context of the impact on the productive economy (i.e. paid employment). Gender issues were likewise explored in relation to trade and investment, company due diligence and potential barriers to accessing remedies. Additional emphasis was placed on the need to explore gender inequalities at the State policy level, the community level and the individual level within households or families.

In essence, adopting a 'gender perspective' or 'integrating gender' thus requires business entities to examine the ways in which they may have a differential, disproportionate or unforeseen impact on women or men as a result of their different social, cultural or legal roles, rights and responsibilities. In 2010, when a draft version of the UN Guiding Principles was published for consultation, a gender analysis of the content was produced. In the final version of the UN Guiding Principles, the following elements specifically address a gender perspective:

•   the need for States to advise companies on how to effectively consider issues of gender, vulnerability and/or marginalization, while further recognizing the specific challenges that may be faced by indigenous peoples, women, national or ethnic minorities, religious and linguistic minorities, children, persons with disabilities, and migrant workers and their families;[20]
•   the need for States to pay special attention to sexual and gender-based violence when helping companies to assess heightened risks of human rights abuses in conflict-affected areas;[21]
•   the need for companies to consider the different risks that may be faced by women and men when looking at the potential human rights impacts of the business;[22]
•   the importance of sex-disaggregated data when tracking performance and using qualitative and quantitative indicators.[23]

It is worth noting that, in the Guiding Principles, women are not included per se as a vulnerable group. This is an important distinction, as persistent inequalities that may render women vulnerable do not automatically confer such a status on all women under broader circumstances. As stated in the Interpretive Guide to the Corporate Responsibility to Respect Human Rights:

> Vulnerable individuals, groups and communities are those that face a particular risk of being exposed to discrimination and other adverse human rights

---

[19] *Integrating a Gender Perspective into the UN 'Protect, Respect and Remedy' Framework*, 29 June 2009, http://www.reports-and-materials.org/Gender-meeting-for-Ruggie-29-Jun-2009.pdf, accessed 6 February 2014.

[20] Commentary to Guiding Principle 3, UN OHCHR, *Guiding Principles on Business and Human Rights: Implementing the United Nations 'Protect, Respect and Remedy' Framework*, (2011), p. 5, http://www.ohchr.org/Documents/Publications/GuidingPrinciplesBusinessHR_En.pdf, accessed 6 February 2014.

[21] Guiding Principle 7 and Commentary, ibid., p. 9.

[22] Commentary to Guiding Principle 18, ibid., p. 20.

[23] Commentary to Guiding Principle 20, ibid., p. 23.

impacts … Vulnerability can depend on context. For example, while women are more vulnerable to abuse than men in some contexts, they are not necessarily vulnerable in all contexts. Conversely, in some situations women from marginalized groups may be doubly vulnerable: because they are marginalized and because they are women.[24]

In the Southeast Asian context, the specific risks to women who are discriminated against both on the basis of their ethnicity and their gender is particularly striking. In Indonesia, for instance, there are at least seventeen main ethnic minority groups and many additional smaller groups. The situation for the Acehnese and the ethnic Chinese minorities has been improving in recent years but certain groups, such as the Papuans, are significantly under-represented in many employment categories.[25] Meanwhile, in Thailand, there have been incidents of minority ethnic groups struggling to survive as large-scale development projects threaten their economic and cultural survival.[26] Similarly, in the rainforests of Sarawak in Malaysian Borneo, indigenous men and women protesting against logging activities have faced death threats and there have been allegations of sexual violence against women in the community.[27] Such challenges, combined with the gendered norms present in such societies, can pose a challenge for women at risk of discrimination based on multiple factors.

Overall, the UN Guiding Principles could have taken a stronger approach to gender issues and incorporated gender-sensitive language into various principles and commentary, such as those relating to meaningful consultation, communication and barriers to access to remedy. Nevertheless, the language incorporated into the final version is welcome and provides a foundation to build upon when considering the three pillars, as will be explored in the following section of this chapter.

Gender in the mandate of the UN working group

In 2011, the Guiding Principles were unanimously endorsed by the UN Human Rights Council. On this occasion, the UN Working Group on Business and Human Rights was established, which brought together five individuals to carry forward the work of Professor Ruggie. The UN Working Group has also been mandated to integrate a gender perspective into its work.[28]

[24] Office of the UN High Commissioner for Human Rights (OHCHR), 'Interpretive Guide to the Corporate Responsibility to Respect Human Rights', (2012), p. 11, http://www.ohchr.org/Documents/Publications/HR.PUB.12.2_En.pdf, accessed 6 February 2014.

[25] Minority Rights Group, 'World Directory of Minorities and Indigenous Peoples', (2008), http://www.minorityrights.org/4430/indonesia/indonesia-overview.html#sthash.lU36pAvW.dpuf, accessed 27 January 2014.

[26] Minority Rights Group, 'State of the World's Minorities and Indigenous Peoples', (2012), pp. 156–157.

[27] Ibid., p. 37.

[28] UN Human Rights Council, UN HRC Res 17/4 (2011) UN Doc A/HRC/RES/17/4, Seventeenth Session, 30 May – 17 June 2011 'Human Rights and Transnational Corporations and Other Business Enterprises', (6 July 2011).

To date, the Working Group has engaged with the UN Working Group on Discrimination against women in law and practice,[29] as well as with the Gender Reference Group – a network of professionals interested in the connections between gender, business and human rights.[30] One challenge moving forward will be ensuring that due focus is given to the potential impacts that companies may have on women's rights at the annual Forum on Business and Human Rights. At the 2013 Forum, the issue was notably absent from the agenda.[31]

Other UN initiatives

In terms of other relevant initiatives at the UN level, in 2010, the UN Global Compact and UN Women (then UNIFEM) created a global code of conduct for companies on the issue of gender equality. These principles set out a useful benchmark in terms of the types of issues that companies should explore, although the inclusion of human rights considerations could be stronger. The code sets out expectations under the following headings: corporate leadership on gender equality; fair treatment at work, including respecting and supporting human rights and non-discrimination; health and safety of workers; education and training for women; supply chain and marketing practices to empower women; community initiatives and advocacy to promote equality; measuring and reporting on progress towards gender equality.

At the time of writing, over 650 company CEOs have signed up to the principles across a wide variety of countries.[32] These include ten companies headquartered in Vietnam, as well as representation from companies in Thailand, Singapore, Malaysia, Korea and the Philippines. While the Women's Empowerment Principles represent a helpful high-level indicator of commitment to gender equality globally, it is the reality of day-to-day corporate practices and policies that will demonstrate over time whether companies are taking a gender perspective into account as part of their responsibility to respect human rights in practice.

---

[29] On 2 and 3 October 2013, the Office of the High Commissioner for Human Rights held a workshop on the topic of 'Business and gender' with the Human Rights Council's Working Group on Discrimination against Women and participation from the UN Working Group on Business and Human Rights.

[30] See, for example, http://www.ohchr.org/Documents/Issues/TransCorporations/Submissions/MultiStakeholder/GenderBusinessAndHumanRightsReferenceGroup.pdf, accessed 24 February 2014.

[31] V. Rouas, 'Business and Human Rights: Women, the Missing Actors?', (Lawyers for Better Business, 2014), http://www.l4bb.org/Blog95A5M8/blog_topic.php?action=view_topic&list_num=7&people_id=Vrouas&people_name=Virginie%20Rouas&people_title=PhD%20student%20in%20Law&people_institution=%20SOAS&people_location=London&people_country=United%20Kingdom&formatted_people_registration_date=6%20Feb%202013&topic_id=49&category_id=&cur_page=1, accessed 8 May 2014.

[32] Women's Empowerment Principles (2010), http://weprinciples.org/Site/Companies, accessed 27 January 2014.

The State duty to protect and gender considerations

States have a duty to protect individuals against human rights abuses caused by business. In terms of protecting gender equality, many states have enacted laws and regulations to do so. The International Labour Organization has played a leading role in ensuring gender equality within the workforce and maintaining interest amongst states on issues that disproportionately affect women, such as home-working and domestic labour.[33]

At present, most communications on the issue of human rights impacts experienced by women are found in the deliberations of the Committee attached to CEDAW. Article 2(e) of CEDAW requires all State Parties to 'take all appropriate measures to eliminate discrimination against women by any person, organization or enterprise'. In addition, as set out in a 2007 study of Committee materials, other Articles have been drawn upon when making links between the private sector and impacts on women.[34] These include Article 11 in relation to employment, Article 12 in relation to health care and Articles 13 and 14 in relation to economic and social life, including financial services.[35] The Committee has also raised on several occasions the need for States to consider the impact of development projects on women's rights – most notably the right to non-discriminatory access to land and water and the need to ensure equal access to land. Examples of recommendations to States Parties relating to the private sector noted in the 2007 analysis of CEDAW communications are set out in Table 3.1.[36]

In more recent communications from the CEDAW Committee, several items relating directly to the private sector have been addressed. These include a call to Djibouti to improve 'technical and vocational training for women including in traditionally male-dominated fields and in the agricultural sector', along with a call to collect 'disaggregated data on the situation of women and men in the private and informal sectors to monitor and improve women's working conditions'.[37] In 2012, Singapore was asked to eliminate occupational segregation, ensure that all women employees can access paid maternity leave without any discrimination based on marital status, apply legislation to guarantee the right of equal pay for equal work and enact legal protections against sexual harassment in the workplace.[38] Similarly, Myanmar was requested to 'provide, in its next report, detailed information, including data disaggregated by sex; an analysis on the situation of

---

[33]   ILO Convention C177: Home Work Convention (1996) and ILO Convention C189: Domestic Workers Convention (2011).

[34]   State Responsibilities to Regulate and Adjudicate Corporate Activities under the United Nations' core Human Rights Treaties, Individual Report on the United Nations Convention on the Elimination of All Forms of Discrimination against Women, Report No. 4, September 2007.

[35]   Ibid.

[36]   Ibid.

[37]   CEDAW, 'Concluding Observations of the Committee on the Elimination of Discrimination Against Women – Djibouti', CEDAW/C/DJI/CO/1–3 (2 August 2011) at paragraph 29(e).

[38]   CEDAW, 'Concluding Observations of the Committee on the Elimination of Discrimination Against Women – Singapore', CEDAW/C/SGP/CO/4/Rev.1 (16 January 2012) at paragraph 30(a)–(d).

Table 3.1 CEDAW Committee recommendations regarding the private sector

Type of actor	Recommendations to State Parties
Employers	States should do more to guarantee equal pay for equal work and monitor working conditions. They should also take steps to combat occupational segregation, including through temporary special measures to promote female representation in decision-making in the private sector. The Committee has discussed a wide range of employers in recommending State action to prevent and punish discrimination, from publicly listed companies to small, family owned enterprises. Concluding Observations express concern about the labor market in particular sectors in certain States. The Committee has referred to the tourism and hospitality sector; light industry; the apparel and clothing sector; and the agricultural sector. It has also recommended that States Parties strengthen control of employment agencies and ensure protection in export processing zones.
Health-care providers	States should report on how private health care providers meet States' duties regarding equal access to services. They should also enact laws and formulate policies to address violence against women, including through health care and hospital protocols. The Committee may be implicitly referring to pharmaceutical companies in General Recommendation 24 when it confirms that women should be fully informed when they agree to participate in research.
Media and advertising agencies	States should take measures to ensure that the media and advertising agencies respect and promote respect for women, including through positive portrayals of women.
Financial institutions	The Committee implicitly suggests regulation of private financial institutions may be necessary when it speaks of temporary special measures regarding credit and loans. Further, the Concluding Observations for one State explicitly recommended proactive steps to ensure financial institutions act in line with the interests of indigent women.
Tourism industry	The Committee has indicated that it might support greater regulation of the tourism industry in order to protect against exploitation of prostitution.
Companies affecting land resources	The Committee implies some necessary regulation of companies whose activities affect land resources when it calls for assessments before development projects and steps to ensure that women can access land and water resources without discrimination.

women in the field of employment, in both the formal and informal sectors, and trends over time; and information about measures taken and their impact on realizing equal opportunities for women in the employment sectors, including in new fields of employment and entrepreneurship'.[39]

Interestingly, CEDAW was the first Convention to direct States specifically to regulate the private sector as part of their duty to protect human rights. As such, it remains a point of interest as to whether the Committee will issue a recommendation on discrimination against women and the private sector in a manner akin to the Committee on the Rights of the Child, following the endorsement of the Guiding Principles by the Human Rights Council. In addition, the CEDAW Committee has issued several General Recommendations which include a private sector dimension. For instance, General Recommendation No. 24 on Women and Health notes specifically that when States work with private actors to provide health functions, the State remains responsible for the fulfilment of the right to health and should report on how they are promoting and protecting women's health.[40] Furthermore, General Recommendation No. 25 deals with temporary special measures, which may be used by States to accelerate de facto equality between men and women. Paragraph 23, in particular, specifically provides guidance on creating and implementing temporary special measures in the employment of women in the private and public sectors, ensuring that questions of qualification and merit are carefully examined 'for gender bias as they are normatively and culturally determined'.[41]

The corporate responsibility to respect and gender considerations

The second pillar of the *Protect, Respect and Remedy* Framework focuses on the corporate responsibility to respect human rights. When it comes to gender equality, many businesses are aware of – and have taken steps to respond to – issues such as equal pay, the need for balanced parental leave and the importance of an equal workforce. The issue of women in senior leadership positions – not least on corporate boards and in CEO positions – has drawn considerable attention also. Such questions are rooted in workplace dynamics.

In addition to the above, many companies are increasingly looking at diversity of suppliers and supporting women-owned businesses in the supply chain. Less well understood are the actual human rights impacts that corporate entities have, and

---

[39] CEDAW, 'Concluding Observations of the Committee on the Elimination of Discrimination Against Women – Myanmar', CEDAW/C/MMR/CO/3 (7 November 2008) at paragraph 37.

[40] CEDAW, 'CEDAW General Recommendation No. 24: Article 12 of the Convention (Women and Health)', A/54/38/Rev.1 (2 May 1999) at paragraph 14, http://www.un.org/womenwatch/daw/cedaw/recommendations/recomm.htm#recom24, accessed 27 January 2014.

[41] CEDAW, 'General recommendation No. 25, on article 4, paragraph 1, of the Convention on the Elimination of All Forms of Discrimination against Women, on temporary special measures', UN Doc. HRI/GEN/1/Rev.7 (2004), http://www.un.org/womenwatch/daw/cedaw/recommendations/General%20recommendation%2025%20(English).pdf, accessed 27 January 2014.

how these affect women and men in different ways. The UN Guiding Principles call upon companies to look at human rights impacts from this angle. The following sections explore three key themes, drawn from the content of the Guiding Principles, where understanding potential gender impacts will be essential.

Local law versus international law

Guiding Principle 23 notes that companies should comply with all applicable laws and respect internationally recognized human rights wherever they operate. The commentary to the Principle goes on to elaborate this point further:

> Although particular country and local contexts may affect the human rights risks of an enterprise's activities and business relationships, all business enterprises have the same responsibility to respect human rights wherever they operate. Where the domestic context renders it impossible to meet this responsibility fully, business enterprises are expected to respect the principles of internationally recognized human rights to the greatest extent possible in the circumstances, and to be able to demonstrate their efforts in this regard.[42]

Essentially, where local law or practice contradicts international human rights law, companies should look to respect the international standards. In the context of gender equality, there are numerous examples of discriminatory practices and laws that run counter to human rights norms. For instance, in certain Southeast Asian countries, employers are obliged to deport female migrant workers who become pregnant.[43] There is clearly a health consideration at play here, but one that has a negative impact on other rights, such as the right to work and freedom from discrimination.

Additional negative human rights impacts commonly experienced by women migrant workers in Malaysia, Cambodia and Thailand have been highlighted.[44] For instance, the focus of these countries on building export-oriented economies and attracting foreign direct investment has led to the creation of several special economic zones, which can lead to workers – most often women migrant workers – being granted temporary work status to ensure a flexible workforce. Furthermore, there has been evidence in all three countries of poor working and living conditions along with low wages being paid.[45] In this respect, living

---

[42] UN Guiding Principles, see n. 20, Commentary to Guiding Principle 23, p. 25.

[43] In addition, there have been incidents reported of migrant women in Malaysia and Singapore being required to sign contracts that state that they will not get pregnant during the term of employment (SOMO, 'Outsourcing Labour: Migrant Labour Rights in Malaysia's Electronics Industry', (SOMO, 2013), http://makeitfair.org/en/the-facts/news/reports/outsourcing-labour, accessed 8 May 2014).

[44] War on Want, 'Restricted Rights: Migrant Women Workers in Thailand, Cambodia and Malaysia', (2012), http://www.waronwant.org/attachments/WOW%20Migration%20Report%20low%20res.pdf, accessed 27 January 2014.

[45] Ibid., p. 3.

areas have been found to be overcrowded and unhygienic, with the additional challenge of being insecure. This lack of security has also been reported to apply in some cases to the commute between the workplace and the living quarters.[46] Reports likewise point to examples of women migrant workers not being entitled to sick pay in Thailand and Malaysia, while being entitled to it in Cambodia, but struggling to access it.[47] Finally, women migrant workers in all three countries have been reported to face difficulties in joining trade unions, which can present a challenge in bringing forward complaints and ensuring fair bargaining power.[48] Such examples point to the challenges in treatment of women migrant workers in three countries of Southeast Asia. Such difficulties are replicated elsewhere globally and serve as a reminder of the challenges in applying standards at the local level.

Several other examples of situations where local laws do not measure up to international standards were set out in a 2008 report sponsored by the Office of the High Commissioner for Human Rights (OHCHR) to explore discrimination against women in the law.[49] It included such examples as obedience laws – the husband's marital power, succession and inheritance, discrimination in employment, night work and mining work. It also addressed barriers to employment – such as the requirement for family or spousal consent, and maternity policies – hampering women's ability to participate in the labour market. These clearly encompass several of the areas that companies will confront as they seek to offer equal opportunities to women in the workforce. Adequate responses to these challenges are likewise essential to ensuring that women members of local communities are not at greater risk of negative human rights impacts by the corporation as a result of these inequalities in the law.

The issue is somewhat trickier for businesses operating in countries where women are unable to participate fully in employment opportunities due to legal or cultural barriers. In Saudi Arabia, for instance, companies have taken various steps to incorporate women into the life of the business in ways that align with the local culture – for instance, by offering opportunities to women as sales representatives to ensure that they only interact with other women. This is a very delicate area for multinational businesses, and companies tend to tread very carefully while finding subtle ways to empower women to access economic opportunities and ensure that their rights can be met in practice.

Community impacts

Oxfam Australia has published various reports that specifically address the gendered nature of extractive industry projects, particularly mining. Their

---

[46] Ibid., p. 27.
[47] Ibid., p. 27.
[48] Ibid., p. 27.
[49] Dr Fareda Banda, 'Project on a Mechanism to Address Laws that Discriminate Against Women', commissioned for the Office of the High Commissioner for Human Rights – Women's Rights and Gender Unit (2008).

2009 report (Oxfam Report) calls on companies to undertake a gender impact assessment as part of their responsibility to respect human rights. In doing so, it emphasizes that:

> [While] recognising that women's rights are human rights, it is equally important that mining companies become aware of, prevent, and address the potential gendered impacts of their activities. This might include a stronger gender focus in recommendations around human rights impact assessments, inclusion of gender impacts in guidance on human rights policy development or better corporate reporting on gender issues.[50]

The Oxfam Report sets out some of the negative impacts and human rights abuses that tend to disproportionately affect women located at or around the mine site, such as:

- a failure to consult with women in a way which enables full participation;
- payment of compensation and royalties to men 'on behalf of' families and communities, thus reinforcing women's economic dependence on men and potentially missing women-headed households;
- loss of land and displacement potentially resulting in loss of livelihoods and increased burdens for women in providing for families;
- environmental damage, which can lead to an increase in women's workloads, such as having to walk further for water sources, fuel/wood and forest products;
- the influx of a transient male workforce, which can bring social and health problems, such as increased alcohol use, domestic violence, sexual violence, sexually transmitted diseases and prostitution;
- women experiencing discrimination in the mine workplace, where employment opportunities often benefit men or where women are only employed for menial low-paid tasks.[51]

To address and mitigate these negative impacts, mining companies should conduct rigorous gender impact assessments in relation to their projects. If properly carried out, a gender impact assessment can provide effective answers to the following business-relevant questions.

- What are the likely impacts of this project on women, their needs and their interests?
- How will addressing the concerns of women and improving gender equality contribute towards a more sustainable project?

---

[50] C. Hill and K. Newell, *Women, Communities and Mining: The Gender Impacts of Mining and the Role of Gender Impact Assessment* (Oxfam Australia, 2009), p. 6.
[51] Ibid., p. 7.

- How can women's practical needs and strategic interests best be supported and advanced by the project?[52]

Again, the Oxfam Report is instructive as it sets out the component elements of a gender impact assessment as follows:

1   sex-disaggregated household, workplace and community data relevant to the project;
2   an understanding of gender relations and their implications, including an understanding of:
   i   the gender division of labour and different responsibilities of women and men, including their productive and reproductive roles;
   ii   the experiences of women as distinct from, and in relation to, the experiences of men;
   iii   who has access to and control over resources, assets and the benefits from the project;
   iv   the ways in which women may be subordinate to men – for example, if women have less access to resources such as land, income and political influence – and through what mechanisms this inequality is maintained and reinforced;
3   an understanding of women's and men's different needs, priorities and strengths. This includes identifying:
   i   women's practical gender needs;
   ii   women's strategic gender interests;
4   an understanding of the barriers to meeting women's and men's needs and interests and the risks related to gender equality issues, including resistance to change from various quarters and possible backlash;
5   the identification of opportunities for greater equality and empowerment for women, and recommendations to address women's practical needs and strategic interests.

A similar report produced in 2009 by the Asia Pacific Forum on Women, Law and Development addresses mining projects and their gendered impacts in a variety of countries, including Thailand, Cambodia and the Philippines.[53] They note also that 'women as informal small-scale miners, or women running small-scale businesses in the service sector in mining communities, or local women engaging in agriculture, herding or fishing, are affected by mining differently than their male counterparts'.[54] Amongst other impacts, the report notes the issue of pollution, particularly mercury poisoning associated with gold mining, which is

---

[52]   Ibid., p. 8.
[53]   Asia Pacific Forum on Women, Law and Development, 'Mining and Women in Asia: Experiences of Women Protecting Their Communities and Human Rights Against Corporate Mining', (APWLD, 2013), http://apwld.org/wp-content/uploads/2013/09/Women-and-Mining-in-Asia1.pdf, accessed 8 May 2014.
[54]   Ibid., p. 2.

highly detrimental to the health of pregnant women. There are, however, a number of examples today of proactive gender impact studies by mining companies and comprehensive guidance provided for community relations staff, which are encouraging.[55]

In addition to the gendered human rights impacts that a mining company may have on a particular community, the topics addressed above could be extended to other large-footprint sectors such as agriculture, forestry or hydropower. For instance, the World Commission on Dams previously noted that due to the gender neutrality during the construction phase for a dam, women often pay a 'disproportionate share of social costs'.[56] This was in the main due to an increased dependence by women on the common natural resources that can disappear as a result of the project and the paying of compensation to the men in the communities.

A lack of equality in land ownership is a particularly pertinent issue when exploring corporate impacts of the extractive industries on women in practice.[57] The gender and land rights database which was launched in 2010 by the Food and Agriculture Organization of the United Nations recognizes that 'disparity on land access is one of the major causes for social and gender inequalities in rural areas, and it jeopardizes, as a consequence, rural food security as well as the wellbeing of individuals and families'.[58] The challenges faced by women in relation to ownership and inheritance of land are multiple and set out here by way of illustration.[59] They include: customary laws and practices which conflict with international human rights standards; registration of land in the name of the husband (or brother and/or son) only; discrimination written into the local laws in certain countries; the process of land registration itself;[60] lack of awareness in

[55] See, for example, case-studies contained in Rio Tinto, 'Why Gender Matters: a Resource Guide for Integrating Gender Considerations into Communities Work At Rio Tinto', (2010), http://www.riotinto.com/documents/reportspublications/rio_tinto_gender_guide.pdf, accessed 8 May 2014.

[56] World Commission on Dams, 'Dams and Development – A New Framework for Decision-Making', (2000), http://www.internationalrivers.org/files/attached-files/world_commission_on_dams_final_report.pdf, accessed 8 may 2014

[57] The Women, Business and the Law database, launched by the World Bank Group in March 2010, draws on several areas of formal law and assesses gender disparities. The 2014 report notes that 128 of the 143 countries examined impose legal differences on the basis of gender in one or more of the main indicators. It also notes that married women continue to experience more legal differences on the basis of gender than unmarried women. The 2012 report from the Women, Business and the Law project found that there were 26 economies that applied different inheritance rights to women and men. They were found across the Middle East and North Africa, with seven in Sub-Saharan Africa (Burundi, Guinea, Mali, Mauritania, Senegal, Sudan and Tanzania), three in South Asia (Bangladesh, Nepal and Pakistan) and two in Southeast Asia and the Pacific (Indonesia and Malaysia). It is important to stress here that this data is limited to the formal laws in place on the statute books and does not yet take into consideration customary laws or parallel legal systems which will sometimes conflict with the formal laws in place.

[58] Food and Agriculture Organization (FAO), 'Gender and Land Rights Database', (2010), http://www.fao.org/gender/landrights, accessed 27 January 2014.

[59] For a more in-depth analysis see M. Benschop, *Women's Rights to Land and Property*, (Nairobi: UN-HABITAT, 2004).

[60] Land registration formalities may be gender blind but not gender neutral. For instance, land registration forms may simply not include the option to register the land in the names of both spouses.

decision-making bodies of gender inequalities and lack of awareness amongst the men and women implicated as to the rights at stake.

Effective consultation with affected and surrounding communities will be a key element of how companies manage their relationship with land from a human rights perspective. The International Finance Corporation (IFC) includes stake-holder consultation as a key element of effective stakeholder engagement by corporations.[61] The guidance put forward includes a section dedicated to gender considerations, recognizing that the arrival of a company into a community is likely to affect women and men differently.[62] An issue closely linked to effective consultation is that of compensation, since most often the plans in place – whether executed at State or company level – will ensure compensation for the heads of households only. There are risks that a gender-neutral approach to compensation can exacerbate existing gender inequalities by paying compensation solely to the male head of the household and not capturing female-headed households, single or widowed women.[63] Further considerations relating to the 'gender neutrality' and effectiveness of remedies for women are outlined below.

Remedy

In situations where companies have caused or contributed to adverse human rights impacts, the Guiding Principles set out that they should either provide for or cooperate in remediation through legitimate processes. Remediation can be judicial and/or non-judicial. In addition, Guiding Principle 29 sets out that companies should establish or participate in 'operational-level grievance mechanisms' for individuals and communities. The intention is that such mechanisms allow for early identification of problem issues and can address grievances early on in the process before they escalate.

In the context of this chapter, one particular example of a grievance mechanism set up explicitly to address a situation of gender-based violence will be explored. In 2011, allegations of gang rape and sexual violence were made against members of the security personnel protecting the Porgera Joint Venture gold mine. The mine, which is 95 per cent owned and operated by Barrick Gold, a Canadian gold-mining company, is based in Enga Province, Papua New Guinea (PNG).[64] A specific operational-level grievance mechanism was implemented to address these

---

An interesting approach exists in Tanzania, where land is presumed to be co-registered unless the spouses indicate otherwise.

[61] International Finance Corporation, 'Stakeholder Engagement: A Good Practice Handbook for Companies Doing Business in Emerging Markets', (2007).

[62] International Finance Corporation, 'Gender Dimensions of the Extractive Industries', (2009). One example of differential impact may be in relation to health impacts of a project that could affect women's reproductive health. For instance, community members near the BTC oil pipeline in Azerbaijan suspected that air pollution from gas flaring was causing increases in stillbirths.

[63] Asian Development Bank, Gender and Development Unit. See: 'Gender Checklist on Resettlement', (February 2003).

[64] Human Rights Watch, 'Gold's Costly Dividend: Human Rights Impacts of Papua New Guinea's Porgera Gold Mine', (2011).

and earlier incidents following an 18-month consultation period. The mechanism in question nonetheless drew criticism for falling short of the effectiveness criteria set out in Guiding Principle 31. Mining Watch Canada, for instance, was particularly concerned about the nature of the agreement to be signed by individual women having completed the process; a process which required a commitment to no further action against Barrick Gold. In a letter dated 22 March 2013, Barrick Gold addressed this point along with other criticisms, noting that the agreement did not preclude parallel claims, and if a claimant was not happy with the final offer, they would be able to opt out of the process and pursue other legal avenues. However, in the event of a resolution being reached with a given claimant, claims against Barrick would then be released in order to reach finality of the process.[65] At the time of writing, the public disagreement between the company and various civil-society organizations over this clause continues.[66]

At its core, this specific case reveals a gender-specific human rights impact caused by security personnel engaged by the company and public security providers. The corrective action plan put in place by the company is substantive and responds to many of the challenges raised by the civil-society groups. Nevertheless, it could be argued that such a risk issue ought to have been identified in advance and mitigated accordingly via appropriate contractual terms and training of the security personnel. An effective gender impact assessment would have raised issues associated with prevalent sexual violence and the gender norms present in the society, which could lead to significant violence against women. It would have likewise signalled the accompanying cultural challenges experienced by women in bringing forward such complaints.

More broadly, in the Southeast Asian context, the United Nations Development Programme (UNDP), the United Nations Population Fund (UNFPA), UN Women and UN Volunteers recently produced a joint report entitled *Why Do Some Men Use Violence Against Women and How Can We Prevent It?*[67] This was the result of a UN multi-country study on men and violence in Asia and the Pacific, and should inform future business practice in the region.

Gender and the ASEAN sectoral commission on women

In 2010, the ASEAN leaders inaugurated the ASEAN Commission on the Promotion and Protection of the Rights of Women and Children (ACWC). The Commission is made up of representatives from the various ASEAN

---

[65] See http://www.business-humanrights.org/media/documents/company_responses/barrick-letter-to-un-high-commissioner-re-porgera-22-mar-2013.pdf, accessed 25 February 2014.

[66] On 14 May 2013, 77 organizations signed a joint letter to the OHCHR on this topic, http://www.miningwatch.ca/sites/www.miningwatch.ca/files/ltr_to_unhchr_may_14_2013_re_porgera_sign-on.pdf, accessed 25 February 2014.

[67] E. Fulu, X. Warner, S. Miedema, R. Jewkes and J. Lang, 'Why Do Some Men Use Violence Against Women and How Can We Prevent It? Quantitative Findings from the United Nations Multi-Country Study on Men and Violence in Asia and the Pacific', (2013) UNDP, UNFPA, UN Women and UNV.

Member States and acts as a consultative body. It has a stronger mandate than the ASEAN Intergovernmental Commission on Human Rights (AICHR) when it comes to engaging with civil society and is designed to advocate on behalf of women and children, in particular with respect to the most vulnerable and marginalized.[68]

In October 2013, a Declaration on the Elimination of Violence Against Women and Elimination of Violence Against Children in ASEAN was adopted by the Heads of State at the 23rd ASEAN Summit. The Declaration recognizes that the Member States can take measures to 'modify the social and cultural patterns of conduct of men and women, with a view to achieving the elimination of prejudices and customary and all other practices which are based on the idea of inferiority or the superiority of either of the sexes or on stereotyped roles for men and women'.[69] Furthermore, the Declaration notes that violence against women and children can take place 'at home, at school, in the workplace, in public or private spaces (including cyber space) as a result of gender bias, discriminatory and harmful traditional practices'.[70]

The Declaration and its implementation are a welcome addition in ensuring gender equality within ASEAN Member States. However, by focusing on women and children within the same instrument, there is a risk that certain stereotypes relating to care and the role of women could be exacerbated. It is also essential that there is strong cooperation between the various related commissions such as AICHR and the ASEAN Committee on Migrant Worker Rights. That said, it is helpful that the Declaration makes specific reference to the workplace and to the risk of stereotyping in this context. In a joint submission to the ACWC by the Southeast Asia Women's Caucus on ASEAN (Women's Caucus), Asia Pacific Forum on Women, Law and Development (APWLD) and the International Women's Rights Action Watch-Asia Pacific (IWRAW-AP) in 2012, the importance of sexual harassment as a form of violence against women, as well as its prevalence in the workplace, was noted. The submission noted that this may especially affect younger women or women in junior positions and that the media and community leaders will often blame the women rather than the perpetrator in such incidents. They call on ASEAN Member States to address sexual harassment, as is the case for all other types of violence against women, as 'an abuse of power and an attempt to erode the human rights of others'.[71] It will be interesting to see over time whether the ACWC and the AICHR can effectively work together to draw attention to the ways in which women's human rights are impacted by

---

[68] Terms of Reference of the ASEAN Commission for the Promotion and Protection of the Rights of Women and Children (ACWC) (2010), Article 5(4).

[69] The Declaration on the Elimination of Violence against Women and Elimination of Violence against Children in ASEAN (2013), http://www.asean.org/images/archive/23rdASEANSummit/6.%20 declaration%20on%20evawc%20in%20asean%20-%20final.pdf, accessed 27 January 2014.

[70] Ibid.

[71] Women's Caucus, APWLD and IWRAW-AP, 'Due Diligence and Violence Against Women: Enhancing Accountability to ASEAN Women and Girls', (2013), http://womenscaucusonasean. files.wordpress.com/2012/05/due-diligence-and-vaw_final.pdf, accessed 27 January 2014.

business. The recent Declaration on violence against women and children serves as a valuable starting point.

Conclusion

There is a pressing need to better understand the gender-specific impacts of company operations. Such risks need to be clearly mapped and understood by companies and states alike. Persistent gender inequalities exist in all countries and societies to varying degrees. Given the global nature and diversity of business operations, these realities need to be factored in to how companies map their risks and discharge their responsibility to respect human rights.

For too long, gender considerations have been an afterthought, thus resulting in further unexpected exacerbations of existing inequalities. Within the relatively young field of business and human rights, due consideration needs to be given to applying a gender lens to operations and ensuring that future human rights abuses are mitigated and eliminated. Now is the ideal time for gender experts and women's rights organizations to understand corporate impacts and hold states and companies accountable for their respective responsibilities.

4 Children's rights and business

A framework to combat ICT-enabled child abuse in Southeast Asia

Philip Cook, Bindu Sharma and Chris Yeomans

Introduction

Children's rights are increasingly intersecting with business practices beyond what has been seen as a narrow focus on exploitive child labour. This chapter will highlight a number of global child rights business challenges, as well as describe guidelines that are being developed to guide good business practice and State obligations in upholding children's rights. Particular attention will be drawn to General Comment No. 16 on State obligations regarding the impact of the business sector on children's rights, which was adopted by the United Nations Committee on the Rights of the Child in February 2013. The chapter will then address specific Southeast Asian regional challenges to supporting children's rights in the context of ASEAN economic integration, with a focus on opportunities to strengthen human rights business standards for children through Southeast Asian regional and national human rights mechanisms. The scope of protection afforded will be examined in the context of the sexual exploitation of children enabled by information and communication technology (ICT), as well as by social media.

Background

There has been a great deal of discussion of the environmental, carbon and governance footprints of private companies and their impact within the communities in which they operate. Now the issue of human rights, specifically, the full breadth of children's rights and business, is coming under greater scrutiny. Often seen as the State's duty to safeguard, human rights are increasingly coming to the forefront as the global community becomes aware of the reality of human trafficking, child labour and child sexual exploitation, which have been referred to as forms of 'modern-day slavery'.[1] Hence, over the last decade, there has been increasing international consensus on the implementation of human rights

[1] K. Srisang, 'Caught in Modern Slavery: Tourism and Child Prostitution in Asia', International Campaign to End Child Prostitution in Asian Tourism (ECPAT), Report and proceedings of the Chiang Mai consultation, 1–5 May 1990.

standards for the business sector. This has culminated in the United Nations Human Rights Council endorsing the Guiding Principles on Business and Human Rights (Guiding Principles) in June 2011.[2] These principles are designed to establish a global standard for preventing and addressing human rights violations linked to business activity.

Following various international human rights and business initiatives such as the Kimberly Process (a certification scheme for conflict diamonds)[3] and the Voluntary Principles on Security and Human Rights,[4] a *Protect, Respect and Remedy* Framework was developed by the United Nations (UN) under the leadership of Professor John Ruggie, to promote greater awareness of – and adherence to – international human rights standards in business practices around the world.

In addressing children's rights in relation to the business sector, leaders of the UN Global Compact, UNICEF, Save the Children and hundreds of business leaders and representatives from civil-society organizations (CSOs) have all looked to develop mechanisms for the implementation of children's rights in various national and global private sector contexts. This led to the *Children's Rights and Business Principles*, which were launched in March 2012.[5] Taken as a whole, these mechanisms constitute a comprehensive set of principles that serve to guide private sector companies on their responsibilities to children within the workplace, marketplace and community. This represents a significant step forward and provides an opportunity for establishing more effective protection measures against violations that disproportionately affect young people.

With a growing global youth demographic and greater consumer and activist power being leveraged by young people, there has been an increase in interest amongst business leaders to focus on (1) child and youth-centred ethical practices,

---

[2] After six years of consultations and work led by the Secretary-General's Special Representative on the issue of human rights and transnational corporations and other business enterprises, Professor John Ruggie (Harvard University) presented the UN *Report and Guiding Principles on Business and Human Rights: Implementing the United Nations 'Protect, Respect and Remedy' Framework* to the UN Human Rights Council in Geneva. See UN Human Rights Council, *Report of the Special Representative of the Secretary General on the Issue of Human Rights and Transnational Corporations and Other Business Enterprises*, (21 March 2011) A/HRC/17/31, http://www.business-humanrights.org/media/documents/ruggie/ruggie-guiding-principles-21-mar-2011.pdf, accessed 20 September 2013.

[3] See official Kimberly Process website for more information on this international certification scheme: the Kimberley Process (KP), http://www.kimberleyprocess.com, accessed 7 Nov 2013.

[4] The Voluntary Principles on Security and Human Rights is a human rights guideline specifically designed for extractive sector companies. See 'What Are The Voluntary Principles?', The Voluntary Principles on Security and Human Rights (2000), http://www.voluntaryprinciples.org/what-are-the-voluntary-principles, accessed 25 January 2014.

[5] For more information on the ten Children's Rights and Business Principles, as well as their application to the business community since being issued in March 2012, see http://childrenandbusiness.org, accessed 25 January 2014. These principles will be discussed in further detail later in the chapter.

and (2) developing standards of good corporate practice that monitor the impact of private sector activities on young people, as well as their families and communities. This trend to foster greater collaboration between child and youth development organizations and the business community is reflected in recent policies within several development agencies.[6] As governments and civil society acknowledge the important role that companies, corporations and private investors play in providing social and economic opportunities for communities, there is growing interest in how private actors are contributing to the overall development agenda and their impact on children and youth. This is a trend that is not without its challenges. In Western industrial nations, many of these non-governmental organization (NGO)–business partnerships (with the extractive sector in particular) have become controversial as child rights advocates have come under criticism for implicitly supporting (as partners), remaining silent on, or condoning the questionable – and in some cases clearly harmful – business practices of their private sector partners.[7]

---

[6] A number of child rights and development organizations like Save the Children and Plan International are teaming up with the private sector to jointly implement development initiatives in the Global South. An example is IKEA's Social Initiative, initiated in 2005, that works together with UNICEF and Save the Children to promote the rights of every child to a healthy, secure childhood and access to quality education. For more information, see: 'IKEA Social Initiative Sides with the Many Children', http://www.ikea.com/ms/fr_CH/about_ikea/read_our_material/ISI_Brochure_WEB_version.pdf, accessed 25 January 2014. While thousands of similar initiatives exist globally, the most controversial are generally associated with the extractive sector, as illustrated by Plan International Canada's partnership with IAMGOLD (global mining company) and the Burkina Faso Government, to provide vocational training to youth in Burkina Faso. See IAMGOLD-Plan Canada, http://plancanada.ca/Page.aspx?pid=4482, accessed 25 January 2014.

[7] In countries like Canada, there has been a great deal of debate concerning a recent push by its national development agency (i.e. Department of Foreign Affairs, Trade and Development) to use public funds to support private investments and companies in the Global South who seek to expand CSR practices with the assistance of international development NGOs conducting poverty alleviation investments. This has been seen as problematic for many reasons. Among them, many public investments have been geared to supporting private sector interests, including cases where operators from the extractive sector have been found to be complicit or even party to human rights violations. There is a wide breadth of literature on this subject. To see a general note of caution by the Canadian development NGO sector, refer to the Canadian Council for International Cooperation (CCIC), 'Comments on the Report of the Standing Committee on Foreign Affairs and International Development', (November 2012). These served to inform a Parliamentary Committee that was tasked with examining the role of the private sector in international development, http://www.ccic.ca/_files/en/what_we_do/2012_29_11_CCIC%20comments%20on%20report%20on%20private%20sector%20and%20development.pdf, accessed 25 January 2014. See also, North-South Institute, 'Investing in the Business of Development: Bilateral Approaches to Engaging the Private Sector', (2013), http://www.ccic.ca/_files/en/what_we_do/2013-01-11_The%20Business_of_Development.pdf, accessed 7 November 2013. This constitutes a more comprehensive study and critique of how many OCED national bilateral development agencies are working with the private sector, and was conducted by Shannon Kindornay at the North-South Institute and Fraser Reilly-King at CCIC).

International standards and practice for business and the development community

Children under 18 years of age account for almost one-third of the world's population and young adults make up close to half the global population.[8] Because children and youth often count amongst the most marginalized and vulnerable members of society, the likelihood of business having a proportionally larger impact on their lives is significant. In recent decades, there have been laudable efforts by business leaders to develop principled codes of conduct and practice when operating in vulnerable communities, both at home and abroad.[9] ECPAT International's contribution is particularly noteworthy in this regard. ECPAT is a global network of organizations that has been working tirelessly for more than two decades to end child prostitution, exploitation and trafficking. Recently, ECPAT has focused on the link between these threats to children and the rising influence of ICT.[10]

The UN has also been a key actor in articulating good practices and has stressed the importance of including children and young people in decisions that affect them. This is enshrined in Article 12 (right to be heard and considered in decision-making) of the Convention on the Rights of the Child (CRC), the UN Secretary-General's Youth 21 Agenda, and the establishment of a UN Secretary-General Special Advisor on Youth, as well as the aforementioned UNICEF and Save the Children business sector guidelines. In addition, the UN Global Compact's recently developed Children's Rights and Business Principles serve to further strengthen the standards for fair, protective and equitable business practices for children.[11] This set of ten principles outlines the corporate responsibility

---

[8] UNICEF, 'The State of the World's Children 2012: Children in an Urban World', (2012), http://www.unicef.org/sowc2012/pdfs/SOWC%202012-Main%20Report_EN_13Mar2012.pdf, accessed 20 September 2013.

[9] An extensive list of positive examples of NGO–private sector initiatives may be found at Business and Human Rights Resource Centre, 'Positive Initiatives', http://www.business-humanrights.org/ChildrenPortal/PositiveInitiatives, accessed 25 January 2014.

[10] See ECPAT International (End Child Prostitution, Child Pornography and Trafficking of Children for Sexual Purposes), 'Corporate Social Responsibility: Strengthening Accountability in the Fight Against Sexual Exploitation of Children', (October 2012), http://resources.ecpat.net/EI/Publications/Journals/ECPAT%20Journal_OCT_2012.pdf, accessed 25 January 2014. This compendium of three articles summarizes efforts to collaborate with the private sector in creating systems of accountability. It likewise points to positive examples relating to the tourism sector and an evaluation of the aforementioned code of conduct. Among its many achievements, ECPAT has been actively working with various major hotel chains to raise awareness and stifle child exploitation and prostitution in their establishments. Its work constitutes a good example of inter-sectoral collaboration between governments, NGOs, children and business to acknowledge and collectively act in concrete terms. This work was part of ECPAT's sector-wide strategy to collaboratively develop a Code of Conduct for the Protection of Children from Exploitation in the Travel and Tourism sector, with modest but important gains for their efforts.

[11] Information on the aforementioned process of engagement with global business leaders working with the UN Global Compact may be found in the following document: UNICEF, the UN Global

to respect the basic rights of children and suggests a corporate commitment to support actions advancing human rights and development in partnership with children and communities. Children's rights to protection are particularly central to these commitments.

The UN Committee on the Rights of the Child General Comment 16 on State obligations regarding the impact of the business sector on children's rights

The UN Committee on the Rights of the Child (Committee) is the body of independent experts that monitors the implementation of the CRC. All State Parties are obliged to submit regular reports to the Committee on steps taken towards this end. States must report initially two years after acceding to the Convention and then every five years. The Committee examines each report and addresses its concerns and makes recommendations to the State Party in the form of 'concluding observations' (CO). The Committee also publishes its interpretation of the content of human rights provisions, known as General Comments (GC), on thematic issues. GCs arise from the Committee's own experience and jurisprudence, input from experts and a thematic day of discussion. Although not legally binding, GCs provide a formal interpretation of the scope and application of the human rights provisions identified in the CRC, and are considered 'soft law'.[12] They thereby serve as a valuable reference point for States as they seek to implement CRC principles through a series of concrete steps taken in light of these recommendations.

In 2011, the Committee began drafting a GC on the intersection between child rights and the business sector. It is the first UN human rights treaty body to prepare a GC on this issue.[13] It highlights States' obligations regarding the impact of business activities and operations on children's rights arising from the CRC, the Optional Protocol on the Sale of Children, Child Prostitution and Child Pornography,[14] and the Optional Protocol on the Involvement of

Compact, and Save the Children, 'Children's Rights and Business Principles', (2012), http://www. unglobalcompact.org/docs/issues_doc/human_rights/CRBP/Childrens_Rights_and_Business_ Principles.pdf, accessed 25 January 2014. Among a number of relevant principles, companies commit to: (1) meet their responsibility to respect children's rights, and commit to supporting the human rights of children; (2) contribute towards the elimination of child labour in all business activities and business relationships (across the business value chain); (3) provide decent work for young workers, parents and caregivers; (4) ensure the protection and safety of children in all business activity and facilities; and (10) reinforce community and government efforts to protect and fulfil children's rights.

12   For more information on the Committee on the Rights of the Child and its monitoring of children's rights, see Office of the UN High Commissioner for Human Rights, http://www.ohchr.org/EN/ HRBodies/CRC/Pages/CRCIndex.aspx, accessed 25 January 2014.

13   Convention on the Rights of the Child (adopted 20 November 1989, entered into force 2 September 1990) 1577 UNTS 3 (CRC).

14   Optional Protocol to the Convention on the Rights of the Child on the Sale of Children, Child Prostitution and Child Pornography (adopted 25 May 2000, entered into force 18 January 2002) A/ RES/54/263.

Children in Armed Conflict.[15] These obligations cover a variety of issues, reflecting the fact that children are both rights-holders and stakeholders in businesses as consumers, legally engaged employees, future employees and business leaders, as well as members of the communities and environments in which businesses operate. This is important to underline, as GC 16 is focused on clarifying State Party obligations in three ways. First, States are expected to respect, protect and fulfil the human rights of children as laid out by the CRC. With respect to the business sector, this means States are to ensure they monitor, implement and outline measures that should be undertaken by different levels of government, their agencies and businesses to meet the obligations under these guidelines. Second, as party to the CRC, States are responsible for undertaking all appropriate legislative, administrative and other measures for the implementation of the rights in the CRC and to devote the maximum amount of available resources to the realization of these rights. Finally, at each five-year interval, States are obligated to report on how they have implemented and acted upon these guidelines.

In turn, under GC 16, the 'business sector' is defined as including 'all business enterprises, both national and transnational, regardless of size, sector, location, ownership and structure'.[16] Under this definition, GC 16 would also cover NGOs that provide services critical to the enjoyment of children's rights. Paragraph 4 is central to GC 16 and the call for State action. It outlines four ways in which children specifically are affected by business activities.

1   They are more vulnerable than adults to certain activities (e.g. economic exploitation, harassment in the workplace, marketing and environmental hazards).
2   The impact of negative business practices can be lifelong as well as irreversible (and can also cross generations).
3   Children are often politically voiceless.
4   Obtaining remedies for vulnerable children and their families often presents a significant challenge.

In addition to drawing on existing international standards pertaining to business and human rights, such as the UN Framework, the Guiding Principles, and relevant ILO Conventions, GC 16 applies the four general principles[17] of the CRC.[18] These are:

---

[15] Optional Protocol on the Involvement of Children in Armed Conflict (adopted 25 May 2000, entered into force 12 February 2002) A/RES/54/263.
[16] General Comment No. 16 (2013) on State obligations regarding the impact of the business sector on children's rights, (CRC/C/GC 16), 2013, paragraph 3.
[17] Ibid., paragraph 12.
[18] The CRC may be grouped into four broad categories of rights, which include: survival; development; protection; and, participation rights, and a set of Guiding Principles that include: non-discrimination; adherence to the best interests of the child; right to life, survival and

1   Article 2, non-discrimination, recognizing the diversity of childhood, lifespan perspective and differing groups of children;
2   Article 3, best interests of the child, focusing on issues of severity and *irremediability*, uniqueness of children and their development;
3   Article 6, life survival and development, applying a holistic ecological approach, importance of families in business interventions;
4   Article 12, child participation, involving young people in decisions regarding judicial proceedings, arbitration and governance. This relates to opinions being heard and considered.

These four CRC General Principles are laid out in a GC framework that encompasses State Party obligations in relation to the role of the informal economy; micro, small, medium and large-scale businesses; children's rights and global operations of businesses, including international organizations, emergency and conflict situations; legislative frameworks; remedial measures and implementation and monitoring of the GC. In regard to monitoring, a key component of State Party obligations is the application of a Child Rights Impact Assessment (CRIA). As with any monitoring and evaluation system, a CRIA is dependent on good baseline information, appropriate child rights-based indicators, social change outcomes, and the involvement of a range of stakeholders – starting with children – in the assessment of how business affects their personal and collective well-being and development. There are a number of questions, however, as to whether and how we can collectively achieve these rights.

Key questions guiding future applications of GC 16 include the following.

1   Can national and multinational companies and NGOs develop a shared vision of local development that takes into consideration the broader impact of a collective influence on such development and its impact on children and youth? The question particularly applies to those companies operating in highly sensitive contexts, such as extractive industry firms.
2   How can this shared vision be applied through the entire value chain of products and services affecting vulnerable populations, and children specifically?
3   Are companies and their NGO partners willing to integrate their contributions into the development vision of local communities? By doing so, can this help strengthen the social licence to operate while maximizing the net benefit to people, local institutions and local governance?
4   Can this work be done in a meaningfully collaborative, rights-oriented and participatory way with vulnerable local populations who stand to benefit or lose the most from these efforts?

development; and the right to participate. This commonly known set of guiding principles represents the underlying requirements for any and all rights to be realized under the CRC. See UNICEF succinct explanation and listing of the articles related to the four broad categories and a brief description of the four guiding principles, http://www.unicef.org/crc/index_30177.html, accessed 4 March 2014.

5   What can States do to ensure that the stipulations of GC 16 are effectively
     implemented by business sectors, both nationally and internationally?

This latter question is particularly critical as so many children's rights abuses are
connected to a global web of business networks impacting vulnerable children at
a very real and local level. Under GC 16, States are obligated to adopt measures
that ensure business enterprises identify, prevent and mitigate their impact on
children's rights across their business relationships and value chains throughout
their global operations. States are further required to ensure that businesses apply
a strict process of due diligence for safeguarding children's rights and protection
in their work, and that they have an adequate monitoring system to uphold
this obligation. Furthermore, the GCs' explicit reference to sexual exploitation
enabled by ICT (e.g. child pornography) highlights that companies are to be held
accountable for their implicit enabling or facilitating of child abuse – whether
through the production, sale or delivery of their products and services.[19] Only with
multi-actor collaboration between various levels of government, State agencies,
businesses, children, communities, and others will it be possible to address the
fundamental rights and protection of children around the world. Collaboration
addressing child sexual exploitation in Southeast Asia provides some key lessons
towards this end.

Children's rights and business in the Southeast Asian region

Southeast Asia is a predominately youthful region, with more than 60 per
cent of the global youth population residing there.[20] It is a region undergoing
rapid change, with many of its economies in transition to becoming full-
fledged democracies. While the general trend in Southeast Asia has been one
of economic growth and increased social prosperity, these benefits have been
experienced unevenly, with certain sub-regions and demographic groups being
socially excluded. Unfortunately, vulnerable children in Southeast Asia are more
socially excluded and comparatively more affected by a range of negative drivers
of economic change, including harmful and exploitive labour, forced migration
and trafficking, sexual abuse and exploitation, ethnic conflict, and harmful natural
resource extraction. Additional factors include the lack of access to education
and information, as well as communication technologies that might increase these
threats.[21]

While governments have yet to specifically apply GC 16 in the Southeast Asian
region, there already exists a body of experience upon which to apply its principles
as they relate to the mixed response to State Parties to private sector involvement
in social policy. These include the COs from the Committee to State Party reports.
Recent examples include the CO to the government of Cambodia criticizing the

---

[19] CRC/C/GC 16, see n. 16, paragraph 60.
[20] UNESCAP 2012 Youth in Asia Pacific Fact Sheet.
[21] S. Petcharamesree, *Women and Children's Rights in the ASEAN Region* (Bangkok: SEARCH, 2008).

government's lack of a regulatory framework for multinational companies working in Cambodia.[22] Similarly, a CO was made to the government of Thailand encouraging improved monitoring (including the development of a CRIA) on the sale of children, trafficking of children, and exploitive child labour practices.[23] Another example includes the CO to the government of Singapore, recommending strengthened corporate social responsibility practices in relation to the many multinational companies operating under the government's jurisdiction.[24] Likewise, the CO to the government of Malaysia drew attention to the need for more targeted budgetary allocations to health, education and special protection measures for vulnerable groups of children affected by Malaysia's rapid economic growth (for example, the Orang Asli children living in economic hardship, children of indigenous populations living in remote places, children of migrant workers and child victims of trafficking).[25]

In 2010, ASEAN officials inaugurated the Commission on the Promotion and Protection of the Rights of Women and Children (ACWC), to augment the ASEAN Intergovernmental Commission for Human Rights (AICHR).[26] The ACWC has a mandate to, among other things, develop policies, programmes and innovative strategies vis-à-vis the rights of women and children in the region. Under the terms of reference of the establishment of the Commission, the ACWC is comprised of representatives from the ten Member States of ASEAN. As yet, the ACWC has not specifically adopted a specific focus examining the impact of business on children. However, its current five-year work plan focuses on issues such as violence against children, trafficking, and children's participation, which will undoubtedly result in opportunities to strengthen private–public sector partnerships in support of children's rights. Given the region's rapidly growing ICT sector and its impact on children and youth, this area offers a particularly rich area for learning.

---

[22] UNCRC, 'Consideration of Reports Submitted by States Parties Under Article 44 of the Convention: Concluding Observations – Cambodia', CRC/C/KHM/CO/2 (20 June 2011) at paragraphs 26–27.

[23] UNCRC, 'Consideration of Reports Submitted by States Parties Under Article 12, Paragraph 1, of the Optional Protocol to the Convention on the Rights of the Child on the Sale of Children, Child Prostitution and Child Pornography: Concluding Observations – Thailand', CRC/C/OPSC/THA/CO/1 (21 February 2012) at paragraphs 8, 13 and 14.

[24] UNCRC, 'Consideration of Reports submitted by States Parties under Article 44 of the Convention: Concluding Observations – Singapore', CRC/C/SGP/CO/2–3 (4 May 2011) at paragraphs 25–26.

[25] UNCRC, 'UN Committee on the Rights of the Child: Concluding Observations – Malaysia', CRC/C/MYS/CO/1 (25 June 2007). More generally, the UN Committee on the Rights of the Child and the International Labour Organization, as well as a number of NGOs in the region, bring a whole range of issues to the attention of ASEAN States and the general public, including concerns relating to young domestic worker abuse, sexual exploitation of children, child labour (particularly in the hospitality, mining and garment industries), poisoning and significant impacts of environmental degradation on children among others. For more information on a list of references to articles and declarations from human rights bodies on abuses in the region, see the Business and Human Rights Resource Centre, 'Alleged Abuses', http://www.business-humanrights.org/ChildrenPortal/AllegedAbuses#127099, accessed 25 January 2014.

[26] Working Group for an ASEAN Human Rights Mechanism, 'Inaugurated: ASEAN Commission on the Promotion and Protection of the Rights of Women and Children', (7 April 2010), http://www.aseanhrmech.org/news/ASEAN-commission-inaugurated.htm, accessed 25 January 2014.

A Southeast Asian area of challenge for business and children's rights: online child sexual exploitation and abuse

In an increasingly interdependent and globalized world, business today has come under considerable scrutiny by all its stakeholders with respect to businesses' operational footprint. The world is no stranger to the adverse impact of business operations. Examples of human rights transgressions where business is in some way complicit or responsible are readily available. However, in this particular case-study, while industry itself is not the perpetrator of child rights abuse, legitimate industry platforms nevertheless have been shown to facilitate such abuse.

While the Internet offers infinite opportunities for children and adults alike to learn about the world we live in, it has also had a considerable negative impact on child safety online. The advent of the Internet and the concomitant ease of communications across borders, together with the success of globalized e-commerce have brought forth a new dimension to the incidence of child sexual abuse, taking it online. Very often, unbeknown to them, both the financial and ICT industries' platforms are used to facilitate the sale, exchange and dissemination of child sexual abuse images, and, more recently, live on-demand web-streaming of child sexual abuse. These platforms are also being used in the trafficking of women and children for sexual exploitation, as well as a tool for grooming/luring young people into situations of exploitation.

Currently in the ASEAN countries, few governments and law-enforcement agencies collate data on the online abuse of children and fewer still make it available in the public domain. There remains a great stigma to the sexual exploitation of young people as it hits close to home and is often not dealt with openly in conservative Asian societies that are deferential to age. Research and data would go a long way in making Internet safety a part of mainstream child protection efforts. This is particularly so as policing the online environment remains in its early stages and requires multi-jurisdictional collaboration. In the case of online commercial child sexual exploitation and abuse, the 'criminal' activity can be hosted in one country, the victims can be in another country, while the offender accessing or purchasing such illegal images could be in yet another country.

The most recent case of live on-demand abuse is the one coming out of the Philippines reported in January 2014, where the UK's National Crime Agency working with Australian and US counterparts in the Philippines and the Philippines police uncovered a paedophile syndicate paying to watch the sexual abuse of children in the Philippines via webcam. The investigation, codenamed 'Operation Endeavor', covered twelve countries and led to the arrest of seventeen Britons, five of whom have been convicted. Fifteen children aged between 6 and 15 were rescued in a raid in Angeles City in the Philippines and several parents were arrested.[27]

---

[27] 'UK, US Police Bust PH Cybersex Ring: Up to 100k Filipino Kids Exploited', (*Inquirer.net* 17 January 2014), http://globalnation.inquirer.net/96835/british-us-and-australian-police-probe-ph-sex-abuse-ring, accessed 24 February 2014.

The above highlights the fact that increased accessibility and use of home-computer technology has revolutionized the distribution of child abuse images by increasing the ease of possession and dissemination, as well as decreasing the cost of production and distribution – especially across international borders. Zoe Hilton, Head of Safeguarding and Child Protection at the Child Exploitation and Online Protection (CEOP) agency in the United Kingdom, aptly states in a 2010 interview that '(t)he Internet hasn't created abuse, but it has created more opportunities for like-minded individuals to contact each other and interact in dangerous and inappropriate ways'.[28] People are now able to form virtual communities, endorse each other's behaviour and normalize such behaviour. What is more, when these images reach cyberspace, they are irretrievable and can circulate in perpetuity, consequently re-victimizing the child every time they are viewed. In the same interview Ms Hilton rightly observes that '(t)he online risks to children are very real, but often the information needed to safeguard them seems very hidden'.[29] In Asia, with the exception of Japan, Singapore and South Korea, the use of computers and the Internet by youth primarily takes place without adult supervision in Internet cafés rather than in the home or school environment. Children are hence at greater risk of exploitation and exposure to inappropriate content in such establishments, exacerbated by the fact that many countries lack legislation or even guidelines for protecting children in these establishments.

Prior to the arrival of the Internet, it was extremely difficult to obtain child sexual abuse images.[30] A person interested in acquiring child sexual abuse images either had to know someone who had such images or take considerable personal risk to obtain or produce such images. Today, distribution on the Internet – via ordinary email, chat groups, peer-to-peer exchange and technologies like Skype and webcam live-streaming – is no longer limited by national boundaries. Furthermore, the Internet provides instant access to images, videos and on-demand live acts to thousands of individuals throughout the world. In addition, the ability to use traditional payment methods such as credit cards and money transfer services, as well as a variety of new payment platforms such as debit cards, third-party payment platforms, mobile banking, and digital wallets has made it easier than ever to purchase child pornography. Using 1995 as the baseline, INTERPOL reported knowing of approximately 4,000 unique child abuse images in total, worldwide.[31] Subsequently, in a June 2010 report, the United Nations Office of Drugs and Crime (UNODC) estimated that the commercial child sexual exploitation industry globally generates an estimated 50,000 new child sexual abuse images each

---

[28] Camilla Pemberton, 'CEOP's Safeguarding Head Zoe Hilton', (29 January 2010), http://www.communitycare.co.uk/Articles/29/01/2010/113679/ceops-safeguarding-head-zoe-hilton.htm, accessed 25 January 2014.

[29] Ibid.

[30] Such images are referred to as child pornography in most national legal statutes, as well as in UN and other international protocols.

[31] John Carr, 'The Unbelievable Truth About Child Pornography in the UK', *The Huffington Post UK* (16 October 2012), http://www.huffingtonpost.co.uk/john-carr/child-pornography-the-unbeliev-able-truth-ab_b_1970969.html, accessed 25 January 2014.

year and is worth approximately US$250 million globally.[32] This finding is in keeping with the findings of Paulo Sergio Pinheiro, first United Nations Special Rapporteur on the Violence against Children, who, in presenting his report to the UN General Assembly in 2006, noted that 'the Internet and other developments of communication technologies ... appear to be associated with an increased risk of sexual exploitation of children as well as other forms of violence against children'.[33]

The extent of the responsibility for business to safeguard children

Are the financial and ICT industries failing today's children? It is difficult to pinpoint where industry responsibility starts and ends in such a dilemma, where business is not a willing or complicit partner in the crime, but nonetheless serves as a facilitator. The knowledge and expertise needed by industry to protect children is not firmly defined. A key underlying factor to building awareness around the issue of child sexual abuse is first acknowledging the existence of such abuse and, in the context of industry, acknowledging that their platforms are being misused in these crimes. Child sexual abuse continues to be an issue often neglected because it is almost always perpetuated in secrecy, is difficult to identify, and even harder to stop. A culture of silence among authorities and adults only perpetuates the suffering of children targeted by such abuse. It also often breeds mistrust of both law enforcement and society, making it harder for victims to report the abuse.

To surpass these hurdles and encourage a cooperative and comprehensive approach, it is imperative to bring all relevant stakeholders to the table. In a globalized world, governments alone cannot solve the social, environmental, and economic challenges faced today. Governments around the world have acknowledged as much and require the active contribution of other sectors of society. Businesses today need to step up and take greater responsibility for externalities stemming from their operations and play a part in addressing these issues with the help of the communities that they support and/or serve. The last decade has seen the emergence of increasingly more public–private partnerships and corporate social responsibility efforts in response to this shift in stakeholder expectations.

Industry response to online child sexual exploitation

In the case of online child safety, industry has responded with a range of self-regulatory initiatives. Almost universally, companies in the ICT industry have

---

[32] UNODC, 'The Globalization of Crime: A Transnational Organized Crime Threat Assessment: Executive Summary', (2010), http://www.unodc.org/documents/data-and-analysis/tocta/TOCTA_Report_2010_low_res.pdf, accessed 25 January 2014.

[33] UNGA, 'Promotion and Protection of the Rights of Children – Note by the Secretary-General', (29 August 2006), UN Doc A/61/299, http://www.unicef.org/violencestudy/reports/SG_violencestudy_en.pdf, accessed 25 January 2014, at paragraph 77.

drawn up Acceptable Use Policies, Terms of Service and Community Guidelines for their platforms.[34] These tools provide guidelines for user-generated content, parental guides and controls, a recognized system of content labelling, reporting options, protocols for cooperation with law enforcement and more.

Microsoft, a member of the International Centre for Missing and Exploited Children (ICMEC) Board of Directors, has been a leader in developing technology tools to combat online child sexual abuse. In 2009, Microsoft, in cooperation with Dartmouth College, developed PhotoDNA, a technology that aids in finding and removing some of the 'worst of the worst' images of child sexual exploitation images from the Internet.[35] Microsoft has donated the PhotoDNA technology to the National Center for Missing and Exploited Children (NCMEC), which established a PhotoDNA-based programme giving online service providers in the USA an effective tool for taking more proactive action to stop the distribution of known images of child sexual abuse online. Microsoft, working with NCMEC, has implemented a gradual rollout of PhotoDNA on its Bing, SkyDrive and Hotmail services. In early 2011, Facebook joined Microsoft in sublicensing the technology for use on its network globally. In Asia, Trend Micro – a Nikkei listed company and a global leader in cloud security, Internet content security and threat management solutions – is in the midst of testing the use of PhotoDNA on its platform. In July 2013 Twitter announced the company would introduce PhotoDNA to block child abuse images.[36]

In the financial industry, as with the fraud and anti-money-laundering efforts, 'Know Your Customer' protocols can also be extended to individuals using their online payments services. Such individual efforts, while commendable, are not sufficient. The need for cross-sector and cross-border efforts to combat a globalized crime that knows no borders is thus evident. The Financial Coalition Against Child Pornography is one such collaborative response.

Financial Coalition Against Child Pornography

First formed in the USA in 2006, the Financial Coalition Against Child Pornography (FCACP) is an alliance between private industry and the public sector in the battle against commercial child pornography. It is managed by the ICMEC and its

---

[34] For example, see PayPal, 'PayPal Acceptable Use Policy', https://www.paypal.com/sg/webapps/mpp/ua/acceptableuse-full, accessed 25 January 2014; PayPal 'Legal Agreements for PayPal Services', https://cms.paypal.com/sg/cgi-bin/marketingweb?cmd=_render-contentandcontent_ID=ua/Legal_Hub_fullandlocale.x=en_GB, accessed 25 January 2014; Facebook, 'Statement of Rights and Responsibilities', https://www.facebook.com/legal/terms, accessed 25 January 2014 or Facebook, 'Facebook Community Standards', https://www.facebook.com/communitystandards, accessed 25 January 2014.

[35] Microsoft, 'PhotoDNA Newsroom', http://www.microsoft.com/en-us/news/presskits/photodna, accessed 25 January 2014.

[36] Twitter to introduce PhotoDNA system to block child abuse images. Microsoft-developed system may be introduced this year once complication of handling pictures posted alongside billions of tweets can be overcome, http://www.theguardian.com/technology/2013/jul/22/twitter-photodna-child-abuse, The Guardian, 22 July 2013.

sister organization, the NCMEC, both headquartered in the USA. The US-based FCACP plays an important role in eradicating the profitability of commercial child pornography by bringing together banks, credit card companies, online third-party payment systems, technology companies, Internet service providers, social networking platforms, and law-enforcement agencies to find ways to disrupt the economics of the child pornography business and develop solutions that are in line with local laws and customs.[37]

The Asia Pacific Financial Coalition Against Child Pornography (APAC-FCACP) was established in 2009 to widen the efforts of its US counterpart in the Asia Pacific region, alerting industry of a crime that was first seen in the OECD countries where the Internet infrastructure and access to the Internet preceded the ICT revolution in Asia.[38] Managed by the Asia Pacific office of ICMEC based in Singapore, it brings together banks, credit card companies, online third-party payment systems, technology companies, social networking platforms, industry associations, and law-enforcement agencies.[39] Recognizing the important role civil society and governments play in protecting children from online child pornography, the APAC-FCACP urges industry to acknowledge its role and to proactively make efforts to combat this crime and safeguard children.

The APAC-FCACP initiative started with a small core group of companies that were founding members of the US-FCACP, with PayPal taking the lead. PayPal supported ICMEC's expansion of the Coalition's efforts in the Asia Pacific region by starting off the APAC-FCACP initiative prior to ICMEC's establishing its Singapore presence, together with other founding members, MasterCard, Visa and American Express.[40] A region-wide approach has resulted in a membership comprised mostly of regional offices of multinational corporations in the financial and technology industries, including American Express, Citi, Facebook, MasterCard, Microsoft, PayPal, Trend Micro, Visa and Yahoo. Law enforcement in Australia, New Zealand and the US Department of Homeland Security – Immigration and Customs Enforcement representatives in the region are active partners. The Thai Bankers Association has been an interested partner since 2010, and the Inter Agency Council Against Trafficking within the Philippines Department of Justice has been an active member since June 2012.

Since August 2009, ICMEC Singapore has hosted ten APAC-FCACP meetings and seminars in the region, with industry, law-enforcement and NGO partners presenting on how each responds to the issue within its own mandate and jurisdiction. ICMEC has been an active partner with ASEAN on the *Working Towards a Child Pornography and Child Prostitution Free South East Asia* initiative led by the Philippines.[41]

[37] ICMEC, 'Financial Coalition Against Child Pornography', http://icmec.org/missingkids/servlet/PageServlet?LanguageCountry=en_X1andPageId=3064, accessed 25 January 2014.
[38] ICMEC, 'Global Efforts to Expand the Financial Coalition', http://www.icmec.org/missingkids/servlet/PageServlet?LanguageCountry=en_X1andPageId=4355, accessed 25 January 2014.
[39] Ibid.
[40] Ibid.
[41] ICMEC, 'Overview of Programs', http://www.icmec.org/en_X1/icmec_publications/Overview_of_Programs_June_2012__FINAL_.pdf, accessed 25 January 2014.

The Coalition's efforts in Asia are still in their early stages. However, in the USA, there are several indicators that point to the FCACP's impact.[42] For example, since the start of the FCACP there has been a 50 per cent drop in the number of unique commercial child pornography websites reported to the US CyberTipline. There is also a trend towards these websites directing buyers away from traditional payment tools and methods, such as credit cards that are easier to track, towards multi-layered alternative payment schemes where tracing the origin of the transaction is a challenge, to say the least. US law enforcements increasingly successful attention to commercial child pornography websites has led some sites to not accept US credit cards. Finally, collaborative action by law enforcement and the payments industry in the USA has resulted in a significant increase in the price of child sexual abuse images.

Challenges to cross-sector partnerships

Cross-sector collaboration raises an important question around the continuity and long-term sustainability of such initiatives. The biggest challenge, at the country level, is the low level of awareness and even lower level of acknowledgement of the existence of child sexual abuse across all stakeholders – governments, industry and civil society. It will require a collective approach to bring the issue out of the shadows and into the open. Child sexual abuse is hard to discuss, making it difficult to raise awareness and design programme initiatives to eliminate this problem from our society.

In addition, weak legal frameworks around cybercrime make it more challenging to keep the issue on industry's radar. It can be difficult to determine the most effective approach in appealing to businesses, such as voluntary corporate social responsibility (CSR), brand-risk management, long-term goodwill, or simply good business practice, when there is a regulation and guidance deficit. The APAC-FCACP draws on the entire range of measures to keep the membership involved and active in combating crime on their platforms. Very often, personal relationships built over time bear fruit, with companies becoming strong supporters and advocates in the fight. But this takes time. Business could make this a more productive partnership by creating internal protocols and procedures, whereby normal staff turnover does not jeopardize the relationship built carefully over a long period of time and allows efforts to continue and flourish.

How does one institutionalize such cross-sector partnership efforts? Are the UN Framework for Business and Human Rights, which places business responsibility to respect human rights at the centre of policy and practice, or UNICEF's Business and Child Rights' Principles a good way forward? Is such supra-national UN guidance adequate or does ASEAN have a role to play in ensuring regional adoption by

---

42 Financial Coalition Against Child Pornography, 'Backgrounder', http://icmec.org/en_X1/pdf/FCACPBackgrounder1–13.pdf, accessed 25 January 2014.

putting forward implementation guidelines for industry within the region? Is such guidance adequate? Does it place sufficient pressure on companies to respond?

In response to this challenge, the European Commission (EC) took the initiative of drafting a *Guidance for the Information and Communication Technologies (ICT) Sector on Implementing the UN Guiding Principles on Business and Human Rights* (EC Guidance).[43] The draft was open for public consultation, input and comment from December 2012 to February 2013, and published in June 2013. While the EC Guidance takes particular account of the situation and experiences of EU businesses, it aims to be globally relevant. UNICEF, in its submission, took the opportunity to suggest specific references to children's rights 'in terms of protecting children from violence and exploitation, including among others, the distribution of child abuse images online and restriction of harmful content for children'.[44] UNICEF further recommended that companies research the long-term impacts of their products and services on children of different ages and engage with children and child rights experts and stakeholders to understand their concerns.[45] The EC Guidance, now finalized, outlines a series of suggested questions to help industry test the extent to which a company's policy commitment and product design embed the respect for and impact on human rights in line with the Guiding Principles across business units.[46] If human rights considerations are embedded from the very start, companies may also find it helpful in keeping up with the fast pace of change in the technology sector, if human rights considerations are embedded from the very start.

The ICT industry hence shoulders an added dimension to its responsibility to respect human rights because it has a global reach transcending national borders. National laws and jurisdictions limit the State in its duty to protect human rights. With limited exceptions, there is no universal framework that addresses ICT services globally. Numerous legal provisions and protections relevant to the sector, such as the right to privacy, data protection and retention requirements and freedom of expression, do, however, pose complex challenges to the ICT sector's ability to meet its own responsibility to respect human rights.

Human rights have been the focus of regulatory bodies such as the UN for many years, but companies have historically been reluctant to take action. Nonetheless, there has more recently been a definite shift in business attitudes. In recent decades,

---

[43] European Commission Human Rights Sector Guidance Project, Guidance for the Information and Communication Technologies (ICT), Sector on Implementing the UN Guiding Principles on Business and Human Rights, pp. 15–16, (2013), http://ec.europa.eu/enterprise/policies/sustaina-ble-business/files/csr-sme/csr-ict-hr-business_en.pdf, accessed 4 February 2014.

[44] UNICEF comments as part of the public consultation on the EC's Draft Guidance for the ICT Sector on Implementing the UN Guiding Principles on Business and Human Rights (19 February 2013), http://www.ihrb.org/pdf/eu-sector-guidance/ICT/UNICEF.pdf, accessed 25 January 2014.

[45] Ibid., p. 2.

[46] European Commission ICT Sector Guide on Implementing the UN Guiding Principles on Business and Human Rights, http://ec.europa.eu/enterprise/policies/sustainable-business/files/csr-sme/csr-ict-hr-business_en.pdf, accessed 4 February 2014.

where companies have responded, the pressure to respond has come from the public. From Nike in Indonesia, Shell in Nigeria and Apple in the USA to Sanlu in China, consumers and the general public have demonstrated their power in making companies respond, albeit sometimes very slowly. Companies realize that public opinion matters not only when it comes to corporate reputations, but also to the bottom line. Accordingly, society needs to step forward and demand that industry take action. Industry players, on the other hand, must visibly signal a significant shift in their attitude and policies. Responsible business is increasingly seeking to be acquainted with and show that they respect human rights through technological and financial investments, as demonstrated by Microsoft. By extension, it is recognized that business can make the Internet a dangerous place for child pornographers.

Currently, most guidance from the UN and other multilateral and international organizations is levelled at child sexual exploitation in the travel and tourism industry or trafficking in children. There is sparse guidance on business's responsibility regarding online child sexual abuse.[47] As noted at the start, GC 16's express reference to child pornography is the first reference to the fact that companies are to be held accountable. In addition, blocking and notice and take down of web pages are seen by many as censorship and going against the grain of the open net, which presents its own challenges in facing down civil liberties and freedom of speech groups. The FCACP and the APAC-FCACP have put together industry best practices papers for the payments and file-sharing and hosting industry for keeping child pornography merchants out of their platforms.[48]

Finally, children must also be recognized as key actors in cross-sector partnerships, both as potential victims and as agents of social change. One interesting example of a child-centred approach to preventing ICT-enabled sexual exploitation is the Child Protection Partnership (CPP). The CPP is based in Thailand, Brazil and Canada and brings together law-enforcement agencies, government ministries, the private sector, universities and child protection NGOs. The initiative supports child-led efforts to identify especially risky places where children are being exploited online, as well as identifying local advocates who can protect them (including community police, child rights advocates, and other persons identified

---

[47] Business and Human Rights Resource Centre, 'Practical Guidance: Business and Children Portal', http://www.business-humanrights.org/ChildrenPortal/Guidance#109414, accessed 21 July 2014.

[48] ICMEC: US-FCACP has put together a Merchant Best Practices Paper and Webinar for the payments industry for keeping child pornography merchants off the platforms. See 'International Merchant Acquisition and Monitoring Best Practices for Prevention and Detection of Commercial Child Pornography', (May 2007), http://icmec.org/en_X1/pdf/InternetMerchantAcquisition.pdf, accessed 25 January 2014. See also The Asia Pacific Financial Coalition Against Child Pornography. 'Best Practices to Help File Hosting and File Sharing Companies Fight the Distribution of Child Sexual Exploitation Content', (2013), http://icmec.org/en_X1/pdf/BestPracticesforFileHostingandSharingIndustrySeptember2013.pdf, accessed 25 January 2014.

as 'safe' by vulnerable children). In Thailand, the CPP worked with children, protection agencies, researchers and police in a Bangkok urban slum community with high levels of cyber café criminal activities and in rural villages prone to trafficking in girls. The initiative has resulted in increased arrests of perpetrators and efforts to strengthen legislation and policy through the creation of a national inter-sectoral round table that is guided by information collected directly from children most affected by ICT-enabled exploitation.[49]

Conclusions

It is clear that the time is ripe for a concerted effort in combating ICT-enabled child sexual exploitation, as the context and disposition of State and business responsibility and children's rights promotion has never embodied so much progress. With UN efforts to promote the private sector taking a leading role in respecting, protecting and even promoting children's rights, the Guiding Principles on Business and Human Rights launched in 2011 have been quickly bolstered by defining those rights as they apply to the context of child well-being and development. Business representatives working with UNICEF and a number of international NGOs – as seen in the Global Compact's Children's Rights and Business Principles and the recent CRC Committee on the Rights of the Child's GC 16 on State obligations regarding the impact of the business sector on children's rights – collectively provide a useful and practical framework for companies and their partners to evaluate their impact on children in a systemic and integral manner.

At present, there has never been a better time to legally and practically operationalize the responsibility that businesses have in both respecting children's rights and also actively participating in fulfilling the realization of their rights by developing their capacity through partnerships. This is no easy task. Nevertheless, such efforts are being supported by a number of recent COs issued by the CRC in response to Southeast Asian State Party reports. This progress would be greatly enhanced by policy guidance at the ASEAN level, as well as from other regional bodies like the South Asian Association for Regional Cooperation (SAARC), similar to the EC Human Rights Guides for enterprises in three business sectors.[50] ASEAN, particularly with the guidance from the ASEAN Commission for Women and Children, could either subscribe to the EC Guides, urging Asian companies to adapt the recommendations made at the operational level, or draw up policy recommendations of their own.

---

[49]   P. Cook, C. Heykoop, A. Anuntavoraskul and J. Vibulphol, 'Action Research Exploring Information and Communication Technologies and Child Protection in Thailand', (2012), *Development In Practice*, 22(4): 574.

[50]   European Commission / Enterprise and Industry / Human Rights Guides for Enterprises in three business sectors, http://ec.europa.eu/enterprise/policies/sustainable-business/corporate-social-responsibility/human-rights, accessed 4 February 2014.

Collaboration between the business sector, States and human rights organizations is still at a relatively nascent stage. As a result, synergies between partners from these three sectors have yet to reach their full potential. It takes a shared moral vision and continual monitoring – using tools such as the GC 16, with its emphasis on appropriate child impact assessment – to strengthen the ability of these actors to serve children's best interests. Future research and learning in this field will help guide this process.

Part II

5 Regulating social and environmental risk in ASEAN financial integration

The Xayaburi dam project in Lao PDR and Thai Banks

Daniel King

Introduction

The road to financial integration is a priority for the ASEAN Economic Community (AEC). However, the region's strategic milestones for financial integration do not incorporate social or environmental risk-management systems for project finance. The Equator Principles (EPs) are regarded as international best practice for environmental risk management for banks in project finance. The EPs are a voluntary framework based on the International Finance Corporation (IFC) Performance Standards on Social and Environmental Sustainability (Performance Standards) and on the World Bank Group Environmental, Health, and Safety Guidelines (EHS Guidelines). There is a strong argument that the decision by banks in Thailand to provide loans to the Xayaburi hydropower dam on the Mekong River in Lao People's Democratic Republic (Lao PDR) did not comply with relevant laws and standards, including the EPs. The project is likely to have significant negative environmental and social implications within Lao PDR and across borders in Cambodia, Thailand, and Vietnam. The project is the first of eleven proposed dams on the Mekong River mainstream below China, with China planning a cascade of up to twenty-one dams. The Xayaburi project has already caused political tension between Cambodia, Lao PDR, Thailand, and Vietnam. From a regional perspective, the Xayaburi dam shows the opportunity for – as well as the responsibility of – ASEAN policy-makers and ASEAN banks to adopt policies consistent with international banking industry standards, by providing a minimum standard for socially and environmentally responsible investment.

This chapter first critically assesses the decision by Thai banks to finance the Xayaburi dam and then provides an outline of the differentiated responsibility of banks compared to other business enterprises. It subsequently outlines the ASEAN frameworks for socially and environmentally responsible project development and ASEAN financial integration, and argues for the need to link standard setting for responsible investment to the process of financial integration in ASEAN. Finally, the chapter outlines policy recommendations on how to link social and environmental risk management with financial integration. The adoption of ASEAN policy to promote such systems would further the overarching aims of the ASEAN Charter to protect the environment and ensure the sustainable use of natural resources and the promotion and protection of human rights.

Proposed hydropower projects on the Lower Mekong River

The Mekong River flows 4,600 km through China, Myanmar, Lao PDR, Thailand, Cambodia, and then Vietnam. The Mekong River Basin is home to about 65 million people, of which two-thirds live in rural areas and rely on subsistence fisheries.[1] There are eleven proposed dams along the mainstream in the Lower Mekong Basin (LMB) countries.[2] The number of dam projects planned for the Upper Mekong (Lancang) in China has recently increased to twenty-one,[3] and there could therefore be over eighty projects on the Mekong River and its tributaries by 2030.[4] The Xayaburi dam is particularly significant as it is the first of these dams scheduled for construction, and decisions made with regard to Xayaburi will set a precedent for future projects on the Mekong River mainstream below China.[5] The construction cost of the Xayaburi dam is estimated at US$3.5 billion (114 billion THB) and has a planned generating capacity of over 1,285 megawatts of electricity.[6]

Thailand and Vietnam are predicted to purchase close to 90 per cent of the power generated by the proposed mainstream projects.[7] However, both the Thai[8] and Vietnamese[9] future electricity demand calculations have been questioned. Regardless of whether or not the demand for electricity has been over-estimated, the eleven mainstream dam projects are not critical to ensure healthy growth in

[1] G. Ziv, E. Baran, I. Rodríguez-Iturbe and A. Levin, 'Trading-off fish Biodiversity, Food Security, and Hydropower in the Mekong River Basin', (2012) 109 *PNAS* 15, http://www.pnas.org/content/109/15/5609.full, accessed 7 September 2013.

[2] Cambodia, Lao PDR, Thailand, and Vietnam.

[3] International Rivers, 'Mekong/Lancang River', http://www.internationalrivers.org/campaigns/mekong-lancang-river, accessed 7 September 2013.

[4] International Centre for Environmental Management (ICEM), 'Strategic Environmental Assessment of Hydropower on the Mekong Mainstream', (October 2010), p. 6, http://www.mrcmekong.org/assets/Publications/Consultations/SEA-Hydropower/SEA-FR-summary-13oct.pdf, accessed 7 September 2013.

[5] Many of the developers and financiers along the Mekong River are Thai and Chinese investors; it is therefore also relevant to the investment in hydropower dams on the Nu Salween River in China, Myanmar, and Thailand with investors from the same countries.

[6] International Rivers, 'The Xayaburi Dam: A Looming Threat to the Mekong River', (January 2011), http://www.internationalrivers.org/files/attached-files/the_xayaburi_dam_eng.pdf, accessed 7 September 2013.

[7] ICEM, see n. 4, at p. 9.

[8] C. Greacen and A. Palettu, 'Electricity Sector Planning and Hydropower in the Mekong Region', in L. Lebel, J. Dore, R. Daniel and Y. S. Koma, *Democratizing Water Governance in the Mekong Region* (Chiang Mai: Mekong Press, 2007).

[9] The ADB's demand calculation for Vietnam is only 54% of the official figure: ICEM, see n. 4, at pp. 7–8.

the LMB regional power sector.[10] Unfortunately, despite the predictions of serious adverse social and environmental consequences in a Strategic Environmental
Assessment (SEA Report) on the impacts of LMB mainstream dams,[11] alternatives to damming the Mekong and blocking the river channel with any dams constructed have not been adequately explored.[12] A SEA of the Asian Development
Bank's Greater Mekong Sub-region Power Development Master Plan (ADB SEA)
has been conducted belatedly and completed in August 2013. The ADB SEA
consultant's recommendations include an urgent need for improved national and
regional power-demand forecasting and genuine cross-sector review of draft power
plans. The recommendations likewise emphasize that SEAs should be mandatory
for all national and regional power planning processes in the Greater Mekong
Sub-region.[13]

As the second most biodiverse river in the world after the Amazon, the Mekong
is a hotspot for fish species.[14] Over one million tonnes of freshwater fish are caught
annually in Cambodia and Vietnam.[15] Accordingly, fish protein represents between
47 and 80 per cent of total animal protein consumed in the lower basin, illustrating
its critical importance to food supply and human health.[16] Substantial decreases
in fish catch will have serious implications for nutrition in the basin. Studies have
shown that it will be very difficult to replace vital elements of human nutrition currently obtained through fish consumption with other food sources.[17] In addition to
subsistence uses, farmers rely on supplementary income from fish catch to support
purchase of tools and supplies or to balance drops in rice yield.[18] The SEA Report
estimates the potential losses for fisheries due to the eleven proposed mainstream
dams at $476 million/year, with 35 per cent or 550,000–800,000 million tonnes
of migratory fish species becoming vulnerable.[19] There is an international human

---

[10] ICEM, see n. 5, at p. 18.

[11] The SEA report was commissioned by the Mekong River Commission Secretariat (MRCS).

[12] ICEM, see n. 5, at p. 18.

[13] International Centre for Environmental Management, Press Release (8 August 2013), http://icem.
com.au/25-target-for-renewable-energy-is-realistic-and-sustainable-in-the-gms/news, accessed 7
September 2013.

[14] See n. 2.

[15] P. J. Dugan, C. Barlow, A. A. Agostinho, E. Baran, G. F. Cada, D. Chen, I. G. Cowx, J. W. Ferguson,
T. Jutagate, M. Mallen-Cooper, G. Marmulla, J. Nestler, M. Petrere, R. L. Welcomme and K. O.
Winemiller, 'Fish Migration, Dams, and Loss of Ecosystem Services in the Mekong Basin', (2010),
Ambio, 39(4): 344–348, http://www.ncbi.nlm.nih.gov/pmc/articles/PMC3357701, accessed 7
September 2013.

[16] K. G. Hortle, *Consumption and Yield of Fish and Other Aquatic Animals from the Lower Mekong Basin*
(October 2007) Mekong River Commission: MRC technical paper no. 16, http://www.mrcme-
kong.org/assets/Publications/technical/tech-No16-consumption-n-yield-of-fish.pdf, accessed 7
September 2013.

[17] E. Baran, 'Mekong Fisheries and Mainstream Dams Prepared as Part of the Mekong River
Commission's Strategic Environmental Assessment', (2010), p. 19, http://www.worldfishcenter.
org/resource_centre/WF_2736.pdf, accessed 7 September 2013.

[18] R. I. Arthur and R. M. Friend, 'Inland Capture Fisheries in the Mekong and Their Place and
Potential Within Food-Led Regional Development', (2011), *Global Environmental Change*, 21(1):
1–274, at p. 219.

[19] ICEM, see n. 4, at p. 11.

rights responsibility to ensure food in a quantity and quality sufficient to satisfy the dietary needs of individuals.[20] Olivier De Schutter, UN Special Rapporteur on the right to food, has worked with numerous stakeholders to elaborate standards on the right to food.[21] Communities and civil-society groups from the region could consider engaging him on the potential crisis in Cambodia caused by dams (and the developers and financiers of those large-scale projects).

Only three of the eleven proposed LMB mainstream dam projects have explicit and detailed plans for fish-pass facilities.[22] However, serious concerns have been raised in relation to the fish-pass designs, which do not constitute efficient mitigation measures and will not address the dramatic changes wrought by the dams on fisheries.[23] Fish-pass technology that can effectively deal with the large biomass and biodiversity of the long-distance migratory fish in the Mekong remains untested. On this basis, independent experts have stated that 'fish passes, whatever their type, are not a realistic measure to mitigate the impact of mainstream dams on mainstream fish migrations'.[24] Such experts have further affirmed that, 'there has never been a successful fish pass built for a dam the size of Xayaburi'.[25] A Mekong River Commission (MRC)-appointed panel of seventeen international experts in fisheries and fish passes supported these findings.[26] More study on the use of this technology on the Mekong River would be required before it could be considered as an effective mitigation option.[27]

Of the numerous risks involved, reduced sedimentation flows will have significant impacts on broader food production, as sediments suspended in the waters of the Mekong contain nutrients that serve as natural fertilizers.[28] Accordingly, sediment plays a fundamental role in supporting agricultural productivity on 18,000 km² of the floodplains of Cambodia and 5,000–10,000 km² of the delta in Vietnam. It is likewise critical to aquatic productivity in the Tonle Sap in Cambodia and the coastal fishery in the Mekong delta of Vietnam.[29] The delta is the primary area for rice growing in Vietnam and is essential for both food supply and economic

---

[20] United Nations Economic and Social Council 'The Right to Adequate Food (Art.11): 05/12/1999.E/C.12/1999/5 (General Comments)', (12 May 1999) E/C.12/1999/5, at [8], http://www.unhchr.ch/tbs/doc.nsf/0/3d02758c707031d58025677f003b73b9, accessed 7 September 2013.

[21] See, for example, Olivier De Schutter, 'Report of the Special Rapporteur on the Right to Food: Agribusiness and the Right to Food, Human Rights Council', A/HRC/13/33 (22 December 2009).

[22] ICEM, see n. 5, at p. 100.

[23] Ibid., at p. 16.

[24] See n. 17.

[25] E. Baran, World Fish Centre, quoted in *The Economist*, 'The Mekong River: Lies, Dams and Statistics', (26 July 2012), http://www.economist.com/blogs/banyan/2012/07/mekong-river, accessed 9 May 2014.

[26] P. Dugan 'Mainstream Dams as Barriers to Fish Migration: International Learning and Implications for the Mekong', (2008), *Catch and Culture*, 14(3): 9–15.

[27] ICEM, see n. 5, at p. 142.

[28] Sediment currently contains an estimated 26,376 tonnes/year of nutrients: ICEM, see n. 5, at p. 78.

[29] Ibid.

development.[30] Further baseline studies are called for to better understand these impacts,[31] but short of preventing the construction of dams in the areas most sensitive to the hydro-sediment regime, mitigation measures such as sluicing would not alleviate these impacts.[32] Sediment build-up also often affects the efficiency of the dams themselves.

Proponents of the dam argue that hydropower development will support economic diversification and growth, and income generated by exporting the electricity can be reinvested in alternative livelihoods and employment for those affected. However, the SEA Report commissioned by the Mekong River Commission Secretariat (MRCS) estimates that inequality and poverty will actually increase as a result of LMB mainstream dam development over the first twenty-five years, as the majority of financial benefits flow to the business enterprises involved in the projects during that period. Moreover, the governments involved do not have adequate programmes in place to effectively share the financial benefits flowing from the dams with affected communities.[33]

In light of the above, the SEA Report recommends that decisions on LMB mainstream dams should be deferred for a period of ten years for further impact assessments to be conducted and options to be explored, with reviews being undertaken every three years to ensure that these studies are being conducted effectively.[34] As a result of the release of the SEA Report, the World Bank Group 'confirmed it will not finance and has no plans to invest in hydro projects on the mainstream of the Mekong'.[35] Similarly, on 30 November 2011, the United States Senate Committee on Foreign Relations approved a resolution calling on US representatives at multinational banks to suspend financial support to environmentally questionable projects on the Mekong River, including the planned Xayaburi dam.

[30] R. E. Grumbine, J. Dore and J. Xu, 'Mekong Hydropower: Drivers of Change and Governance Challenges Frontiers', (2012), *Ecology and the Environment*, 10(2): 91–98, at p. 92.

[31] Pöyry Energy AG, 'Xayaburi Hydroelectric Power Project, Run-of-River Plant', commissioned by the government of the Lao PDR recognized the need for significant further studies to comply with MRC requirements (2011) pp. 20, 21, and 38, http://www.poweringprogress.org/download/Reports/2012/July/Compliance%20Report%20Xayaburi%20Main%20Final.pdf, accessed 7 September 2013. Other reports calling for further studies include Mekong River Commission Sediment Expert Group Report 'Report of Sediment Transport, Morphology, and Nutrient Balance', (2010), http://www.mrcmekong.org/assets/Consultations/2010-Xayaburi/Annex3-Sediment-Expert-Group-Report.pdf, accessed 7 September 2013; Compagnie Nationale du Rhône, 'Xayaburi Hydroelectric Power Project – Peer Review of the Compliance Report made by Pöyry', (30 March 2012), p. 60, http://www.poweringprogress.org/download/Reports/2012/April/Final-report-V1.pdf, accessed 7 September 2013; ICEM, 'Strategic Environmental Assessment of Hydropower on the Mekong Mainstream', (October 2010), p. 160, http://www.mrcmekong.org/assets/Publications/Consultations/SEA-Hydropower/SEA-Main-Final-Report.pdf, accessed 7 September 2013.

[32] ICEM, see n. 5, at p. 168.

[33] ICEM, see n. 5, at p. 12.

[34] ICEM, see n. 5, at p. 24.

[35] The World Bank, 'World Bank Group Welcomes Strategic Environmental Assessment of Mekong Mainstream Dams', (22 October 2010), http://web.worldbank.org/WBSITE/EXTERNAL/COUNTRIES/EASTASIAPACIFICEXT/CAMBODIAEXTN/0,,contentMDK:22740418~menuPK:293875~pagePK:2865066~piPK:2865079~theSitePK:293856,00.html, accessed 7 September 2013.

Regional and local concerns about the Xayaburi dam

Concerns have been raised repeatedly that the process by which decisions on the Xayaburi dam have been made violate the *1995 Agreement on the Cooperation for the Sustainable Development of the Mekong River Basin* (1995 Mekong Agreement), under which Lao PDR, Thailand, Cambodia, and Vietnam have agreed to cooperate in the management of the flows of the Mekong River mainstream. Observers argue that the MRC Procedures for Notification, Prior Consultation and Agreement (PNPCA), which form part of the 1995 Mekong Agreement framework, have not been complied with. It is further argued that the conduct of the project is in violation of general requirements of international law, including international human rights law and the customary international legal requirement for a transboundary environmental impact assessment.[36]

As there is no independent MRC mechanism for determining compliance with the 1995 Mekong Agreement framework, it cannot be stated definitively whether there has been a breach by Lao PDR. However, a number of independent experts have found that the main environmental consultant hired by Lao PDR, namely Pöyry Management Consultants from Finland, is likely to have breached the MRCS Design Guidance. In particular, it seems Pöyry did not adequately address the concerns formally raised by the Thai, Cambodian, and Vietnamese governments during the PNPCA; nor did they address the concerns outlined in MRCS 'Prior Consultation Project Review Report' on the Xayaburi Project.[37] These findings apply to the design as it was in 2011 – a final design is yet to be publicly released but the concerns of Pöyry's design are so fundamental that they are not likely to be adequately addressed without the ten-year deferment for further study of impacts recommended in the SEA Report.

In December 2011, all four MRC member governments committed to commission a further report on the impacts of dams on the Mekong River mainstream,[38] and the Vietnamese government has commissioned an additional report on the impacts of mainstream hydropower development on the Mekong Delta.[39] However, the Lao PDR and Thai governments have not followed the recommendations of

[36] International Rivers, 'Xayaburi Dam: How Laos Violated the 1995 Mekong Agreement', (13 January 2013), http://www.internationalrivers.org/blogs/267/xayaburi-dam-how-laos-violated-the-1995-mekong-agreement, accessed 7 September 2013.

[37] See World Wildlife Fund, 'Critical Review of the Pöyry Compliance Report about the Xayaburi Dam and the MRC Design Guidance – Fish and Fisheries Aspects', (November 2011), http://awsassets.panda.org/downloads/review_of_fisheries_aspects_in_the_poyry_report.pdf, and ICEM, 'Comments on the Xayaburi Hydropower Project Compliance Report: Gains and Losses for the LMB', (23 November 2011), http://www.icem.com.au/documents/envassessment/mrc_sea_hp/VUSTA%20poyry%20review.pdf, both accessed 7 September 2013.

[38] Mekong River Commission Secretariat, 'Further Study on Impact of Mekong Mainstream Development to Be Conducted, say Lower Mekong Countries', (8 December 2011), http://www.mrcmekong.org/news-and-events/news/further-study-on-impact-of-mekong-mainstream-development-to-be-conducted-say-lower-mekong-countries, accessed 7 September 2013.

[39] ICEM, 'Technical Support to the Ministry of Natural Resources and Environment (MONRE) Project Management Unit (PMU) for Implementation of the Mekong Delta Study', (2013, ongoing), http://icem.com.au/portfolio-items/mekong-delta-study, accessed 7 September 2013.

the SEA Report, nor have they waited for the MRC and Vietnam government studies to be completed before allowing the project and the power purchase to proceed. Thai National Energy Policy Council and the Thai Cabinet both approved the Electricity Generating Authority of Thailand's (EGAT) power purchase agreement (PPA) to buy 95 per cent of the energy produced by the Xayaburi dam.[40] This approval by Thai State bodies of the PPA is currently under investigation by three administrative bodies with respect to its compliance with Thai law. The investigations under Thai law consist of: (1) two investigations by Senate Commissions, one on Good Governance and the other on Community Natural Resources; (2) an investigation by the Sub-committee on Community Natural Resources of the National Human Rights Commission; and (3) the Administrative Court of Thailand, by way of a case filed against the Thai government for approval of the PPA by community representatives from eight Thai Mekong River Provinces. The lawsuit argues that the approval of the PPA by both the National Energy Policy Council and Cabinet was unconstitutional and therefore illegal because it did not include impact assessment or public consultation.

The findings of these three investigations on balance suggest that further impact assessment and consultation should have been carried out under Thai law before the project's approval and financing. In response to these findings, a Senate Committee on Community Rights has called for a transboundary impact assessment of the dam's impacts on Thailand. Similarly, the National Human Rights Commission of Thailand (NHRCT) has released a statement calling on the Thai Prime Minister to review the implementation of the Xayaburi dam's construction, comply with the MRC Council resolution to study the impacts of mainstream hydropower development and suspend the PPA until an investigation into its approval is conducted.[41] The Thai Senate Commission and the NHRCT have likewise questioned the decision-making processes surrounding the dam. Although the Administrative Court dismissed a challenge to the Thai government's approval of the PPA for lack of jurisdiction, the Supreme Administrative Court has overruled this on appeal and said the Court does have jurisdiction to hear the case, and State agencies have an obligation to conduct impact assessment and consultations.

It is important to note that, regardless of the Thai judicial and administrative system's response to the complaints, the feasibility studies and environmental and social impact assessments prepared by project proponents were incomplete. Furthermore, they were not made publicly available to potentially affected communities. Crucially, the project's potential transboundary social, health, or environmental impacts have not been assessed, despite MRCS studies indicating that

[40] Energy Policy and Planning Office, Ministry of Energy, 'Resolution of the National Energy Policy Committee on Draft PPA Xayaburi Project', (2010), http://www.eppo.go.th/nepc/kpc/kpc-133.htm, and Energy Policy and Planning Office, Ministry of Energy, 'Resolution of Cabinet to Approve Draft Power Purchase Agreement Xayaburi Project on Conditions', (2011), http://www.eppo.go.th/admin/cab/cab-2554-01–11.html, accessed in Thai, 7 September 2013.

[41] National Human Rights Commission of Thailand, 'National Human Rights Commission of Thailand's Press Release on Xayaburi', (Unofficial English Translation) (4 May 2012), https://lists.kepa.fi/pipermail/mekong-l/2012-May/000180.html, accessed 7 September 2013.

significant negative impacts are likely. Thus, there could not be any meaningful consultation with potentially affected communities in Thailand without this impact assessment. It is also important to note that the dam developer still has not released the final design of the dam, meaning it is still not currently possible to fully assess the project's impacts. Despite the serious flaws in impact assessment, as well as the local, regional, and international concerns about the dam, Lao PDR and Thailand are moving ahead with the project. Thai banks have also agreed to finance the project.

Differentiated responsibility of banks under international standards

For a large infrastructure project such as the Xayaburi dam, securing funding is one of the biggest challenges that the project developer will face and thus constitutes a critical stage of project development. Although the influence of banks financing large hydropower dams and other infrastructure projects will vary from project to project, they are in a powerful position to influence decisions made by developers. In this regard, '…"but for" their financial role, many human rights abuses would not happen'.[42] Thailand's four largest banks – Bangkok Bank, Kasikorn Bank, Krung Thai Bank and Siam Commercial Bank – are key stakeholders in the Xayaburi dam and have provided financing for the project from the beginning.[43] A further two banks, the Export-Import Bank of Thailand (EXIM Bank) and Thai Investment and Securities Company Limited (TISCO), have also subsequently committed to provide finance.[44]

Although the Thai banks by no means stand alone as influential stakeholders, without the financing they are providing, the Xayaburi dam could not be built. This is particularly evident in light of international financial institutions such as

[42] BankTrack, 'Human Rights Responsibilities of Private Sector Banks: the Policy Required to "Respect" and Provide "Access to Remedy"', (2010), p. 2, http://www.banktrack.org/manage/ems_files/download/the_human_rights_responsibilities_of_banks/310715_hr_responsibilities_of_banks_submission_to_dr_ruggie.pdf, accessed 7 September 2013.

[43] The Xayaburi hydropower project will cost approximately US$3.5 billion to build. Between them, they are responsible for 61.9% of all lending by Thai banks and account for 65.3% of all deposits made to Thai banks. These four banks state that they will contribute US$1.86 billion to the project and an undisclosed amount will be provided to fund equity for the lead project developer Ch. Karnchang. See International Rivers. 'The Xayaburi Dam, A Looming Threat to the Mekong River', (21 January 2011), http://www.internationalrivers.org/resources/the-xayaburi-dam-2635, accessed 7 September 2013. See also Japanese Research Institute Limited, 'The Roles and Functions of the Banking Sector in the Financial System of the ASEAN+3 Region', (March 2012), p. 66, http://www.asean.org/images/archive/documents/ASEAN+3RG/2012/120314Final%20Report_JRI_.pdf, accessed 7 September 2013. And finally, National Human Rights Commission of Thailand, 'Transcript of the Fact Finding Meeting on Xayaburi Hydropower Dam Construction', (21 February 2012) (unpublished). More information on the meeting is available http://www.nhrc.or.th/2012/wb/en/news_detail.php?nid=79andparent_id=1andtype=hot, accessed 7 September 2013.

[44] To date, the extent of these banks' involvement is unknown. See P. Yuthamanop, 'Vientiane Says Sorry for Broken Xayaburi Ground', *Bangkok Post*, (25 November 2012), http://www.bangkokpost.com/print/322967, accessed 7 September 2013.

the World Bank Group (WBG)[45] and the Asian Development Bank (ADB) declining to provide funding to this project due to the social and environmental risks in the SEA Report. This position is particularly striking in light of the WBG and ADB track record of providing technical and financial support for dams in Lao PDR, such as the Nam Theun 2. Through their lending decisions, therefore, Thai banks are responsible for supporting a project that potentially has very serious negative environmental and social impacts and that has caused regional political tensions.

The differentiated responsibility of banks compared to other business enterprises involved in project finance is recognized in two key international standards.[46] First, the EPs, which are voluntarily adopted by financial institutions and are applied where total project capital costs exceed US$10 million.[47] If the project does not comply with the EPs, adopting institutions commit to not fund that project. Since the EPs' inception in 2003, they have been revised in 2006 and 2013, and adopted by seventy-eight financial institutions in thirty-five countries, covering over 70 per cent of international project finance debt in emerging markets.[48] Despite the widespread adoption by global banks such as HSBC, Citi Bank, and Standard Chartered, banks from ASEAN countries have not yet adopted the EPs or sector-specific policies to guide project finance lending decisions.

However, the key weakness of the Equator Principles regime is the lack of any independent accountability mechanism, as the Equator Principle Secretariat does not have a mandate to investigate the compliance of individual banks. In contrast, the IFC does provide a non-judicial remedy for problem projects that it financially supports. The Compliance Advisor Ombudsman (CAO) is an independent body established to oversee the implementation of IFC Performance Standards. Although there have been many well-documented studies questioning the IFC's compliance with its own mandate and safeguards in projects it finances, and criticism of the effectiveness of the CAO to remedy such problems, the CAO remains an important opportunity for communities to raise concerns about IFC-funded projects. It also serves as an effective means of accessing information and meetings with government and business stakeholders. Such a mechanism for large-scale development projects is not provided by Equator Principle banks or at the national level in ASEAN countries. National Human Rights Institutions (NHRIs) constitute the most analogous

[45] The World Bank, 'World Bank Group Welcomes Strategic Environmental Assessment of Mekong Mainstream Dams', (22 October 2010), http://web.worldbank.org/WBSITE/EXTERNAL/COUNTRIES/EASTASIAPACIFICEXT/CAMBODIAEXTN/0,,contentMDK:22740418~menuPK:293875~pagePK:2865066~piPK:2865079~theSitePK:293856,00.html, accessed 5 September 2013.

[46] In addition, the OECD is reviewing human rights implementation in the broader financial sector and the UNEP Finance Initiative has commissioned a paper on banking and human rights.

[47] The Equator Principles III (4 June 2013), http://www.equator-principles.com/resources/equator_principles_III.pdf, accessed 7 September 2013.

[48] As of 5 September 2013. The Equator Principles Association, 'About the Equator Principles', http://www.equator-principles.com/index.php/about-ep, accessed 5 September 2013.

non-judicial mechanism,[49] but NHRIs only exist in half of the ASEAN States, with varying degrees of independence and efficiency. The Thai National Human Rights Commission has called the Thai banks financing the Xayaburi dam to a meeting, but has not yet released any findings on the Thai banks.

In addition to the EPs, the United Nations 'Protect, Remedy and Respect' Framework (UN PRR Framework) and its Guiding Principles (UN Guiding Principles) apply to all business enterprises, including banks. The UN Guiding Principles were not intended to be industry specific, so the banking sector is not explicitly referred to. However, the responsibility of banks to uphold human rights is implicitly recognized in both.[50] Guiding Principle 13(b), for instance, states that companies must 'seek to prevent or mitigate adverse human rights impacts that are directly linked to their operations, products or services by their business relationships, even if they have not contributed to those impacts'.[51] The explanatory comment on this principle clarifies that '(b)usiness relationships are understood to include relationships with business partners, entities in the value chain ... directly linked to its business operations, products or services'.[52] As banks have business relationships with clients by providing the clients' money, and human rights violations from a project can be linked to banking products and services, this formulation includes banks and their financing activities. This link is made explicit in the Office of the High Commissioner for Human Rights (OHCHR)'s *The Corporate Responsibility to Respect Human Rights: An Interpretive Guide*, where 'providing financial loans to an enterprise for business activities that, in breach of agreed standards, result in the eviction of communities' is cited as an example of an adverse impact directly linked to business operations.[53]

Following the release of the UN PRR Framework and UN Guiding Principles, the EPs were revised to explicitly state the importance of human rights with reference to the latter. The Equator Principle institutions have 'recognize(d) that (their) role as financiers affords (them) opportunities to promote responsible environmental stewardship and socially responsible development, including fulfilling (their) responsibility to respect human rights by undertaking due diligence in accordance with the Equator Principles'.[54] The use of 'due diligence' refers to the concept of human rights due diligence outlined in the UN Guiding Principles.

[49] The National Human Rights Commission of Thailand is an exception as it accepts complaints against Thai development projects, both inside Thailand and overseas Thai investment like the Xayaburi project. Not all ASEAN countries have an NHRI and they vary in effectiveness.

[50] BankTrack letter to the UN OHCHR, 'Banks and the "Protect, Respect and Remedy" Framework', (26 March 2012), http://www.business-humanrights.org/media/documents/banktrack-submission-unsg-report-business-human-rights-26-mar-2012.pdf, accessed 5 September 2013.

[51] UN OHCHR, *Guiding Principles on Business and Human Rights: Implementing the United Nations 'Protect, Respect and Remedy' Framework*, (2011), p. 14, http://www.ohchr.org/Documents/Publications/GuidingPrinciplesBusinessHR_EN.pdf, accessed 5 September 2013.

[52] Ibid., at p. 15.

[53] UN OHCHR, 'The Corporate Responsibility to Respect Human Rights: An Interpretive Guide', (2012), p. 17, http://www.ohchr.org/Documents/Publications/HR.PUB.12.2_En.pdf, accessed 7 September 2013.

[54] The Equator Principles III (4 June 2013), p. 2, http://www.equator-principles.com/resources/equator_principles_III.pdf, accessed 7 September 2013.

In October 2013, the Thun Group of Banks[55] released its *Discussion Paper for Banks on Implications of Principles 16–21 of the UN Guiding Principles on Business and Human Rights* (Thun Group Discussion Paper). Guiding Principles 16–21 relate to policy development and commitment, due diligence in terms of scope, accountability and implementation, as well as tracking and reporting. Some of the banks in the Thun Group are also members of the Equator Principles Association's Steering Committee, and Appendix 2 of the Thun Group Discussion Paper specifically relates to standards for project finance, with reference to the Equator Principles and IFC Performance Standards as the relevant standard. The Thun Group Discussion Paper constitutes an important starting point and road map for the banking sector's implementation of the Guiding Principles. However, it could be strengthened in two key respects.

First, the Thun Group Discussion Paper underestimates the leverage of banks on human rights issues by stating that, despite a common perception of their considerable sway over their clients' behaviour, 'in practice, the degree of leverage is often a great deal less than popularly believed'.[56] This suggests that expectations relating to how far banks can and should seek to influence client actions to promote good practice should be tailored accordingly. Although influence will vary between deals, banks are well placed to set effective standards and to effectively monitor their borrowers' conduct.[57] Banks do understand existing norms on managing environmental and social risk, as illustrated by the EPs and IFC Performance Standards.

Second, the Thun Group Discussion Paper could be strengthened with an analysis of access to remedies under principles 22, 29 and 30 of the UN Guiding Principles. In project finance, this places a responsibility on the Equator Principles' Secretariat and members of the Thun Group of Banks to assess and provide a grievance mechanism, rather than placing this sole responsibility on their clients. Principle 22 states that business enterprises should 'provide for or cooperate in' remediation if they have caused or contributed to human rights abuses. Principle 29 of the Guiding Principles states that, 'business enterprises should establish or participate in effective operational-level grievance mechanisms for individuals and communities who may be adversely impacted'. Guiding Principle 30 states that '(i)ndustry, multi-stakeholder and other collaborative initiatives that are based on respect for human rights-related standards should ensure that effective grievance mechanisms are available'. On this point, Appendix 2 of the Thun Group Discussion Paper states that '(g)rievance mechanisms should also be put in place by the client'.[58] While this constitutes an important acknowledgement, it should

---

[55] In May 2011 and May 2012, discussions between major Swiss banks took place in Thun, Switzerland. The group includes Barclays, BBVA, Credit Suisse AG, ING Bank N.V., RBS Group, UBS AG, and UniCredit.

[56] Thun Group of Banks, 'Discussion Paper for Banks on Implications of Principles 16–21 of the UN Guiding Principles on Business and Human Rights', (October 2013), p. 5, http://www.business-humanrights.org/media/documents/thun-group-discussion-paper-final-2-oct-2013.pdf, accessed 25 January 2014.

[57] D. Sarro, *Do Lenders Make Effective Regulators: An Assessment of the Equator Principles on Project Finance*, Osgoode Law School, York University, Toronto (Research Paper No.4/2013), p. 1524.

[58] See n. 56, at p. 22.

not detract from the banks' own responsibility under the UN Guiding Principles to have a grievance mechanism like the IFC CAO.

Despite the significant momentum gained in support of the UN PRR Framework or UN Guiding Principles internationally, no ASEAN bank has yet endorsed them. Moreover, ASEAN banks are generally known not to acknowledge human rights responsibilities or to have social and environmental risk-management systems. However, some of the global banks that have financial interests in ASEAN banks may serve to increase the relevance of the Thun Banks initiative within the region. At a minimum, the global banks in question should work to inform business practice within the region in accordance with Thun findings. It is likewise necessary that ASEAN policy-makers take action to ensure that ASEAN banks meet international standards.

Although not specific to banks, one final initiative of note is the Global Reporting Initiative (GRI), a leading organization in improving the reporting practices of business enterprises across the world. GRI's Sustainability Reporting Guidelines (the Guidelines) is another reference tool for ASEAN policy-makers to consider for a regional social and environmental reporting policy. It offers 'Reporting Principles, Standard Disclosures and an Implementation Manual for the preparation of sustainability reports by organizations, regardless of their size, sector or location'.[59] The Thai Stock Exchange has recently adopted reporting guidelines consistent with GRI standards. There is an increasing trend of voluntary corporate social responsibility (CSR) and GRI adoption by business enterprises within the ASEAN-5.[60] However, these businesses are still choosing to 'disclose items that improve legitimacy while omitting others'.[61] Thus, ASEAN policy-makers need to discuss how to eventually strengthen implementation of reporting guidelines across the region, as discussed further below.

Responsibility of Thai banks financing the Xayaburi dam

Thailand has seven major commercial banks.[62] Although some of these commercial banks have taken steps towards adopting CSR policies, such efforts remain focused on philanthropic support for environmental and community projects.[63] Where banks do have CSR policies or commitments in place, the wording

[59]   GRI, 'Reporting Principles and Standard Disclosures', (2013), https://www.globalreporting.org/resourcelibrary/GRIG4-Part1-Reporting-Principles-and-Standard-Disclosures.pdf, accessed 7 September 2013.
[60]   Indonesia, Malaysia, the Philippines, Singapore, and Thailand.
[61]   The ASEAN-5 membership is comprised of Indonesia, Malaysia, the Philippines, Singapore, and Thailand. See also R. Liong, *Carrot Or Stick: Corporate Social Responsibility Disclosures By South East Asian Companies*, Dissertation at University of Exeter Business School (May 2013), p. i.
[62]   Bangkok Bank, Krung Thai Bank, Kasikornbank, Siam Commercial Bank, Bank of Ayudhya, Thai Military Bank (TMB), and Siam City Bank.
[63]   Philanthropic projects noted in annual reports include youth and community development programmes, education and training (including environmental awareness), arts and culture, charity and relief work, sport, nurturing Thai values, and religious activities. Other activities include training and courses for small and medium enterprises.

tends to be vague, and treatment of CSR in public documents (such as annual reports) is generally indistinguishable from discussions of corporate governance policy and codes of conduct. Meanwhile, the adoption and implementation of social and environmental due diligence systems – including human rights impact assessments – do not meet international standards or best practice. The fact that this applies to the four major Thai banks involved in the financing of the Xayaburi dam reflects the extent to which the management of these risks remains a marginal concept that has not yet been incorporated into the industry's core business practice within the region.[64] Against this backdrop, Kasikorn is the only Thai bank to have a publicly available CSR policy in accordance with UN Guiding Principle 16(d).[65] Others in the region should therefore join Kasikorn in doing so. That said, while Kasikorn should be commended for publishing its CSR policy, its value and effectiveness depends on the bank eventually detailing how this commitment will be implemented across actual business operations.

More broadly speaking, the Secretary-General of the Thai Bankers' Association has cautioned its membership that, while costs may increase in the short term, the EPs 'must be adopted to avoid unexpected costs, difficulties in project management, and reputational risks'.[66] There is also growing evidence that socially and environmentally responsible investment is good business. However, the Thai banks and the Thai Bankers' Association have not yet taken any public steps towards adopting the EPs. The Thai Bankers' Association cites Thai Government budget constraints as an obstacle to adoption of the EPs, due to expenses arising out of compliance with these standards.[67] However, project developers are responsible for shouldering a portion of the associated costs (such as conducting improved due diligence and community consultations) with the Thai government. For the Xayaburi project, the estimated annual return for the US$3.5 billion project is

---

[64] For instance, while the four banks in question publicly stated in shareholder meetings in 2013 that they commissioned their own independent impact assessment report for the project, it is not clear whether this was commissioned before or after their decision to finance the project. This, coupled with their refusal to provide a copy to the public, raises questions over the value of the exercise at hand.

[65] Kasikorn, 'CSR Policies and Activities', (2013), http://www.kasikornbank.com/TH/ SocialActivities/Policy_Responsibility/Pages/Policy_Main.aspx, accessed 7 September 2013. UN Guiding Principle 16(d) states that human rights policies should be 'publicly available and communicated internally and externally to all personnel, business partners and other relevant parties'. An alternative standard is the Global Reporting Initiative (GRI), a global voluntary sustainability-reporting framework that has been adopted by many companies worldwide and is referred to in the Stock Exchange of Thailand's Guidelines for CSR. However, the GRI has so far not been adopted widely in ASEAN. Moreover, despite efforts at standardization, it does not meet the specific but diverse needs of potential audiences for the data ranging from issue-specific social activists to risk-assessing investors.

[66] International Finance Corporation, 'Are Thai Banks Ready for the Equator Principles?', (2012), http:// www1.ifc.org/wps/wcm/connect/region__ext_content/regions/east+asia+and+the+pacific/ news/are+thai+banks+ready+for+the+equator+principles, accessed 7 September 2013.

[67] Ibid. As the majority of infrastructure projects are sponsored by the Thai government, the Bankers' Association considers that the short-term costs of complying with the EPs would fall to the government.

approximately US$462 million.[68] As such, the availability of an adequate budget for social and environmental risk management of such projects should not pose difficulty. The adherence of seventy-seven global banks to the EPs further suggests that budgetary constraints – either on the part of the bank, their client, governments or other parties involved in large projects – do not constitute a valid basis for the failure to adopt them. The IFC likewise implements similar standards.

Furthermore, if such social and environmental standards were adopted across ASEAN, the administration costs associated with implementation would be integrated into project finance deals without any competitive disadvantage to ASEAN banks across the region. This would ensure that projects such as the Xayaburi dam – and other controversial projects financed by Thai banks across the ASEAN region[69] – would not be financed before adequate social and environmental risk-management systems have been adopted and implemented. These broader regional implications highlight the urgency for an integrated approach to the management of social and environmental risk across the ASEAN finance sector, in a manner consistent with international standards. This would ensure that profitability of the bank lending to large projects in the medium term was increased *and* that human rights and environmental standards were better implemented.

Responsibility of export credit agencies

The EXIM Bank is not a commercial bank but an export credit agency wholly owned by the Thai government and under the control of the Ministry of Finance.[70] It is tasked with supporting Thai investment overseas.[71] UN Guiding Principle 4 directly addresses the role of export credit agencies (ECAs):

> States should take additional steps to protect against human rights abuses by business enterprises that are owned or controlled by the State, or that receive substantial support and services from State agencies such as export credit agencies and official investment insurance or guarantee agencies, including, where appropriate, by requiring human rights due diligence.[72]

---

[68] Chapters 4 and 5 of the Xayaburi Dam Power Purchase Agreement between Lao PDR, EGAT and the Xayaburi Power Company Limited available on LaoFab.

[69] The Siam Commercial Bank also provided financing for the Khon Kaen Sugar Company's 20,000-hectare sugar plantation and factory in Sre Ambel District, Koh Kong Province in Cambodia. This project has been the subject of regional and international attention for the alleged forced eviction of local communities. Siam Commercial Bank and Bangkok Bank have also provided bridge loans of US$325 million to support the controversial Special Economic Zone in Dawei Division in Myanmar, which will transform 200 km^2 into Southeast Asia's largest industrial complex.

[70] It is worth noting that Krung Thai bank is majority-owned by the Thai government.

[71] Export-Import Bank of Thailand (EXIM), (2013), http://www.exim.go.th/en/about_exim/about.aspx, accessed in Thai, 7 September 2013.

[72] See n. 53, at p. 6.

The accompanying commentary states that, '(t)he requirement for human rights due diligence is most likely to be appropriate where the nature of business operations or operating contexts pose significant risk to human rights'.[73] In this context, the financing of large infrastructure projects like the Xayaburi hydropower dam do potentially pose significant risks to human rights. ASEAN policy-makers should therefore also consider uniform policies consistent with international standards for ECAs involved in project finance in ASEAN, but have so far been silent on the issue.

ASEAN has not made any public commitments on standards for ECAs or the possibility of an ASEAN ECA. The Japanese government, however, wants to 'continue the exchange of information, networking, and cooperation in trade financing between JBIC (Japan Bank for International Cooperation) and ASEAN export credit agencies'.[74] JBIC has adopted the World Bank Group safeguard policies as a guideline in its activities, and could therefore also engage ASEAN policy-makers on adopting similar standards for national ECAs.[75]

Socially and environmentally responsible investment in the ASEAN economic community

The ten ASEAN Member States adopted the ASEAN Charter in 2007 to provide a legal basis and institutional framework for the creation an ASEAN Community, comprised of the ASEAN Security Community (ASC), the ASEAN Economic Community (AEC) and the ASEAN Socio-Cultural Community (ASCC).[76] All three pillars are expected to work in tandem in establishing the ASEAN Community.[77] The stated purposes of ASEAN in its Charter that relate to the promotion of socially and environmentally responsible development include: (1) '(T)o promote and protect human rights and fundamental freedoms … with due regard to the rights and responsibilities of the Member States of ASEAN';[78] (2) 'To promote sustainable development so as to ensure the protection of the region's environment, the sustainable development of its natural resources, the preservation of its cultural heritage and the high quality of life of its people';[79] and (3) 'To enhance the well-being and livelihood of the peoples of ASEAN by providing them with equitable access to opportunities for human development, social welfare and justice'.[80] In practice, the AEC has received the most attention

---

[73] See n. 53, at p. 7.

[74] ASEAN-Japan Plan of Action, (2013), http://www.asean.org/asean/external-relations/japan/item/the-asean-japan-plan-of-action, accessed 7 September 2013).

[75] In the past, there has been discussion of both an Asian and ASEAN ECA. However, there does not appear to have been further progress on either.

[76] Charter of the Association of Southeast Asian Nations, 'Preamble', (January 2008), http://www.asean.org/archive/publications/ASEAN-Charter.pdf, accessed 7 September 2013.

[77] ASEAN Secretariat, 'ASEAN Economic Community Blueprint', (2008), p. 5, http://www.asean.org/archive/5187-10.pdf, accessed 7 September 2013.

[78] ASEAN Charter 2008, Article 1(7).

[79] ASEAN Charter 2008, Article 1(9).

[80] ASEAN Charter 2008, Article 1(11).

and the human rights component of the ASCC has been peripheral. There is thus a need to revisit the wording of the relevant instruments to enable an interpretation that better integrates environmental and social considerations in the process of economic integration.

The ASEAN Economic Community Blueprint (2008) was designed to set 'clear targets and timelines for implementation of various measures as well as pre-agreed flexibilities to accommodate the interests of all ASEAN Member Countries', in order to accelerate the establishment of the AEC.[81] An overarching objective includes providing 'an open, outward-looking, inclusive, and market-driven economy consistent with multilateral rules as well as adherence to rules-based systems for effective compliance and implementation of economic commitments'.[82] One of the elements of a single market and production base in the AEC is the freer flow of investment.[83] A key pillar for a more comprehensive investment regime within the AEC is 'more transparent, consistent and predictable investment rules, regulations, policies and procedures'.[84] Rules or guidelines for banks consistent with international standards of providing project finance loans are at least consistent with these aims for the AEC and have the potential to promote one of the AEC aims of 'international best practices that would increase the investor confidence in ASEAN'.[85]

The primary goal of the ASEAN Socio-Cultural Community Blueprint 2008, on the other hand, is to contribute to realizing an ASEAN Community that is 'people-centered and socially responsible ... where the wellbeing, livelihood, and welfare of the peoples are enhanced'.[86] A strategic objective of the ASCC Blueprint is to '[ensure] that Corporate Social Responsibility (CSR) is incorporated in the corporate agenda and to contribute towards sustainable socio-economic development in ASEAN Member States'.[87] An agreed action under this objective is to '[develop] a model public policy on Corporate Social Responsibility or legal instrument for reference of ASEAN Member States by 2010'.[88] However, this initiative has stalled. It further invites Member States to refer to the relevant international standards and guides such as ISO 26000, titled 'Guidance on Social Responsibility'.[89] The ASCC Blueprint also encourages the 'adoption and implementation of international standards on social responsibility'.[90]

While ASEAN has yet to adopt a model public policy on CSR, a policy specific to banks should be considered in this process, in order to meet the ASEAN

[81] ASEAN Secretariat, 'ASEAN Economic Community Blueprint', (2008), p. 5, http://www.asean.org/archive/5187-10.pdf, accessed 7 September 2013.
[82] Ibid.
[83] See n. 81, at p. 12.
[84] See n. 81, at p. 13.
[85] See n. 81, at p. 12.
[86] ASEAN Secretariat, 'ASEAN Socio-Cultural Community Blueprint 2008', (June 2009), p. 1, http://www.asean.org/archive/5187-19.pdf, accessed 7 September 2013..
[87] Ibid., at p. 13.
[88] See n. 86.
[89] See n. 86.
[90] See n. 86.

Charter's overarching objectives of sustainable development. Furthermore, Thai banks and regulators have refused to adopt CSR policies that incorporate the EPs, partly because this may put them at a competitive disadvantage to other ASEAN banks in the short term. An ASEAN model public policy for banks consistent with the EPs would thus constitute an important step in integrating international best practices of social and environmental risk management into project finance and place ASEAN banks in an equal regulatory space. Such a policy would also enhance the process of ASEAN's financial and investment integration, and is an opportunity for strengthening national financial institutions in managing social and environmental risk. Although ASEAN's financial integration is uneven, with ASEAN-5 countries being much more advanced, ASEAN members have shown the ability to innovate in institutional strengthening in the finance sector, as discussed further below. Once such a policy is developed, progressive steps towards a regional mechanism for enforcement – or at least an advisory service on the implementation of social and environmental standards in project finance – would be an important part of ensuring adequate implementation and ensuring that the 'remedy' pillar of the UN Guiding Principles is realized.

In a significant step towards this end, the ASEAN Infrastructure Fund Limited (AIF) has been established to support and integrate infrastructure development in ASEAN. The AIF is administered by the ADB and was set to begin its lending operations in the second half of 2013, with approximately US$1 billion in projects for the next three years.[91] It is worth noting that the ADB's Safeguard Policy Statement will apply to all the AIF projects.[92] The ADB's Safeguard Policy Statement and EPs are similar frameworks, albeit that the ADB has an independent Compliance Advisory Ombudsman, which acts as an independent grievance mechanism, while the Equator Principles Secretariat does not have such a mandate. The adoption of an ASEAN model public policy on CSR for banks or any other rules or guidelines on socially and environmentally responsible loans in project finance would thus be consistent with the AEC, ASCC, and AIF, and is likely to enhance regional integration by providing baseline common rules and procedures.

Another key element of the ASEAN Economic Community investment regime is the ASEAN Comprehensive Investment Agreement 2012 (ACIA).[93] Under Article 17(1)(b) of the ACIA, ASEAN Member States are permitted to adopt and enforce measures 'necessary to protect human, animal or plant life or health'. Consistent rules or guidelines for project finance loans at the national or regional level would

---

[91] Asian Development Bank, 'ASEAN Infrastructure Fund Readies $1 Billion Pipeline for Lending Operations', (1 May 2013), http://www.adb.org/news/asean-infrastructure-fund-readies-1-billion-pipeline-lending-operations, accessed 7 September 2013.

[92] Asian Development Bank, 'Framework for Operation of the ASEAN Infrastructure Fund', (1 May 2013), http://www.adb.org/sites/default/files/linked-docs/45097–001-reg-oth-01.pdf, accessed 7 September 2013.

[93] ASEAN Comprehensive Investment Agreement, Article 41 (1). ACIA supersedes two precursor investment agreements – the ASEAN Investment Guarantee Agreement ('ASEAN IGA') and the Framework Agreement on ASEAN Investment Area ('AIA Framework Agreement').

fit into the general exception falling under Art.17(1)(b) and promote integration by guaranteeing a minimum standard of protection by ASEAN banks in this regard. However, the ACIA does not derogate from existing rights and obligations of ASEAN Member States under existing bilateral investment agreements.[94] Other existing investment obligations and stabilization clauses in investor–State contracts in the region have used more restrictive wording.[95] For example, in the Power Purchase Agreement for the Xayaburi dam between the Lao government, EGAT and the developer, the application of Lao environmental laws to the project was excluded altogether. There would thus need to be discussion among national governments and ASEAN policy-makers on how best to ensure that there is sufficient financial regulatory space to develop a model banking policy that meets international laws and standards to adequately protect human rights, as well as animal or plant life.

Process of financial cooperation and integration in ASEAN

Another important part of the ASEAN Economic Community is a process of financial cooperation and integration. Following the Asian Financial Crisis in 1998 and the Global Financial and Economic Crisis in 2008, there has been political will amongst ASEAN policy-makers to adopt policies that are designed to improve financial stability and cooperation in ASEAN to combat future crises. In order to reach the aims in the ASEAN Charter and ASCC for sustainable development, and to avoid the financing of projects like the Xayaburi dam without proper impact assessment and consultation, there is a need to integrate social and environmental risk-management policies into the process of financial integration. The adoption of an ASEAN model public policy on CSR for banks – as well as the adoption of any other rules or guidelines relating to socially and environmentally responsible loans – should be explored further by ASEAN policy-makers as the process of financial integration in ASEAN continues to move forward. It is worth going into some of the detail of this process to identify how much progress has been made and to identify the opportunities for the integration of additional social and environmental considerations.

ASEAN hosts four major initiatives to strengthen financial cooperation and further the process of financial integration.[96]

1   The ASEAN Swap Arrangement (ASA) establishes reciprocal currency or swap arrangements to provide liquidity support to ASEAN Members experiencing balance of payments difficulties.
2   The ASEAN+3 (China, Japan and Korea) Finance Ministers Process aims to strengthen policy dialogue, coordination, and collaboration on common financial, monetary, and fiscal issues. It is comprised of four components:

94   ASEAN Comprehensive Investment Agreement, Article 44.
95   See Human Rights Resource Centre, University of Indonesia, 'Business and Human Rights in ASEAN: A Baseline Study', (2013), pp. 47–49.
96   Asian Development Bank, *Institutions for Regional Integration: Toward an Asian Economic Community East Asian Regional Integration* (Manila: ADB, 2010), pp. 129–132.

    i   the Economic Review and Policy Dialogue (ERPD);

    ii   Chiang Mai Initiative multilateralization is reserve pooling with a foreign exchange reserves pool of US$120 billion;

    iii the Asian Bond Markets Initiative (ABMI) aims to develop efficient and liquid bond markets in Asia, and

    iv the ASEAN+3 Research Group.[97]

3   The ASEAN Surveillance Process (ASP) initiative reviews global, regional, and individual country developments, monitors exchange rate and macro-economic aggregates, as well as sectoral and social policies, along with facilitating the consideration of better policy options.[98]

4   A road map for financial and monetary integration based on the four pillars of capital market development, capital account liberalization, financial services liberalization, harmonised payments and settlement systems.

The road map for ASEAN and financial integration has been progressively articulated in the ASEAN Vision 2020, the Roadmap for Integration of ASEAN, the Roadmap for Monetary and Financial Integration of ASEAN, and the ASEAN Economic Community Blueprint. The ADB and ASEAN Secretariat recently published a study suggesting plans for capital account liberalization (CAL) and financial services liberalization (FSL) in the ASEAN banking sector, together with institutional and policy reforms and an ASEAN framework for policy coordination and mutual assistance over 2011–2020.[99] By 2015, ASEAN aims to have integrated financial and capital markets. Financial regulations are to be integrated by 2020.[100] Two reference frameworks guide planning for financial integration – one for the five original ASEAN-5 members and another for the five newer members (Brunei, Cambodia, Lao PDR, Myanmar, and Vietnam).[101] This road map could be amended to include milestones for the gradual implementation of social and environmental policies in the ASEAN banking sector. Like the CAL and FSL processes, this road map could also distinguish between ASEAN-5 and the newer members.

The endorsement of the ASEAN Banking Integration Framework (ABIF) by the regional central bank governors in 2011 constitutes an additional prospect of note. One model that was proposed under the ABIF was for each ASEAN Member State to designate one or more local bank, as a Qualified ASEAN Bank (QAB) to expand and operate within the region.[102] Now, there is a broad multilateral

---

[97] Asian Development Bank, 'ASEAN+3 Finance Ministers Process', (2013), http://www.aric.adb.org/initiativetable.php?iid=64andssid=2andtitle=ASEAN+3%20Finance%20Ministers%20Process, accessed 7 September 2013.

[98] Asian Development Bank, 'ASEAN Surveillance Process Initiative', (2013), http://aric.adb.org/initiative/asean-surveillance-process, accessed 7 September 2013.

[99] ADB, 'The Road to ASEAN Financial Integration: a Combined Study on Assessing the Financial Landscape and Formulating Milestones for Monetary and Financial Integration in ASEAN', p. 1.

[100] Ibid.

[101] See n. 99.

[102] See n. 99, at p. 4.

framework for QAB but the number of banks so designated will depend on bilateral agreements between ASEAN countries. In order to meet the socially and environmentally responsible development objectives of ASEAN, the EPs could be integrated into the QAB process.

ASEAN's banking market has so far seen little integration and there are only three ASEAN banks, which the ADB considers to have the 'widest regional presence'.[103] These three banks are Maybank of Malaysia, Bangkok Bank of Thailand, and United Overseas Bank of Singapore.

None of these three regional banks has adopted the Equator Principles or operationalized social and environmental risk-management systems into their lending practices. Maybank has joined the Carbon Disclosure Project,[104] but does not have a social or environmental policy to guide its lending. Bangkok Bank has a code of conduct and business ethics practice that commits the bank to respecting individual rights under the law and that prohibits human rights violations.[105] However, the financing of the Xayaburi project shows that this bank has yet to operationalize these commitments adequately. United Overseas Bank of Singapore (UOBS), for its part, has an Operational Risk and Compliance Committee overseeing the implementation of policies and procedures for risk management. However, the body in question is solely focused on risks to the bank, thus failing to consider the environment or communities in their own right.[106]

The non-ASEAN global banks that have a wider presence in the region include Citibank, HSBC, and Standard Chartered Bank, all of which have adopted the EPs.[107] ASEAN policy-makers should ensure that the adoption of the EPs is a prerequisite before a bank is permitted to become a QAB. Furthermore, the adoption of an ASEAN social and environmental risk-management policy should be a milestone in the ASEAN process of financial integration, in line with the objective of sustainable development in the ASEAN Charter, which would mean an application to all banks operating in ASEAN, not just the QAB.

Linking social and environmental responsible investment with financial integration

The standards and institutions outlined above are aimed at strengthening economic and financial risk management and integration in ASEAN. However, a similar level of attention and commitment to social and environmental risk

---

[103] See n. 99, at p. 4.

[104] Maybank, 'Environment', (2013), http://www.maybank.com/en/about-us/sustainability/environment.page, accessed 7 September 2013.

[105] Bangkok Bank, 'Code of Ethics and Business Ethics Practice', (2013), http://www.bangkokbank.com/BANGKOKBANK/ABOUTBANGKOKBANK/ABOUTUS/CORPORATEPROFILE/CORPORATEGOVERNANCEPOLICY/Pages/CodeofConductandBusinessEthics.aspx, accessed 7 September 2013.

[106] United Overseas Bank of Singapore, 'Operational Risk', (2013), http://www.uobgroup.com/investor/risk/operational_risk.html, accessed 7 September 2013.

[107] See n. 99, at p. 4.

management should be strengthened amongst ASEAN policy-makers, in a manner that is consistent with ASEAN's aims of socially and environmentally responsible investment. As the Xayaburi dam case-study shows, there is a need for banks in ASEAN to implement policies on social and environmental risk-management systems that are consistent with international standards.

The joint ADB and ASEAN Secretariat study on financial integration makes some recommendations on the necessary regional mechanism and the capacity-building that is required for financial integration to be successful.[108] The study has concluded that:

> If financial integration is to succeed, the ASEAN financial regulatory agencies must be adequately equipped with relevant software and hardware. By software is meant the human resource capacity to monitor and manage domestic financial market deregulation under the new environment of an integrated ASEAN financial market. By hardware is meant the legal, tax, and regulatory systems that are required to support the financial market infrastructure.[109]

This statement focuses only on the financial aspects of the process of integration, and ASEAN financial regulatory agencies need to be much more aware of the social and environmental impacts of projects financed by the sector. The ADB and World Bank Group have already integrated social and environmental systems into their lending practices and could do more to facilitate a regional dialogue in ASEAN about a common policy.

The joint ADB and ASEAN Secretariat study suggests there are three options available for building such a regional mechanism for financial system integration: '(i) the ASEAN Secretariat could take up this work; (ii) existing ASEAN mechanisms, such as a working group or committee, could be expanded; or (iii) an entirely new organization could be built'.[110] Whatever structure is ultimately chosen, the mechanism in question should ensure the integration of the administration of ASEAN social and environmental risk-management rules that are consistent with international standards.

Conclusion

In conclusion, commercial banks and export credit agencies have a differentiated responsibility compared to other business enterprises when it comes to international standards for implementing social and environmental risk-management systems in project finance. The financing of the Xayaburi dam in Lao PDR shows that Thai banks have not developed the risk-management systems that meet international standards, such as the UN PRR Framework, the UN Guiding Principles, and the Equator Principles. However, the Thai banks are not alone, as no ASEAN bank

---

[108] See n. 99, at p. 19.
[109] See n. 99.
[110] See n. 99.

has adopted such measures. ASEAN policy-makers need to show leadership in initiating a regional discussion on how to implement ASEAN's aims for socially and environmentally responsible investment in the context of bank lending in project finance. This would further the implementation of laws and standards, as well as provide a basis for regulatory harmonization across ASEAN in the future. There should also be discussion of how to administer these standards at the national and regional levels, as part of a wider strategy for regional institutional regulatory strengthening in the process of financial integration. Meanwhile, ASEAN banks themselves have the responsibility and opportunity to develop and implement social and environmental risk-management systems in project finance consistent with international laws and standards.

6 Corporate sustainability and palm oil industries in Southeast Asia

A principled pragmatism

Puvan Selvanathan and Vani Sathisan

Introduction

The growing global demand for palm oil is expected to double in less than a decade. The consequences of illegal land clearing and unsustainable sourcing by several palm oil industries are all too familiar – deforestation, forest fires, gas emissions and a serious loss of endangered species in Southeast Asia. While laws exist to prohibit such burning and deforestation of land, they are poorly enforced and do not reflect the reality of the economic drivers and the accompanying environmental risks. The willingness of key actors to address complex challenges by adopting a holistic environmental, social and governance perspective has led to successful collaborations across sectoral, institutional and organizational divides. Such multi-stakeholder collaboration in addressing context-specific issues underscores the need both to gain support and to take action on a range of related issues that contribute toward and may ultimately overcome complex challenges. However, it is also of much concern that, while several companies have taken steps to reduce their liability in the environmental sector, there is an absence of a serious human rights focus in policy. This chapter aims to underscore the importance of incentivizing businesses to embed human rights responsibly and will lay out well-coordinated regional developments and approaches in the Association of Southeast Asian Nations (ASEAN) by businesses, governments and civil society that attempt to abide by key international standards governing business and human rights. This chapter will also recommend that governments should stop privatizing human rights and support a compliance-driven agenda and align national regulations to attract and incentivize companies to plan for sustainability, and that companies could back governance initiatives and target resource security.

Corporate sustainability: a principled pragmatism

Traditionally, corporations have addressed the social impact of their business operations through corporate social responsibility (CSR) programmes as justifiable and necessary actions outside of their core operations. But the responsibilities of businesses with regard to environmental and social impact are no longer limited to the realm of traditional CSR. The United Nations Guiding Principles on

Human Rights and Business (GPs), proposed by Harvard Professor John Ruggie and unanimously adopted by the UN Human Rights Council in 2011, affirm the duty of States to protect against human rights abuses committed by third parties, including businesses (Pillar 1), the responsibility of corporations to respect human rights, which requires them to act with due diligence to avoid infringing those rights (Pillar 2), and the joint responsibility to ensure access to effective judicial and non-judicial remedies (Pillar 3) where business-related human rights abuses do occur.

Significantly, the GPs require companies to respect human rights law. They further recommend that companies not confine themselves only to issues of compliance with national law, which may impose less stringent requirements than internationally recognized norms. The UN Human Rights Council's endorsement of the GPs was indicative of the growing consensus in this arena. This was not surprising, as the GPs were the product of six years of research and consultations with corporations, civil society, States and concerned individuals. They explain how the *Protect, Respect and Remedy* Framework can be implemented by governments, business and the international community, and a multi-stakeholder forum is organized annually in Geneva to take stock of progress, with a working group overseeing and promoting implementation.

Today, risk management extends beyond regulatory compliance. In fact, global enterprises such as Coca-Cola and Nestlé have invested significant resources in their sustainability strategies, as well as in the due diligence departments which are required to implement them. These new departments apply fresh perspectives and approaches on how businesses ought to function.

Therefore, instead of casting CSR as an afterthought, global enterprises consider a broad spectrum of cascading risks that may arise from human rights violations, corrupt practices, labour abuses and environmental damage. These corporations recognize that it is vital to protect themselves not only from expensive and protracted litigation, but also from reputational damage in the court of public opinion. Accordingly, the UN Working Group on the issue of human rights and transnational corporations and other business enterprises, has stated that:

> [B]usinesses will play a major role in developing the green economy and human rights safeguards are necessary to ensure that policies and business plans intended to advance environmental or development goals do not negatively impact people, communities and their livelihoods.[1]

Sustainable development and 'the green economy'

The scope and scale of the global sustainable development challenge have been unprecedented in the last century, with multi-sector stakeholders scrambling to

---

[1] 'Business must respect human rights for truly sustainable development – UN expert body on Rio+20', http://www.ohchr.org/en/NewsEvents/Pages/DisplayNews.aspx?NewsID=12306&LangID=E, accessed 26 March 2014.

tackle the problem at national and global levels.[2] The international community has quite consistently mobilized scientific and technical expertise to address issues of environmental sustainability, poverty eradication and the composition of economic growth.

For example, at the Rio+20 United Nations Conference on Sustainable Development in 2012 (Rio+20), international organizations, governments, civil-society and private sector participants, as well as other stakeholders determined sustainable development to be a balance of social, economic and environmental hopes. Of thematic importance at Rio+20 was the 'green economy'[3] in the context of sustainable development and eradicating poverty, where the roles and commitments of multi-sectoral actors were articulated and emphasis was placed on both 'intra-generational and inter-generational equity'.[4] In Rio+20's 'outcome document', compellingly entitled 'The Future We Want', global leaders pledged more than US\$513 million towards sustainable development initiatives.[5] The current iteration of global development objectives agreed by Member States after Rio+20 is geared toward the process of developing a set of Sustainable Development Goals (SDGs). These were devised to complement and enhance the Millennium Development Goals (MDGs) due to expire in 2015, and converge with the post-2015 development agenda. In efforts to shape public policy and influence national development targets around the world, the United Nations Development Programme (UNDP) has forged numerous country-level partnerships with governments. In turn, the United Nations Environment Programme (UNEP) has proposed a framework this year for embedding the environment in the SDGs.[6]

Rio+20 and 'The Future We Want' have provided an opportunity for international organizations, governments, business and civil society to come together in productive and innovative ways. The United Nations Global Compact (UNGC) was established in 2000 as a policy initiative for businesses committed to implementing ten principles within their strategies and operations.[7] These principles include human rights, labour, environment and anti-corruption.[8] The UNGC has

[2] Puvan Selvanathan, Alexander J. Orona and Mahdev Mohan, 'Sustainable Agriculture and Development: A Forecast of the Post-2015 Corporate Sustainability Landscape', (forthcoming, 2014), *Asia Europe Journal.*

[3] The Green Economy Initiative defined 'green economy' as: 'one that results in improved human well-being and social equity, while significantly reducing environmental risks and ecological scarcities', http://www.unep.org/greeneconomy/AboutGEI/WhatisGEI/tabid/29784/Default.aspx, accessed 24 March 2014.

[4] Rio+20 United Nations Conference on Sustainable Development:, http://www.uncsd2012.org/index.html, accessed 1 November 2013.

[5] Millennium Development Goals and Beyond 2015, http://www.un.org/millenniumgoals/environ.shtml, accessed on 4 December 2013.

[6] United Nations Environment Programme Report, http://post2015.org/2013/08/06/unep-report-embedding-the-environment-in-sustainable-development-goals/, accessed on 4 December 2013.

[7] UN Global Compact, http://www.unglobalcompact.org/AboutTheGC/index.html, accessed 1 November 2013.

[8] UN Global Compact's Ten Principles, http://www.unglobalcompact.org/AboutTheGC/TheTenPrinciples/humanRights.html, accessed 26 March 2014.

over 10,000 corporate and other participants from 130 countries.[9] Along with enabling participants to implement these principles into their organizations with the help of management tools and resources, the UNGC's mission includes linking these actions to the broader UN goals, such as the MDGs.[10] The UNGC is a global action network (GAN), a term coined by Steve Waddell to describe 'multi-stakeholder change networks that are addressing critical global issues'.[11] GANs combine local and global strategies to achieve their objectives, and are able to bring flexibility to their approach. GANs operate on the basis of a 'tipping point' model;[12] that is, when enough organizations adopt a business model incorporating principles such as UNGC's, they establish an operating norm for that sector that eventually compels peers to adopt the same principles.[13] Principles are codified and declared when a critical mass of organizations have 'crystallized' common sentiments and agreed that they are commonly pertinent. For example, the Principles and Criteria of the Roundtable for Sustainable Palm Oil (RSPO) codify practices that are sufficiently well accepted among actors in the palm oil sector as being pertinent in the production of sustainable palm oil. A set of principles is declared when they reasonably capture the concepts, policies, customs and practices deemed as being most indicative of the corpus and discourse of sustainable development in a particular context.

Such conceptions and practices have also been shaped by international standards set by a multitude of global initiatives, including the Voluntary Principles on Security and Human Rights (VPSHR), the UN Principles for Responsible Investment (UNPRI), the Equator Principles,[14] the International Finance Corporation (IFC) Performance Standards.[15] The Organisation for Economic Co-operation and Development (OECD) Guidelines, which also count among these standards, provide for a 'specific instance' complaint to be filed against companies that are from – or operate in – an OECD-adhering country.[16]

A report published by the UN in 2013 under the auspices of the UN Secretary-General Ban Ki-moon laid out an action agenda to support global sustainable

---

[9] Ibid.

[10] Ibid.

[11] Steve Waddell, 'The Global Compact: An Organizational Innovation to Realize UN Principles', (2011), paper prepared in collaboration with the UN Global Compact and presented to the Global Compact Donor Group on 26 October 2011, p. 5, http://networkingaction.net/wp-content/uploads/UNGC_Organizational_Innovation_Note.pdf, accessed 9 May 2014.

[12] Malcolm Gladwell, *The Tipping Point: How Little Things Can Make a Difference* (Back Bay Books, 2002).

[13] Ibid., p. 13.

[14] The Equator Principles is a credit risk management framework for determining, assessing and managing environmental and social risk in project finance transactions, http://www.equator-principles.com, accessed 26 March 2014.

[15] The newly revised IFC performance standards – Guidance on implementation by EP association members from 1 January 2012, http://www.equator-principles.com/index.php/all-ep-association-news/254-revised-ps, accessed 26 March 2014.

[16] An archive of specific instances that have been or are being considered by National Contact Points as of June 2011, http://www.oecd.org/investment/mne/33914891.pdf, accessed 2 January 2014.

development efforts for the period 2015–2030. The report, entitled 'An Action Agenda for Sustainable Development', outlines ten sustainable development priorities, covering the four main dimensions of sustainable development: economic growth and the end of poverty, social inclusion, environmental sustainability, and good governance.[17] Secretary-General Ban stated that, 'the post-2015 process is a chance for the global community to work towards a new era in sustainable development'.[18] He further highlighted that the latest report from the Sustainable Development Solutions Network stressed that, 'the result of a collaboration between top scientists, technologists, businesses, and development specialists, is a critical input to the work we are doing to shape an ambitious and achievable post-2015 agenda'.[19] The report discusses the complexity of the required transformations in agriculture and underscores the importance of achieving a coordinated approach by business, government and civil society and the need for all actors of society to be mobilized to increase investments in research and teaching to share knowledge and promote sustainable solutions to agricultural problems. It also discusses the need to adopt sustainable technologies for agriculture, to improve agriculture systems, promote and raise rural prosperity, and develop farming practices, rural infrastructure and access to resources for food production.

Palm oil industries and environmental sustainability

While many countries are on track to meet their 2015 MDG targets, some are likely to fall behind. The haze in the summer of 2013 – an almost annual occurrence in Southeast Asia, which engulfed Malaysia and Singapore in foul smoke and sent the Air Pollution Index rising precipitously – has jolted ASEAN into questioning its commitment to the seventh MDG relating to the goal of ensuring environmental sustainability. MDG 7 calls for the integration of the principles of sustainable development into country policies and programmes and the reversal of the loss of environmental resources. It specifically highlights how forests are a 'safety net for the poor' but continue to disappear 'at an alarming rate'.[20]

On 21 June 2013, the Pollutant Standard Index reading in Singapore reached an all-time high of 401.[21] This resulted in Singaporeans scrambling for respiratory masks. Poor visibility also prompted shipping companies to issue warnings of potential accidents involving oil tankers in the Malacca Straits, which could

[17] An Action Agenda for Sustainable Development<http://unsdsn.org/2013/06/06/action-agenda-sustainable-development-report, accessed on 2 January 2014.

[18] Ibid.

[19] UN Millennium Development Goals and Beyond 2015, http://www.un.org/millenniumgoals/beyond2015-news-archive.shtml, accessed 2 January 2014.

[20] UN Millennium Goals, http://www.un.org/millenniumgoals/environ.shtml, accessed 4 December 2014.

[21] Normal PSI reading is in the 0 to 50 range. Air quality in the 51 to 100 range places it in the 'moderate' category, while anything above 100 is considered 'unhealthy', http://yourhealth.asiaone.com/content/spore-air-quality-reaching-unhealthy-range-psirises#sthash.Z1a0WkdG.dpuf, accessed 2 January 2014.

trigger devastating oil spills. Governments and environmental activists were quick to blame palm oil companies and the slash-and-burn cultivation allegedly utilized by the industry. NASA satellite images and the Indonesian government's plantation concession maps were used by the World Resources Institute to conclude that half of the hot spots occurred in pulpwood concessions or palm oil plantations in Sumatra. They equally pointed fingers at local farmers who widely view slash-and-burn as the most cost-effective method of clearing clogged peat land on the east coast of Sumatra, home to most of Indonesia's palm oil producers. News reports claimed that about half of the land in Sumatra that was subject to deforestation belongs to huge palm oil conglomerates that are mostly Malaysian-owned.[22] Meanwhile, palm oil companies argued that an opportunistic link was being conveniently conjured by anti-deforestation activists between slash-and-burn cultivation and their industry. Finally, both the Malaysian and Indonesian governments chose not to share concession maps that could have helped identify, and hold accountable, plantation companies for causing the fires that sparked the haze.[23]

Against this backdrop, Indonesia remains the only member of ASEAN not to have ratified the Agreement on Transboundary Haze Pollution (ATHP) brokered in 2002. The ATHP requires parties to '(i) cooperate in developing and implementing measures to prevent, monitor, and mitigate transboundary haze pollution by controlling sources of land and/or forest fires, development of monitoring, assessment and early warning systems, exchange of information and technology, and the provision of mutual assistance; (ii) respond promptly to a request for relevant information sought by a State or States that are or may be affected by such transboundary haze pollution, with a view to minimising the consequence of the transboundary haze pollution; and (iii) take legal, administrative and/or other measures to implement their obligations under the Agreement.'[24] The Agreement is the 'first regional arrangement in the world that binds a group of contiguous States to tackle transboundary haze pollution resulting from land and forest fires' and 'has also been considered as a global role model for the tackling of transboundary issues'.[25]

In the weeks that followed the haze furore, a series of regional governmental meetings were held, environmental activists circulated petitions and various multi-stakeholder governance initiatives were announced. At the 15th Meeting of the Technical Working Group and Sub-Regional Ministerial Steering Committee on Transboundary Haze Pollution hosted by the Malaysian government, the

---

[22] *The Economist*, 'Unspontaneous Combustion: Forest Fires Bring Record Levels of Air Pollution', (29 June 2013), http://www.economist.com/news/asia/21580154-forest-fires-bring-record-levels-air-pollution-and-end-not-sight-unspontaneous, accessed 26 March 2014.

[23] *The Guardian*, 'Singapore Tells Indonesia to Share Forest Fires Map', (17 July 2013), http://www.theguardian.com/environment/2013/jul/17/indonesia-forest-fire-maps-singapore, accessed 26 March 2014.

[24] See n. 8.

[25] ASEAN Agreement on Transboundary Haze Agreement, http://haze.asean.org/?page_id=185, accessed 4 December 2014.

Indonesian government finally agreed to ratify the ATHP by year-end or early 2014.[26] Accordingly, in a Trilateral Cooperative Process, the governments of Singapore, Malaysia and Indonesia agreed to mobilize their respective national resources to tackle the haze.[27] The Singaporean government, in a more stringent move, began to consider the introduction of extra-territorial legislation to enhance penalties for errant companies whose actions damage the environment and cause the haze. Specifically, Singapore's Law Minister K. Shanmugam announced in Parliament that the Attorney-General was considering 'what legal options are available, if credible and usable evidence is received that Singapore-linked companies are involved'.[28]

In February 2014, a new law on transboundary haze, named the 'Transboundary Pollution Bill', was proposed in Parliament, aimed at targeting errant firms with haze-producing fires on their land that affect Singapore.[29] Under the proposed law, errant businesses can be fined up to US$300,000 or up to US$450,000 if they actively ignore requests to prevent or control the haze. After public feedback, however, the bill was strengthened to include fining errant companies up to $2 million, nearly seven times its original suggestion, as well as widened its net to target firms that who have agreements or arrangements with companies that cause haze in Singapore by having fires in their land.[30] Though praised for its efforts to curtail the haze problem, the bill was criticized by several environmental and legal experts as unproductive in tackling the haze issues sustainably in the long term and fraught with difficulties in procuring evidence. The bill purports to impose both criminal and civil liability upon commercial entities responsible for the land-clearance fires but has not placed monetary limits on the damages recoverable via civil claims, and the implications of such a bill on regional agricultural conglomerates, health insurance providers and Singapore residents affected by the haze remain to be seen. The Singaporean government undertook such efforts at legislation despite considerable discussion that some of the big palm companies that operate in Indonesia are based in Singapore or have Singaporean investors. Singaporean Prime Minister Lee Hsien Loong had even stated that local companies or those with a presence in Singapore that had contributed to the forest fires would be held accountable.[31]

[26] http://www.channelnewsasia.com/news/asiapacific/asean-welcomes-indonesia/747976.html
[27] First trilateral meeting on transboundary haze in Jakarta, http://www.todayonline.com/singapore/first-trilateral-meeting-transboundary-haze-jakarta, accessed 26 March 2014.
[28] Elgin Toh, 'Extra-Territorial Laws on Haze Being Considered: Shanmugam', *The Straits Times*, (8 July 2013), http://www.straitstimes.com/the-big-story/the-haze-singapore/story/extra-territorial-laws-haze-being-considered-shanmugam-201307, accessed 1 November 2013.
[29] M. Kotwani, 'Experts Say Draft Haze Bill Won't Solve Issue in Long Term', Channel NewsAsia, (28 February 2014), http://www.channelnewsasia.com/news/singapore/experts-say-draft-haze/1015752.html, accessed 9 May 2014.
[30] http://www.straitstimes.com/news/singapore/environment/story/haze-bill-firms-cause-haze-could-be-fined-100000-day-20140707
[31] Hunter Stuart, 'Indonesia Fires, Singapore Smog Likely Caused By Palm Oil Companies', http://www.huffingtonpost.com/2013/06/21/indonesia-fires_n_3479727.html, accessed 9 May 2014.

Over in Indonesia, implementing laws to ban companies from using fire in large-scale land conversion has been a major challenge at the federal and provincial levels. Governmental legislation is still tenuous in Indonesia, where slash-and-burn is a way of life in Sumatra, and regulation alone has failed to govern how land can be cleared. Rusli Zainal, the governor of Riau since 2003, was recently charged, inter alia, with approving illegal logging permits to finance his re-election campaign.[32] A critical disconnect continues to exist between the enforcement of regulations against slash-and-burn and the human rights of the people involved.

Wilmar International, the world's largest palm oil trader, Singapore-based Golden Agri-Resources and Sime Darby, the world's largest producer of sustainable palm oil, have all been censured for their role in unethical land use contributing to the recent haze. Asia Pulp and Paper and Golden Agri-Resources pledged to stop clearing natural forests within their concessions after being targeted in campaigns by leading international non-governmental organizations (NGOs) such as Greenpeace for their involvement in forest clearing and burning. Wilmar International, while having banned burning on its own plantations, still relies on third-party suppliers for more than 90 per cent of its crude palm oil.[33] Sime Darby similarly prohibits burning on its own plantations but purchases almost half of its commodity from external buyers.[34] However, even if a company's own environmental policies and operational standards are sound and manageable, it maintains an obligation to include a stipulated number of smallholders in its buying programme to ensure the viability of the local community and contribute to improving livelihoods. These external smallholder suppliers, however, are not always provided with the necessary means to engage in cultivation practices that respect the environment.

The complexity of this situation means that some of these larger businesses do not necessarily control or can be accountable for 'their' palm oil production, and that some of the governments involved evidently default on their duty to protect and mitigate the adverse human rights impacts that can be caused by unsustainable agricultural practices. Businesses may lead or fund capacity-building initiatives to equip communities with the required tools for sustainable development and thus contribute to providing human rights safeguards to communities, but these efforts should not presume to substitute the government's duty to protect as stipulated under Pillar 1 of the Guiding Principles.

Yet, the delicate balance between what may be reasonably expected of a company and what is necessarily required of a government is a complementary process involving costs, benefits and stakeholders common to both actors. It is further complicated when the effects of the problem – in this case, both environmental and social (health and well-being) – are transboundary, with actions and impacts

---

[32]   Eco-Business.com, 'How Corruption Is Fuelling Singapore's Haze', http://www.eco-business.com/news/how-corruption-fuelling-singapores-haze, accessed 9 May 2014.

[33]   *Jakarta Post*, 'Wilmar to cut ties with RI palm oil suppliers, http://www.thejakartapost.com/news/2013/07/01/wilmar-cut-ties-with-ri-palm-oil-suppliers.html, accessed 9 May 2014.

[34]   Eco-Business.com, 'Name and Shame Companies Behind Haze: Singapore', http://www.eco-business.com/news/name-and-shame-companies-behind-haze-singapore, accessed 9 May 2014.

of companies and governments not necessarily falling within the same jurisdictions. Making things less complicated suggests adopting a 'rights-holder-centric' approach to development that is both environmentally responsible and economically sustainable. Chronic global development problems do not exist in isolation but are often interlinked and mutually reinforcing. Protecting the environment in developing countries depends on the provision of practical economic opportunities for local populations.[35] Ill-equipped and unable to afford modern farm machinery, farmers continue to engage in slash-and-burn as the arguably quickest and most cost-effective method of land cultivation to meet subsistence needs and carve out a living. When what's being burned is peat land, the fire is extremely difficult to control or stop and results in the emission of greenhouse gases.[36]

Fortunately, a number of key actors are trying to address these complex challenges through a holistic environmental, social and governance approach. This has led to successful collaborations across sectoral, institutional and organizational divides. Such multi-stakeholder collaboration in addressing context-specific issues underscores the need to take action on a range of related issues that may ultimately overcome these complex challenges. For example, an expert group convened by the UN Global Compact in early 2013 to consider the challenges in sustainable agriculture identified at least sixteen issue areas that are shaping the concept: yield and productivity; land use and rights; soil and water; biodiversity; energy efficiency; climate change; waste; small-scale producers; family farmers and cooperatives; gender equality; children and youth; workers' rights and conditions; health and nutrition; animal and marine welfare; supply chains and trade; institutions and infrastructure; and financing.[37] The group concluded that these factors are interdependent and progress towards sustainability in agriculture will depend on action all of them.[38]

We must acknowledge that gaps still exist in the current sustainable development efforts of palm oil companies, which tend to overlook the human element in human rights problems. Many have supported RSPO, where plantations that are RSPO-certified are forbidden from using burning to clear forests.[39] For instance, Sime Darby, a founding member of RSPO, has certified all its estates in Malaysia and Indonesia.[40] Environmental benefits, or at least the avoidance of negative

---

[35] See n. 1: The green economy is 'one whose growth in income and employment is driven by public and private investments that reduce carbon emissions and pollution, enhance energy and resource efficiency, and prevent the loss of biodiversity and ecosystem services'.

[36] BBC News, 'South East Asia Haze: What Is Slash and Burn?', http://www.bbc.co.uk/news/business-23026219, accessed 24 March 2014.

[37] UN Global Compact, White Paper: *Towards Sustainable Agriculture Business Principles*, New York, (2013).

[38] Alejandro Litovsky and Puvan Selvanathan, *Reaping the Dragon's Teeth – How Business Will Support the Transition of Global Food and Agriculture* (UN Global Compact, 2013).

[39] World Wildlife Fund for Nature, 'Singapore's Haze Underscores Need for Action Against Irresponsible Companies', (22 June 2013), http://www.wwf.sg/?209155/singapore-haze-underscores-need-for-action-against-irresponsible-companies, accessed 9 May 2014.

[40] 'Sime Darby Surges Ahead in RSPO Compliance', press release, Sime Darby (November 2010), www.simedarbyplantation.com/sime_darby_surges_ahead_in_RSPO_compliance_.aspx, accessed 1 November 2013.

environmental impacts, define the sustainability policies of palm oil companies that claim to have responsible operations. However, the promotion and protection of human rights is generally less apparent or immediately recognizable in these same policies.

There is an increasingly urgent need to acknowledge and recognize that the spectrum of human rights is wide and that they individually and collectively impact upon each other. The more sustainable position for businesses is to internalize human rights in both principle and practice to inform their role in inclusive and equitable development.

Incentivizing responsible businesses to embed human rights

How companies work with civil society and other stakeholders to create political momentum for sustainability will also be a key factor of success. In 'Reaping the Dragon's Teeth – How business will support the transition of global food and agriculture', three priorities were outlined for business and government cooperation. First, government leaders can align national regulations to attract and incentivize companies that behave responsibly and plan for sustainability, and can provide pre-commercial investment support to make rural communities attractive places to live, work and invest in.[41] Second, government support for a compliance-driven agenda would make sustainability an easier choice for all actors in the agricultural sector, and mandatory operating requirements could be introduced into some basic sustainability criteria.[42] Last, companies should target resource security and back governance initiatives aimed at fighting corruption and improving public management capacities.[43] In the same vein, the OECD echoes that 'responsible business conduct' emerges from a well-coordinated approach by businesses, government and civil society that is 'complementary and interdependent'.[44]

Singapore's move towards a 'comply or explain' basis for Corporate Sustainability Reporting Guidelines 2011 offers an opportunity for companies to 'assess and disclose the environmental and social aspects of their organizational performance, in addition to the financial and governance aspects',[45] and the bourse 'encourages the company to disclose its sustainability policy, including mitigation of risks, performance data and other material information, which deepens stakeholders' understanding of corporate performance'.[46] Contributing to community development is legally mandated in Indonesia by the Corporate Law (2007), with an implementing regulation (2012) for the responsibility to do so. The Indonesian

---

[41] 'SGX Guide to Sustainability Reporting for Listed Companies', p. 20, http://rulebook.sgx.com/net_file_store/new_rulebooks/s/g/SGX_Sustainability_Reporting_Guide_and_Policy_Statement_2011.pdf, accessed 1 November 2013.

[42] Ibid., p. 21.

[43] Ibid.

[44] OECD, 'Policy Framework for Investment: User's Toolkit', http://www.oecd.org/investment/toolkit/policyareas/responsiblebusinessconduct, accessed 9 May 2014.

[45] See n. 41.

[46] See n. 41.

Capital Market and Financial Institutions Supervisory Agency requires publicly listed companies to report on labour issues, social and community development, and consumer safety. Similarly, Bursa Malaysia Listing Requirements (2006) call for corporate annual reports to include a 'description of the corporate social responsibility activities or practices undertaken by the listed issuer and its subsidiaries or if there are none, a statement to that effect'.[47]

From the market perspective, a key foundation for such priorities in cooperation between actors was the Forest Stewardship Council (FSC) pioneering certification label for sustainably sourced timber in the 1990s. Similar initiatives multiplied for other global commodities such as cotton, palm oil, sugar and agricultural outputs for biofuels.[48] Certification systems were created to focus on specific aspects such as fair trade, fair labour and the avoidance of deforestation.[49] Multilateral banks, donor nations and private foundations have been 'aligned in variously leading and supporting roles', bolstering the notion of certification as a 'solution for sustainability'.[50]

Beyond certification, the Earth Security Initiative and UNGC have underscored the need for agriculture businesses to begin the transition towards sustainable agriculture, including embedding human rights in their sustainability policies by:

- working with governments to design and execute market strategies for sustainable intensification in agriculture;
- championing the evolution of national regulation to measure, value and enforce sustainability performance;
- setting corporate targets that build resource-resilient supply chains and support government efforts to better manage resource scarcity and food.[51]

Companies across the agricultural value chain must be able to address the systemic risks they face and develop new market opportunities by supporting broader governance of environmental resources.[52] Unilever, for example, has been actively involved in trying to break the link between palm oil and deforestation and was one of the first big companies to commit to moving to 100 per cent certified sustainable palm oil. Publicly committing in 2008 to purchasing all palm oil from sustainable sources by 2015, as well as supporting a moratorium on further deforestation for palm oil in Southeast Asia, Unilever reached its 2015 targets three years in advance. Since 2012, Unilever's palm oil use has been supported mainly by Greenpalm Certificates.[53] Furthermore, the Unilever 'Sustainable Living Plan'

---

[47] World Federation of Exchanges, http://www.world-exchanges.org/sustainability/m-6-4-4.php, accessed 13 March 2014.

[48] See n. 37.

[49] See n. 37. Examples include: Fairtrade International. www.fairtrade.net, Social Accountability International, www.sa-intl.org, Rainforest Alliance Certification, www.rainforest-alliance.com.

[50] Ibid.

[51] Ibid.

[52] See n. 37.

[53] Unilever Australasia, 'Our Commitment to Sustainable Palm Oil', http://www.unilever.com.au/sustainable-living/Concerns/PalmOil, accessed 1 March 2014.

aims to improve health and well-being, reduce environmental impact and source 100 per cent of agricultural raw materials sustainably, and enhance the livelihoods of people across their value chain by 2020.[54] Over in Myanmar, steps are being undertaken to develop its palm oil sector sustainably. In June 2014, the Union of Myanmar Federation of chambers of Commerce & Industry brought together plantation companies, government agencies and civil society organizations at a multi-stakeholder meeting in Yangon to set up a sustainable palm oil learning group and to discuss sustainable growth of the palm oil sector.[55]

Conclusion

Ban Ki-moon, Secretary-General of the United Nations, writing in the *Economist* in 2007, said 'complex problems must be dealt with comprehensively, in their full economic, social and political dimension'.[56] The myriad issues in relating sustainability and development to food and agriculture exemplifies complexity. Addressing them means recognizing the convergence in systems that govern and affect the planet and its people universally, and requires solutions that demand cooperation, collaboration and collective action. States and their multilateral institutions have recognized that the private sector is a powerful lever for solutions, particularly when operating strategically and in partnership with civil society. Secretary Ban evokes the 'spirit of principled pragmatism', which confronts the rhetoric of principles that do not translate into action – in other words, the imperative 'to deliver results, not mere promises'. Principles, such as UNGC and the Guiding Principles, are a call to action. They provide functional guidance and fuel for a race to the top by peers, whether government, business or NGO, or for partnerships among these actors. The pragmatic application of functional principles offers opportunities for meaningful results from relevant innovations suited to evolving contexts and varying circumstances. Traditionally prescriptive regulation, compliance, policing and enforcement remain necessary to transition from an environment of pursuing singular interests at the expense of others, to one where individual risks and rewards are aligned to mutual benefits and collective outcomes.

---

[54] Unilever, 'Unilever Sustainable Living Plan Summary', http://www.unilever.com/sustainable-living/uslp/, accessed 1 March 2014.

[55] http://www.fauna-flora.org/news/myanmars-palm-oil-industry-heads-for-a-sustainable-path/.

[56] Ban Ki-moon, 'The Spirit of Principled Pragmatism', *The Economist*, (November 15th 2007), http://www.economist.com/node/10120161, accessed 9 May 2014.

7 Human rights risks amidst the 'gold-rush'

Cambodia, Laos, Myanmar and Vietnam

Mahdev Mohan

Introduction

Cambodia, Laos, Myanmar and Vietnam, the 'CLMV States' in the Association of Southeast Asian Nations (ASEAN), are the regional bloc's emerging economies. As one commentator writes of Myanmar, 'imagine ... a country rich in natural resources, ruled for nearly half a century by a military regime that had obsessively chosen severe external isolation and harsh internal control, now opening up both internally to some political changes and externally to foreign trade and investment. The opportunities – both for those interested in profit and for external do-gooders – are almost boundless'.[1] The European Union, the United States, and other Western governments have responded by agreeing to ease certain financial and investment sanctions on the Southeast Asian nation. This has spurred a 'gold-rush' of sorts amongst many transnational corporations, which are attracted to Myanmar's vast, and largely untapped, natural resources and immense economic potential. For every opportunity, however, Myanmar and the other CLMV States have a daunting challenge to face: poor infrastructure, pervasive corruption, ethnic conflict and human rights abuses.

These States and their investors should understand their investment risks and live up to their responsibility to protect and respect human rights. In several countries in the past, large infrastructure and extractive-sector projects have led to significant human rights abuses, including, in some cases, forced labour, displacement and land-grabbing. These abuses intensify conflict and invariably affect the most marginalized and vulnerable sectors of society, especially women, children, ethnic minorities and indigenous peoples. This chapter seeks to temper the great gold-rush into the CLMV States with caution.

The risk of transnational litigation relating to adverse human rights impacts allegedly caused by extractive industries has increased following the adoption of the UN Guiding Principles (GPs), notwithstanding the US Supreme Court decision in *Kiobel*.[2] Where traditional legal recourse does not produce results,

---

[1] Jayati Ghosh, 'Nothing Is Simple in Burma's Great Gold-rush', *The Guardian*, (2012), http://www.theguardian.com/commentisfree/2012/apr/09/great-burma-gold-rush.

[2] *Kiobel v. Royal Dutch Shell Petroleum Co*, No. 10–1491 (U.S. 2012), 621 F. 3d 111, affirmed. See the *American Journal of International Law* special issue, 'Agora: Reflections on Kiobel', October 2013, 107(4).

aggrieved parties will have other means of publicizing allegations against the extractive sector, and in this context it can be expected that the GPs will be used as a yardstick. If the CLMV States, ASEAN and the extractive sector do not voluntarily embrace the GPs as international standards evolve, the pressure for meaningful regulatory responses will be increased.

Much has been written about the legacy of *Kiobel* through the lens of US jurisprudence. This chapter considers the import of *Kiobel* for Southeast Asia in light of recent developments, specifically in relation to the extractive sector in its CLMV States. It will first examine supranational regulatory standards, namely the GPs on business and human rights. Next, it will analyse the domestic human rights obligations imposed on the CLMV States in view of the greater economic integration within ASEAN. Third, it will analyse the applicable legal and regulatory frameworks in the CLMV States and how these States address, or ought to address, business-related human rights abuses. Finally, it will examine an ongoing seminal case regarding the acquisition of sugar plantations in Cambodia's Koh Kong province that is before the courts of the United Kingdom, and consider how strategic lawyering has served the plaintiffs well, and may offer a way forward through analogy.[3]

Transnational human rights litigation

Corporate accountability for human rights and environmental violations in connection with the extractive industries is typically discussed in the light of transnational human rights litigation (THRL) – often referred to as 'transnational public interest litigation'[4] or 'plaintiff's diplomacy'[5] – pursuant to statutes such as the US Alien Torts Claim Act (ATCA), which gives US federal courts jurisdiction to hear foreign claims for human rights abuses committed elsewhere. Although ATCA has largely lain dormant, throughout the 1990s it began to be used as a means by which non-State actors sought damages from transnational corporations in response to alleged violations of international human rights law. Well-publicized cases have been brought in US Courts against transnational business enterprises operating in the oil and gas sector for their alleged roles in perpetrating human rights abuses in developing countries in Asia and Africa.[6] Certain European

---

[3] The research findings in this chapter are part of a larger project led by the author as principal investigator and supported by the Centre for Corporate & Investor Responsibility at the Sim Kee Boon Institute for Financial Economics in the Singapore Management University (SMU). Special thanks to project researchers Delphia Lim, Beverly Ng and Nadia Samdin.

[4] S. Joseph, *Corporations and Transnational Human Rights Litigation* (Oxford: Hart Oxford, 2004).

[5] A.-M. Slaughter and D. Bosco, 'Plaintiff's Diplomacy', (2002), *Foreign Affairs*, 79(5): 102–116.

[6] Malgosia Fitzmaurice, 'Case Study: Wiwa and Royal Dutch Petroleum and Shell Transport and Trading Company Before the US Court of Appeals for the Second Circuit (the Alien Tort Claims Act and the Doctrine of *Forum non Conveniens*', in Wybo P Heere (ed.), *From Government to Governance: The Growing Impact of Non-State Actors on the International and European Legal System: 2003 Hague Joint Conference on Contemporary Issues of International Law* () (T M C Asser Press, 2004) at pp. 203–205.

countries also have similar routes for access to justice and remedy thorough the domestic courts.[7]

These cases have been cited by international lawyers and scholars to illustrate that corporate responsibility to respect human rights extends beyond the domestic legal and regulatory sphere and can be adjudicated by foreign courts.[8] Legal barriers can deter legitimate cases involving corporate human rights violations from being addressed and obstruct access to justice, especially when these violations do not attract domestic criminal liability for the company.[9] This can occur when 'the way in which legal responsibility is attributed among members of a corporate group under domestic criminal and civil laws facilitates the avoidance of appropriate accountability', when claimants are denied justice in both their home and host States, and where certain groups are excluded from the same level of legal protection of human rights as others enjoy.[10]

In his speech to the UN Human Rights Council (UNHRC) in 2011, Professor John Ruggie, former UN Special Representative for Business and Human Rights, remarked that multilateralism – that is, finding common ground rules for global action – works.[11] It has been said that THRL helps to generate 'a transnational legal process approach whereby techniques of process are used to internalize into transnational actors – here, multinational corporations – standards of right and wrong behaviour'.[12] In 2013, however, Professor Ruggie lamented that, if the respondents' arguments persuaded the Supreme Court in *Kiobel* v. *Royal Dutch Petroleum Co.* (*Kiobel*),[13] its decision may 'destroy an entire juridical edifice for redressing gross violations of human rights'.[14]

---

[7] E. A. Engle, 'Alien Torts in Europe? Human Rights and Tort in European Law', (2005), Zentrum fur Europaische Rechtspolitik an der Universitat Bremen ZERP-Diskussionspapier.

[8] Harold Hongju Koh, 'Separating Myth from Reality About Corporate Responsibility Litigation', (2004), *Journal of International Economic Law*, 7(2): 263, at 264–268; Justine Nolan and Luke Taylor, 'Corporate Responsibility for Economic, Social and Cultural Rights: Rights in Search of a Remedy?', (2009), *Journal of Business Ethics*, 87, at 433–434.

[9] On whether (and when) States are obliged to impose criminal responsibility on companies for human rights violations, see Piet Hein van Kempen, 'The Recognition of Legal Persons in International Human Rights Instruments: Protection Against and Through Criminal Justice?', in Mark Pieth and Radha Ivory (eds), *Corporate Criminal Liability: Emergence, Convergence, and Risk* (Springer, 2011), at pp. 379–386.

[10] John Ruggie, 'Report of the Special Representative of the Secretary-General on the Issue of Human Rights and Transnational Corporations and Other Business Enterprises', (21 March 2011), http://www.business-humanrights.org/media/documents/ruggie/ruggie-guiding-principles-21-mar-2011.pdf, accessed 9 May 2014.

[11] Ibid.

[12] Hongju Koh, see n. 8, at pp. 267–268. For elaboration, see also Harold Hongju Koh, 'Bringing International Law Home', *Hous. L. Rev.*, (1998), 35: 623; Harold Hongju Koh, 'Why Do Nations Obey International Law?', (1997), *Yale L.J.*, 106: 2599; Harold Hongju Koh, 'How Is International Human Rights Law Enforced?', (1999), *Ind. L.J.*, 74: 1397.

[13] The respondents' supplemental brief argued that ATCA does not apply to corporations, including US companies, and that its previous judicial interpretation and application amounted to a violation of international law and comity.

[14] John Ruggie, 'Kiobel and Corporate Social Responsibility – An Issues Brief', (4 September 2012), http://www.hks.harvard.edu/var/ezp_site/storage/fckeditor/file/KIOBEL%20AND%20CORPORATE%20SOCIAL%20RESPONSIBILITY.pdf, accessed 9 May 2014.

The unanimous Supreme Court decision in *Kiobel* on 17 April 2013 determined that international claimants could not bring civil suits in US courts under ATCA against foreign corporate defendants that have a mere corporate presence in the US for alleged egregious human rights violations.[15] This case involves a joint subsidiary of the Royal Dutch Petroleum Company, based in the Netherlands, and Shell Transport and Trading Company, based in England. Nigerian plaintiffs residing in America sued the former for its alleged complicity in human rights violations, including rape, murder, theft and destruction of property, that were committed by Nigeria's armed forces in Ogoniland.

This suit was initially dismissed by a federal appeals court on the grounds that the ATCA provided no basis for corporate-liability lawsuits.[16] Dismissing the appeal to the Supreme Court, Chief Justice Roberts' majority opinion held that the presumption against extraterritoriality aims to avoid judicial interference with foreign policy.[17] The decision underscored a strong general presumption against the extra-territorial application of American law. Chief Justice John Roberts stated that 'there is no indication that the ATCA was passed to make the United States a uniquely hospitable forum for the enforcement of international norms'.[18] He further added that 'even where the claims touch and concern the territory of the United States, they must do so with sufficient force to displace the presumption against extraterritorial application'.[19]

Businesses operating in Southeast Asia are no strangers to ATCA litigation. Notably, an early high-profile lawsuit under ATCA was filed against energy giant Unocal. Unocal, the suit alleged, knowingly subjected villagers to forced labour, murder, rape and torture at the hands of the Myanmar military when constructing the Yadana natural gas pipeline together with the State-owned Myanmar Oil and Gas Enterprise (MOGE). Unocal denied those charges. That case has since been settled out of court without the company admitting any wrongdoing, but, as we shall see, similar concerns persist in Myanmar and other countries in the Southeast Asian region today. While the Unocal case was ultimately settled out of court, it has been seen as a strategy by which private actors can leverage formal enforcement actions in domestic courts to regulate overseas conduct in aid of supranational policy goals and regulation.[20]

However, the narrowing of ATCA's scope – which has been described as the only practical avenue of redress for business-related human rights abuse in

---

[15] *Kiobel* v. *Royal Dutch Petroleum Co*, 133 S. Ct. 1659, 185 L. Ed. 2d 671 (2013) (majority opinion of Chief Justice Roberts), at 6.

[16] *The Economist*, 'The Shell Game Ends – Some Good News for Multinationals', (22 April 2013), http://www.economist.com/news/united-states/21576393-some-good-news-multinationals-shell-game-ends, accessed 9 May 2014.

[17] *Kiobel* v. *Royal Dutch Petroleum Co*, 133 S. Ct. 1659, 185 L. Ed. 2d 671 (2013) (majority opinion of Chief Justice Roberts), at 6.

[18] *Kiobel* v. *Royal Dutch Petroleum Co.* () 621 F. 3d 111, affirmed: http://www.law.cornell.edu/supremecourt/text/10–1491#writing-10–1491_OPINION_3.

[19] Ibid.

[20] See n. 3.

Southeast Asia – is a blow to victims: such legal barriers may leave them without opportunity for effective remedy.[21] The US Supreme Court's determination of ATCA's future applicability to corporations in *Kiobel* is significant in light of the crucial preventive role effective and dissuasive remediation processes can have. The fate of ATCA will turn, in part, on how US courts decide two further cases under this statute which concern corporate accountability for mass human rights violations in Southeast Asia.

More specifically, they involve ExxonMobil's alleged conduct in Aceh[22] and Rio Tinto's in Papua New Guinea.[23] At the time of writing this chapter, the proceedings for the former case, where fifteen Acehnese villagers have accused former Indonesian soldiers working for Exxon Mobil of murder, torture and other atrocities against their family members during the period of civil unrest from 1999 to 2001, are ongoing, following a motion by ExxonMobil to have the case reheard *en banc*. In the latter case, the Court of Appeals has had its earlier decision, which acknowledged that corporate liability for aiding and abetting international crimes exists under ATCA, vacated by the Supreme Court. The Court of Appeals has been directed by the Supreme Court to reconsider the case in the light of *Kiobel*,[24] which has held that a claim under ATCA will rebut the presumption against extraterritoriality if it can 'touch and concern the territory of the US ... with sufficient force'.[25] In any event, in the light of *Kiobel*, it is likely that lower US courts will

---

[21] Changrok Soh, 'Extending Corporate Liability to Human Rights Violations in Asia', (2013), *Journal of International and Area Studies* 1(23), at 32, 34.

[22] In 2001, eleven Indonesian villagers filed suit against ExxonMobil in the US federal court alleging that the company was complicit in human rights abuses committed by Indonesian security forces in Aceh. The plaintiffs maintain that ExxonMobil hired the security forces, who were members of the Indonesian military, to protect the natural gas extraction facility and pipeline which ExxonMobil was operating. The plaintiffs allege that they suffered grave human rights violations at the hands of these security forces. On 8 July 2011, the Court of Appeals held that a corporation should not be immune from liability under ATCA. See http://www.business-humanrights.org/LegalPortal/Home for more details.

[23] Residents of the island of Bougainville in Papua New Guinea (PNG) filed suit against Rio Tinto under ATCA in the US federal court in 2000. The plaintiffs allege, inter alia, that: Rio Tinto was complicit in war crimes and crimes against humanity committed by the PNG army during a secessionist conflict on Bougainville; Rio Tinto sought dismissal of the case, which the district court granted in 2002. Rio Tinto argued to the trial court that the case raised questions that are 'non-justiciable' because they involve acts of State and political questions, and because ruling on them would breach standards of international comity. The trial court agreed. After four years of protracted litigation, on 25 October 2011, the Ninth Circuit Court of Appeals reversed the lower court's dismissal of the case. See http://www.business-humanrights.org/LegalPortal/Home for more details.

[24] This statement was true at the time of writing. Since then, on 28 June 2013, the US Court of Appeals for the Ninth Circuit upheld the dismissal of the case. See *Sarei* v. *Rio Tinto, PLC; Rio Tinto Limited*, Order dated 28 June 2013, http://cdn.ca9.uscourts.gov/datastore/opinions/2013/06/28/02–56256%20web.pdf.

[25] The door is not closed on ATCA's scope. As Breyer J held in his opinion partially concurring with the judgment, the court 'leaves for another day the determination of just when the presumption against extraterritoriality might be "overcome"'. Kennedy J, who joined the majority opinion, too

confirm that 'foreign-cubed' cases against corporations must be dismissed and are categorically barred.[26]

UN's *Protect, Respect and Remedy* Framework: towards a supranational regulatory framework

Even if ATCA litigation may not be as prevalent or successful following *Kiobel*, corporate responsibility has existed independently and beyond ATCA, or more specifically, beyond the scope of liability that the US Supreme Court has been prepared to accept in the wake of *Kiobel*.

In 2008, the UNHRC approved Professor John Ruggie's proposed framework on business and human rights, otherwise known as the UN's *Protect, Respect and Remedy* Framework.[27] This framework is based on three pillars, being the duty of States to protect human rights, the responsibility of corporations to respect human rights, and the need to ensure access by victims to both judicial and non-judicial remedies where business-related human rights abuses do occur.[28]

In 2011, the UN Guiding Principles on Business and Human Rights, comprising thirty-one Guiding Principles (GPs), were unanimously adopted by the UNHRC to implement all three pillars of the UN's *Protect, Respect and Remedy* Framework.[29] In Professor John Ruggie's words, 'the Council's resolution establishes the guiding principles as the authoritative global reference point for business and human rights'.[30] Impressively, all twenty-eight members of the Council voted for the endorsement.[31] The resolution also envisions a multi-stakeholder forum to address and solve challenges and roadblocks encountered while implementing the principles.[32]

Whereas the UN's *Protect, Respect and Remedy* Framework addressed, in Professor Ruggie's words, the 'what' question: what do States and businesses need to do to

opined that this decision left open questions about the 'proper implementation of the presumption against extra-territorial application'. See n. 2.

[26] Anupam Chander, 'Unshackling Foreign Corporations: *Kiobel's* Unexpected Legacy', (2013), *American Journal of International Law*, 107, at 830–831; Matteo M. Winkler, 'What Remains of the Alien Tort Statute After *Kiobel?*', (2013), *North Carolina Journal of International Law and Commercial Regulation* 39: 171 at 186–189.

[27] John Ruggie, *Protect, Respect and Remedy: A Framework for Business and Human Rights – Report of the Special Representative of the Secretary – General on the Issue of Human Rights and Transnational Corporations and Other Business Enterprises*, 8th session, Agenda Item 3, UN Doc A/HRC/8/5 (7 April 2008) paras 51–81 (*Protect, Respect and Remedy* Framework), http://www.reports-and-materials.org/Ruggie-report-7-Apr-2008.pdf.

[28] Ibid.

[29] Human Rights Council, *Guiding Principles on Business and Human Rights: Implementing the United Nations 'Protect, Respect, and Remedy' Framework*, A/HRC/17/31 (21 March 2011).

[30] Ibid.

[31] Additionally, the UNHRC resolution has established a working group which consists of five experts. The working group is tasked with the promotion and implementation of the GPs.

[32] This and a complete list of actions requested of the Working Group in its mandate is contained in ten sub-paragraphs and can be found in Human Rights Council resolution 17/4 (A/HRC/RES/17/4).

ensure business respect for human rights; the GPs address the 'how' question: how we move from concept to practical, positive results.[33] The GPs seek to provide companies with a set of comprehensive standards built upon existing laws. They advise public and private companies on how to conduct their activities in accordance with human rights. Additionally, the GPs outline human rights due diligence processes that seek to prevent and address human rights abuses. Finally, the GPs take remediation into concern in the event that a human rights violation occurs and is attributable to a business entity.

This chapter is concerned with the first pillar. The State duty to protect under Pillar 1 of the UN's *Protect, Respect and Remedy* Framework does not concern human rights abuses directly caused by the State itself. Instead, as GP 1 states, the duty is to protect against human rights abuse within its territory and/or jurisdiction by third parties, including business enterprises. As stated in the commentary to the GPs, States will not be considered to have violated their treaty obligations simply because a private actor has abused rights; there must be some act or omission by the State that evidences a failure to exercise due diligence in fulfilling its duty.

Accordingly, GP 1 defines the State duty to protect as requiring 'taking appropriate steps to prevent, investigate, punish and redress such abuse through effective policies, legislation, regulations and adjudication'. More broadly, a key aspect of this duty is that States should help foster corporate cultures respectful of rights both at home and abroad, through all available avenues.[34]

This component considers the extent to which the State has fulfilled and/or failed in its duty to protect by applying the UNGP's 'operational principles' for this duty. These 'operational principles' are divided into the following four broad issue areas: (i) the State's regulatory and policy functions, (ii) the State's involvement in business (State-Business nexus), (iii) the role of States in respect of businesses operating in conflict-affected areas, and (iv) ensuring policy coherence within and among the State's human rights and business regimes both domestically and internationally. This chapter will consider the GPs relating to the first and second issue areas.

With regard to the first issue area, GP 3 states that:

> [i]n meeting their duty to protect, States should: (a) [e]nforce laws that are aimed at, or have the effect of, requiring business enterprises to respect human rights, and periodically to assess the adequacy of such laws and address any gaps; (b) [e]nsure that other laws and policies governing the creation and ongoing operation of business enterprises, such as corporate law, do not constrain but enable business respect for human rights; (c) [p]rovide effective guidance to business enterprises on how to respect human rights throughout

---

[33] See Mahdev Mohan and Delphia Lim, 'Securing Human Rights in Business', *Business Times*, 3, June 2011.

[34] See n. 29. See also 'Human Rights and Corporate Law: Trends and Observations from a Cross-National Study Conducted by the Special Representative', Addendum to the Report of the UNSRSG on Business and Human Rights to the Human Rights Council, 23 May 2011 ('UNSRSG's Corporate Law Report').

their operations; (d) [e]ncourage, and where appropriate require, business enterprises to communicate how they address their human rights impacts.

The GPs make clear that the primary responsibility to promote and protect human rights law lies with the State. Although the GPs do not purport to create new legal obligations, they emphasize that the area of business and human rights is not a 'law-free zone'.[35] Existing domestic laws or regulations, for example, may impose requirements on business enterprises that are based on a State's international human rights obligations. These duties to protect human rights are enshrined in the constitutions of Cambodia,[36] Laos,[37] Myanmar,[38] and Vietnam.[39] This chapter seeks to provide a snapshot of each State's regulatory regime relevant to the above-mentioned areas of focus and to identify any gaps in the relevant laws and/or regulations, as well as in their enforcement.

ASEAN as a 'regulatory State'?

The Southeast Asian region has taken strides towards adopting common human rights standards, even though such efforts have not attained full integration or singularity of purpose in respect of the GPs. ASEAN has long been regarded as a group of sovereign nations operating on the basis of *ad hoc* understandings and informal procedures.[40]

As a multilateral institution, ASEAN has been criticized for failing to adequately promote and protect human rights, due to its long-standing policy of non-interference in Member States' internal affairs. Nevertheless, noting the development of a network of ASEAN treaties governing trade and investment, former ASEAN Secretary-General Rodolfo Severino predicted that 'this developing rules-based economic regime will gradually extend to other areas of ASEAN cooperation, [as] ASEAN is more than an economic association'.[41] This prediction has come to pass. Although the Southeast Asian region has not codified the GPs in the form of a regional treaty, it has taken strides towards adopting common human rights standards. Efforts are underway in laying the groundwork for an institutional framework to facilitate free flow of information based on each country's national laws and

---

[35] *Report of the Special Representative of the Secretary-General on the Issue of Human Rights and Transnational Corporations and Other Business Enterprises,* John Ruggie, Human Rights Council 14th Session (9 April 2010) UN Doc A/HRC/14/27, 66.

[36] Articles 31 and 48, the Constitution of the Kingdom of Cambodia.

[37] Articles 6, 8, 16, 17, 21, 22, 27, 29, and 46, Constitution of the Lao People's Democratic Republic.

[38] Articles 22, 23, 24, 28, 36(c), 45, 347, 348, and 356, Constitution of the Republic of the Union of Myanmar (2008).

[39] Article 112(5), 1992 Constitution of the Socialist Republic of Vietnam (as amended 25 December 2001).

[40] R. Severino, 'ASEAN Way and the Rule of Law', address at the International Law Conference on ASEAN Legal Systems and Regional Integration sponsored by the Asia-Europe Institute and the Faculty of Law, University of Malaya, Kuala Lumpur, 3 September 2001.

[41] Severino, see n. 40.

regulations, preventing and combating corruption, and cooperation to strengthen the rule of law, judiciary systems and legal infrastructure, and good governance.[42]

With the adoption of the ASEAN Charter in November 2007, ASEAN moved toward becoming a single polity. The 2007 ASEAN Charter states, inter alia, that members should adhere to 'principles of democracy, the rule of law and good governance, respect for and protection of human rights and fundamental freedoms'.[43] In 2009, ASEAN Member States designed a 'road map', which envisions the creation of a 'rules-based Community of shared values and norms' built on three pillars, namely, the ASEAN Political-Security Community, the ASEAN Economic Community and the ASEAN Socio-Cultural Community, each with its own blueprint and infrastructure for implementation and integration.

Significantly, human rights compliance has become an established part of ASEAN's discourse and stated goals.[44] The ASEAN Intergovernmental Commission on Human Rights (AICHR) is an important mechanism established under the ASEAN Charter to develop 'common approaches and positions on human rights matters of interest to ASEAN'.[45] AICHR's progress of work as ASEAN's 'overarching body ... for the promotion and protection of human rights and fundamental freedoms in accordance with the ASEAN Charter' was noted at the 18th ASEAN Summit.[46]

AICHR has also completed its first thematic study, a baseline study relating to business and human rights in ASEAN,[47] although there is a need for sustained systematic analysis by regional experts to inform and support initiatives by businesses, governments and civil society committed to business and human rights.[48] Corporate social responsibility (CSR) is also mentioned in the blueprint for the ASEAN Socio-Cultural Community. But business impacts on human rights pertain to all three pillars and need to be holistically understood and addressed.[49]

---

[42] Ibid., para. 15.

[43] Charter of the Association of Southeast Asian Nations, Singapore, 20 November 2007, http://www.asean.org/archive/publications/ASEAN-Charter.pdf, accessed 9 May 2014.

[44] ASEAN Secretariat, ASEAN Political-Security Community Blueprint (1 March 2009), http://www.asean.org/communities/asean-political-security-community, accessed 9 May 2014.

[45] Terms of Reference of ASEAN Intergovernmental Commission on Human Rights (July 2009), para 4.11, http://www.refworld.org/docid/4a6d87f22.html, accessed 20 May 2014.

[46] 2011 Chair's Statement of the 18th ASEAN Summit, issued by the Chair of ASEAN in Jakarta, Indonesia on 8 May 2011, http://www.asean.org/archive/Statement_18th_ASEAN_Summit.pdf, accessed 9 May 2014.

[47] See Study Team on Business & Human Rights of the ASEAN Intergovernmental Commission on Human Rights (AICHR), Baseline Study on the Nexus Between Corporate Social Responsibility & Human Rights: An Overview of Policies & Practices in ASEAN (13 June 2014). Copy of the study on file with author.

[48] AICHR faces constraints in executing its wide-ranging functions. AICHR representatives have highlighted the difficulties faced in terms of the capacity of AICHR members and its limited budget. They have indicated that assistance is needed in, inter alia, capacity-building for AICHR members and staff and AICHR's thematic studies. See UNDP Asia Pacific Regional Centre and OHCHR Regional Office for Southeast Asia, Report on 'Regional Dialogue on UN Engagement with the ASEAN Human Rights System', Bangkok, 6 September 2010.

[49] Ibid.

AICHR has also drafted the ASEAN Human Rights Declaration (AHRD), which has since been adopted by all ten ASEAN States.[50]

The UN High Commissioner for Human Rights Navanetham Pillay has positively observed that the newly promulgated ASEAN Declaration of Human Rights 'will set the tone for the emerging ASEAN human rights system'.[51] The High Commissioner has also noted that Southeast Asia (SEA) benefits from an 'energetic and sophisticated' civil society.[52] ASEAN's efforts to reinforce its commitment to human rights through this Declaration are laudable.[53]

Yet, it bears mentioning that the strength of extra-territorial jurisdiction and the legacy of the GPs depends on their uniform enforcement, especially since a multilateral treaty or international court devoted to regulating business-related human rights abuses remains unlikely (though not impossible).[54] Although supranational regulations can sometimes regulate trans-border issues more effectively than national institutions, they rarely provide an institutional framework that clearly caters to the community to which they are accountable above and beyond the State. Further, with some exceptions,[55] there has not been uniform or consistent acknowledgement by the region's businesses of the relationship between the impact of their operations and human rights. For such implementation to take place in SEA there needs to be a keen appreciation of regional developments and sustained enforcement action, including THRL, to embed the GPs and clarify their implications. As ASEAN works towards articulating its norms and values, it is therefore vital that business and human rights standards be included throughout the ASEAN system.

[50] ASEAN Human Rights Declaration (Cambodia, 18 November 2012), http://www.asean.org/news/asean-statement-communiques/item/asean-human-rights-declaration.
[51] Seventh Official Meeting of the ASEAN Intergovernmental Commission on Human Rights Address by the United Nations High Commissioner for Human Rights, 28 November 2011.
[52] Ibid.
[53] Gerard Clarke, 'The Evolving ASEAN Human Rights System: The ASEAN Human Rights Declaration of 2012', (2012), *Northwestern Journal of International Human Rights*, 11.
[54] UNHRC, 26th Sess, UN Doc A/HRC/26/L.22 (24 June 2014). This resolution directs the UNHRC to establish an inter-governmental working group with the mandate to "elaborate an international legally binding instrument to regulate, in international human rights law, the activities of" business. See also John Ruggie, *A UN Business and Human Rights Treaty?*, 28 January 2014, http://www.hks.harvard.edu/m-rcbg/CSRI/UNBusinessandHumanRightsTreaty.pdf. ('At the September 2013 session of the UNHRC, the delegation of Ecuador delivered a statement stressing "the necessity of moving forward toward a legally binding framework to regulate the work of transnational corporations and to provide appropriate protection, justice and remedy to the victims of human rights abuses directly resulting from or related to the activities of some transnational corporations and other business enterprises." Ecuador was speaking not only in its own behalf but also for the African Group, the Arab Group, Pakistan, Sri Lanka, Kyrgyzstan, Cuba, Nicaragua, Bolivia, Venezuela and Peru. Following up on its statement, Ecuador is convening an expert workshop during the Council's March session. This proposal potentially brings the business and human rights agenda to a new inflection point.')
[55] One exception is Malaysia's Sime Darby Berhad. See letter dated 20 May 2011 from Sime Darby Berhad to the SRSG, http://www.global-business initiative.org/Home%20files/Letter%20from%20Sime%20Darby%20supporting%20UN%20GPs.pdf.

ASEAN's CLMV States and the extractive sector

The speed of economic change and growth in the extractive sector in the CLMV States is startling and may even be disconcerting. Laos has recognized mining as a critical sector of the economy and continued to support development of the sector by promoting domestic and foreign investment. In 2010, the significant producers of copper, gold and silver in Laos were the Australian companies Minerals and Metals Group Lane Xang Minerals Ltd. and PanAust Ltd.[56] Mining has, as at 2011, come to account for 80 per cent of Laos' foreign direct investment inflows, and provides 45 per cent of foreign exchange profits from exports.[57] Laos' first formal mine went into operation at Sepon, Savannaket Province, in 2002. The Sepon Mineral District is a highly mineralized 400 square kilometre area that has primarily gold and copper operations.[58]

According to Laos' Department of Mines, Ministry of Energy and Mines, as of November 2010, there were 263 mining projects in Laos.[59] Corporations have suggested that these mines were a 'welcome addition' to communities, due to reported 'big leaps' in average incomes and greater income equality.[60] However, this purported positive impact of mining has also been questioned. Notwithstanding fiscal rules imposing a uniform annual profit tax of 20 per cent on foreign investors, and royalty rates from 2 to 5 per cent payable by all mineral producers,[61] only one mining project in Laos is reportedly paying profit taxes and seventeen are paying royalties.[62]

Second, adverse social and environmental impacts have also reportedly arisen as a result of mining projects in the region. There have been spills of harmful and toxic pollutants in Laos,[63] and the National Assembly has acknowledged that there are serious environmental concerns.[64] For example, Oz Mineral's Sepon copper

---

[56] US Geological Survey, *2010 Minerals Yearbook. Laos* (Advance Release).

[57] International Council on Mining and Metals, *In Brief. Utilizing Mining and Mineral Resources to Foster the Sustainable Development of the Lao PDR*, (July 2011), http://www.icmm.com/page/62109/icmm-presents-summary-of-recent-lao-pdr-country-case-study, accessed 9 May 2014.

[58] See http://www.ozminerals.com/2008-sustainability-report/Sustainability/Company_Overview/regional_exploration.htm

[59] Poverty Environment Initiative (PEI) Lao PDR Issues Brief 08 /2010: Economic, social and environmental impacts of investments in mining [UNDP]

[60] A 2010 country case study by the International Council on Mining and Metals on the economic and social contribution of mining drew from the experiences of two existing large-scale mines in the country, namely, MMG Sepon, owned by MMG, the subsidiary of China Minmetals Corporation, and ICMM's first Chinese-owned member company, and the Phu Bia Mining Phu Kham Copper-Gold Operation owned by PanAust Ltd. Biannual household surveys conducted by the two companies reported that mining revenues had been distributed across the country, favouring low-income districts with a high representation of ethnic minority groups. It was argued that the decline in income inequality evidenced the positive impact of mining. It observed that the mines had thus far experienced to a lesser degree the social tensions associated with resource extraction in some other countries. *Inbrief. Utilizing Mining and Mineral Resources to Foster the Sustainable Development of the Lao PDR*, (July 2011), http://www.icmm.com/page/62109/icmm-presents-summary-of-recent-lao-pdr-country-case-study, accessed 9 May 2014.

[61] From the website of Lao PDR's Department of Geology and Mines, http://www.dgm.gov.la.

[62] Ibid.

[63] Poverty Environment Initiative (PEI) Lao PDR Issues Brief 08 /2010: Economic, social and environmental impacts of investments in mining [UNDP].

[64] Amendments needed in the Lao mining industry legislation, Land Issues Working Group.

mine has been criticized as 'a huge project with detrimental environmental and social impacts which will do next to nothing for the population'.[65] Local communities have also apparently been paid inadequate compensation for their loss of land as a result of mining activities.[66]

In Vietnam, plans to begin the exploitation of about 5.3 billion tonnes of bauxite in the Central Highlands,[67] and to take advantage of its estimated 210 billion tonnes of coal in the Red River Delta,[68] have attracted controversy. Vietnam's Central Highlands are inhabited by ethnic minority groups with agricultural livelihoods. There is great concern that large-scale bauxite mining in the area will displace these communities, have adverse environmental impacts due to deforestation and toxic mining waste, and destroy their livelihoods.[69] With regard to coal-mining in the Red River Delta, exploitation plans will likely result in the permanent displacement of rice farmers in the area, which is the country's second largest rice-growing region.[70]

Third, there are many instances in the CLMV States in which the combination of conflict, corruption and corporate complicity has contributed to flagrant human rights abuses. CLMV States are notorious for weak governance, and it is here that the challenge of operationalizing the GPs is greatest. All four countries have extractive-sector exploration projects which merit close examination. In particular, there are fears that these countries with rapidly developing extractive industries will fall prey to the 'resource curse', i.e. the paradox that countries with an abundance of natural resources tend to have less economic growth than countries without these natural resources.[71]

A key area in which such conflict, corruption and corporate complicity have heightened human rights abuses is in the area of land concessions. Domestic judicial avenues for recourse against State action in granting concessions appear unpromising in CLMV States. In Myanmar, new laws such as the Vacant, Fallow and Virgin Lands Management Law substantially amended the legal framework of the land and reintroduced the concept of private ownership – where such land remains as State property and can be nationalized by the government if necessary, resulting in a removal of protections for farmers by allowing their land to be repossessed if they fall into debt.[72]

[65] The Akha Heritage Foundation, 'Campaigners Say No to Funding for Copper Mine in Laos', http://www.akha.org/content/akhainlaos/docs/copperminesinlaos.html, accessed 9 May 2014.

[66] Amendments needed in the Lao mining industry legislation, Land Issues Working Group.

[67] Third World Network, 'Legendary Vietnamese General Fights to Save Environment', (2009), http://www.twnside.org.sg/title2/resurgence/2009/225/eco1.htm, accessed 9 May 2014.

[68] Agriviet.net, 'Farmers Worry About Mining in Red River Delta', http://agriviet.net/23108-farmers-worry-about-mining-in-red-river-delta, accessed 9 May 2014.

[69] *The Economist*, 'Bauxite Bashers: the Government Chooses Economic Growth Over Xenophobia and Greenery', (23 April 2009), http://www.economist.com/node/13527969, accessed 9 May 2014.

[70] Agriviet.net, 'Farmers Worry About Mining in Red River Delta', http://agriviet.net/23108-farmers-worry-about-mining-in-red-river-delta/, accessed 9 May 2014.

[71] *The Guardian*, 'Cambodia's Oil Must Not Be the Slippery Slope to Corruption and Catastrophe', 21 June 2011, 'Revenues from Oil, Gas and Mining Must Benefit All Cambodians, New Coalition Urges'; Cambodians for Resource Revenue Transparency press release, 12 June 2009; *The Economist*, 'Cambodia's Oil Resources: Blessing or Curse?', 26 February 2009.

[72] Vacant, Fallow and Virgin Lands Management Law, unofficial translation available at http://www.burmalibrary.org/docs13/VFVLM_Law-en.pdf. Article 4: 'The Central Committee shall permit

Cambodia

Economic land concessions

Even though national laws prevent officials from granting permits on protected land and cap concession sizes at 10,000 hectares,[73] officials have routinely flouted these rules, granting commercial leases to plots of rural land that have already been occupied by residents, offering them little or no compensation. Over time, the government has seized almost 5 million acres of land – 10 per cent of the nation's entire land mass.[74] A number of cases involving violence and detention carried out by company personnel, military police and/or private security have been reported.

Although the Land Management and Administration Project (LMAP) was designed to improve land tenure security, the land titling system is open to manipulation (not titling contentious land, re-titling public land as State private land). Resettlement sites lack tenure, security and basic amenities (lack of access to health services, employment opportunities, education, potable water, electricity, etc. in new resettlement areas.)

Despite the fact that the LMAP is committed to providing over US$30 million to increasing tenure security, many observers suggest that the land crisis has actually worsened over the period of its implementation. It has become apparent to groups working with threatened communities that LMAP is not providing tenure security to the most vulnerable members of Cambodian society. LMAP was designed so that areas 'likely to be disputed' would not be titled and 'informal settlements' would not be titled without the approval of the Government. Communities living in these areas face the greatest risk of being evicted and becoming landless.

Despite the fact that systematic titling is supposed to be implemented across all project provinces, titling of households in urban areas has been extremely slow, especially in Phnom Penh. For example, LMAP originally aimed to adjudicate 198,000 titles in Phnom Penh by the end of 2007.[75] Figures obtained to the end of 2009 show that 83,655 titles were adjudicated, and fewer than half of these were actually issued to owners.[76] In light of the fact that possession rights are not being consistently recognized by the Government, many urban communities face imminent forced eviction. It is foreseeable that the problem will be exacerbated in the near future as the city continues to develop and expand.

the right to do, (and) right to utilize land of vacant, fallow and virgin land in the country, for the following purposes: – (a) Agriculture; (b) Livestock Poultry Farming and Aquaculture; (c) Mining; (d) Government allowable other purposes in line with law; 5. The following persons and organizations may apply to Central.'

[73] Land Law 2001, Article 59. See also http://www.cambodiainvestment.gov.kh/investors-information/land-site-development.html.

[74] Joel Brinkley, 'Private Property, Public Greed in Cambodia', *POLITICO*, (6 May 2013), http://www.politico.com/story/2013/05/lawyer-works-to-put-end-to-cambodia-land-grabbing-90985.html accessed 9 May 2014.

[75] Natalie Bugalski, Mark Grimsditch and David Pred, 'Land Titling in Cambodia: Lessons from the Land Management and Administration Project', April 2010, referring to LMAP project appraisal document, 2002, at 43.

[76] Ibid.

For the most part, the beneficiaries of systematic titling have been those living in undisputed rural areas that generally have little appeal to businesses wishing to acquire the land for development. With few real incentives for the Government to title at-risk households, the donor-funded titling process is largely impotent in the face of illegal land-grabbing and forced evictions throughout the country.

Forced evictions are frequently justified by statements that the communities in question 'do not have title', are 'illegal' or are 'squatters'. In this dual system of access, an absence of title is equated with illegal occupation, contrary to the provisions of the Land Law and the spirit of the titling system.

Judicial recourse against such violations remains illusory. For example, On 27 May 2008, an Economic Land Concession (ELC) was awarded to a Cambodian company named CIV for a rubber plantation in Snoul district, Kratie province. The 769-hectare ELC, one of thirty-five awarded in Kratie in recent years, is on ancestral land communally owned by hundreds of Stieng minority families – despite the fact that the 2001 Land Law bars acquisition of indigenous land. The affected families say they were never consulted about the plans, in contravention of the sub-decree on ELCs. After the company sent in bulldozers to clear the villagers' rice and cassava crops, the villagers decided to take collective action. On 5 October 2008, 300 villagers held a peaceful protest at the site, demanding that company workers remove the camp they had set up.

Two weeks later, four community members were invited to Kratie provincial court for questioning on allegations of robbery and property destruction relating to the protest – despite the fact that no violent confrontation had taken place. No evidence has been presented against the men, beyond a criminal complaint from the CIV company, and one of the men was not even present at the protest.[77] The community attempted to utilize various means to resolve the dispute and keep their land, or at least receive adequate compensation. This included complaints to the court for the cancellation of the land swap contract between the former community representatives and the company, and also a breach of trust claim against the same representatives.

The community also complained to the Ministry of Land Management Urban Planning and Construction, Cadastral Commission, Municipality of Phnom Penh, and National Assembly, without resolution of the dispute. None of the complaints the community filed were ever resolved by the courts or Cadastral Commission, as should have been done before any title was issued. Furthermore, in the absence of the provision of any legal aid, as should have occurred under LMAP, Dey Krahorm residents had to seek out private legal counsel themselves at great expense.

---

[77] See Surya P. Subedi, Report of the Special Rapporteur on the situation of human rights in Cambodia, A human rights analysis of economic and other land concessions in Cambodia, 24 September 2012. See also LICADHO, 'Land Grabbing and Poverty in Cambodia: the Myth of Development', May 2009, http://www.licadho-cambodia.org/reports/files/134LICADHORE portMythofDevelopment2009Eng.pdf; Human Rights Now, 'Human Rights Now, Fact Finding Report for Cambodia In Cambodia, People are Deprived of Land', (October 2012), http://hrn. or.jp/eng/activity/HRN%20Cambodia%20Report%20on%20Land%20Rights%202012.pdf.

Laos

There are a number of legal safeguards available in Laos to prevent and address the adverse human rights and environmental impacts of mining operations, specifically in the context of general legislation, environmental impact assessments, environmental performance bonds and community-development funds.

General obligations

The Environment Protection Law states that '[a]ny person or organization engaged in commercial production, service or other undertaking that causes a disaster is obligated to mitigate the damage and to restore the affected area under the supervision of the local authority or the concerned sectoral agency'.[78] The law states that persons and organizations have an obligation to actively participate in environmental restoration,[79] but it does not specify under what conditions these obligations are applied.

Particular obligations are imposed on investors under the Law on Investment Promotion of 2009. Domestic and foreign investors must, under this law, 'introduce a social insurance and social security system for the workers in their enterprises in compliance with the relevant law; promote the employment of Lao labour; place emphasis on labour skill development, upgrading of specialized skill and transfer of technology to Lao workers',[80] and 'pay compensation for the damages which are caused by their business; make a contribution to the eradication of poverty of the peoples and to the local development in the area where their projects are located'.[81] Investors must also 'protect and develop the environment, ensure that the business operations have no significant negative impacts to the public, the security and social order or to the health of the labourers'.[82] Should environmental problems occur, 'investors have an obligation to take necessary measures to solve such situation in a timely manner in accordance with the laws and regulations'.[83] The law provides for a procedure for issuing warnings prior to termination of business operations that are in breach of the concession agreement, laws and regulations, and that have a harmful impact on the environment.[84]

Similarly, the Law on the Promotion of Foreign Investment 2004 provides for the following obligations on foreign investors: the obligation to pay the necessary taxes, duties and other fees; to give priority to recruiting Lao workers and to train and upgrade their skills; to address matters of social security, health and safety of

[78] Article 28 Environmental Protection Law 1999.
[79] Article 27 Environmental Protection Law 1999.
[80] Article 69.3 Law on Investment Promotion 2009.
[81] Article 69.5 Law on Investment Promotion 2009.
[82] Article 70 Law on Investment Promotion 2009.
[83] Article 70 Law on Investment Promotion 2009.
[84] Article 76(1) Law on Investment Promotion 2009.

their employees; and to protect the environment and ensure that their activities do not severely impact the public, national security or public order.[85]

Environmental performance and impact assessments

Development projects and activities that have the potential to affect the environment must submit an environmental impact assessment report for an environment compliance certificate before starting the project.[86]

An Environmental Impact Assessment (EIA) Regulation (No. 1770/STEA) was passed in 2000, and an updated ESIA Regulation (2010) was enacted in February 2010. At the national level, the Water Resource and Environment Administration is responsible for ESIAs, including coordination with other departments, review and approval of ESIAs and a role in monitoring compliance.[87]

Mineral Exploration and Production Agreements in Laos require mining operators to submit Environmental and Social Management Plans and a bond guaranteeing environmental quality: prior to closure, the Government of Laos will inspect the mine and if the Environmental and Social Management Plan has been violated, the bond can be seized.[88] In the mining sector, performance bonds are generally required to insure the State against the costs of repairing any environmental damage that may be caused by operations and rehabilitating the site after the end of a project. It is essential that projects that could cause impacts on the environment are registered and that the government has the power to require performance bonds and to confiscate the bond in the event of breaches.[89]

In Laos, the Minerals Law of 2008 makes it a requirement for investors to contribute to community-development funds.[90] Such funds are a positive example of a government–company–community partnership. Community-development funds channel revenues generated by mining operations back into communities, including strengthening weak public services.

Funds in Laos have been used to deliver community investment programmes or even transfer mining profits directly back to local inhabitants. Such funds can be used to manage compensation funds and to continue local community support even after the mine has been closed.[91]

---

[85]   Article 13 Law on Promotion of Foreign Investment 2004.

[86]   Article 8.3 Environmental Protection Law 1999.

[87]   Poverty Environment Initiative (PEI) Lao PDR Issues Brief 08 /2010: Economic, social and environmental impacts of investments in mining [UNDP].

[88]   Ibid.

[89]   Ibid.

[90]   Morten Larsen, *Lao PDR Development Report 2010, Natural Resource Management for Sustainable Development*, http://siteresources.worldbank.org/LAOPRDEXTN/Resources/293683–1301084874098/LDR2010_Mining.pdf, accessed 9 May 2014.

[91]   Ibid.

Regulatory weaknesses

Not all mining companies adopt environmentally sound practices.[92] Inadequate implementation has been identified as factors contributing to adverse corporate social and environmental impacts.

Mining concessions have reportedly been used by companies for sites or minerals not stipulated in the relevant concessions; companies are also said to have repeatedly extended their concessions, whether or not contractual conditions are complied with.[93] Officials have alleged that some companies did not intend to develop proposed projects but planned to reserve them for other purposes.[94] Government officials have cited loopholes in the law as the cause of the lack of regulation.[95]

The implementation of the required environmental impact assessments has been problematic. There is a lack of capacity and resources to monitor investments through systematic inspections, resulting in corporate misconduct going unpunished.[96] High-level government approval is often given to investment proposals even before environmental impact assessments are conducted.[97]

Implementation is not uniformly poor; there have been positive examples of government enforcement. For example, the government recently requested the Sino-Lao Corporation to account for fifty items of concern raised in its environmental impact assessment. The government also revoked sixteen concessions in December 2010 for non-compliance with laws.[98]

Myanmar

Gold mining

Myanmar has banned mining of mineral resources along the country's four major river courses or near the river banks in a bid to preserve the natural environment, according to an order of the Ministry of Mines. The four rivers are the Irrawaddy, Thanlwin, Chindwin and Sittoung.[99] Exploration and production of minerals along the river courses or closer than 90 metres to the riverbanks is prohibited as a result. These gold-mining operations have reportedly drained water sources, increased

---

[92]   Report on Implementation of the Brussels Programme of Action for the Least Developed Countries (2001–2010) at 18.

[93]   Amendments needed in the Lao mining industry legislation, Land Issues Working Group.

[94]   Ibid.

[95]   Ibid.

[96]   Report on Implementation of the Brussels Programme of Action for the Least Developed Countries (2001–2010) at 18; Poverty Environment Initiative (PEI) Lao PDR Issues Brief 08 /2010: Economic, social and environmental impacts of investments in mining [UNDP] at 4.

[97]   Poverty Environment Initiative (PEI) Lao PDR Issues Brief 08 /2010: Economic, social and environmental impacts of investments in mining [UNDP] at 4.

[98]   Ibid.

[99]   'Myanmar Bans Mining Near Rivers for Environmental Reasons', (29 March 2013), http://news.xinhuanet.com/english/world/2012–03/29/c_131497308.htm, accessed 9 May 2014.

soil erosion and polluted rivers with mercury and other chemicals. Mercury is highly toxic to the environment and poses serious risks to public health.[100]

The vast majority of toxic wastes from gold extraction processes are disposed of untreated directly onto land and into waterways, effectively poisoning the soil and compromising water quality. Mercury and other toxic materials are biomagnifying in food chains and accumulate in the tissues of living organisms, with negative effects on flora and fauna, local biodiversity and human health. In early 2013, it was uncovered that a member of a Myanmar government-backed Kachin militia was behind the expropriation of large tracts of land in the Kachin State from local farmers in order to carry out lucrative gold-mining operations.[101] Such operations have led to land seizures and illegal evictions of residents with little or no compensation, contrary to the GPs.

As the gold-mining process that is used involves mercury, cyanide and other toxic chemicals, and affects local rivers in the vicinity, environmental activists from the Kachin Development Networking Group have stated that these will have serious and long-term repercussions. Mount Pinpet in the eastern Burmese state of Shan has also been destroyed due to Russian and Italian engineering companies working together to develop a massive iron ore mine.[102] This has already led to the confiscation of vital farmlands without adequate compensation to resident farmers and is expected to destroy twenty-five villages, permanently displace 7,000 ethnic Pa-Ohs from their traditional farmlands and impact another 35,000 people relying on the Thabet watershed on the eastern side of the mountain.[103]

Oil and gas

The Shwe natural gas and Myanmar–China oil transport projects are two of Myanmar's largest energy projects. Two pipelines running through Myanmar will transport gas from the Shwe fields in Myanmar and oil from the Middle East and Africa to China. The Chinese National Petroleum Corporation (CNPC) operates the pipelines and works with other companies on various aspects of operations. However, it has been reported that human rights abuses are taking place in the construction of the Shwe gas pipeline, including displacement, forced labour, discrimination, sexual violence and other forms of violence, and killings.[104] With a May 2013 deadline imposed by the companies for the completion of the pipelines,

---

[100] 'Burma's Pro-Government Kachin Militia Leader Grabs Land for Gold Mining', (10 July 2013), http://www.kachinnews.com/news/2533-burma-s-pro-government-kachin-militia-leader-grabs-land-for-gold-mining.html, accessed 9 May 2014.

[101] Ibid.

[102] Earth Rights, 'Alumni Report: PYO on Iron Mining in Burma', http://www.earthrightsalumni.org/content/alumni-report-pyo-iron-mining-burma, accessed 9 May 2014.

[103] Ibid.

[104] See 'Sold Out: Launch of China Pipeline Project Unleashes Abuse Across Burma', (September 2011), http://www.burmalibrary.org/docs11/SoldOut%28en%29.pdf, accessed 9 May 2014.

which has since lapsed, there has been renewed attention on the projects' human rights impacts.[105]

There are concerns that exploration contracts entered into by the Myanmar Oil and Gas Enterprise (MOGE) with Malaysian and Thai State oil companies, or concessions it has granted to Chinese ones to construct oil and gas pipelines, may not be consistent with the GPs and international standards. Both Daw Aung San Suu Kyi and President Thein Sein have called for ethical and responsible invest-ment. To give effect to these calls, investors seeking entry into Myanmar will have to carefully select who they partner with. Like other companies that have done business in Myanmar, they run the risk of allegations of complicity if they asso-ciate with businesses with close relationships to members of the former military government – or others whose names appear on sanctions lists – who face credible allegations of human rights abuses.

Businesses acquiring land in Myanmar should also ensure that people are not forcibly evicted from their land, and obtain free, prior and informed consent of affected communities before any proposed relocation. A resettlement plan provid-ing sufficient compensation, the guarantee of basic standard of living and access to livelihoods should be implemented when relocation becomes unavoidable.

Combating corruption

Foreign investors should note that they may be subject to anti-corruption legislation that has extra-territorial effect, such as the US's Foreign Corrupt Practices Act, the UK's Bribery Act and Singapore's Prevention of Corruption Act. The UK Bribery Act not only makes bribery committed extra-territorially an offence,[106] it also contains a unique provision requiring companies to prevent bribery committed by persons performing services for or on behalf of the company, and thus has a wide reach.[107]

At the same time, it affords companies a defence if they have in place adequate procedures designed to prevent such persons from bribing in the course of per-forming services for or on behalf of the company. A creative 'with, not against' approach has been adopted in respect of enforcement.[108] In determining whether to prosecute, public interest factors will be considered. Factors against prosecution include proactive corporate compliance measures, self-reporting (whistle-blowing)

---

[105] See Huang Kaixi, 'CNPC's Dreams of Pipelines from Myanmar All Blocked Up', (18 June 2013), http://english.caixin.com/2013–06–18/100542666.html

[106] The offences created by the Act apply to bodies incorporated in the UK in respect of acts committed anywhere in the world; the offence of failing to prevent bribery applies to the same, as well as bodies wherever incorporated carrying on business in the UK. See 2010 UK Bribery Act, ss. 7 and 12.

[107] 2010 UK Bribery Act, ss. 7 and 8.

[108] See Charlie Monteith, 'The Bribery Act 2010: Part 3: Enforcement', (2011) 2 Crim. L.R. 111, (Sweet and Maxwell) at 114 ('To work with business, in other words, not against it, has meant the SFO pla-cing a huge emphasis on raising awareness, education, persuasion, and ultimately prevention'.)

and remedial actions.[109] Companies are therefore, in a rather novel manner, given a role in anti-bribery regulation and enforcement. To comply, companies are encouraged to include anti-bribery provisions in, for example, their supply chain contracts or joint venture agreements.[110] They are also discouraged from doing business with companies that pose corruption risks that anyone should reasonably know of.[111]

Further, the approach to prosecutions encourages companies to report possible violations by their business associates and partners, even if they are not directly involved. This approach gives effect to GP 13(b), which states that '[t]he responsibility to respect human rights requires that business enterprises … [s]eek to prevent or mitigate adverse human rights impacts that are directly linked to their operations, products or services by their business relationships, even if they have not contributed to those impacts'. Further, the extra-territorial reach of the offence of failing to prevent bribery spurs this company-driven regulation and enforcement to cross borders and have a region-wide impact. A company-driven approach to addressing regional corruption, as opposed to one dominantly driven by States, is apposite in the ASEAN context, where the principle of non-interference means that Member States are reluctant to directly address systemic rule-of-law weaknesses in another Member State.

Notably, Singapore, for instance, is moving towards an approach similar to that in the UK by urging companies to cooperate with enforcement and prosecutorial agencies to avoid or deter corporate crime prosecutions.[112] As such, in addition to their liability for gross human rights abuses and international crimes, investors of these countries could also be held criminally liable through prosecution for contravening their respective domestic anti-bribery laws which have extra-territorial effect. For example, given the close ties between the government and business community in Myanmar and the other CLMV countries, US, UK and Singapore investors should vigilantly guard against corruption in Myanmar lest this trigger legal obligations at home.

Vietnam

Laws and regulations

Vietnam's mining-related laws contain substantial environmental safeguards. All investors are required to submit investment dossiers to the authorities that

---

[109] Ibid.

[110] UK Ministry of Justice, 'The Bribery Act 2010 Guidance about procedures which relevant commercial organisations can put into place to prevent persons associated with them from bribing', at 16 to 17.

[111] The UN Corporate Responsibility to Respect Human Rights: An Interpretive Guide 2012, at 7.8 ('…not knowing about human rights abuses linked to the enterprise's operations, products or services is unlikely by itself to satisfy key stakeholders, and may be challenged in a legal context, if the enterprise should reasonably have known of, and acted on, the risk through due diligence').

[112] *Business Times*, 'Prosecutors May Do Deals to Seal Justice', 4 October 2011. Straits Times, Thumbs-up all round for tougher MAS regulations: those involved say rules against money laundering, terror funding are crucial, 17 July 2014.

include an environmental impact assessment and solutions.[113] Under the 1996 Mineral Law (amended in 2005) (1996 Mineral Law), mining operators bear the responsibility for protecting mineral resources in their areas of operation.[114] They are to bear the costs of protecting and rehabilitating the environment and land, as determined by environmental impact assessment reports, feasibility studies or exploration proposals.[115] Such costs are guaranteed by requiring mining operators to make a deposit in a bank for the purposes of rehabilitating the environment.[116]

The 2005 Environment Protection Law requires all business enterprises to lodge environmental protection commitments with the local people's committees.[117] Owners of certain types of projects are required to submit detailed environmental impact assessment reports, which must include the opinions of the local people's committees and representatives of the communities residing at the project's location, including opinions opposing the project location or environmental protection solutions.[118] Appraisal councils or appraisal service organizations will appraise environmental impact assessment reports,[119] and are required to make these public by posting them at their project sites.[120]

Further, the 1996 Mineral Law contains a policy for the protection of the locals residing at mining sites.[121] In particular, mining organizations are required to give

[113] 2005 Investment Law, Article 48. English translated version is available at http://moj.gov.vn/vbpq/en/Lists/Vn%20bn%20php%20lut/View_Detail.aspx?ItemID=594, accessed 9 May 2014.

[114] 1996 Mineral Law (amended in 2005), Article 9(4). English translated version is available at http://moj.gov.vn/vbpq/en/Lists/Vn%20bn%20php%20lut/View_Detail.aspx?ItemID=216, accessed 9 May 2014.

[115] 1996 Mineral Law (amended in 2005), Article 16. English translated version is available at http://moj.gov.vn/vbpq/en/Lists/Vn%20bn%20php%20lut/View_Detail.aspx?ItemID=216, accessed 9 May 2014.

[116] 1996 Mineral Law (amended in 2005), Article 16. English translated version is available at http://moj.gov.vn/vbpq/en/Lists/Vn%20bn%20php%20lut/View_Detail.aspx?ItemID=216, accessed 9 May 2014.

[117] 2005 Environment Protection Law, Articles 24, 25 and 26. English translated version is available at http://moj.gov.vn/vbpq/en/Lists/Vn%20bn%20php%20lut/View_Detail.aspx?ItemID=596, accessed 9 May 2014.

[118] 2005 Environment Protection Law, Article 14 and 18. English translated version is available at http://moj.gov.vn/vbpq/en/Lists/Vn%20bn%20php%20lut/View_Detail.aspx?ItemID=596, accessed 9 May 2014.

[119] 2005 Environment Protection Law, Article 21. English translated version is available at http://moj.gov.vn/vbpq/en/Lists/Vn%20bn%20php%20lut/View_Detail.aspx?ItemID=596, accessed 9 May 2014.

[120] 2005 Environment Protection Law, Article 32. English translated version is available at http://moj.gov.vn/vbpq/en/Lists/Vn%20bn%20php%20lut/View_Detail.aspx?ItemID=596, accessed 9 May 2014.

[121] 1996 Mineral Law (amended in 2005), Article 7. English translated version is available at http://moj.gov.vn/vbpq/en/Lists/Vn%20bn%20php%20lut/View_Detail.aspx?ItemID=216, accessed 9 May 2014.

priority to the recruitment of local labour for mineral activities and related services.[122] Vietnam has enacted several pieces of labour legislation, including those relating to child labour. Minors may not be employed in dangerous jobs or jobs allowing exposure to noxious substances prescribed in the list published by the Ministry of Labour, Invalids and Social Affairs and the Ministry of Health.[123] The work hours of an employee who is a minor may not exceed seven hours per day or forty-two hours per week.[124]

Enforcement and implementation

The local Provincial People's Committees is the body tasked with managing extractive activities and revenues.[125] Inspections to monitor compliance with the Environment Protection Law are conducted across industrial zones and provinces by inspectorates of the Ministry of Natural Resources and Environment and the General Department of Environment Protection.[126]

Despite the requirements for all business enterprises to lodge environmental assessment reports under the 1996 Mineral Law, the implementation of such requirements is uneven. While most mining operators have at least one environmental impact assessment report, extended environmental impact assessment reports, which are required when the scale of operations has been expanded, for example, are often not conducted.[127] Also, mining plans issued by provincial and central government authorities do not appear to have included strategic environmental assessments.[128] There has also been limited reported involvement of civil-society and local communities in monitoring the process and extractive activities.[129]

Poor implementation may be partly attributed to problems in coordination between the central government and the local provincial authorities. Pro-investment local authorities have reportedly not considered or have disregarded environmental impacts when reviewing investment dossiers. Failures or delays in

---

[122] 1996 Mineral Law (amended in 2005), Article 7. English translated version is available at http://moj.gov.vn/vbpq/en/Lists/Vn%20bn%20php%20lut/View_Detail.aspx?ItemID=216, accessed 9 May 2014.

[123] 2012 Labor Code, Article 121, available in Vietnamese at http://vanban.chinhphu.vn/portal/page/portal/chinhphu/hethongvanban?class_id=1and_page=1andmode=detailanddocument_id=163542, accessed 9 May 2014.

[124] 2012 Labor Code, Article 122, available in Vietnamese at http://vanban.chinhphu.vn/portal/page/portal/chinhphu/hethongvanban?class_id=1and_page=1andmode=detailanddocument_id=163542, accessed 9 May 2014.

[125] The Extractive Industries Transparency Initiative and the Implementation Perspective of Vietnam (May 2011) at 20.

[126] Vietnam Report, HRRC Business and Human Rights Baseline Study, Section III.2.3.

[127] The Extractive Industries Transparency Initiative and the Implementation Perspective of Vietnam (May 2011) at 18.

[128] Ibid. at 18.

[129] Ibid. at 18.

enacting and implementing environment protection regulations by local provincial authorities prompted the central government to issue a circular directing them to do so promptly.[130]

Prudent use of resources can help developing countries overcome poverty, but there are many instances where the combination of conflict, corruption and corporate complicity in the CLMV States has contributed to flagrant human rights abuses. Corruption can affect the implementation of legal protections, and may allow mining licence applicants to obtain licences without meeting legal requirements. Government representatives have acknowledged corruption in mining and have attributed these to loopholes in institutions, State management and supervision; they also noted that scope for officials to impose requirements for approvals allowed them to seek bribes, and contributed to corruption. Nepotism and cronyism are viewed as prevalent problems, as appointments to the public sector are often based on relationships with the ruling communist party.[131] In a survey conducted by the World Bank and IFC in 2012, more than 50 per cent of the companies surveyed expected to make 'facilitation payments' such as informal payments or gifts to public officials.[132]

Like the other CLMV countries, corruption in Vietnam is exacerbated by a lack of transparency and accountability in the grant of extractive licences. Regulations are frequently changed without prior notice, and they are often applied in an opaque manner.[133]

Summary

From the preceding analysis, it appears that laws and regulations on human rights and environmental concerns in the CLMV countries have been enacted on different scales and have met with varying degrees of success.

On one end of the spectrum lies Myanmar, where limited legislation has been enacted to address human rights and environmental concerns and where such abuses are committed on an ongoing basis. On the other end of the spectrum lie Vietnam and Laos, both of which have enacted legal frameworks for human rights and the environment (although they tend to focus on the latter). Their implementation, despite lacking true comprehensiveness and consistency, has shown partial successes. At the middle of this spectrum lies Cambodia, in which some laws have been enacted in relation to the protection of land, but which have yet to be meaningfully implemented.

Despite the differences in the regulatory frameworks across the CLMV countries, a common theme appears in all of them. In each country, limited data has

---

[130] Vietnam Report, HRRC Business and Human Rights Baseline Study, Section III.2.3.
[131] Overview of corruption and anti-corruption in Vietnam (January 2012) at 3.
[132] The World Bank and the International Finance Corporation, Doing Business in a more transparent world: comparing regulation for domestic firms in 183 economies, 2012.
[133] Overview of corruption and anti-corruption in Vietnam (January 2012) at 2 to 5.

been published on the effectiveness of domestic remedies for victims of human rights abuses, including victims' ability and willingness to obtain domestic remedies. In light of the lack of success of domestic remedies, THRL plays an even more significant part in allowing human rights victims to obtain effective redress of wrongs. This is where the US Supreme Court's limit of the extra-territorial application of the ATCA in *Kiobel* further constrains the remedies available to human rights victims. Given the CLMV States' historical resistance to binding human rights commitments, the prospect of an ASEAN human rights court seems far off.[134]

Garden-variety transnational litigation

In March 2013, 200 Cambodian villagers of Koh Kong Province filed a complaint in the UK courts against Tate & Lyle Sugars Limited.[135] The plaintiffs maintain that they remain the legal owners of the land on which the Koh Kong companies grew sugar. Therefore, they claim that under Cambodian law they are the rightful owners of the crops grown on their land, and are claiming compensation for the profit from selling the sugar.[136] The defendants argue that they do not have knowledge of the facts asserted by the plaintiffs and seek to be declared the rightful owners of the sugar purchased from the Koh Kong companies.[137]

The UK High Court has accepted jurisdiction of the suit, and it remains pending before the courts.[138] This recent THRL case before the UK courts arising from Cambodia is significant in several respects, and ought to be contrasted with the litigation strategy deployed by the appellants in *Kiobel*. Instead of selecting a forum, such as courts in the USA that do not have a direct nexus to the nationality of the alleged perpetrator, victim or site of human rights abuse, the plaintiffs in *Song Mao* carefully selected the UK courts as the forum because the defendants allegedly complicit in the abuses are domiciled in the UK. The *Song Mao* claim sets out how the size (more than 10,000 hectares) and type of land (private property as opposed to State land) acquired was contrary to Cambodian law and that the Cambodian government did not comply with the requisite conditions for an economic land concession (ELC).

134 Donald E. Weatherbee, *International Relations in Southeast Asia: The Struggle for Autonomy* (Rowman and Littlefield, 2nd edn, 2008), pp. 250–252.
135 Statement of Claim, *Song Mao* v. *Tate & Lyle Indus. Ltd*, Claim No. 2013, Folio 451 (EWHC (Comm), Mar. 28, 2013) (QB), http://www.business-humanrights.org/media/documents/tate-lyle-particular-of-claim-28-mar-2013.pdf, accessed 9 May 2014 ('Song Mao SoC').
136 Song Mao SoC, para. 23–27, 32–33.
137 Defence and Counterclaim of the First and Second Defendants, *Song Mao* v. *Tate & Lyle*, Claim No. 2013, Folio 451 (EWHC (Comm), May 2, 2013) (QB), http://www.business-humanrights.org/media/documents/tate-lyle-defence-counterclaim-2-may-2013.pdf, accessed 9 May 2014.
138 Joel Brinkley, 'Private Property, Public Greed in Cambodia', *POLITICO*, (6 May 2013), http://www.politico.com/story/2013/05/lawyer-works-to-put-end-to-cambodia-land-grabbing-90985.html, accessed 9 May 2014.

Further, the *Song Mao* claim shows that all available remedies, including domestic litigation have been exhausted, and that the law is often used against victims of land grabs in Cambodia. Importantly, civil-society organizations assisting the plaintiffs with the claim filed a complaint to the Thai national human rights commission as the Cambodian sugar companies in question are substantially (50%) owned by Khon Kaen Sugar PC Ltd (KKS), a Thai company.

The Thai commission in turn found evidence that KKS had violated the human rights of the impacted communities through their ELCs. It confirmed its commitment 'to ensure that communities and their natural resources remain protected, and that various human rights principles are applied in meeting the economic, social and environmental pillars for fairness and sustainable development'.[139] Consistent with Cambodian law, the GPs, and reports by the UN Special Rapporteur for Human Rights in Cambodia,[140] the *Song Mao* claim suggests that the defendants did not ensure that people were not forcibly evicted from their land – they did not obtain free, prior and informed consent of affected communities before any proposed relocation. Although human rights abuse is alleged, the cause of action that the plaintiffs have chosen is the tort of conversion, akin to theft, on the basis that the defendants have acquired raw sugar through illegal contracts which wrongfully deprived the plaintiffs of the ownership, use and possession of the sugar and had converted the same to their own use.[141]

Conclusions

The extractive industry operates in complex environments where human rights issues are a central concern. It is imperative that the extractive industry conducts business in a responsible way. This chapter has sought to consider each CLMV State's unique legal and regulatory frameworks and the steps they have each taken to address relevant business-related human rights abuses. ASEAN countries are indeed increasingly affected by the linkage of their free trade and investment prospects with compliance with international labour standards. It is critical for ASEAN to recognize the importance of business and human rights to its development as an integrated economic community by the year 2015.

Next, the *Song Mao* case demonstrates that THRL need not be rooted in jurisdictional statutes such as ATCA, which are confined to narrow grounds – i.e. international law violations that substantially and adversely affect an important

---

[139] 'Findings of the Subcommittee of the National Human Rights Commission of Thailand on the Koh Kong Sugar Cane Plantation Case in Cambodia', (25 July 2012), at 3, http://www.boycottbloodsugar.net/wp-content/uploads/2012/07/NHRC-Findings-on-Koh-Kong-25-July.pdf, accessed 9 May 2014.

[140] Surya P. Subedi, 'Report of the Special Rapporteur on the Situation of Human Rights in Cambodia, a Human Rights Analysis of Economic and Other Land Concessions in Cambodia', (24 September 2012).

[141] Song Mao SoC.

American national interest. THRL can look to regional human rights institutions and UN fact-finding bodies for corroboration. Significantly, THRL cases should be commenced in the courts of a State with a connection to the parties and select garden-variety causes of action in tort or contract law where the elements and standard of proof can be met. The UK has been receptive to such tortious claims (usually on the basis that the company had assumed a duty of care to the victims of its subsidiary overseas),[142] although this re-characterization has been criticized as failing to capture the severity of such acts which constitute egregious human rights violations.[143]

As appealing as a war crimes or genocide litigation may be to human rights lawyers, in domestic courts, a more pedestrian cause of action founded on tort or contract may be far more attractive to courts concerned with ensuring that they do not run afoul of international comity or embarrass the Executive. Similarly, the extent to which extractive companies operating in CLMV States may be involved with negative human rights impacts will be heavily influenced by both their operating context and the practices of their business partners. Both factors will shape the policies, processes and practices they need in order to prevent and address such impacts. The locations where such companies operate (whether on- or off-shore) are determined by where resources exist. The exploitation of natural resources can generate large revenues that enable states to foster growth, reduce poverty and help ensure the realization of human rights.

However, in the CLMV States where governance is weak, such exploitation may instead contribute to poverty, corruption, crime and conflict, with all the associated negative impacts on individuals' human rights. When states fail to meet their duty to protect human rights, the responsibility of extractive companies to respect human rights does not change; however, it can become all the more challenging for them to meet that responsibility in practice. The UN Working Group on Business and Human Rights[144] has recommended that the GPs be domestically incorporated into national or regional development and action plans consistent with the UN's post-2015 development agenda.[145]

---

[142]   Robert McCorquodale, 'Waving Not Drowning: *Kiobel* Outside the United States', (2013), *American Journal of International Law*, 107, 846 at 847–849; Michael D Goldhaber, 'Corporate Human Rights Litigation in Non-U.S. Courts—A Comparative Scorecard', (2013), *U C Irvine Law Review*, 3, at 127.

[143]   Jennifer Zerk, 'Corporate Liability for Gross Human Rights Abuses: Towards a Fairer and More Effective System of Domestic Law Remedies', report commissioned by the OHCHR, 2013, http://www.ohchr.org/Documents/Issues/Business/DomesticLawRemedies/StudyDomesticLawRemedies.pdf, at 53.

[144]   UNHRC, 26th Sess, UN Doc A/HRC/26/L.1 (24 June 2014). This resolution notes the important role that national action plans ... on business and human rights can play as a tool for promoting the comprehensive and effective implementation' of the GPs.

[145]   Joanne Bauer, 'Presentation on Behalf of Centre for Applied Legal Studies, Wits University (CALS) and Partners to the UN Working Group on Business and Human Rights Open Consultation on National Action Plans on Business and Human Rights', (Geneva, 20 February 2014) at para 7.

National / regional action plans

National action plans need to be flexible to respond to the concrete needs of each society. At the same time, states and other stakeholders in Southeast Asia require concrete guidance with information on how to deploy the GPs and need context-sensitive advice on what is expected of them, taking into account that the implementation of the GPs will take time and is a process made up of cumulative steps, with long-term goals.

Sabel and Zeitlin suggest that regulatory policy-making in any field comprise these four elements: (1) joint definition by Member States/stakeholders of initial objectives (general and specific), indicators and guidelines; (2) national reports or action plans which assess performance in light of the objectives and metrics and propose reforms accordingly; (3) peer review of these plans, including mutual criticism and exchange of good practices, backed up by recommendations in some cases; and (4) re-elaboration of the individual plans and, at less frequent intervals, of the broader objectives and metrics in light of the experience gained in their implementation.[146]

It bears mention that these kinds of 'soft' law-making techniques have emerged within the EU, and are a complement to 'hard' domestic legislation and transnational adjudication. ASEAN, too, should follow this example, especially where the legal basis for action is weak, the issues are domestically sensitive or where diversity among the CLMV (and other ASEAN) States precludes harmonization. In fact, AICHR's above-mentioned baseline study on corporate social responsibility and human rights is an example of one or more of these four elements and should pave the way for iterative deliberation, policy learning and implementation of business and human rights standards in the region.

It is proposed that such national/regional action plans are the way forward, and they should consider issues that are underexplored in the global conversation about business and human rights, such as those that have been considered in this chapter in the context of the specific concerns, risks and opportunities for these emerging economies in Southeast Asia. In light of the above, States and businesses should not only examine the role of a State's national institutions and foreign courts and commissions, but also carefully consider the 'role of markets, consultation processes, third party auditing and accreditation mechanisms, private grievance procedures and so forth'.[147] Legitimation of the GPs, and the manner in which they are deployed in these States such that these processes and methodologies enjoy a broad community acceptance, is required.

This pluralistic and decentralized approach to regulation is crucial in securing regulatory legitimacy and compliance in the face of the specific human rights challenges that CLMV States face. This author would recommend therefore that strategic national/regional action plans for regulation and enforcement should

---

[146]   See generally, C. Sabel and J. Zeitlin, (2003), 'Active Welfare, Experimental Governance, Pragmatic Constitutionalism: The New Transformation of Europe', on file with the author.

[147]   B. Morgan and K. Yeung, *An Introduction to Law and Regulation* (Cambridge University Press, Law In Context series, 2007), p. 11.

be devised that can provide guidance on how to address business and human rights challenges in the region, bearing in mind Professor Ruggie's refrain that any such action plan should 'follow the approach that has enabled us to get to this point: based on the premise that any course of action – voluntary, mandatory, or hybrid – should produce practical improvements in the lives of affected individuals and communities'.[148]

---

[148] John Ruggie, 'A UN Business and Human Rights Treaty?', (28 January 2014), p. 5.

Part III

8 Tigers, dragons, and elephants on the move in Myanmar

The case for responsible investment and three recommendations for Asian leaders

Mark Hodge and Salil Tripathi[1]

Introduction

In lifting most restrictions on investment in Burma/Myanmar following tangible signs of political reform in 2012,[2] governments that had imposed sanctions on the country since the mid-1990s have said that new investments should be 'responsible'.[3] The Myanmar Government has echoed this call, and it increasingly applies to foreign companies already operating in Burma. Well documented are the potential gains from investment in a country pursuing rapid economic growth,

---

[1] The authors wish to thank Donna Guest, Institute for Human Rights and Business, and Vicky Bowman, Myanmar Centre for Responsible Business, for their review and comments on an earlier version of this chapter. The authors bear the responsibility for any factual errors or misunderstandings. The authors also wish to note that circumstances in Myanmar, including investment and economic projects, are changing on a daily basis, so certain details may be out of date by the time of publishing. Nonetheless, they hope the sentiment and messages of the chapter remain relevant. The authors write here in their personal, not institutional, capacity.

[2] Following Burma's independence from Britain in 1948, civilian governments struggled to exert control over the ethnically diverse country, until a military coup deposed a civilian government in 1962, and subsequent nationalization and the Burmese Way to Socialism led to economic stagnation. Following the quashing of the 1988 pro-democracy uprising, the government also sought foreign investment to revive the economy, and held elections in 1990 whose results the military refused to recognize. Western nations imposed economic sanctions, which slowed Myanmar's economy significantly but did not cripple it. In April 2012, Myanmar held parliamentary by-elections to fill 45 seats vacated by representatives who were required to resign their seats upon assuming ministerial office, as per Myanmar's 2008 constitution. Moreover, hundreds of political prisoners have been released, although scores remain in detention or serving sentences. The government and ethnic minority armed opposition groups have embarked on a peace process, although it presents significant challenges. There is a greater degree of freedom of expression, peaceful assembly, and association today, although important restrictions are still in place. These political and human rights changes, coupled with promise of economic deregulation, convinced Western governments to relax, and later remove, some of the restrictions and sanctions.

[3] White House Press Office, 'Statement by the President on the Easing of Sanctions on Burma', (2011), http://www.whitehouse.gov/the-press-office/2012/07/11/statement-president-easing-sanctions-burma, accessed 11 December 2013; The Republic of the Union of Myanmar President Office, 'Press statement by co-Chairs Catherine Ashton, EU High Representative/ Vice President of the Commission U Soe Thane, Union Minister from Ministry of President's Office', (2013), http://www.president-office.gov.mm/en/?q=briefing-room/announcements/2013/11/17/id-2948, accessed 11 December 2013.

rich in natural resources and with 60 million prospective consumers. Investors will face daunting risks, which include unclear land ownership, questionable linkages of military personnel to State-owned or private enterprises, a nascent labour movement struggling to find its voice, and ongoing ethnic conflict.

Herein, we discuss the responsible investment imperatives and challenges for Asian investors, and offer a three-pronged framework for action for Asian companies to succeed. While Asian investors have been present in Myanmar for a long time, including during the sanctions period, they now face a new set of social challenges as well as competition from investors from the United States, Europe, Australia, New Zealand, Canada, and other countries that had imposed restrictions on economic ties with Myanmar. Asian firms may need to renegotiate agreements, address past social impacts, rehabilitate their reputation, or alter project time lines in order to address concerns regarding the social licence to operate that in an earlier period they could ignore.

The chapter is organized into three parts. Part one maps the special economic and commercial significance of Myanmar for Asia. Sandwiched between Asian powerhouses India and China, and part of the dynamic ASEAN grouping, Myanmar's strategic location is important. Myanmar could unlock trade routes and create important economic opportunities for its immediate neighbours. The section ends with a reflection on the ASEAN project, and what a stable, democratic, economically strong, and internationally accepted Myanmar could mean for it. Part two argues that Asian corporations must adapt and meet their responsibility to respect human rights in the face of recent developments in Myanmar. This starts with an acknowledgement that the culture of doing business is changing from a reliance on back-room deals and informal networks to more accountable and transparent corporate conduct. Many Asian investors have developed good relationships with the government, the military, and key Myanmar businesses. While such relationships have provided the legal licence to operate, they are not sufficient, in that they do not imply the social licence to operate. The focus should then turn to the substantive human rights and social challenges that all companies will have to confront when investing or operating in Myanmar. While Asian investors have not been confronted by sanctions, there are multiple recent developments regarding responsible business conduct and human rights that Asian investors should take seriously (including the UN Guiding Principles on Business and Human Rights,[4] the ASEAN Human Rights Declaration,[5] and Asian NGO proposals regarding corporate accountability[6]). Ultimately, though, the most significant drivers of responsible investment will come from within Myanmar itself.

---

[4] UN Human Rights Council, *Report of the Special Representative of the Secretary – General on the Issue of Human Rights and Transnational Corporations and Other Business Enterprises, John Ruggie: Guiding Principles on Business and Human Rights: Implementing the United Nations 'Protect, Respect and Remedy' Framework*, (2011), 16 June 2011, A/HRC/17/31.

[5] *ASEAN Human Rights Declaration* (Adopted 19 November 2012), http://www.asean.org/news/asean-statement-communiques/item/asean-human-rights-declaration?category_id=26, accessed 2 January 2014.

[6] For example, Yap Swee Seng and John Liu (eds), 'Corporate Accountability in ASEAN: A Human Rights-Based Approach', (2013), Asian Forum for Human Rights and Development,

Existing cases, reports, and campaigns indicate that scrutiny of Asian companies by Myanmar's people, communities, and grassroots organizations is increasing, supported by an interconnected Asian civil society. The concluding part offers a three-pronged framework for governments and companies from across Asia to invest responsibly in Myanmar.

1   First, investment and trade agreements should uphold the protection and respect of human rights. This should apply to bilateral investment treaties, free trade agreements, concessions/licences to exploit natural resources and large-footprint projects in Myanmar.
2   Second, Asian governments should encourage, even require and resource, human rights due diligence and responsible business reporting by corporations that they support via trade missions, investment guarantees, and public finance.
3   Third, Asian corporations should evolve well beyond corporate social responsibility (CSR) or traditional corporate philanthropy in order to address the social impacts of business throughout the lifecycle of projects. Companies should meet their responsibility to respect human rights, with special attention to land, conflict, and complicity in international crimes.

Part one

Myanmar's special significance for Asia

Up and down littoral Myanmar all of Asia's big economies are opening up new trade routes to reach neglected parts of the Asian land mass. The results could transform large swathes of the continent.'Rites of Passage', *The Economist*, May 2013.[7]

Asian companies and economies have much to gain from an economically resurgent and politically stable Myanmar. Part of this concerns cementing their first-mover advantage gained, in part, as a consequence of Western sanctions. Data from the European Commission shows that in 2012 the top ten import, export and trade countries for Myanmar were all Asian.[8] A 2013 Asia Development Bank Report emphasizes the natural wealth of Myanmar and reiterates the current prominence of Asian trade partners, stating:

Myanmar is endowed with rich natural resources, including petroleum, timber, tin, antimony, zinc, copper, tungsten, lead, coal, marble, limestone,

http://www.forum-asia.org/uploads/publications/2013/September/Corporate-Accountability-ASEAN-FINAL.pdf, accessed 28 November 2013.
[7] *The Economist*, 'Special Report on Myanmar: Rites of Passage', (2013), http://www.economist.com/news/special-report/21578174-opening-up-myanmar-could-transform-rest-asia-rite-passage, accessed 11 December 2013.
[8] EU Directorate-General of Trade, 'European Union, Trade with Myanmar', (2013), http://trade.ec.europa.eu/doclib/docs/2006/september/tradoc_113423.pdf, accessed 18 December 2013.

precious stones, natural gas, and hydropower. In 2011, natural gas, wood products, pulses, beans, fish, rice, clothing, jade, and gems were its largest export commodities. Its top export destinations in 2011 were the PRC, India and Thailand, while its top import sources were the PRC, Singapore and Thailand.[9]

With the easing of Western sanctions, Asian countries and their enterprises will now have to compete with Western actors for market share, as governments and multinational corporations seek to unlock Myanmar as one of the final frontiers of globalization.

For capital-surplus Asian countries, Myanmar is an attractive destination for foreign direct investment (FDI). Once integrated fully with the global economy, Myanmar's value to Asia may be disproportionately large, since it lies at the crossroads of China, India, and Southeast Asia. While the mantra of globalization is that the world is 'flat', the fact is that even in a globalized world, hard geographical contours matter. The success and global influence of trading ports and cities such as the seventh-century Srivijaya, the fifteenth-century Malacca, the nineteenth-century Bombay, and the twenty-first-century Hong Kong and Singapore demonstrate the very physical drivers of Asia's economic place in the world. Myanmar fits into this narrative. Myanmar has approximately 6,000 kilometres of international borders with Bangladesh, China, India, Laos, and Thailand. The country's coastline runs south from the Bay of Bengal for almost 3,000 kilometres, jutting into major international shipping lanes in the Indian Ocean.[10] Beyond its importance for regional integration, the economic development of Myanmar may significantly address the energy needs, internal security imperatives, and economic growth aspirations of its largest neighbours – China, India, and Thailand. All of this has led to efforts by Asian actors – many ongoing for some time – to upgrade or establish major ports, roads, railways, export processing zones, and pipelines across Myanmar.

Investments and business interests

In June 2013, the *Wall Street Journal* reported a 'sharp fall' in Chinese investment in Myanmar (US$1.42 billion in 2012–2013, down from US$4.62 billion the year before).[11] Nonetheless, the article notes 'still, China remains Myanmar's largest trading partner. Myanmar imported $175 million of Chinese goods in

[9] Asian Development Bank, 'Connecting South Asia and South-East Asia – Interim Report', (2013), Japan: Asian Development Bank Institute., http://www.adbi.org/files/2013.05.05.book.connecting.south.asia.southeast.asia.interim.report.pdf, accessed 18 January 2014.

[10] D. Steinberg, *Burma/Myanmar: What Everyone Needs to Know* (Oxford: Oxford University Press, 2013), p. 8.

[11] J. Gronholt-Pedersen, 'Chinese Investment in Myanmar Falls Sharply', *Wall Street Journal*, (2013), http://online.wsj.com/news/articles/SB10001424127887324063304578525021254736996?mg= reno64-wsjandurl=http%3A%2F%2Fonline.wsj.com%2Farticle%2FSB10001424127887324063 3045785252021254736996.html, accessed 10 December 2013.

March – mainly machinery, base metals and transportation equipment – making up nearly a third of total imports for the month'. In 2008, a report from Earth Rights International listed eighty hydropower and extractive corporations from China in the country.[12] Myanmar holds a strategic significance for China. First, Chinese access to the Indian Ocean, South and Southeast Asian markets requires routing through Myanmar to avoid the congested Straits of Malacca. To this end, China already has or is in the process of constructing new oil and gas pipelines that will serve as arteries and capillaries for hydrocarbons between China, Africa, and the Middle East. The main example of this is the Shwe Gas pipeline that runs from Kyaukphyu in Rakhine State in the west, up to Mandalay, and then across the border to Yunnan province. Second, economic activity in Yunnan province is key for China. Yunnan shares an extensive border with Myanmar, and Beijing sees trade through Yunnan as a key tool to maintain internal stability in remote, south-western, ethnically diverse provinces that have not benefited from the boom in China's eastern seaboard. Economic development here, the theory goes, will partly address the growing discontent in inland China.[13] Other economic activities in Yunnan linked to Myanmar include tourism and markets for Myanmar's jade (extracted from mines exploited by the military and Kachin and other armed opposition groups).

Looking further afield in East Asia, in a May 2013 visit to Myanmar, Japan's Prime Minister Shinzo Abe pledged to lend Myanmar US$500 million and to cancel US$1.74 billion of debt.[14] A portion of Japanese Overseas Development Assistance will be focused on infrastructure development around the Thilawa port, south of Yangon.[15] A Japanese consortium made up of three major Japanese companies (Mitsubishi Corporation, Marubeni Corporation and Sumitomo Corporation)[16] is set to lead development of the Burmese-led 2,500 hectare Special Economic Zone at Thilawa. In 2012, Japan and Myanmar agreed a plan to make communications network improvements (including a high-speed, high-capacity core optical transmission network between Naypyitaw, Yangon, and Mandalay). This involves another Japanese consortium.[17] For its part, South Korea

[12] Earth Rights International, 'China in Burma: the Increasing Investment of Chinese Multinational Corporations in Burma's Hydropower, Oil and Natural Gas, and Mining Sectors', (2008), http://www.burmalibrary.org/docs5/China_in_Burma-ERI.pdf, accessed 10 December 2013.

[13] M. Lubina, 'China's Burma Policy Seen from Yunnan', (2012), EU-Asia Centre, http://eu-asiacentre.eu/pub_details.php?pub_id=69, accessed 10 December 2013.

[14] S. Roughneen, 'Japan Making up for Lost Time', (2012), *The Irrawaddy*, http://www.irrawaddy.org/japan/japan-making-up-for-lost-time-in-burma.html, accessed 10 December 2013.

[15] Japan International Cooperation Agency, 'Press Release: ODA Loan Agreements signed with the Republic of the Union of Myanmar', (2013), http://www.jica.go.jp/english/news/press/2013/130607_01.html, accessed 10 December 2013.

[16] Mitsubishi Corporation Website, 'Establishment of a Consortium for the development of the Thilawa SEZ', (2013), http://www.mitsubishicorp.com/jp/en/pr/archive/2013/html/0000022732.html, accessed 10 December 2013.

[17] Web RTC World, 'Sumitomo Corporation, NEC Corporation and NTT Communications Corporation Provide Communications Infrastructure in Myanmar', (2013), http://www.webrtc-world.com/news/2013/12/04/7576866.htm, accessed 10 December 2013.

has committed fresh loans (US$500 million from 2014 to 2017), and is building a bridge to link Yangon to Dala (where an industrial zone may be established). The *Wall Street Journal* reports that official statistics show South Korean investment in Myanmar amounted to US$2.98 billion in seventy-seven projects as of March 2013.[18] South Korea's major corporations such as POSCO and Daewoo are already being touted as implementers of these schemes.[19]

After China, Thailand is the largest investor in Myanmar,[20] but Thailand has a long and complicated history with Myanmar. According to one Myanmar NGO, the Thai government is interested in the energy sector in particular, with a focus on hydropower along the Salween River and the Tasang dam, in which the Thai government invested US$6 million. The NGO also estimated that Thailand relies on Myanmar for some 20 per cent of its domestic energy consumption.[21] Both the Thai government (since 2008) and the Japanese government (more tentatively since 2010) have been in discussions with Myanmar regarding the Dawei deep-water port and Special Economic Zone in the south-east of the country. Consequently, multiple companies from these countries are involved, or interested, in developing or servicing the project. The most prominent of these has been Ital-Thai Development Plc (ITD – an Italian–Thai Joint Venture). As we note below (in Part two), the Dawei project has been highly controversial with unions, local populations and NGOs criticizing land acquisition, environmental impacts, and ITD business practices.

A 2012 *Asia Times* article notes that 'As of October 2011, Singapore was the sixth-largest source of foreign direct investment in Myanmar, with 74 Singaporean companies contributing a total of US$1.8 billion, according to Myanmar's Ministry of National Planning and Economic Development.'[22]

---

18 *The Wall Street Journal*, 'Myanmar, S. Korean Firms Sign Memo on Economic Cooperation', (2013), http://online.wsj.com/article/BT-CO-20130518–700105.html, accessed 10 December 2013.

19 It should, however, be noted that companies from Asia, including POSCO and Daewoo are increasingly facing the scrutiny of international investors over their conduct in emerging markets. In 2011 and 2012, the Council of Ethics in Norway, which recommends to the State authorities how to invest the country's oil revenues, had named Daewoo and Korean Gas Corp, along with two Indian companies (ONGC and GAIL India) to exclude them from the portfolio of investments of the government global pension fund. The companies were building an 800 km pipeline in Myanmar, and the Council of Ethics felt that it represented unacceptable human rights risks. In 2013, noting that the pipeline had already been constructed, the Council of Ethics revoked the recommendation to exclude the companies. http://www.regjeringen.no/en/sub/styrer-rad-utvalg/ethics_council/Recommendations/Recommendations/recommendations-on-human-rights/recommendations-from-2011–2012-and-2013-.html?id=748076, accessed 4 March 2014.

20 Directorate of Investment and Company Administration – Government of Myanmar, 'Data on Foreign Investment, Local Investment and Company Registration', (2013), http://www.dica.gov.mm/dicagraph1.htm, accessed 13 January 2013). See original article at Mizzima, 'Foreign Investment Figures Highlight China's Dominance', (2013), http://www.mizzima.com/business/investment/item/10445-foreign-investment-figures-highlight-china-s-dominance, accessed 13 January 2014.

21 Arakan Rivers Network, 'Thai-Burma Relations', (2009), http://www.arakanrivers.net/?page_id=152, accessed 10 December 2013.

22 M. Wijaya, 'Myanmar Lures Singapore Inc', (2013), *Asia Times*, http://www.atimes.com/atimes/Southeast_Asia/NC20Ae01.html, accessed 10 December 2013.

Singaporean companies operating in the country, seeking joint ventures or bidding for licences include Yongnam (currently bidding for two airport projects), Ezion (shipping), Interra Resource (the largest onshore oil producer in Myanmar), and a range of mining and minerals firms.[23] In 2013, a Malaysian news agency reported that investment in Myanmar from Malaysia amounted to US$1 billion in 2012, and noted that this as mainly in the areas of oil and gas, hotels, plastics, and seafood.[24] Palm oil is Malaysia's major export to Myanmar, with the main import being crude rubber. Major Malaysian oil companies have been in Myanmar for some time, including Petronas (who purchased in 2002 the interests of the British firm Premier Oil, which had faced a sustained campaign and pressure to divest)[25] and the diversified group UMW Holdings (who were targeted by the UK Burma Campaign in 2008).[26] In 2012/2013, several new deals involving Malaysian companies were announced or under discussion, including the manufacturing and distribution of car parts by APM[27] and Tan Chong (a joint venture with Japanese car maker Nissan);[28] a US$750 million power plant to supply the Mandalay Region led by Mudajaya Holdings;[29] and the purchase of 30,000 hectares of land for sugarcane by FELDA Global Ventures Holdings (a government-linked corporation considered to be the world's largest plantation operator).[30]

[23] *Singapore Business Review*, 'Check Out Why These Firms Invest in Myanmar', (2013), http://sbr.com. sg/markets-investing/news/check-out-why-these-singapore-firms-invest-in-myanmar, accessed 10 December 2013.

[24] Mizzima News, 'Myanmar-Malaysia Trade Expected to Top $1 billion', (2013), http://mizzimaenglish.blogspot.com/2013/02/myanmar-malaysia-trade-expected-to-top.html, accessed 10 December 2013.

[25] T. Macalister, 'Premier Oil Gets Out of Burma', (2002), *The Guardian*, http://www.theguardian. com/business/2002/sep/17/oilandpetrol.news1, accessed 10 December 2013. See also Petronas Website 'Myanmar', (2002), http://www.petronas.com.my/community-education/community/global-outreach-programme/Pages/global-outreach-programme/myanmar.aspx; and http://www.premier-oil.com/premieroil/about/history, accessed 14 January 2014.

[26] At the time of writing, the Burma Campaign no longer publishes this list (see http://www.burmacampaign.org.uk/index.php/campaigns/more-info/dirty-list). This letter from UMW to the Business and Human Rights Resource Centre (London-based NGO) provides information about UMW investment in Myanmar and references the Burma Campaign. See. Business and Human Rights Resource Centre, 'UMW Holdings Berhard Responds to Burma Campaign UK', (2009), http://www.reports-and-materials.org/UMW-response-re-Burma-20-Jan-2009.pdf, accessed 10 December 2013.

[27] *The Star Online*, 'APM Automotive Gets Myanmar Nod to Set up Plant', (2013), http://www.thestar. com.my/Business/Business-News/2013/10/17/APM-Automotive-gets-Myanmar-nod-to-set-up-plant.aspx, accessed 13 January 201).

[28] NTD Television, 'Japan's Nissan to Produce Cars In Myanmar', (2013), http://www.ntd.tv/en/news/world/asia-pacific/20130920/82795-japan39s-nissan-to-produce-cars-in-myanmar.html, accessed 13 January 2014.

[29] C. Myers, 'Mudajay Outlines MDY Power Plant', (2013), *Myanmar Times*, http://www.mmtimes.com/index.php/business/3924-mudajaya-outlines-mdy-power-plant.html, accessed 10 December 2013.

[30] *New Straits Times*, 'Felda Global to Develop Complete Supply Chain in Myanmar', (2012), http://www.nst.com.my/latest/felda-global-to-develop-complete-supply-chain-in-myanmar-1.150933, accessed 10 December 2013.

To the immediate west, India also has interests in Myanmar. India's *Economic Times* reported in June 2013 that investment 'is expected to soar to $2.6 billion over the next few years'.[31] Several major Indian companies already operate in Myanmar, such as ONGC Videsh Limited, Essar Energy, and Jubilant Oil and Gas. Others, including Tata Motors, have trading relationships. In turn, several health-care and pharmaceutical enterprises have distribution relationships.[32] The centrepiece of India's interest is the construction of the Sittwe deep-water port on the Bay of Bengal, underway since 2010. The port is being financed by India to the tune of over US$100 million and is part of a larger effort to link Myanmar and north-east Asia – the Kaladan Multi-Modal Transit Transport Project.[33] Like the Dawei port and other projects, the Kaladan project is also the subject of criticism and concern from local communities.[34]

Not dissimilar to China's Yunnan strategy, India is seeking to address its own domestic challenges in its north-eastern states. These states have historically challenged rule from New Delhi, with some states having experienced insurgencies. A 2013 Chatham House report notes:

> The land border includes four of India's unstable and politically-sensitive northeastern states and the influx of drugs, arms, immigrants and militants from Burma has long been a cause of concern for the Indian government. As well as these threats, the shared border also presents opportunity. There is potential to greatly increase border trade, and a mooted gas pipeline between the two countries would be of great benefit to India's underdeveloped North East.[35]

ASEAN and Myanmar

Myanmar will be the chair of ASEAN for 2014, which places further scrutiny upon the sincerity of the country's reforms. In the past, Myanmar's membership in ASEAN caused tension between ASEAN and Western countries that objected to Myanmar joining in 1997. Beyond impacting the social project of ASEAN, the steps Myanmar takes to deregulate its economy will be closely watched as the region prepares to set up the ASEAN Economic Community (AEC), scheduled for launch

---

[31] *The Economic Times*, 'Look East Policy: India Underperforming Its Role in Myanmar', (2013), http://articles.economictimes.indiatimes.com/2013-10-02/news/42617389_1_foreign-investment-total-trade-volume-china, accessed 10 December 2013.

[32] G. Price, *India's Policy Towards Burma* (London: Chatham House, 2013), http://www.chathamhouse.org/sites/default/files/public/Research/Asia/0613pp_indiaburma.pdf, accessed 10 December 2013.

[33] Ministry of Development for North Eastern Region (MDONER), 'Kaladan Multi-Modal Transit Transport Project', Government of India, http://mdoner.gov.in/content/introduction-1, accessed 10 December 2013.

[34] Kaladan Movement, 'One Cannot Step into the Same River Twice: Making the Kaladan Project People-Centered', (2013), https://dl.dropboxusercontent.com/u/102872850/KM_Report_Eng.pdf, accessed 10 December 2013.

[35] Ibid. Price, *India's Policy Towards Burma*, p. 2, see n. 32.

in 2015. Myanmar could gain economically from the AEC. One US-sponsored study estimates a 4.4 per cent increase in national income and 66 per cent increase in exports to its fellow ASEAN Members. [36] If Myanmar stutters on reforms, or fails to manage its internal conflict in ways that protect human rights, the impact will be felt by ASEAN Member States. The ambitious infrastructure plans such as those set out above will no doubt falter or hit dead end. On the flip side, the AEC could pose specific problems for Myanmar, such as accentuating competition with neighbours in relation to agriculture and low-skilled manufacturing exports such as textiles. Indeed, some in Myanmar have expressed the view that the country is not ready for the AEC.[37]

Myanmar is key to considering ASEAN linkages to the South Asian sub-continent. A 2013 joint interim study of the Asian Development Bank, 'Connecting South Asia and South-East Asia' addresses the economic ties between the two Asian sub-regions.[38] The report focuses on trade and investment links, physical transport infrastructure, energy infrastructure and trading, trade facilitation, financing infrastructure, and policy reforms. The premise of the report is that, while trade between the two sub-regions has grown dramatically in the past decade (increasing nearly twenty-two times from US\$4 billion to US\$86 billion between 1990 and 2011), it is still below potential. The report notes that: 'By virtue of its strategic location straddling South Asia and Southeast Asia, the recent opening up of Myanmar in political, economic, and financial terms presents a significant new opportunity for enhancing these integration efforts, with the promise of substantial gains for both sub regions',[39] and that the 'key physical barriers or hindrances to sub-regional trade are located mainly in Myanmar, the only land bridge between these sub-regions'.[40] The report then catalogues multiple infrastructure projects underway and a number of sub-regional trade/connectivity programmes. Many of these involve Myanmar, such as the Bay of Bengal Initiative for Multi-Sectoral Technical and Economic Cooperation (established in 1997); the Greater Mekong Sub-region (est. 1992); Mekong-Ganga Cooperation (est. 2000) and the Mekong-India Economic Corridor (est. 2008).[41]

It is important not to exaggerate economic activity or conflate ideas, diplomatic overtures, photo-shoot pronouncements, and intentions with actual money invested, people employed, and assets created on the ground in Myanmar. The *Wall Street Journal* struck a realistic note among the chorus of investor enthusiasm

[36] Peter A. Petri, Michael G. Plummer and Fan Zhai, *The Economics of the ASEAN Economic Community*, (2010). Brandeis University, Department of Economics and International Businesss School Working Paper 13, pp. 21 and 18.

[37] Z. Mann, 'Burma Not Ready for ASEAN Economic Community, Businesspeople Say', (2013). *The Irrawady*, http://www.irrawaddy.org/economy/burma-not-ready-for-asean-economic-community-businesspeople-say.html, accessed 3 January 2014.

[38] Asian Development Bank (ADB) and Asia Development Bank Institute (ADBI), 'Connecting South Asia and South-East Asia: Interim Report', (2013), http://www.adbi.org/files/2013.05.05.book.connecting.south.asia.southeast.asia.interim.report.pdf, accessed 3 January 2014.

[39] Ibid. ADB: 2013, p. 11.

[40] Ibid. ADB: 2013, p. 13.

[41] Ibid. ADB: 2013, pp. 58 and 59.

following the Asia meeting of the June 2013 World Economic Forum in Naypyitaw. They reported that 'foreign direct investment in the year that ended in March amounted to just $1.4 billion. Lao PDR, with about a 10th of Myanmar's population, received the same amount of FDI in calendar 2012'.[42] It went on to discuss various barriers to rapid investment in Myanmar, such as decades of sanctions, power shortages, lack of a skilled workforce, and unclear regulation. To that, add uncertainty about the future direction the country will take after presidential elections in 2015. But two things are clear. First, Asia's major powers want a stake in the future of Myanmar and are *already* invested – presumably, they do not want their dominant position to be disrupted. Second, several high-profile Asian investments are being challenged or criticized by local communities and civil society across the region. A February 2013 report titled 'Developing Disparity: Regional investment in Burma's Borderlands', published by the Transnational Institute, provides an excellent and comprehensive overview of these challenges and states that, '(w)ithout basic and democratic protections in place) … the development of Asia's final frontier will only deepen disparity between the region's poorest and most neglected peoples and the military, business and new political elites whose wealth is rapidly consolidating'.[43] Myanmar could be the final piece in the puzzle of ensuring the twenty-first century is the 'Asian Century'. But Asian investors now need to tread more carefully and act responsibly.

Part two

No immunity from social realities and expectations

> Foreign direct investment that results in job-creation should be invited. Investors should adhere to codes of best practices. Track records in regards to internationally recognized labour standards and environmental responsibility should be examined. Aung San Suu Kyi, *Speech to International Labour Conference*, Geneva, June 2012[44]

To grow its economy, Myanmar needs investment as well as access to global markets and technology. This can have profoundly positive effects on the realization of human rights, even if investors' primary interest may not have anything directly to do with human rights. Good jobs improve living standards, companies can create healthy and safe employment opportunities, and their taxes fund urgently needed public services. But economic activities or corporate conduct may

---

[42] N. Bereton-Fukui, 'Myanmar Still Lags in Foreign Investment', (2013), *The Wall Street Journal*, http://online.wsj.com/news/articles/SB10001424127887324063304578520633473332690, accessed 3 January 2014.

[43] M. Smith (ed.), 'Developing Disparity – Regional Investment in Burma's Borderlands. Transnational Institute', (2013), http://www.burmalibrary.org/docs14/Burmasborderlands-red.pdf, accessed 3 January 2014.

[44] ILO Press Release. 'Statement by Aung San Suu Kyi at the 101st International Labour Conference', (2012), http://www.ilo.org/global/about-the-ilo/media-centre/statements-and-speeches/WCMS_183369/lang--en/index.htm, accessed 3 January 2014.

sometimes have adverse impacts that pose major risks to human rights. This can fuel social discontent and conflict, which in turn undermines economic growth. Asian public and private investors were not necessarily required to comply with Western governments' sanctions on Myanmar, and many continued to do business. Affected communities are already using newfound freedoms to protest against old and new investments, including questioning the basis on which concessions, licences and investments were approved in the first place. While Asian investors may not face the same scrutiny in their home countries home as Western investors do, changes in Myanmar society are so profound that it will not be business as usual. The question is whether Asian business leaders and their governments have the capacity, skills, and ability to manage the new dynamics and navigate the path ahead.

A new business culture: from 'know-who' to 'know-how'

Western investor interest in Myanmar poses a multi-pronged challenge for Asian businesses already operating there without global scrutiny or attention. The absence of such scrutiny has enabled Asian businesses to operate without necessarily making significant investment in health and safety, without setting standards for wages, and by pursuing deals with powerful local business entities without necessary due diligence concerning their antecedents. The Cantonese word *guanxi*, or connections, essentially embodies the idea that connections can substitute for expertise, capability, and performance. Kinship provides comfort level and breeds trust – as sociologists have noted in what they call the bamboo network, an overseas Chinese investor in another country would seek out a trader from his background, possibly from the same village of his ancestors or speaking the same dialect. Indian attitudes when operating abroad and in India itself can be similar. Indian companies often seek out employees or representatives from Indians settled in the country where operations are to be located.

To the Western investor this seems like nepotism, even corruption. But the Asian investor would argue: how different is it from a consortium of European companies working together, or American companies buying only from American suppliers? In any case, Myanmar lacks institutions that can intermediate between market players (e.g. stock markets, information vendors, rating agencies, brokerage houses)[45] and in this context, informal networks often take over. Those networks tend to develop organically, based on trust or prior contact. Cultural and social factors do influence these choices, but the absence of other independent or fair means to assess partners leaves them with little choice. This, however, is a somewhat benign explanation. In reality, in many emerging markets, striking business deals with the *nomenklatura* – or people from the privileged, elite classes – ensures success. A former dean of a business school in Southeast Asia told one of the authors of this chapter: 'In Southeast Asia it is not know-how, but know-who.' This is changing and the change

---

[45] Tarun Khanna and Krishna Palepu, *Winning in Emerging Markets* (Harvard Business School Press, 2012).

is more pronounced in Myanmar. For example, Myanmar's decision to participate in some international initiatives concerning corporate responsibility and transparency shows the State's willingness to reform. The title of an April 2013 *Wall Street Journal Blog* about developments in Myanmar captures the mood – 'Myanmar's clean house – China's worst nightmare?' The article dealt with Myanmar's moves to sign the Extractive Industries Transparency Initiative (addressed below), and quoted a Hong Kong-based consultant who notes that, after decades of favourable deals with Myanmar generals, China now needs to get used to 'doing it the hard way (and increasingly in Myanmar) it is the only way'.[46]

Myanmar has historically been suspicious of all its neighbours, including China. Its recent closeness with China had more to do with Myanmar's isolation from the rest of the world than any specific affinity towards China. The recent changes, suggesting an about-turn, may have as much to do with Myanmar needing some space between itself and China as with its desire to re-engage the West.[47] In the past, some of Myanmar's generals fought battles with the Communist Party of Burma that received support from China. For such generals, for entrepreneurs keen to access the latest technology, and for many people who do not like the influx of Chinese workers in Myanmar, the opening to the West is a boon.

All companies, both Western and Asian, should welcome the changes in Myanmar and respect international labour standards and human rights wherever they do business. Asian companies should seize the opportunity to raise their game. This is not to suggest that Western companies always have higher standards or always abide by those standards. But the sophistication of Western markets, longer traditions of accountability, vibrant free press, and an active civil society have combined to create accountability mechanisms and countervailing institutions that apply pressure to and, in turn, improve practices of companies.

Social realities in factors of production

Classical economics hold that there are three basic factors of production (inputs into any value creation or production process) – land, labour, and capital. In Myanmar, securing these inputs carries risk of exposure to human rights challenges and possible abuses. Risks are compounded by a history of ethnic conflict. The London-based Institute for Human Rights and Business laid out these issues in a paper titled 'Responsible Investment in Myanmar: The Human Rights Dimension.'[48] The following sections draw on that analysis.

46 G. Robinson, 'Myanmar Clean House – China's Worst Nightmare?', (2013), *The Financial Times*, http://blogs. ft.com/beyond-brics/2013/04/15/myanmar-cleans-house-chinas-worst-nightmare/#axzz2qrI5kqdu, accessed 3 January 2014.

47 Bertil Lintner, 'China Behind Myanmar's Course Shift', (2011), *Asia Times*, http://www.atimes. com/atimes/Southeast_Asia/MJ19Ae03.html, accessed 31 Jan 2014.

48 Salil Tripathi, 'Responsible Business in Myanmar: The Human Rights Dimension', (2012), London: Institute for Human Rights and Business (IHRB), http://www.ihrb.org/pdf/Occasional-Paper-1-Burma-Myanmar-FINAL.pdf, accessed 3 January 2014.

LAND

Any business will need access to land – to build a retail store, develop a port, erect power lines or telecom towers, construct factories, develop golf courses, create tourism complexes, or establish export processing zones. Human rights groups have criticized the land-acquisition process in Myanmar as being non-transparent. Customary users of land may not have legal title, and registering land titles is complicated. There are allegations of 'land grabs'. Forced eviction is often the norm. Under new land laws, people have to register their land with the State. But civil-society groups contend that small farmers, including farmers in ethnic and/or remote areas, may not know of the proposed changes, and companies or well-connected individuals may end up acquiring such plots, regardless of having identified legal or customary owners. Once the new owners acquire legal title, they can seek access to land, and should they meet resistance, security forces intervene to ensure access. Sometimes force is used to evict people, leading to further human rights violations.

Establishing land titles is not easy in Myanmar. Under international standards, indigenous communities have the right to Free Prior Informed Consent, but in Myanmar there are no communities recognized as 'indigenous'.[49] However, many companies consider it good practice to seek the informed consent of all affected parties and vulnerable groups before using or acquiring land. But consultation with local communities is not always practical. In Myanmar's case, local communities sometimes fear the consequences of speaking freely to outsiders. Historically, many businesses have come upon land acquired forcibly or after paying inadequate or no compensation to the legal or customary owners. Communities may be reluctant to be frank in consultation processes. Any business investing in Myanmar will struggle to ensure that they have obtained consent after a fully consultative process and without force. They will have to use their leverage over security forces to ensure they follow international norms and principles governing use of force.[50]

LABOUR

Until recently, Myanmar did not allow independent trade unions, and workers' rights have been violated routinely. New labour laws provide for independent trade unions for the first time in fifty years. But workers are frequently required to

[49]   UN General Assembly, 'United Nations Declaration on the Rights of Indigenous Peoples: reso-lution/adopted by the General Assembly', 2 October 2007, A/RES/61/295, http://www.refworld. org/docid/471355a82.html, accessed 22 January 2014. Article 10 explicitly states: 'Indigenous peoples shall not be forcibly removed from their lands or territories. No relocation shall take place without the free, prior and informed consent of the indigenous peoples concerned and after agree-ment on just and fair compensation and, where possible, with the option of return.'

[50]   United Nations, 'Code of Conduct for Law Enforcement Officials', (1979), adopted by General Assembly resolution 34/169 of 17 December 1979, http://www.ohchr.org/EN/ProfessionalInterest/ Pages/LawEnforcementOfficials.aspx, accessed 31 January 2014; and United Nations (1990) 'Basic Principles on the Use of Force and Firearms by Law Enforcement Officials', adopted by the Eighth United Nations Congress on the Prevention of Crime and the Treatment of Offenders, Havana, Cuba, 27 August to 7 September 1990, http://www.ohchr.org/EN/ProfessionalInterest/Pages/ UseOfForceAndFirearms.aspx, accessed 31 January 2014.

work far longer than the legally permitted hours; their wages remain low; women workers have been sexually harassed; and gender-based discrimination is common. In many cases, employees receive few benefits, and jobs are terminated without due process. Since early 2012, workers have begun forming unions at the enterprise level and have faced resistance in some cases. Myanmar has also historically faced allegations of forced labour. For companies that poses a challenge. There is a tradition in Myanmar whereby communities perform collective labour for public works. Experienced executives distinguish between such collective public work and cases where military or local authorities have forced villagers to work on a public project. In the latter case, people are working against their will, offered no payment, and are required to work as porters, or to build infrastructure, or on farming projects. Executives say it is difficult to sift through nuances to find out if every individual in a collective effort has consented to do so. While forced labour has been decreasing, it remains a serious problem, especially in the ethnic minority states, where conflict persists or is likely, and the army presence is still strong. With Myanmar communities reopening old cases, companies will need to be aware of such legacy issues – how was the infrastructure they now own or use built? Can they satisfy themselves that the infrastructure they use was not built using forced labour? Was due process followed in acquiring land?

CAPITAL

Access to capital is a major challenge in Myanmar. Transactional inconveniences are easing slowly. With the opening of a few cash points where foreign cards can be used, transactions for foreign visitors have become simpler. But other concerns remain. Money laundering is an old allegation affecting some banks that operated through the sanction years. Recent reforms suggest that standards might improve, but risk of exposure to allegations of links with past illicit trade remains. Companies will have to undertake enhanced due diligence of their financial intermediaries. This means not only checking financial soundness and liquidity, but also business practices, including current and previous business relationships.

CONFLICT

Investors also must note Myanmar's fragile ethnic balance, with several groups – Karen, Shan, Kachin, Karenni, Mon, Rakhine, Palaung, Pa'O, Wa, Kokang, and Chin – having historically fought for greater autonomy or independence. The national government has had to struggle to establish control over the seven ethnic minority states in Myanmar's borderlands. Many of those areas have precious minerals and natural resources in which companies have an interest. Human rights groups have researched smuggling of jade and other precious stones from these areas.[51] Some companies have also struck lucrative relationships

---

[51]   Human Rights Watch, 'Burma: Foreign Investment Finances Regime', (2013), http://www.hrw.org/ news/2007/11/11/burma-gem-trade-bolsters-military-regime-fuels-atrocities, accessed 6 January

with field commanders – from government forces or armed opposition groups. Disentangling those relationships will not be easy for legitimate businesses. These areas expose companies to complicity risks of the type that are described in the Red Flags Initiative.[52] The Red Flags cover exposure risks to grave international crimes where the statute of limitations may not apply, and depending on their gravity, universal jurisdiction may apply. Companies operating in Myanmar are not always going to be at risk of being complicit in such abuses, but some areas are unstable and the situation is critical, which may escalate risks. Rigorous due diligence is, therefore, essential and companies should operate in areas where they can be reasonably certain that their actions will not cause or contribute to any human rights abuses.

International, national and regional standards

One of the most significant recent international developments with regard to corporate responsibility is the UN endorsement of the Guiding Principles or UNGPs in 2011.[53] Chapter 1 of this volume provides an overview of the UNGPs, approved unanimously by the UN Human Rights Council, as the Council did with the UN *Protect, Respect and Remedy* Framework in 2008. Endorsing governments included many major Asian investors in Myanmar – China, India, Thailand, Indonesia, Malaysia, Japan, and South Korea.[54]

Ignoring the normative expectations of the UNGPs in conducting business is becoming less and less feasible. This is partly because other corporate social responsibility standards (both voluntary and mandatory) converge around them – for example, the OECD Guidelines for Multinational Enterprises[55] and ISO 26000.[56] In Asia, there are early signs of convergence: the Indonesian Capital Market and Financial Institution Supervisory Agency requirement that listed companies report information on social responsibility (labour, community development

2014; and *Asia Times*, 'Illicit Trade Imperils Burma's Reforms', (2013), http://www.atimes.com/atimes/Southeast_Asia/SEA-02–230713.html, accessed 6 January 2014.

[52] International Alert, 'Red Flags: Liability Risks for Companies Operating in High Risk Zones', (2008), http://www.redflags.info, accessed 10 December 2013. These are: (a) expelling people from their communities, (b) forcing people to work, (c) handling questionable assets, (d) making illicit payments, (e) engaging abusive security forces, (f) trading goods in violation of international sanctions, (g) providing the means to kill, (h) allowing the use of company assets for abuses, and (i) financing international crimes.

[53] UN Human Rights Council. 'Report of the Special Representative of the Secretary – General on the issue of human rights and transnational corporations and other business enterprises, John Ruggie: *Guiding Principles on Business and Human Rights: Implementing the United Nations 'Protect, Respect and Remedy' Framework*, (2011), 16 June 2011, A/HRC/17/31.

[54] UNHRC, Membership of the Human Rights Council 19 June 2010–18 June 2011 by regional groups, http://www.ohchr.org/EN/HRBodies/HRC/Pages/Group20102011.aspx, accessed 7 January 2014.

[55] OECD, 'OECD Guidelines for Multinational Enterprises', (2011), OECD Publishing, http://dx.doi.org/10.1787/9789264115415-en, accessed 7 January 2014.

[56] International Organization for Standardization, 'Discovering ISO 26000', (2011), http://www.iso.org/sites/iso26000launch/documents.html, accessed 7 January 2014.

and consumer safety are included);[57] Bursa Malaysia's Business Sustainability Programme launched in 2010 to encourage listed companies to include sustainability considerations into their business strategies;[58] the 2011 Singapore Stock Exchange publication of its Sustainability Reporting Guidance for listed companies, which 'encourages the company to disclose its sustainability policy, including mitigation of risks, performance data and other material information';[59] and the development of mandatory business reporting for some listed companies in India,[60] with reference to the National Voluntary Guidelines on Responsible Business. In the Indian case, Principle 5 of the Guidelines addresses human rights and draws heavily from the UNGPs.[61]

Turning to Myanmar's biggest trade partner, China, there are also important domestic developments. In 2012, the Chinese State Council announced plans to require major industrial projects within China to pass a social risk assessment, aimed at preventing social incidents and grievances that might have operational consequences.[62] In February 2013, the Ministry of Commerce released 'Guidelines for Environmental Protection in Foreign Investment and Cooperation',

> to direct enterprises in China to further regularize their environmental protection behaviours in foreign investment and cooperation activities, timely identify and prevent environmental risks, guide enterprises to actively perform their social responsibilities of environmental protection, set up good international images for Chinese enterprises, and support the sustainable development of the host country.[63]

An increasing number of international organizations and governments are working with Chinese businesses to try to address societal concerns. In a conference in April 2013 titled 'Sustainable business and investment in the global context: rights,

[57] Decision of the Chairman of Bapepam-LK No. Kep-431/BL/2012 ('Rule No. X.K.6') on 'Submission of Issuer or Public Company Annual Report' dated 1 August 2012.

[58] Bursa Malaysia, 'Powering Sustainability: A Guide for Directors', (2010), http://www.bursamalaysia.com/misc/sustainability_guide_for_directors.pdf, accessed 15 November 2013.

[59] Singapore Exchange, 'Guide to Sustainability Reporting for Listed Companies', (2011), http://rulebook.sgx.com/net_file_store/new_rulebooks/s/g/SGX_Sustainability_Reporting_Guide_and_Policy_Statement_2011.pdf, accessed 15 November 2013.

[60] Security and Exchange Board of India, 'Circular: Business Responsibility Reports', (2011), http://www.sebi.gov.in/cms/sebi_data/attachdocs/1344915990072.pdf, accessed 15 November 2013.

[61] Ministry of Corporate Affairs, Government of India, 'National Voluntary Guidelines on Social, Environmental and Economic Responsibilities of Business', (2011), http://www.mca.gov.in/Ministry/latestnews/National_Voluntary_Guidelines_2011_12jul2011.pdf, accessed 15 November 2013.

[62] K. Bradsher, '"Social Risk" Test Ordered by China for Big Projects', (2012), *New York Times*, http://www.nytimes.com/2012/11/13/world/asia/china-mandates-social-risk-reviews-for-big-projects.html?r=0, accessed 3 December 2013.

[63] Ministry of Commerce, PRC, 'Notification of the Ministry of Commerce and the Ministry of Environmental Protection on Issuing the Guidelines for Environmental Protection in Foreign Investment and Cooperation', (2013), http://english.mofcom.gov.cn/article/policyrelease/bbb/201303/20130300043226.shtml, accessed 3 December 2013. The quoted excerpt is Article 1 of the Notification.

risks and responsibilities', which brought together over 100 business executives from Chinese private and State-owned enterprises in Beijing, a Peking University Law School professor noted:

> As Chinese companies become more international, the voice of stakeholders like NGOs is becoming stronger. As a result, Chinese companies are incorporating human rights into their management systems. Even within China they cannot avoid this topic. International conventions are being translated into Chinese law and the enforcement of these laws is becoming more stringent. Chinese companies must comply, either voluntarily or involuntarily.[64]

By way of illustration, consider the currently stalled Myitsone dam in Myanmar, led by CPI Yunnan, a Chinese company. In September 2011, Myanmar President Thein Sein announced the suspension of the project due to public pressure and lack of adequate social and environmental impact assessments on the part of the company. He stated, 'Being the government elected by the people, it upholds the aspiration and wishes of the people … It is also responsible to solve the problems that worry the public. Therefore, the government will suspend the Myitsone dam project during its tenure.'[65] CPI Yunnan reported in September 2013 that 60 per cent of the total US$3.6 billion investment[66] had already been paid and reports suggest that China remains confident the project – like the other five projects agreed at the same time – will go ahead.

There are multiple angles to this case, but two dimensions signal interesting trends. First, the project was planned as a bilateral government-to-government project, which CPI Yunnan was simply expected to implement. Since the suspension, the project has been changed to a purely commercial enterprise. This no doubt eases any diplomatic tensions, but the Chinese firm now has responsibilities that go beyond commercial project implementation, such as acquiring the social licence to operate, dealing with legacy issues, and building its own capacity to address human rights and environmental challenges that in the past were 'managed' by the governments and generals. Chinese investment setbacks in Myanmar (including the China–Myanmar pipeline and the Monywa/Letpadaung copper mine) have received attention from commentators in Beijing,[67] representing a

---

[64] Global Business Initiative on Human Rights, 'Event Report – Sustainable Business and Investment in the Global Context: Rights, Risks and Responsibilities', (2013), http://www.global-business-initiative.org/wp-content/uploads/2012/05/Report-of-Business-Executives-Conference-and-Roundtable-for-Practitioners-16–17-April-2013-Beijing-English.pdf, accessed 10 December 2013

[65] T. Fuller, 'Myanmar Backs Down, Suspending Dam Project', (2011), *New York Times*, http://www.nytimes.com/2011/10/01/world/asia/myanmar-suspends-construction-of-controversial-dam.html, accessed 25 November 2013.

[66] M. Kha, '60% of Investment Already Paid for Suspended Myitsone Dam: Chinese Developer', (2013), *The Irrawady*, http://www.irrawaddy.org/china/60-of-investment-already-paid-for-suspended-myitsone-dam-chinese-developer.html, accessed 10 December 2013.

[67] See, for example, Li Yi, Wang Yu and Yang Yue, 'Commercial Outlook for China-Myanmar Pipeline Bleak', (2013), Caijing, http://english.caijing.com.cn/2013–06–18/112920308.html, accessed 3 January 2014.

growth in national dialogue about China's reputation in Myanmar and globally. Some reports argue that pressure on Chinese companies is a result of NGO action sponsored by Western governments or motivated by Western interest.[68] Others concur with the idea that there are growing expectations in China for Chinese companies to operate responsibly. Either way, domestic space for dialogue has opened.

Western investment in Myanmar is a test for decades of responsible business developments because it draws on lessons learnt from previous experiences of sanctions, impacts on society, and using levers to stop abuses. If so, it is surely also an ongoing test for the region's human rights declarations. ASEAN is consensus driven, so any development at the ASEAN level will ideally add force to ensuring responsible investment in Myanmar from ASEAN Member States. The ASEAN Human Rights Declaration (AHRD),[69] adopted by Member States in November 2012, is not without contention. A joint civil-society statement published by Human Rights Watch on the day the AHRD was adopted highlighted the ways in which it fell well below international standards, and noted: 'The Declaration that was adopted, through some of its deeply flawed 'General Principles', will serve to provide ready-made justifications for human rights violations.'[70] Nonetheless, the Declaration addresses a number of rights that are inherently linked with economic activity and business conduct. These include restrictions on the State and affirmative rights of the people including: protection of migrant workers and child labourers; protection from slavery and trafficking, and arbitrary deprivation of property; and the right to effective remedy, privacy, freedom of expression, peaceful assembly, and an adequate standard of living.

An immediate challenge to ASEAN's human rights commitment could be the actions it takes to promote the ASEAN Economic Community. For example, some have pointed to rules governing free trade areas (FTAs) in ASEAN in relation to investor–State disputes that potentially give foreign investors stronger protection than home governments, leading to fears that fundamental labour rights will be compromised.[71] To be sure, ASEAN's record in protecting labour rights is not exemplary. Myanmar is party to six FTAs under ASEAN (with Australia and New Zealand, India, Japan, South Korea, and China).[72]

---

[68] Li Jing, 'Western-Funded Green Groups "Stir up Trouble" in China', (2013), *South China Morning Post*, http://www.scmp.com/news/china/article/1298716/western-funded-green-groups-stir-trouble china?utm_source=edmandutm_medium=edmandutm_content=20130823andutm_campaign=scmp_today, accessed 7 January 2014.

[69] ASEAN Human Rights Declaration (adopted 19 November 2012), http://www.asean.org/news/asean-statement-communiques/item/asean-human-rights-declaration?category_id=26, accessed 2 January 2014.

[70] Human Rights Watch, 'Civil Society Denounces Adoption of Flawed ASEAN Human Rights Declaration', (2012), http://www.hrw.org/news/2012/11/19/civil-society-denounces-adoption-flawed-asean-human-rights-declaration, accessed 10 December 2013.

[71] M. Smith (ed.), 'Developing Disparity – Regional Investment in Burma's Borderlands. Transnational Institute', (2013), http://www.burmalibrary.org/docs14/Burmasborderlands-red.pdf, accessed 3 January 2014.

[72] Ibid.

Meanwhile, regional civil-society institutions are increasingly building their own blueprint and expectations for corporate accountability, including active campaigns and legal efforts focused on investors from China, India, Thailand, Malaysia, and Singapore. In October 2013, FORUM-ASIA (a grouping of forty-seven human rights organizations) published an extensive report titled 'Corporate Accountability in ASEAN: A Human Rights-Based Approach'.[73] As well as setting out the broad context and business and human rights issues across ASEAN, the report cites twenty-five cases of alleged human rights abuses involving businesses. The case-studies span several ASEAN countries and mention several Asian corporations from sectors including extractives, industrial development and manufacturing, agriculture, and energy (hydropower). Two of these are in Myanmar – the Shwe gas pipeline[74] and the Dawei deep-water seaport and Special Economic Zone. The report makes eighty-four recommendations on 'Legal Frameworks, the State-Business Nexus, Access to Information and Public Participation, and Access to Justice and Redress'. These are addressed to governments, business, commercial banks, ASEAN, the ASEAN Intergovernmental Commission on Human Rights (AICHR), and individual National Human Rights Institutions. Without getting into a debate about the merits of those twenty-five cases, what is clear is that ASEAN civil society is demanding that human rights be protected and respected by all investors, including those from Asia.

But Myanmar is the host

The most significant and sustainable influencers of responsible investment will come from within Myanmar itself. In a March 2012 speech to parliament, President Thein Sein noted: 'The national development strategy of our government is not aimed at developing a class or a community but aimed at developing every aspect of all walks of life, all classes or all the people of the Myanmar polity.'[75] Likewise, in a number of speeches in Europe in 2012, Aung San Suu Kyi urged that investments into Myanmar be responsible and supportive of democracy, rule of law, and human rights.[76] On the other hand, citizens will scrutinize corporate conduct to safeguard their rights and dignity as economic plans and activities are implemented. Foreign – including Asian – investors should watch, anticipate, and adapt to Myanmar's commitments in relation to labour standards, transparency, land, and human rights protection.

[73] Yap Swee Seng and John Liu (eds), 'Corporate Accountability in ASEAN: A Human Rights-Based Approach, Asian Forum for Human Rights and Development', (2013), Bangkok, http://www.forum-asia.org/uploads/publications/2013/September/Corporate-Accountability-ASEAN-FINAL.pdf, accessed 28 November 2013.

[74] Ibid., footnote 19.

[75] Burma Library, 'Translation of the Address Delivered by President of the Republic of the Union of Myanmar', (2012), http://www.burmalibrary.org/docs13/PYIDH-NLM2012–03–02-day17-STspeech.pdf, accessed 28 November 2013.

[76] See, for example, S. Nebehay and T. Miles, 'Suu Kyi Says Myanmar Needs Responsible Investment', (2012), *Reuters*, http://www.reuters.com/article/2012/06/14/us-myanmar-swiss-suukyi-idUSBRE85C1NA20120614, accessed 10 December 2013; S. Mahtani, 'Suu Kyi Seeks

In 2012, the Myanmar government stated its intent to implement the Extractives Industry Transparency Initiative (EITI).[77] As the EITI website states:

(C)ountries implement the EITI standard to ensure full disclosure of taxes and other payments made by oil, gas and mining to governments. These payments are disclosed in an annual EITI report. This report allows citizens to see for themselves how much their government is receiving from their country's natural resources.[78]

By September 2013, Myanmar had completed three of the four requirements to make its final application to join, including appointing a senior official to lead implementation and pledging to work with civil society and the private sector on implementation. In an August 2013 interview, Deputy Minister for Finance U. Maung Maung Thein, said: 'If we become an EITI member, corruption in resource based industries will be wiped out automatically. The other benefit we will get from it is more foreign investment ... Money received from sale of natural resources is the property of all citizens.'[79] Asian investors should note that transparency about their own payments would fall under this mechanism, even if their governments have not joined the EITI.

Myanmar has also committed to improve labour standards. In June 2013, the International Labour Organization (ILO) voted[80] to lift its remaining restrictions on Myanmar in large part due to President Thein Sein's commitment to eradicate forced labour, consistent with Myanmar's obligations under ILO Convention 29 (1930).[81] The resolution calls on ILO Member States to:

(p)rovide financial support for the elimination of forced labour and invites the Governing Body (the executive body of the ILO) to review the situation in Myanmar on issues relating to ILO activities, including freedom of association and the impact of foreign investment on decent working conditions in the country.[82]

Responsible Investment in Myanmar', (2012), Wall Street Journal Blog, http://blogs.wsj.com/searealtime/2013/09/21/suu-kyi-seeks-responsible-investment-in-myanmar, accessed 10 December 2013; and *The Scotsman*, 'Aung San Suu Kyi Would Welcome "Ethical" UK Investment in Burma', (2012), http://www.scotsman.com/news/politics/top-stories/aung-san-suu-kyi-would-welcome-ethical-uk-investment-in-burma-1-2360900, accessed 10 December 2013.

[77]   Extractive Industry Transparency Initiative (EITI) website, 'Myanmar Considers the EITI', (2012), http://eiti.org/news-events/myanmar-considers-eiti, accessed 3 January 2014.

[78]   Extractive Industry Transparency Initiative (EITI) website. 'What is the EITI?', (2012), http://eiti.org/eiti, accessed 18 November 2013.

[79]   S. Thitsar, 'Extractive Industries Transparency Initiative', (2012). *The Myanmar Times*, http://www.mmtimes.com/index.php/national-news/7765-extractive-industries-transparency-initiative.html, accessed 15 November 2013.

[80]   International Labour Organization, 'ILO Lifts Remaining Restrictions on Myanmar', (2013), http://www.ilo.org/ilc/ILCSessions/102/media-centre/news/WCMS_216355/lang--en/index.htm, accessed 15 December 2013.

[81]   ILO, Forced Labour Convention, C29, 28 June 1930, C29, http://www.refworld.org/docid/3ddb621f2a.html, accessed 22 January 2014.

[82]   Ibid.

Other commitments that will increase scrutiny of international investors include the Parliamentary Land Investigation Committee's[83] investigation of land-grab complaints and the establishment of a National Human Rights Commission in September 2011.[84]

Legislative developments will also be key. There are some positive – albeit nascent – signs. For example, Myanmar's new Foreign Investment Law requires Environment and Social Impact Assessments to be submitted as part of the application for certain large-scale and environmentally sensitive projects.[85] The Myanmar Investment Commission may also prohibit foreign investments such as, among other things, 'activities that affect culture and ethnic traditions' and 'activities that can be harmful to people's health or harmful to the environment'. But laws can only do so much. What is not known is Myanmar's longer-term political will or capacity to draft the details of such laws and then enforce them. And Myanmar's efforts to promote inward investment, establish trade relations, and incentivize enterprise growth may either reinforce or undermine the protection and respect of human rights in the economic/business sphere. In September 2012, the Brookings Institution published a working paper, 'The Myanmar Economy: Tough Choices',[86] which addresses traditional macro-economic questions such as fiscal policy, taxation, the exchange rate system, moving away from the cash economy, and the establishment of a sovereign wealth fund. But the report also highlights environmental, social and governance questions linked to economic policy, such as revenue transparency, steps to ensure socially beneficial infrastructure and communications development, job creation in the context of the Special Economic Zone Law, channelling foreign aid in appropriate directions, and new land laws. It seems inevitable that Myanmar's economic policies will be expected to address such matters far more specifically than in the past, when governments and companies could strike deals with generals or their relatives.

---

[83] A. Noe Noe, 'Commission Will Report Over 300 Land Grabs to Myanmar MPs', (2012), *The Myanmar Times*, http://www.mmtimes.com/index.php/national-news/3591-commission-will-report-over-300-land-grabs-to-hluttaw.html, accessed 28 November 2013.

[84] See Myanmar National Human Rights Commission (MNHRC) website: http://www.mnhrc.org.mm/en, 'The Myanmar National Human Rights Commission was established on 5 September 2011 by Notification No. 34/2011 of the Government of the Republic of the Union of Myanmar with a view to promoting and safeguarding the fundamental rights of the citizens enshrined in the Constitution of the Republic of the Union of Myanmar. Its establishment was based on the principles relating to the status of national institutions (Paris Principles) contained in United Nations General Assembly Resolution A/ Res/ 48/ 134. Taking into consideration the principle of pluralism, the Commission was formed with the following fifteen retired persons from different professions and various national races as members'.

[85] See Foreign Investment Rules at website: http://www.investinmyanmar.com/myanmar-investment-laws; Foreign Investment Rules. Note Chapter 5, Article 33. – 'Proposals for the economic activities that are considered capital intensive by the Commission, and that are prescribed to undergo environmental impact assessment by the Ministry of Environmental Protection and Forestry have to be submitted along with Environmental and Social Impact Assessment'.

[86] L. Rieffel, 'The Myanmar Economy: Tough Choices', (2012), The Brookings Institution, Working Paper 51, http://www.brookings.edu/~/media/research/files/papers/2012/9/myanmar%20economy%20rieffel/09%20myanmar%20economy%20rieffel.pdf, accessed 11 December 2013.

Asian companies will have to prepare for this new environment and not view it as a public relations exercise through philanthropic endeavours. Their licence to operate is at stake. International and domestic civil-society organizations are demanding responsible corporate behaviour and accountability from companies because of concern over potentially adverse social and environmental impacts. An April 2013 report from a US non-profit centre, titled 'Conducting Meaningful Stakeholder Consultation in Myanmar',[87] provides an overview of the key international actors, local networks, sector-specific organizations (addressing land, labour, environment, sustainable development, youth, and gender), and ethnic representatives.

Beyond the growing and vibrant NGO community and media, individuals and communities directly affected by investments are rightfully demanding responsible behaviour from companies. Protests have become common, as an expert notes,[88] and among the recent projects facing enhanced scrutiny are:

- **Letpadaung Mine project**: In the 1990s, a Canadian company entered into a joint venture with the Myanmar State-owned mining enterprise to explore for copper in the Monywa area west of Mandalay. The Canadian company sold its stake to Wanbao Mining, a Chinese copper mining company owned by Norinco, the business arm of the Chinese military, and in the process of the deal, the military-owned Union of Myanmar Economic Holdings obtained the Myanmar government's stake, and with it, the responsibility for resettlement. Wanbao sought to extend the mine's area, against local opposition, which got national-level support from environment and human rights activists and Buddhist monks. Police used disproportionate force in breaking up protests using white phosphorus, and many people, including monks, were severely injured. The Government appointed a commission headed by Aung San Suu Kyi, who recommended that the project should continue, provided there was greater transparency, more benefit for the State, better environmental management, greater compensation and livelihoods support, and training for the security forces. Wanbao Mining has since renegotiated the agreement and offered to pay higher compensation, but communities remain dissatisfied with their approach and are calling for the full implementation of the Enquiry's recommendations, particularly on transparency.

- **Dawei SEZ**: A Thai-Italian company called Ital-Thai Group had won a 75-year concession to create a US$300 million special economic zone in Dawei. With its proximity to Thailand's industrial zone, the project has considerable economic potential. But it was controversial – local farmers had

---

[87] The Shift Project, 'Conducting Meaningful Stakeholder Consultation in Myanmar', (2013), http://shiftproject.org/sites/default/files/Conducting%20Meaningful%20Stakeholder%20 Consultation%20in%20Myanmar_1.pdf, accessed 11 December 2013.

[88] D. Guest, 'Responsible Investment in Myanmar: Getting down to the Grass Roots', (2013), Institute for Human Rights and Business, http://www.ihrb.org/commentary/staff/responsible-business-in-myanmar-getting-down-to-the-grassroots.html, accessed 11 December 2013.

occupied vast tracts in the area to prevent road construction, alleging inadequate compensation for land acquired. Others claimed that proper environmental impact assessment had not been carried out. In November 2013, the Government withdrew the concession, promising to compensate Ital-Thai. Japanese investors are now likely to invest.

- **Shwe Gas Pipeline:** The Shwe gas project is controversial because it passes through contested regions that have seen protracted warfare. There have been several violent incidents in Rakhine unrelated to the pipeline, and more recently the ethnic violence has spread beyond, to other parts of Myanmar, pitting Myanmar's Buddhists against Muslims. Meanwhile, people in Rakhine – Buddhists and Muslims alike – are opposed to the project and have courted arrest. A local watchdog group, the Myanmar China Pipeline Watch Committee, is monitoring the pipeline and its effect on the region.[89]
- **Bagan-Nyaung Oo:** In October 2012, the township of Bagan-Nyaung Oo protested against a tourism project being planned in their area. More hotels are being planned in the historic Bagan area, and the local communities are resisting.[90] There has been increased concern over encroachment.[91] Unless their concerns are taken into account and resolved through a proper grievance mechanism, civil unrest may devastate the appeal of a monument that personifies the nation's cultural and aesthetic identity. For Myanmar, Bagan has a cultural resonance similar to what Borobudur has for Indonesia or Angkor Wat has for Cambodia, personifying the national aesthetic.

It can be seen that land is often the single most important cause creating friction between communities and companies. The people being adversely affected are poor. Many lack their own land titles but they have customary rights. Companies face protests if they disregard those rights. State security forces often clamp down using harsh force. That violates human rights, alienates communities, and undermines the company's licence to operate. Communities in Myanmar have been ignored for nearly fifty years and are now finding their voice, and, using their new assertiveness, they are changing the political environment. Businesses – local or foreign – can no longer afford to ignore it.

---

[89] The Committee has its own Facebook page (https://www.facebook.com/MyanmarChinaPipeline Watch) and has been monitoring the project closely. See also A. Min Thein and T. Kyaw, 'Myanmar Rights Groups to Monitor Effects of Controversial China Petroleum Pipeline', (2013), *Radio Free Asia*, http://www.rfa.org/english/news/myanmar/pipeline-09242013163443.html, accessed 20 January 2014.

[90] K. Thett, 'The Run on Myanmar: Stumbling Blocks on the Way to Responsible Tourism', (2013), Tourism Watch, http://www.tourism-watch.de/node/1920, accessed 20 January 2014.

[91] A. Kyaw Zin, 'Encroachment Is the Main Problem in Bagan', interview with U. Naing Win, the director of Bagan Department of Archaeology, National Museum and Library under Ministry of Culture, *Myanma Freedom Daily*, http://www.mmfreedom-daily.com/?p=17019, accessed 20 January 2014.

Part three: conclusion

Getting it right: a framework for Asian leaders

Corporations from Delhi to Beijing and from Bangkok to Tokyo will need to build new awareness and capacities if they are to secure their social licence to operate in fast-changing Myanmar. Their governments can either incentivize and support the necessary behaviour or risk seeing their business leaders and investments failing dramatically. By way of example, some Chinese firms have been ill prepared for this change and have suffered in parts of Africa and the European Union in the past decade. Using the UN Guiding Principles for Business and Human Rights as a starting point, below we set out a three-part framework for what we see as imperatives for Asian States and companies as they continue to invest in Myanmar.

Uphold protection and respect of human rights

First, investment and trade agreements, including around specific projects, should uphold the protection and respect of human rights. This should apply to bilateral investment treaties, free trade agreements, concessions/licences to exploit natural resources and large-footprint projects in Myanmar. ASEAN should show leadership by commissioning an independent impact assessment of the ASEAN Economic Community blueprint. This would include reviewing the impact of investor–State dispute settlement (ISDS) with attention to how to protect investor rights without undermining policy and legal space in Myanmar to protect workers and affected populations. An internationally agreed reference point for this action can be found in the 'Principles for responsible contracts: integrating the management of human rights risks into State-investor contract negotiations: guidance for negotiators' (an addendum to the UN Guiding Principles).[92] The guide includes '10 key Principles to help integrate the management of human rights risks into investment project contract negotiations between host State entities and foreign business investors'.[93] The principles cover human rights in relation to:

- project negotiations preparation and planning
- management of potential human rights impacts
- project operating standards
- stabilization clauses
- additional goods and services provision
- physical security

[92] UN Human Rights Council, 'Principles for Responsible Contracts: Integrating the Management of Human Rights Risks into State-Investor Contract Negotiations: Guidance for Negotiators', (2011), Addendum A/HRC/17/31, http://www.ohchr.org/Documents/Issues/Business/A.HRC.17.31. Add.3.pdf, accessed 10 December 2013.
[93] Ibid.

- community engagement
- project monitoring and compliance
- grievance mechanisms for non-contractual harms to third parties
- transparency/disclosure of contract terms.

Leaders from business and government can find guidance and tools in this area. An example of such a resource is 'The Investment and Human Rights Project' at the London School of Economics,[94] which has developed a free resource aimed at building awareness about how international investment works and what might its relationship be to peoples' enjoyment of their human rights. The project also sought to create constructive spaces for learning, research, discussion and sharing of practical tools in the area of investment and human rights.

Encourage human rights impact assessments and responsible business reporting

Second, Asian governments should encourage, even require and resource, human rights impact assessments and responsible business reporting by State-owned enterprises and by enterprises that they support through export finance or loans. A number of governments in Asia have discussed or legislated some form of mandatory CSR requirements. However, many of these efforts do not address the operational impacts of business activity and favour philanthropic models of CSR. In Myanmar, as in other situations of high human rights risk, Asian governments should recognize that requiring human rights impact assessments and periodic responsible business reporting is a sensible risk-management approach. The Asian Development Bank should do the same for all projects it participates in. By way of example, at a national level, China's 2012 State Council requirement for social impact assessments should include human rights impact assessments for all investments in Myanmar. This could be implemented via two financing entities that sit under the State Council – the State-owned Assets Supervision and Administration Commission and the Export-Import Bank of China. All Asian governments should follow the lead of the United States by adopting responsible business reporting requirements consistent with the UN Guiding Principles. Because a vast amount of Asian investment into Myanmar is publicly financed, governments should set aside funds to resource this work, including contributing to existing efforts by national and international organizations to build knowledge and capacity.

---

[94] The Investment and Human Rights Project at the London School of Economics: http://www.lse. ac.uk/humanRights/research/projects/theLab/investmentHumanRights.aspx. In early 2014, the Project will launch 'an innovative website that will be a free learning tool on investment and human rights for a range of practitioners, including lawyers, institutional investors, lenders, investment consultants and advisors, government and civil society. The site will also serve as a focal point for documents, relevant materials, and tools making them available in an easy-to-access way.'

Meet the responsibility to respect human rights with special attention to rights-based social dialogue

Third, Asian corporations should meet their responsibility to respect human rights with special attention given to rights-based social dialogue. Business leaders should implement the road map set out by the UN Guiding Principles – i.e. adopt a public statement of policy to respect human rights, carry out human rights due diligence, and cooperate in remediation (including establishing operational-level grievance mechanisms). In order to build capacity and credibility, Asian companies would benefit from participating in multi-stakeholder and industry initiatives such as the Voluntary Principles for Security and Human Rights (extractive sector),[95] the Global Network Initiative (information and communication technologies),[96] and the Fair Labour Association (textiles).[97] Due diligence responses from companies should apply international standards in relation to land, labour, and ethnic conflict. Asian companies need to pay special attention to ensuring worker and community interactions are based on rights-based principles, not the philanthropic, patriarchal or charity-based CSR models often dominant at home.

Economic development and growth in Myanmar is certainly an opportunity for foreign investors, from Asian and beyond. Asian corporations have had the early-mover advantage – often supported by financing from their governments. But this has changed with the lifting of sanctions. Rather than play the game by old rules, Asian companies should come up to speed on current trends and follow international standards, including through conducting human rights due diligence. Responsible Asian investment in Myanmar is now essential, with transparency and accountability increasingly the norm. This is due, in large part, to an increasingly free and vibrant civil society in Myanmar and across Asia that is concerned about corporate accountability. Excelling at operating in this new context

---

[95] See Voluntary Principles website, http://www.voluntaryprinciples.org: 'Established in 2000, the Voluntary Principles on Security and Human Rights are a set of principles designed to guide companies in maintaining the safety and security of their operations within an operating framework that encourages respect for human rights.'

[96] See Global Network Initiative website, http://www.globalnetworkinitiative.org: 'All over the world – from the Americas to Europe to the Middle East to Africa and Asia – companies in the Information and Communications Technology (ICT) sector face increasing government pressure to comply with domestic laws and policies in ways that may conflict with the internationally recognized human rights of freedom of expression and privacy. In response, a multi-stakeholder group of companies, civil society organizations (including human rights and press freedom groups), investors and academics spent two years negotiating and creating a collaborative approach to protect and advance freedom of expression and privacy in the ICT sector, and have formed an Initiative to take this work forward.'

[97] See Fair Labor Association website, http://www.fairlabor.org: 'Since 1999, FLA has helped improve the lives of millions of workers around the world. As a collaborative effort of socially responsible companies, colleges and universities, and civil society organizations, FLA creates lasting solutions to abusive labour practices by offering tools and resources to companies, delivering training to factory workers and management, conducting due diligence through independent assessments, and advocating for greater accountability and transparency from companies, manufacturers, factories and others involved in global supply chain.'

will also enhance Asian competitiveness globally, beyond Myanmar. Most importantly, all companies investing in Myanmar must act in ways that raise the chances of the country's economic growth, leading to tangible and positive human rights outcomes for its people, rather than bringing more confusion, suffering, disruption, and tension.

9 The new frontier

Due diligence and developing and implementing human rights audits in Southeast Asia

James Kallman

Introduction

The potential for human rights abuse in the course of business practice, either by design or ignorance, is significant, and business-related human rights abuse can be just as devastating to individuals and communities as State-sponsored human rights violations. In response to this reality, multinational corporations are increasingly aware of the importance of monitoring their performance against global human rights frameworks and policies. Auditing to assess human rights policy compliance is seen as a vital way to ensure that these commitments are kept. Such major operations as Suez Environnement, for example, have been producing in-house sustainability reports for a number of years that have been submitted for external assurance using Global Reporting Initiative (GRI) indicators.[1] Meanwhile, in Southeast Asia, the Asia Pulp and Paper Group (APP) has reversed previous negative public sentiment by the publication of its 'Sustainability Roadmap Vision 2020' in June 2012.[2]

For Moores Rowland – Mazars Indonesia, this realization of the need to develop a methodology suitable for measuring company compliance with the UN Guiding Principles on Business and Human Rights (Guiding Principles) was largely in response to a gnawing disquiet that financial audits were not adequately providing a complete picture of a company's DNA. While all the financial data may be available, most experts in the industry appear increasingly to favour scanning key financial ratios over reading annual reports in their entirety. Moreover, given the major corporate scandals and collapses in recent decades, something more is obviously needed to provide reporting of greater dimension and value, both to the companies themselves and their diverse stakeholders. As a first step towards addressing such challenges, Moores Rowland – Mazars Indonesia began to provide assurance on company sustainability reports in 2010, as in the broadest sense

[1] Suez Environnement Commitments and Performance Report 2011, http://www.suez-environnement.com/wp-content/uploads/2012/12/sustainable_report_2011.pdf, accessed 14 February 2014.
[2] Latest developments on the APP commitment are available at http://www.asiapulppaper.com/sustainability, accessed 14 February 2014.

of the term, audit attestation need not be restricted to financial data.[3] Since that time, assurance services have been provided for companies in a variety of sectors ranging from telecommunications and consumer goods production to renewable and non-renewable energy resource operators.[4]

The drawback of this approach, however, is that this exercise relies on reports that are prepared by the company under review, and thus only those specific areas that the company itself wishes to address are selected.[5] Instead, what is needed for a proper human rights audit is a comprehensive set of indicators that the assessor can apply to any company, based on those best suited to determine human rights risk or compliance for a particular sector or context.

This chapter highlights the progress that Moores Rowland – Mazars Indonesia has made in developing and applying these indicators, based on its experience in advising and auditing companies in the mining, plantation, industrial, and retail sectors with regard to their compliance with environmental and human rights standards and policies. The chapter equally outlines the next steps on the journey in finding ways to make respecting human rights an integral part of doing business in Southeast Asia and elsewhere.

Challenge of development

While recognizing the need for such externally validated human rights audits marked a vital first step, identifying where to begin was an entirely different matter. In contrast to financial statements, there were no internationally recognized standards for conducting human rights audits. This remains the case to date. Indeed, the discussions of the Moores Rowland – Mazars Indonesia working group, which was tasked with developing the initial guidelines, were marked by spirited argument in support of views that – while not disparate – were certainly not harmonious at first. 'Human rights due diligence is surely a legal matter', claimed the lawyers, 'but materiality must be considered', countered the audit department, while the internal control, marketing communications and corporate social responsibility (CSR) experts all chipped in with their own views which they believed to be preeminent. While much work had already been and continues to be done on the subject in Europe and Africa,[6] it nevertheless took nearly six

---

[3] This involves carrying out an assurance engagement on the company-prepared sustainability report in accordance with standards issued by the International Auditing and Accounting Board, and AccountAbility.

[4] Specifically, PT Telekomunikasi Indonesia (Indonesia's largest telecommunications operator, listed on the New York Stock Exchange), Unilever (multinational consumer goods producer), PT Perusahaan Indonesia (gas distribution), Star Energy Geothermal Ltd. (geothermal energy supplier) and its associated oil company Star Energy, among others.

[5] One has to appreciate the legal liability of companies for the public statements they make, which has led to reluctance on their part to include assurance of operations not under their direct control, such as those of companies in the supply chain.

[6] It was at a breakfast meeting in Jakarta in 2011 that Prof. Christine Kaufmann of the University of Zurich Competence Centre for Human Rights first focused the author's attention on the valuable role that auditors could play in evaluating compliance with the due diligence standards contained

months before an initial set of indicators was finally agreed upon. These were based upon prevailing Indonesian labour, human rights, and environmental laws, in addition to key international human rights standards such as the Universal Declaration of Human Rights (UDHR); the OECD Guidelines for Multinational Enterprises; the International Covenant on Civil and Political Rights (ICCPR); the International Covenant on Economic, Social and Cultural Rights (ICESCR); and the International Labour Organization (ILO) Conventions.

These Mazars Indicators for Human Rights and Social Compliance, or MIHRSC as they have become known, provide guidelines for performing an in-depth assessment on human rights compliance, being categorized by indicators that address the following issues:

- forced labour
- child labour and young workers
- conditions of employment and work
- non-discrimination
- freedom of association
- workplace health and safety
- community and environmental impact
- supply chain management.

This chapter will examine each of these issues in turn. The MIHRSC were developed with the expert guidance of Marzuki Darusman, Executive Director of the Human Rights Research Centre for ASEAN and former Indonesian Attorney-General, who drew on his considerable human rights experience.[7] The MIHRSC measure how well a company is complying with basic human rights. They are assessed against local laws and consolidated at an international level. The MIHRSC have won international accolades,[8] which is not only a vindication

within the Guiding Principles. Separately, in partnership with Shift, the Institute for Human Rights and Business (IHRB) issued for the European Commission three Guides on implementing the Guiding Principles in June 2013. The Guides target employment and recruitment agencies, information and communications technology (ICT), and the oil and gas sectors: see, http://www.ihrb.org/publications/reports/human-rights-guides.html, accessed 10 February 2014. Further afield, IHRB has collaborated with the Kenya National Commission on Human Rights on the 'Nairobi Process: A Pact for Responsible Business', an initiative aiming to embed human rights due diligence in Kenya's emerging oil and gas sector through the application of the Guiding Principles: see The Nairobi Process, http://www.ihrb.org/about/programmes/nairobi-process.html, accessed 10 February 2014.

[7] The author extends his sincere thanks to Marzuki Darusman for sparking the beginning of this journey by pressing Moores Rowland – Mazars Indonesia as to whether it could carry out human rights audits on companies. The author is grateful for the encouragement and sage counsel that he continues to provide to this day.

[8] The International Accounting Bulletin declared the Mazars human rights audit practice 'Audit Innovation of the Year' at their inaugural annual awards in March 2012. The award had been granted on the basis that 'Mazars ha(d) taken a lead role in assessing audit clients against the Mazars Indicators for Human Rights Compliance.' In keeping with this, judges expressed the view that 'the Mazars Human Rights Audit was pertinent, innovative and could set a benchmark for global best

of Moores Rowland – Mazars Indonesia's efforts, but an indication of Southeast Asia's interest in being a thought-leader in the realm of business and human rights and embedding the Guiding Principles in the region.[9] With respect to accounting and auditing, it marks an inflection point for a profession that earns its living by looking backwards at past results instead of towards the future.

The MIHRSC are used in the identification and examination of a company's process in respecting human rights as required by the Guiding Principles. This examination includes assessing the adequacy of the following components of a company's corporate strategy:

1 high-level policy commitment to respect human rights, including the supporting operational-level policies, processes, training, and incentive structures;
2 human rights due diligence process under which the company: (a) assesses the actual and potential impacts on human rights arising from its own activities and through its business relationships; (b) integrates the findings from these assessments and takes action to prevent or mitigate adverse impacts; (c) tracks the effectiveness of the efforts taken to address human rights impacts; and (d) communicates these efforts to the affected stakeholders;
3 remediation processes (including non-judicial operational-level grievance mechanisms) for human rights damage that the company has either caused or contributed to.

In providing guidelines for the performance of an external audit of company compliance, the MIHRSC are used to specify the following:

1 objectives, i.e. listing of targets to be reached and the aim of the indicator;
2 scope, i.e. specifying the range within which the indicator is applied, plus defining key elements of the indicator;
3 processes, i.e. suggesting step-by-step work to be carried out to reach the indicator's overall objective;
4 collection of information, i.e. suggesting what to obtain, from whom, and how this can be used in the process;
5 creation of a working paper, hyperlinked to a standardized Excel spreadsheet, in order to gather and process the information required to draw out the underlying conclusions of the final report;

practice'. See International Accounting Bulletin Editorial Board, 'IAB Award winners revealed', (12 March 2012), http://www.internationalaccountingbulletin.com/news/iab-award-winners-revealed, accessed 14 February 2014.
9 Prior to this, due diligence has been the sole/dominant preserve of international experts and organizations of business and human rights based in Europe or North America. For example, see IHRB and the Global Business Initiative (GBI), 'The "State of Play" of Human Rights Due Diligence: Anticipating the Next Five Years', examining how 23 companies were interpreting the concept and describing the efforts made to apply it in practice, http://www.ihrb.org/pdf/The_State_of_Play_of_Human_Rights_Due_Diligence.pdf, accessed 10 February 2014.

6   reporting of material information, formatted to report results and conclusions;

7   proposing practical recommendations that address potential and actual human rights issues.

Engaging business

Having developed the necessary tools, ensuring their successful implementation in practice then depended on the ability to convince business of their utility. To this end, the first strategy adopted was to employ terms that business knew and could more easily relate to. This was crucial in light of the politically charged connotations often associated with the term 'human rights', as well as the costly reputational damage arising from their violation. Linking human rights with corporate social compliance, on the other hand, made matters more palatable, as did the use of the word 'audit', a concept and process with which business is both familiar and comfortable.

The key to securing cooperation has been to reassure companies that the core purpose of this human rights compliance and auditing exercise is to seek out mutually beneficial solutions to existing challenges, rather than passing judgement on companies for real or perceived failures. On this basis, efforts have been focused on identifying the areas where human rights issues are most likely to arise and to implement preventative measures or – in the event of prior occurrence – to undertake remedial action. It has also been important to stress that companies taking part in such audits are not alone, for gremlins lie in wait in all operations. Even lawyers and accountants can fall foul of forced labour practices, requiring employees to work a minimum number of billable hours that most likely are not achievable within the standard work schedule. Nevertheless, irrespective of the size or nature of the problems, there is value to be found by a company addressing human rights-related challenges in a constructive manner, without losing sight of the fact that the whole purpose of running a commercial enterprise is to obtain profit.[10] Although not always immediately apparent, the direct benefit that companies can draw from constructively engaging can be determined on several levels, not least in the savings of time and effort required to deal with the fallout from human rights issues. The trend towards ever greater corporate disclosure through auditing should work its way through to the field of human rights as well. Clients may be offered new specialized audit and assurance services in any area where there is an information need or exposure to litigation arising from errors, misstatements and/or distortions in the published financial statements.

How a company deals with its human rights and social compliance issues is important. If done correctly, it engenders camaraderie that brings the parties closer together, be they employees, the local community, or society at large. This

---

[10]   'Corporations may be "organs of society", in short, but they are specialized organs, established to perform specialized economic functions, and the obligations imposed on them must recognize that fact.' J. G. Ruggie, *Just Business* (New York, Norton, 2013), pp. 51–52.

is particularly true for companies in the extractive industry, whose operations, by their very nature, often run counter to the traditional lifestyle of the local community. In this respect, in addition to securing the formal government contracts and licences, it is vital for such companies to also obtain a 'social licence to operate' (SLO) from the local community if their operations are to run smoothly and efficiently. An SLO is based 'on the degree to which a corporation and its activities meet the expectations of local communities, the wider society, and various constituent groups'.[11] Obtaining an SLO is essential for reducing the risks of social conflict and for enhancing a company's reputation. So crucial is this factor to present-day operations that a manager of mining assets in the Asia Pacific region can be expected to devote up to 35 to 50 per cent of his or her time to managing social risk.[12]

Forward-thinking companies often tend to get it right from the start, being well aware that even the smallest issues must be resolved at inception, rather than being left to fester and later erupt into a major problem with far greater consequences. In this sense, it is very much a case of paying now, or being forced to pay later when the costs are significantly higher.[13] An independent assessment or 'audit' using guidelines such as the MIHRSC can assist a company in identifying those areas that have the greatest potential to be problematic from a human rights viewpoint, thus enabling preventative measures to be put in place or, in the case of non-compliance, remedial action to be taken. It is usually in relation to this added value that management's initial reticence begins to change to realization of the potential benefits that can be gained by paying more than just lip service to human rights. Moreover, this can lead to a request for audit to ascertain the company's respect for human rights as outlined in the Guiding Principles. As in any other aspect of business, companies seek reassurance that they are on the right track and have robust processes in place and embedded throughout their operations, with a view to reducing the prospects of unpleasant surprises in the near or distant future.

MIHRSC in practice

One of the greatest challenges related to implementing MIHRSC is the immensity of the task and the time involved in undertaking a full audit of a company's human

---

[11] N. Gunninham, R. Kagan and D. Thornton, 'Social License and Environmental Protection: Why Business Go Beyond Compliance', (2004), *Journal of the American Bar Foundation*, 39(2): 307–341.

[12] Rachel Davis and Daniel M. Franks, 'The Costs of Conflict with Local Communities in the Extractive Industry', (2011), p. 4, http://shiftproject.org/sites/default/files/Davis%20and%20 Franks_Costs%20of%20Conflict_SRM.pdf, accessed 14 February 2014.

[13] Toronto-based Barrick Gold Corp was forced to book a US$5.1 billion impairment charge on its Pascua-Lama project in northern Chile in the second quarter of 2013, having been fined approximately US$16 million by the Chilean authorities in July. It also had its operations suspended following 'very serious' violations of its environmental permit by failing to fully implement its promises to safeguard the local community's water rights. This also led to the August 2013 filing of a class-action lawsuit in a US court by a group of investors. See also Davis and Franks, see n. 12.

rights commitment, as several months are often required in order to complete the exercise. The initial planning stage alone can take upwards of a month, encompassing the following steps:

1   determination of the scope of the audit;
2   gathering an understanding of the nature of the company's business;
3   considering the environment and community within which the company carries out its operations;
4   identification of the human rights laws and regulations applicable to the company's business;
5   risk identification, mapping and assessment;
6   design and tailoring of the audit procedures to best fit the requirements of the company's business operations.

The result of the planning stage is a specific risk-based approach, tailored to the needs of producing an efficient and effective audit of the company's compliance with the measures laid out in the Guiding Principles. Putting this plan into action involves taking a series of coordinated steps, beginning with understanding and assessing the company's policies and procedures. This is followed by examining what actually takes place in practice, as well as interviewing executive management, relevant staff, and other relevant parties. It is only then that compliance with the Guiding Principles and MIHRSC can be assessed. At this stage, reported cases of non-compliance should be evaluated and validated by confirmation with management. Finally, the remediation process is observed to see how the company embeds this learning into better operational procedures to avoid repeating past mistakes.

Although simple enough to list and define, the practical completion of the above stages can be time-consuming, as some need to be revisited in light of operational realities. At times, this may be due to a breakdown in the internal communication process, whereby the processes and policies set in place by a company's senior management or human resources department are in fact not being carried out at the operational level. A case in point can be drawn from a company in India, where the head of security maintained that his personnel were not in any way armed, yet on our site visit, the security guards were quite openly seen to be carrying a *lathi*, the traditional Indian fighting stick. This emphasizes the need for suitably trained internal auditors with the authority to ensure that the Guiding Principles are embedded in every department throughout the operation. Remediation, of course, plays a major part in this, and besides an open-door policy enabling employees to express their concerns to the internal auditors, the auditors themselves must have sufficient authority to investigate reports of non-compliance and report their findings, plus suggested remedy, to the highest levels. External audits, too, are dependent on the freedom of employees to express their concerns, which in itself is an indicator of the management's commitment to the whole audit process.

In other instances, the independence of the auditor must be upheld. While collaboration with the company is essential in many respects, the final call must always lie with the auditor. This is particularly relevant with respect to the choice of parties selected for interview, as well as in the arrangements for conducting such meetings. While the company may suggest that certain individuals are perhaps not entirely trustworthy, it is up to the auditor to ensure that all relevant parties are afforded the opportunity to state their case without let or hindrance and free from fear of retaliatory action. It may well be true that a particular non-governmental organization (NGO), for example, does indeed have a vested interest in taking a certain position, but it is the responsibility of the auditor to provide a balanced judgement on the matter based on the facts provided by all relevant parties.

Moreover, while the company's statement on its human rights practice should provide a road map of steps to be taken towards a better future, the auditors' final report on this statement also goes beyond simply pointing out current deficiencies. Recommendations that assist the company to improve in this field are vital. The latter focus underscores the importance attributed to the process rather than to outcomes, and ensures that steps taken are in line with the shift from 'blaming and shaming' tactics to the more forward-thinking 'know(ing) and show(ing)' approach outlined by Professor John Ruggie.[14] Not only does this encourage improvement in the attitude of business towards respecting human rights, but it also shifts management thinking from a defensive to a progressive posture. All this, of course, is totally dependent on management's commitment to human rights, for the auditors' hands are rather tied when management deliberately sets out to mislead, by telling underage workers to stay at home when the auditors pay a visit, for example.

Part of the financial audit process already includes evaluating contingent liabilities, such as pending and threatened litigation, as well as liability for environmental damage. Adding measurable and quantifiable human rights standards to the accounting and auditing procedures would protect public companies from contingent punitive liabilities and other potential associated costs by providing them with both processes to inhibit or mitigate human rights abuses and annual feedback on their effectiveness. It is important to again stress, however, that assessments such as the MIHRSC are designed to deal with process rather than outcome, whereby the company's statement of the processes embedded in its operations to minimize the risk of human rights issues is assessed against the Mazars' indicators. As such, this does not constitute an examination or a review in accordance with generally accepted audit or attestation standards. To put this in simpler terms, a financial audit carried out to accepted standards deals with facts that enable the auditor to quantify items, with profit or loss clearly stated and numerical projections made under specific criteria. An assessment under the MIHRSC, meanwhile, deals with

---

[14] UN OHCHR, *Guiding Principles on Business and Human Rights: Implementing the United Nations: 'Protect, Respect and Remedy' Framework*, (2011) p. 16, http://www.ohchr.org/Documents/Publications/ GuidingPrinciplesBusinessHR_EN.pdf, accessed 14 February 2014.

systems and thus, while areas that could lead to potential liability may be identified, it is far harder to assign a financial value to the failure to implement equal hiring practices, for example.

Such generally accepted standards have yet to be developed for the audit of human rights. Moores Rowland – Mazars Indonesia and other auditors thus turn to international human rights law, which provides a unique framework with which to assess the worldwide practices of transnational corporations, their subsidiaries and their suppliers. By virtue of their widespread acceptance by States, international standards have entered the legal, moral, and public discourses of the world's nations. Rooted in international legal standards such as the UDHR, the ICCPR, and the ICESCR, as well as relevant ILO Conventions, the indicators are aimed at providing a means to assess the company processes covering the broad objectives mentioned earlier and discussed in more detail now.

Forced labour

Verify that the company has taken all necessary measures to ensure that it does not participate in, nor benefit from, any form of forced labour; this may include bonded labour, debt bondage, forced prison labour, slavery, servitude, or human trafficking. This sphere also seeks to ensure that workers are not coerced or compelled into voluntary overtime work due to physical intimidation or threats of withholding wages.[15]

Child labour and young workers

The evaluation of business practices in relation to this indicator seeks to ensure that the company is in compliance with the respective minimum age standards and conditions. This is an area where local regulation must be taken into account, as the legal minimum working age can vary by country: from 14 years old in India, for example, to the age of 18 in Indonesia.[16]

---

[15] While the UDHR formed the initial basis, considerations were also taken of the ICCPR and the ICESCR. Relevant provisions are as follows: UDHR (adopted 10 December 1948) UNGA Res 217 A(III): Art. 4 (prohibition against slavery or servitude), Art. 23(2) (right to equal pay for equal work), Art. 23(3) (right to just and favourable remuneration), and Art. 24 (right to rest and leisure and periodic holidays with pay); ICCPR (adopted 16 December 1966, entered into force 23 March 1976) 999 UNTS 171: Art. 8 (prohibition against slavery and to perform forced or compulsory labour); ICESCR (opened for signature 16 December 1966, entered into force 3 January 1976) 993 UNTS 3: Art. 7 (the right to just and favourable conditions of work, healthy working conditions, as well as to rest and remuneration for public holidays).

[16] The background to the formulation of this indicator may be found in the conventions and recommendations published by the ILO. For instance, Art. 2(3) of the ILO Convention concerning Minimum Age for Admission to Employment (adopted 26 Jun 1973, entered into force 19 June 1976) 1015 UNTS 297 (ILO Convention No. 138) stipulates that '(t)he minimum age specified in pursuance of paragraph 1 of this Article shall not be less than the age of completion of compulsory schooling and, in any case, shall not be less than 15 years'.

Conditions of employment and work

In this case, the auditor assesses the extent to which a company provides healthy, suitable, and safe working conditions for all its employees. It equally explores whether employees are provided with the necessary support, training, and equipment to fulfil their assigned tasks. Included in this field is the payment of a living wage for basic working hours, provision of sick leave, maternity leave, etc.[17]

Non-discrimination

This indicator serves to ensure that the company's compensation, benefit plans and employment-related decisions are based solely on relevant and objective criteria. Coming under this heading are hiring practices that ensure equal opportunity of employment to disabled persons, for instance, unless their disability actually precludes them from performing the job requirements.[18]

Freedom of association

This indicator requires that a company recognizes the rights of its workers, including the freedom of association and the right to bargain collectively. Here again, the workers' representatives should not be subject to restriction or recrimination for merely carrying out their role in representing the workers in seeking their legitimate aspirations.[19]

Workplace health and safety

This indicator assesses whether the company's workers are afforded safe, suitable and sanitary working facilities. Where government regulation is not specific, best

---

[17] UDHR, see n. 15, Art. 24 (right to rest and leisure), ICESCR, see n. 15, Art. 7 (right to just and favourable conditions of work, healthy working conditions, as well as to rest and remuneration for public holidays).

[18] UDHR, see n. 15, Art. 2 (non-discrimination), Art. 7 (equality before the law), Art. 23(2) (right to equal pay for equal work); ICCPR, see n. 15, Art. 2 (non-discrimination), Art. 26 (equality before the law); ICESCR, see n. 15: Art. 2 (non-discrimination), Art. 7(a) (right to just and favourable conditions of work, Art. 7(c) right to fair wages and equal opportunity).

[19] UDHR, see n. 15, Art. 20(1) (freedom of peaceful assembly and association), Art. 23(4) (the right to form and to join trade unions); ICESCR, see n. 15: Art. 8 (a) the right to form trade unions, (b) the right of trade unions to establish national federations or confederations, (c) the right of trade unions to function freely subject to no limitations other than those prescribed by law, (d) the right to strike provided that it is exercised in conformity with the laws of the particular country; ICCPR, see n. 15: Art. 22 (restrictions on the freedom of association must be prescribed by law, necessary in a democratic society and in the interests of national security or public safety. See also, ILO Convention concerning Freedom of Association and Protection of the Right to Organize (adopted 9 July 1948, entered into force 4 July 1950) (ILO Convention No. 87), Arts. 2, 5 and 11, as well as the Convention concerning the Application of the Principles of the Right to Organize and to Bargain Collectively (adopted 1 July 1949, entered into force 18 July 1951) (ILO Convention No. 98), Arts 1 and 2.

practices should be adopted, especially in ensuring that all personnel undergo proper training on a regular basis to respond to workplace emergencies and that periodic fire and safety drills are conducted.[20]

Community and environmental impact

In this case, auditors will examine whether the company's operations are causing any harm to the local community or the environment in which it operates. This, however, merely states things in their broadest sense, for it includes such things as security, land issues, rights of the community, contingency plans for health and safety of the community in the case of industrial accidents, as well as fair business practice and corruption, which all fall under the human rights umbrella.[21]

Supply chain management

This final indicator serves to ensure that the company screens and monitors all major suppliers, contractors, sub-suppliers, joint-venture partners, and other major business associates with respect to their commitment to human rights and social issues. Again, this merely states things in the most simplistic of terms, for one has to rationalize what the company can and cannot achieve in this field. This rests on the degree of control and power that the company can exert over the supplier and other relevant stakeholders, for this is far greater if it is the supplier's primary income source. Nevertheless, companies should never forgo efforts to determine their position on such matters, no matter how little individual influence they can exert, for like gnat bites, outside pressures from numerous sources can eventually sway even the most stoic defender of the status quo. Moreover, the wise words of mother come to mind, 'Be careful of your choice of friends, for it is on them that you yourself will be judged.'

Lessons learned

Professor Ruggie often talks about 'the tone at the top' and this indeed is a primary determinant on how successful efforts are likely to be in implementing a productive

---

[20] The health and safety of workers is covered in both the ICESCR and ILO Convention No. 155 – Occupational Safety and Health, 1981. See also, ICESCR, see n. 15, Art. 7(b) (the right to just and favourable conditions of work which ensure, in particular: safe and healthy working conditions), Art. 12(1) (the right to the highest attainable standard of physical and mental health), Art. 12(2), 'The steps to be taken by the States party to the present Covenant to achieve the full realization of this right shall include those necessary for: ... (b) The improvement of all aspects of environmental and industrial hygiene; (c) The prevention, treatment and control of epidemic, endemic, occupational and other diseases; (d) The creation of conditions that would assure to all medical service and medical attention in the event of sickness).' See also Part II of the Occupational Safety and Health Convention (1981), relating to Principles of National Policy, Arts 4(1), 4(2) and 5.

[21] The right to a healthy environment is recognized in both international and regional conventions, including Art. 12 (2) of the ICESCR (see n. 15).

human rights audit.[22] The first clue is the level to which human rights and CSR issues are reported, and indeed whether such issues are dealt with by a dedicated department or simply viewed as another chore to be handled by human resources. The latter provision will, of course, depend on the size of the operation, but it is always encouraging when CSR matters are reported directly to top management. Indeed, this was one of the deciding factors for the choice of Berau Coal as the subject company for Moores Rowland – Mazars Indonesia's initial human rights audit using the MIHRSC, as its president director at the time, Rosan Roeslani, was not only a strong supporter but took a hands-on role in determining human rights policy. The decision was to be vindicated by the positive outcomes and feelings of satisfaction shared by both parties, resulting in particular from one of the audit's recommendations, whereby job advertisements were no longer gender or age specific. This led to female employees successfully performing roles that in the past had been looked upon as solely a male preserve.

Nevertheless, while the 'tone at the top' provides a first indication of how seriously a company takes its human rights responsibilities, what goes on behind the scenes is not always what the public might perceive. Despite adverse criticism at times, the Bakrie family, for example, has in the main retained the teams responsible for human rights matters in Bumi's major coal operations of Kaltim Prima Coal and Arutmin.[23] In fact, in a nationalistic spirit, they have not only supported the strengthening of programmes but empowered those put in place by previous owners BP and Rio Tinto, and BHP Billiton, respectively. However, at times, well-perceived companies are not as ardent in their support of human rights. We have also met with those responsible for human rights issues bemoaning the fact that they do not always have top management's ear.

From the other side of the picture, meanwhile, the auditor must also develop a strong bond of trust not only with the company, but with all relevant stakeholders. As financial auditors, this is something of which Moores Rowland – Mazars Indonesia was already well aware. The fact that APP and WWF are both on the firm's client list – despite at times being perceived as adversaries – only goes to highlight the fact that it is possible to be independent and impartial in treating each appointment strictly on its own merits. In the case of human rights audits, however, the importance of trust cannot be overstated. This is particularly so in the absence of confidentiality mechanisms akin to the attorney–client privilege where auditors are concerned. The building of such trust is thus an essential precursor to companies and relevant stakeholders feeling comfortable in openly revealing their challenges. Nevertheless, this is often easier said than done in instances where

---

[22] Ruggie has referred to the importance of this matter in various instances, including at the *First Annual Forum on Business and Human Rights* in Geneva on 4–5 December 2012.

[23] The family-controlled Bakrie Group is one of Indonesia's largest conglomerates with ten major companies listed on the Indonesia Stock Exchange. The cornerstone of the group is PT Bumi Resources, reputedly Asia's largest exporter of thermal coal, the production of its Kalimantan-based miners Kaltim Prima Coal and Arutmin. The former group chairman (eldest brother Aburizal Bakrie) retired in 2004 to enter politics. He is currently Chair of the Golkar Party and is standing as its official candidate for Indonesia's presidential election in 2014.

management's conviction of the advantages of human rights compliance clashes with the perception of grizzled veterans on the shop floor who do not see why they should suddenly have to change the way they may have been doing things for years or even decades. It is therefore essential for the company not only to introduce policies and practices that promote respect of human rights at all levels, but to explain the reasoning that lies behind their introduction. This is crucial in enabling employees to understand why new practices may be necessary and that they have not simply been introduced at the whim and caprice of management. All this forms part of embedding the whole concept of respect for human rights into the core fabric of the organization, which, if done correctly, can create a greater sense of shared ownership by breaking down barriers between management and the rank and file.

Patience and understanding are also key attributes for the human rights auditor to espouse, in addition to a deep-rooted commitment to help strengthen the respect for human rights as part of mainstream business practice. However, such enthusiasm must be tempered by an acknowledgement that human rights audit practice is a very new field of expertise, which is evolving at ground-breaking pace. As such, every audit must be approached with an air of caution in view of the diverse challenges brought on by assignments of this nature. In keeping with the demands of an ever-changing world, the MIHRSC themselves thus require constant updating as new laws and regulations come into force, in itself a time-consuming business. It is thus essential for the audit process to be individually tailored to address the specific challenges that each company faces, particularly in relation to industry sector and size of company, as these two variables can have major effects on the areas of concentration. This necessitates the auditors first surveying the landscape in order to determine what areas pose the greatest risk for that particular company. For instance, the running of a mining operation presents distinct problems to those involved in running a factory. This approach is consistent with the Guiding Principles, which calls upon companies to understand those areas of their operation that can negatively impact on human rights and put effective processes in place to deal with them.[24] However, the whole process has not solely been to build the capacity of companies in embedding respect for human rights into their corporate culture, for it has also built our own capacity, particularly in contributing resources. This has brought with it a need to incorporate specialists into the team on an assignment basis. For example, while much of *adat* land in Indonesia has now been officially transferred to State land, there

---

[24] See Commentary to Guiding Principle 12, which states that '[b]ecause business enterprises can have an impact on virtually the entire spectrum of internationally recognized human rights, their responsibility to respect applies to all such rights. In practice, some human rights may be at greater risk than others in particular industries or contexts, and therefore will be the focus of heightened attention. However, situations may change, so all human rights should be the subject of periodic review.' See n. 14 at pp. 13–14. See also, Guiding Principles 17–21, which elaborate on steps that businesses should take towards that end: see n. 14 at pp. 17–24.

still remains a need to understand and, wherever possible, respect the traditions, rights, and beliefs of the diverse local cultures spread across the archipelago.[25]

Cost is a major factor, of course, and while large mining operations can afford to hire a team of independent auditors to carry out an assessment of their human rights compliance across the whole of their operation, which may take three or four months or more to complete, the same is obviously not true of smaller companies in different fields. It was with this in mind that the MIHRSC were developed so that individual indicators can be used independently to address specific areas where human rights issues are most likely to arise. In a pilot project with GBI in India, for instance, Moores Rowland – Mazars Indonesia used only a single indicator for each of the subject companies. A lesson learned from this project, meanwhile, was that difficulties can arise in reaching agreement on the terms of reference for the audit, as one company wished to restrict the range of those interviewed, fearing that its workers would be emboldened to demand further rights.

In Indonesia, the majority of Moores Rowland – Mazars Indonesia's initial audits have involved large companies in the mining and plantation sectors. Both sectors are open to human rights issues involving the communities in which they operate, quite often with regard to land rights. Considerable tensions often arise from the fact that many affected communities occupy their traditional lands under forms of customary tenure and may therefore not benefit from formal legal titling. Similar problems also exist in Cambodia.[26] Meanwhile, following Indonesia's decentralization of government, the local administrations have come to view these large business operations as potentially lucrative sources of funding. On occasions, this has led to dubious tariffs being levied on the company. At other junctures, the local community faces significant disadvantage. This can heighten resentment of the perceived interloper and even lead to confrontation, in which the local police or army units may become involved. In such instances, the local community may view the security forces as acting on behalf of the company, whereas the security forces look upon it as merely carrying out their duty to protect the State's land that the government is currently leasing to the company. In one case, a foreign mining company, mindful of the damage this could cause to its carefully nurtured relationship with the local community, had to plead with the local police not to arrest local villagers merely for stopping on the road outside its operation. This reinforces the fact that it is not just business that needs to factor respect for human rights into its daily operations, but also the security forces – and by association – administrations at both the local and national level.

---

[25] In his landmark 1918 study on Indonesia's customary legal system, the Dutch scholar van Vollenhoven identified 19 geographical areas of jurisdiction in the Indonesian archipelago: see J. F. Holleman (ed.), *Van Vollenhoven on Indonesian adat law: selections from Het Adatrecht van Nederlandsch-Indië* (Volume I, 1918; Volume II, 1931, M. Nijhoff, 1981).

[26] Traditionally, in Cambodia, ownership of land has been based on land use instead of formal title. See http://www.aprodev.eu/files/Trade/landgrab_aprodev.pdf, accessed 16 February 2014, at p. 9. Though the Land Laws of 1992 and 2001 allow people to apply for formal title, only a small proportion of applicants received formal land certificates (ibid., at pp. 7–8). Meanwhile, a new

Alternative dispute resolution

The complex nature of these intersecting relationships emphasizes the need for compromise. While this is perhaps most relevant in securing an effective remedy following harmful business impacts, experience gained from carrying out human rights audits has revealed a great need for skilled mediators to address issues in their early formative stages before the realities become obscured by emotion. A mediated solution is far more likely to achieve this than legal recourse, which by its very nature is confrontational. Thus in the vast majority of cases, mediation offers by far the most logical and effective means of resolution, as it avoids the win–lose outcome of legal recourse that can breed ongoing resentment.

Sadly, however, resources facilitating such courses of action are extremely limited in countries across ASEAN. In Indonesia, for instance, alternative dispute resolution is regulated under two laws, but neither specifically addresses business-related human rights disputes.[27] Moreover, existing mediation training centres focus solely on procedural rather than human rights aspects, thus meaning that knowledge of such matters – as well as of applicable laws – relies solely on the individual mediator's own background. This at times results in inconsistency and a lack of sufficiency in the way the mediators comprehend the issue at hand. It is in view of such challenges that Moores Rowland – Mazars Indonesia and the Human Rights Resource Centre for ASEAN have committed to establishing a Business and Human Rights Mediation Centre, to both train mediators and offer mediation services. Although the courses will vary in accordance with differing needs, training will be available for personnel from companies, NGOs and government entities, as well as for those seeking to become professional mediators attached to the Centre. It is all a matter of putting lessons learned into practice, and learning together as we move forward.

Looking ahead

Human rights in business involve three key players – government, the company, and civil society. The interdependence between these actors cannot be overstated. At the time of writing (May 2013), the collapse of Rana Plaza in Bangladesh – which resulted in the death of over 1,100 workers – is fresh in everyone's minds. Initial reports suggest that all the Bangladeshi stakeholders were complicit to one degree or another: government for not enforcing enacted legislation on the building owner; the individual companies for forcing their staff to work in unsafe conditions; and civil society for its apathy in accepting what was known to be the status quo. Yet, in this era of globalization, responsibilities extend far

---

titling initiative launched on 14 June 2012 has not been fully effective in addressing titling issues in disputed areas. See http://www.adhoc-cambodia.org/wp-content/uploads/2013/02/ADHOC-A-Turning-Point-Land-Housing-and-Natural-Resources-Rights-in-2012.pdf, accessed 16 February 2014, at p. 35.

27 Law No. 30 Year 1999 – Arbitration and Alternative Dispute Resolution; and Indonesian Supreme Court Resolution No.1 Year 2008 on Court Annexed Resolution Procedure.

beyond the borders of any individual country, for the tragic events in Bangladesh impinge on the supply chains of a number of major labels in the Western world. Several of these European companies have quickly accepted their collective responsibility, since signing on to the 'Accord on Fire and Building Safety in Bangladesh', a legally binding agreement which aims to ensure the safety of all garment factories in Bangladesh.[28] Signatories are required to establish a fire and building safety programme in the country for a five-year period.[29] While this is very much a case of locking the stable door once the horse has bolted, it also shows their awareness that today's 'connected' society is far more aware of events, and is increasingly becoming the world's conscience in regard to acceptable behaviour by both business and governments.

This sheds light on one of the most difficult problems to overcome, which is to create a common understanding at both the local and global level. While the Member States of the United Nations have endorsed the Guiding Principles at an international level, certain clients have stressed the significant distance between the august halls of diplomacy and their own operational bases, thus underscoring the need for the concepts to be endorsed at a national level. This does not solely involve companies, or even auditors; all three key players must play their part. As far as government is concerned, involvement cannot be limited to simply passing legislation, as the Rana Plaza affair has shown. Each government department must determine the most effective and complementary role that it can play to pro-mote respect for human rights within the business sphere, as well as across society as a whole. An introspective look into its own operating practices would often con-stitute an important starting point.

Civil society, too, must also accept its responsibilities to advance the cause, while being mindful of the value of constructive engagement. This is particu-larly so given the counterproductive effects of antagonistic strategies that may not adequately take into account all the various complexities of a situation. It is here that use of the MIHRSC or a similar approach can build on the standing of auditors as a trusted independent voice on fiscal matters in providing assur-ance on financial statements and encouraging best practices in corporate behav-iour. Translated to the realm of human rights, the Moores Rowland – Mazars Indonesia audit concept can hopefully break the deadlock between civil society and corporations by providing independent third-party monitoring that is accept-able to all three key players.

Conclusion

There are two words that business especially adheres to – certainty and consistency – with the latter being particularly important for financial audit practice, as it enables

---

[28] European signatories include H&M, Mango, and Benetton: see 'The Bangladesh Accord on Fire and Building Safety', http://www.bangladeshaccord.org/signatories, accessed 11 February 2014.

[29] The full text of the Accord is available at http://www.bangladeshaccord.org/wp-content/uploads/2013/10/the_accord.pdf, accessed 11 February 2014.

comparisons to be made. Efficient capital markets cannot exist without accounting, which is the figuring and recording of financial transactions, and auditing, which is the formal checking of financial recordings. The audit of company human rights statements is no less important. Just as there are internationally accepted standards to conduct the audit of financial statements, there is also a need for internationally accepted auditing standards in respect of human rights. It is for this precise reason that Moores Rowland – Mazars Indonesia and Shift have partnered to undertake a two-year project that seeks to develop a twin set of standards for auditing companies, in line with the Guiding Principles. This initiative is being carried out in close cooperation with the Human Rights Research Centre for ASEAN, which serves as a primary research and outreach partner. The proposed standards seek to encompass global and widely accepted (a) reporting standards for businesses to report on their implementation of appropriate risk-management procedures, in accordance with the UN Guiding Principles, and (b) assurance standards to assess companies' performance with regard to human rights risk management. The latter in particular is being conceptualized on the basis of the experience gained in developing and utilizing the MIHRSC, together with input from interested parties, especially in the ASEAN region. The hope is that these twin standards will be adopted at both national and international levels in a similar manner to the standards for financial audit today. The desired outcome is that regulators eventually insist that companies listed on the world's stock markets commit to their implementation.

How soon that can be brought about depends on the will of the three key players. From the State perspective, an increasing number of governments are becoming receptive to the idea of greater reporting on matters concerning human rights and social compliance. This is reflected, for example, in a growing number of countries becoming compliant with the Extractive Industries Transparency Initiative, while there has been increasing regulation in both the USA and Europe in reporting on human rights and social compliance matters. The business sector, for its part, is normally swift to adapt once matters are clearly explained, and certainty and consistency set in place, though given human nature, there will always be a diminishing few who do not wish to comply. That leaves society, for whom expectations must be balanced against the practicalities of implementation. While paradigm shifts cannot be expected overnight, support must be offered to companies that are willing to overcome their current shortcomings. Patience will be a key, but in its role as the ultimate regulator, it will be society that in the end determines the degree to which the Guiding Principles are in fact put into practice.

10 Making human rights a core business practice

The finance sector's role in the promotion and protection of human rights

Kerri-Ann O'Neill

Introduction

Christine Lagarde, head of the International Monetary Fund, said in a 2013 speech on finance sector reform, 'we have made progress, but there is more to do'.[1] The same sentiment can be carried through to the discussion on the finance sector's efforts to make human rights a core business practice.

The size and scale of financial services is a reminder of its significant influence on everyday lives across the world. McKinsey estimates that the world stock of equity and debt at the end of 2010 stood at US$212 trillion.[2] The global fund management industry assets alone totals around US$120 trillion.[3] This is a snapshot of the industry, without even the inclusion of the '2.5 billion estimated adults with discretionary income who are not part of the formal financial system'.[4] In Southeast Asia, the industry is growing faster than GDP, with the Singapore financial services sector expanding 13.1 per cent in 2012 from the previous year.[5] Meanwhile, the number of banks in the Philippines has increased to approximately 700.[6]

The financial services industry is admittedly large and complex. This reality is reflected in the infamous assertion during the global financial crisis that the banking sector was 'too big to fail'.[7] Financial institutions are generally classified as asset managers, banks, private equity institutions or insurance companies.

---

[1] Speech by Christine Lagarde entitled 'The Global Financial Sector – Transforming the Landscape', (*International Monetary Fund*, 19 March 2013), https://www.imf.org/external/np/speeches/2013/031913.htm, accessed 8 March 2014.

[2] C. Roxburgh, S. Lund and J. Piotrowski, *Mapping Global Capital Markets 2011* (McKinsey Global Institute Updated Research Series, 2011), p. 3.

[3] Mary Dowell-Jones, 'Financial Institutions and Human Rights', *Human Rights Law Review*, (2013), 13(3): 423–468, p. 451.

[4] Roxburgh, Lund and Piotrowski, see n. 2.

[5] Department of Statistics Singapore, 'IMF Special Data Dissemination Standard – Economic and Financial Data for Singapore', (2013), http://www.singstat.gov.sg/SDDS/data.html, accessed 8 March 2014.

[6] Deloitte Navarro Amper & Co, *The Philippines: What's Next for the Chosen Land?* (2013), http://www.deloitte.com/assets/DcomPhilippines/Local%20Assets/Documents/Philippines%20state%20of%20the%20nation.pdf, accessed 8 March 2014, p. 3.

[7] Speech by Christine Lagarde, see n. 1.

They provide services around asset-based finance, retail banking, private banking, corporate and investment banking, capital markets, insurance, reinsurance and investment amongst other financial products and services.[8] The sector is heavily interconnected and the global nature of the industry has been long commented upon, leading to the strengthening of the cross-border regulatory regime with the 2009 introduction of the Financial Stability Board (FSB).

This chapter will provide an overview of the current progress that the financial services sector has made in its role to protect and promote human rights, as well as suggesting how the sector may be able to accelerate such progress. It will further explore how financial services can be a substantial force for the strengthened protection and promotion of human rights and assess to what extent the industry is committed to complying with the UN Guiding Principles, which provide the ideal platform for collaboration and change. This will require a review of what is being disclosed by the industry, particularly with respect to how relevant actors across Southeast Asia are integrating the Guiding Principles within their operations. The chapter will then finally discuss what further engagement is needed from the industry in order to consolidate advances.

The core purpose of financial services

The World Trade Organization (WTO) states that 'the bundle of institutions that make up an economy's financial system can be seen as "the brain of the economy", providing the bulk of the economy's need for many functions'.[9] The UK's Financial Conduct Authority believes that 'from insurance contracts for ships negotiated in coffee shops of Mr. Edward Lloyd, to goldsmiths acting as safe depositors of money for merchants, the financial services industry was built on the needs of its customer and functioned in order to meet those needs'.[10]

When stripping the sector of its complexity, it becomes evident that the financial services industry accelerates our society's economic development, which is arguably its core purpose. It can, taking into account risk, make capital available to entrepreneurs and valued companies to grow the economy, improve productivity and provide goods and services which enhance people's lives. It can help pool risks and smooth the shocks of catastrophic events at both the individual and the social level. As such, capital markets enable society to 'bridge the past, present and future';[11] and at its most aspirational is 'the currency of stewardship'.[12]

---

[8] Sustainable Finance Advisory, *Environment and Social Risk Due Diligence in the Financial Sector*, report commissioned by the Netherlands in support of the Proactive Agenda of the OECD Working Party on Responsible Business Conduct Amsterdam, 2013, p. 4.

[9] WTO, 'Financial Services', http://www.wto.org/english/tratop_e/serv_e/finance_e/finance_e.htm, accessed 8 March 2014.

[10] Financial Conduct Authority, *FCA Risk Outlook 2013* (2013), http://www.fca.org.uk/static/fca/documents/fca-risk-outlook-2013.pdf, accessed 8 March 2014, p. 5.

[11] Tomorrow's Company, *Tomorrow's Capital Markets: A Private Invitation to Work with Tomorrow's Company to Set New Incentive Structures for a Sustainable World*, report for the Participants of the PRI in Person Annual Event, (2012), http://www.unepfi.org/fileadmin/publications/investment/Tomorrow_s_Capital_Markets_web.pdf, accessed 8 March 2014, p. 3.

[12] Ibid.

Clearly the responsible provision, management and allocation of capital and credit, as well as the facilitation of the exchange of goods and services, ultimately enable us to grow wealth and care for ourselves and others now and in the future. The transfer and apportionment of risk, as well as the protection and strengthening of assets and savings likewise serves this end. Such services also provide the means for businesses, enterprises and wider economies to innovate and evolve. This is true of every country and region in the world, including Southeast Asia, which is on a robust economic growth trajectory as its emerging economies develop and productivity improves, with the possibility of lifting millions out of poverty.[13]

It is exactly this ability to transform businesses and economies that builds pride in the institutions of finance. For example, DBS, one of Asia's largest financial services groups, tells us that 'DBS was established in 1968 as the Development Bank of Singapore. It was the catalyst to Singapore's economic development during the nation's early years.'[14] Such outcomes powerfully intersect with the original ethos and spirit of the global human rights movement.[15]

The ability to facilitate the enjoyment of key human rights provides the sector with its positive social force. For example, by providing the means to grow the economy, the sector makes it easier for States to provide the right to work,[16] right to a standard of living adequate for health and well-being,[17] the right to education,[18] and the right to own property.[19] Equally, as a sizeable and influential sector in its own right, it is well placed to advise and conduct business with governments, businesses and individuals on human rights factors and crucially it can choose to withdraw support to avoid, contain and mitigate violations. An example of this positive social force extends to institutions which have focused on providing financial services for vulnerable people. Grameen Bank constitutes one such example, stating that its objective 'is to bring financial services to the poor, particularly women and the poorest'. In doing so, it prides itself on being 'almost the reverse of the conventional banking methodology'. This Bangladeshi bank 'starts with the belief that credit should be accepted as a human right … [and] believes that all human beings, including the poorest, are endowed with endless potential'.[20] In doing so, it has proven to stay true to the core purpose of banking, which is to help people save for the future and to provide credit to fuel entrepreneurism.

---

[13] ICAEW, *Economic Insight South East Asia Quarterly Briefing Q3 2013* (2013), http://www.icaew.com/~/media/Files/About-ICAEW/What-we-do/economic-insight/7805-5-icaew-sea-q3-2013-web.pdf, accessed 8 March 2014, p. 2.

[14] See http://www.dbs.com/about/aboutus/default.aspx, accessed 8 March 2014.

[15] The Universal Declaration of Human Rights 1948 preamble states 'the peoples of the United Nations have in the Charter reaffirmed their faith in fundamental human rights, in the dignity and worth of the human person and in the equal rights of men and women and have determined to promote social progress and better standards of life in larger freedoms'.

[16] Universal Declaration of Human Rights 1948, Art. 23.

[17] Universal Declaration of Human Rights 1948, Art. 25.

[18] Universal Declaration of Human Rights 1948, Art. 26.

[19] Universal Declaration of Human Rights 1948, Art. 17.

[20] Grameen Bank, 'Is Grameen Bank Different From Conventional Banks?', (October 2011), http://www.grameen-info.org/index.php?option=com_contentandtask=viewandid=27andItemid=176, accessed 8 March 2014.

Additional initiatives for the promotion of human rights

Project finance for large-scale commercial lending constitutes a relatively small proportion of the commercial lending book of most banks, but is very well supported by policies, practices and governance in terms of assessing non-financial risk, including human rights.[21] The Equator Principles[22] created in 2003 – following controversies involving several financial institutions in the early 2000s, such as the 2002 condemnation by the UN Security Council of eighty-five multinationals for aiding the plunder of the Democratic Republic of Congo's wealth[23] – have served as the basis for sustainable project finance for over a decade now. This work is important to reduce the risk of complicity in human rights abuses through the provision of finance. As at 1 January 2014, the third edition of the principles has been released and includes a reference to the Guiding Principles.[24]

The work of the United Nations Principles for Responsible Investment (UNPRI), launched in 2006, constitutes an additional example of the sector's capacity to facilitate the enjoyment of human rights. UNPRI now counts 1,247 signatories[25] and covers assets under management worth US$34 trillion (or 15 per cent of the world's investable assets), up from US$4 trillion at the UN PRI's launch.[26] The impetus for this work comes from the acceptance of the view that investment and the flow of capital can influence positive social and environmental outcomes. The UNPRI group has spawned many complementary initiatives, such as Sustainable Stock Exchanges Initiatives,[27] which are contributing to the development of a more robust benchmark of environmental, social and governance (ESG) perform-ance for financial investors and wraps in human rights concerns. The benchmarks make it easier for investors to assess what impact their investment may have on social dimensions. The 2012 Annual Report highlights several examples showcas-ing progress in relation to the protection and promotion of human rights, includ-ing the fact that since 2009, 'a coalition of 11 investors has been encouraging 10 companies from the extractive industry to adopt better policies for managing indi-genous rights risks. According to the group's analysis, five companies (3 of which are Canadian) have improved their overall performance.'[28]

---

[21] The Thun Group of Banks, *UN Guiding Principles on Business and Human Rights: Discussion Paper for Banks on Implications of Principles 16–21* (Geneva, 2013), http://www.business-humanrights.org/media/documents/thun-group-discussion-paper-final-2-oct-2013.pdf, accessed 8 March 2014, p. 21.

[22] See http://equator-principles.com, accessed 8 March 2014.

[23] F&C Asset Management and KPMG LLP UK, *Banking on Human Rights: Confronting Human Rights in the Financial Sector*, (September 2004), http://us.kpmg.com/microsite/fslibrarydotcom/docs/Banking%20on%20Human%20Rights_FC_KPMG.pdf, accessed 8 March 2014, p. 6.

[24] See http://equator-principles.com/index.php/equator-principles-3, accessed 8 March 2014.

[25] United Nations Principles for Responsible Investment, http://www.unpri.org/signatories/signator-ies, accessed 8 March 2014.

[26] See http://www.unpri.org/news/pri-fact-sheet, accessed 8 March 2014.

[27] Sustainable Stock Exchanges Initiative, http://www.sseinitiative.org, accessed 8 March 2014.

[28] UNPRI, *Annual Report 2012* (Geneva: UNPRI, 2012), http://www.unpri.org/viewer/?file=wp-content/uploads/Annualreport20121.pdf, accessed 8 March 2014, p. 11.

Aviva[29] serves as an example of the leadership potential of financial organizations to choose to not support activities that can lead to the violation of human
rights. For instance, as a founding signatory of the UNPRI and its commitment
to abide by the Covenant on Cluster Munitions, Aviva does not hold any securities which relate to the cluster munitions industry. Accordingly, in 2013, Aviva
confirmed that it had completed the full audit of its shareholder investments and
made a statement 'confirm(ing) that we have no such holdings'.[30] This work has
now been extended to review policy-holder funds and to publishing its Stop List to
further educate investors about who is producing cluster munitions.[31]

The promotion of human rights is further advanced through the sector's
corporate responsibility practices, which usually involves community investment or philanthropic practices. There are examples of large community
investment programmes within the financial services sector which promote
rights – such as HSBC's Future First initiative on supporting education for
vulnerable children,[32] Barclays Bank's 'Banking on Change' initiative to
improve financial inclusion,[33] ING's partnership with UNICEF,[34] State Street's
US$117 million investment in affordable housing via the Massachusetts Housing
Investment Corporation,[35] as well as Bank Mandiri's 'Self-reliant With Mandiri'
scheme,[36] and Aviva's 'Street to School' programme, to name but a few.

Aviva is also actively involved in such practices, with initiatives dedicated specifically to helping promote the rights of street children. In doing so, it has worked
closely with Plan International and Indonesia's Ministry of Social Affairs to ensure
that 1,500 of Jakarta's street children secure birth registration documents. These
documents are essential for these children to be recognized as citizens and are also
critical for their effective access to education, health services and work.[37] Without
documentation, the children are prone to exposure to the worst forms of human
rights abuses, including trafficking, by criminal actors who prey on the anonymity

---

[29] Aviva is the UK's largest insurance company and operates in 17 markets worldwide including India,
   China, Hong Kong, Vietnam, Taiwan, Indonesia and Singapore.
[30] Aviva, 'Aviva's Position on Cluster Munitions: An Update', (1 March 2013), http://www.aviva.com/
   media/news/item/avivas-position-on-cluster-munitions-an-update-17101, accessed 8 March 2014.
[31] Ibid. A Stop List is a list of institutions that asset managers will not trade in through any of its
   funds.
[32] See http://www.hsbc.com/citizenship/sustainability/youth-education, accessed 8 March 2014.
[33] See http://group.barclays.com/about-barclays/citizenship/our-programmes/community-programmes/
   banking-on-change, accessed 8 March 2014.
[34] See https://www.ingforsomethingbetter.com/our-approach/communities/ing-unicef/, accessed 8
   March 2014.
[35] See http://www.statestreet.com/wps/portal/internet/corporate/home/aboutstatestreet/corporate-
   citizenship/communitydevelopment/!ut/p/c4/04_SB8K8xLLM9MSSzPy8xBz9CP0os3i_0CADCy
   dDRwN3A0tzA09vE0Nvfw9nY3dnQ_3g1Lz40GD9gmxHRQBOwkY4, accessed 8 March 2014.
[36] See http://csr.bankmandiri.co.id/en/menu-self-reliant-mandiri-15.html, accessed 8 March 2014.
[37] CSR Asia, *Joining the Dialogue – Vulnerable Children and Business* (London: CSR Asia, 2013), http://
   www.csr-asia.com/report/Joining_the_dialogue-Vulnerable_children_and_business.pdf, accessed
   8 March 2014, p. 24.

of those without registration. Furthermore, supporting the Jakarta street children increases the likelihood of other cities and regions in Indonesia drawing on the lessons learned, and thus increases the number of actors able to effectively reach out to some of the country's most vulnerable citizens.

Aviva has contributed also to the reduction of child labour in New Delhi, India by supporting Save the Children to conduct a local campaign in a local wet market that encourages stall-holders and small business owners to advertise that their stalls do not use child labour. The project builds on the relationship that the company had already cultivated with the locality through the funding of a drop-in centre for street children in Nehru Place. This successful activity helped to extend the influence of International Labour Organization (ILO) conventions to segments of Delhi previously unaware of such standards.[38] Likewise, Aviva's hosting of a Southeast Asia street-connected child rights conference in Singapore – with partners United Nations Office of the High Commissioner for Human Rights and the NGO Consortium for Street Children – brought together experts from the government, NGO and business sectors to discuss key actions necessary to protect and promote street children's rights.[39] This helped strengthen a dialogue, which until then was largely invisible to society. These are active examples of finance companies taking their role to respect human rights to the core of their business.

In addition, major global financial services companies have been active in ensuring that their own workforce is afforded rights often beyond the national norm, where relevant. This is particularly significant in view of the sector's role as a major employer – e.g. financial services account for 1.3 million jobs in the UK alone.[40] The large, multinational financial institutions have been generally supportive of rights-based agendas within their own workforce, such as elimination of discrimination and in particular promoting women in the workplace. As a starting point, in this respect, Credit Suisse has published research on gender diversity.[41] Barclays Bank, in turn, serves as the Diversity sponsor at the Singapore British Chamber of Commerce.[42] Meanwhile, the Singapore chapter of the Financial Women's Association boasts a healthy and growing corporate members base comprised of the leading financial institutions in Singapore. It regularly holds events with government and NGOs to advance the dialogue of women in financial services.[43]

[38] See http://www.savethechildren.in/85-latest-news/255-street-children-of-delhi-ask-for-their-safety.html, accessed 8 March 2014.
[39] See http://www.business-humanrights.org/Links/Repository/1023916/link_page_view, accessed 8 March 2014.
[40] Equality and Human Rights Commission, *Financial Services Enquiry: Follow Up Report* (London, 2011), http://www.equalityhumanrights.com/uploaded_files/Inquiries/fsi_follow-up_report.pdf, accessed 26 March 2014.
[41] Credit Suisse, 'Does Gender Diversity Improve Performance?', (31 July 2012), https://www.credit-suisse.com/sg/en/news-and-expertise/research/credit-suisse-research-institute/news-and-videos.article.html/article/pwp/news-and-expertise/2012/07/en/does-gender-diversity-improve-performance.html accessed, accessed 8 March 2014.
[42] See http://www.britcham.org.sg/index.php/topmenu/about/sponsors, accessed 8 March 2014.
[43] See http://www.fwasg.org, accessed 8 March 2014.

Together, the Equator Principles, the UNPRI, the Global Compact and other such initiatives have helped transform the policies and practices of financial organizations to be more human rights compliant. The emerging consensus in this regard is reflected in the 2008 United Nations Environment Programme (UNEP) statement by financial institutions that, 'beyond the core business activities, companies in the financial sector may have a role to play in creating an enabling environment for the realization of human rights'.[44] This view has been echoed by the Institute of Human Rights in Business (IHRB), which stated that:

> As an important connector in the world economy, the finance sector is in a privileged position to support or undermine respect for human rights. As most financial institutions have clients and investments in a wide range of sectors, the finance sector's exposure to human rights risks is potentially broader than any other sector.[45]

Yet, further analysis is needed on how the finance sector can most effectively support the realization of human rights. For instance, academics have signalled that, 'there is an urgent need for an informed understanding of the ways that economic policies conducive to people-centred development can support the realization of human rights, and the ways that a human rights focus can support progressive economic policies'.[46] This gap in understanding is exacerbated by the view that financial services are not trustworthy because they are perceived as complex. The Edelman Trust Barometer in fact shows that financial services is the least trusted sector of them all.[47] Multiple opinion polls further suggest that people do not believe that the financial services sector is living up to its core purpose – focusing instead on activities that benefit itself and its investors. This perception is largely underpinned by the fact that 'over the past three decades, economic policy has been geared toward achieving economic growth, underwritten by assumptions about the virtues of the market. Efficiency rather than ethics has been the focus of concern'.[48] This lack of trust means that financial institutions often encounter accusations of violations that may have little to do with them. Institutions must therefore review issues of trust as a new risk to reputation. This state of affairs highlights a breakdown of the traditional view that financiers are the middlemen of the economy and that 'the provision of capital is seen as a neutral act'.[49] The financial sector is no longer perceived as playing a neutral role in society, and this

[44] R. Sullivan and P. Birtwell, *CEO Briefing: Human Rights* (Geneva: UNEPFI, 2008). p. 4.
[45] See http://www.ihrb.org/top10/business_human_rights_issues/2014.html, accessed 8 March 2014.
[46] R. Balakrishnan, D. Elson and R. Patel 'Rethinking Macro Economic Strategies from a Human Rights Perspective', (2010,) *Development*, 53(1): (27–36), at p. 28.
[47] Edelman, '2013 Edelman Trust Barometer Reports Financial Services is Least Trusted Industry Globally', (9 April 2013), http://www.edelman.com/news/2013-edelman-trust-barometer-reports-financial-services-is-least-trusted-industry-globally, accessed 8 March 2014.
[48] Balakrishnan, Elson and Patel, 'Rethinking Macro Economic Strategies', see n. 46, p. 27.
[49] R. Roca and F. Manta, *Values Added: The Challenge of Integrating Human Rights into the Financial Sector* (Copenhagen: Danish Institute for Human Rights, 2010), p. 6.

factor is crucial to the dialogue and debate underpinning the emerging changes within the industry.

While momentum is being gained, it remains challenging to reach a consensus on where financial services and the human rights agenda intersect. In 2004, a KPMG report specifically pointed to these challenges, stating that '(the task of) identifying how human rights issues interplay with the financial services sector can be elusive' in contrast to the extractive and retail industries, which have been 'the prime focus of pressure groups concerned with the protection and promotion of human rights'.[50] In light of such challenges and limited alignment of financial services with the Guiding Principles and other relevant human rights standards, can the industry be said to be taking its human rights responsibilities seriously?

Where has progress been made?

The finance sector's important role in creating an eco-system which protects and promotes human rights has been gaining pace following the adoption of the Guiding Principles and the incorporation of human rights provisions within the OECD Guidelines for Multinational Enterprises (the OECD Guidelines) – both of which relate to financial services.[51] This has served as a fresh opportunity to review current human rights practice within financial services organizations, as evidenced by the OECD Ministerial Council Meeting raising (as one of the first Proactive Agenda items) 'the need to better understand what proper observance of the OECD guidelines by the financial sector entails'.[52] However, ten years on, the Sustainable Financial Advisory review of human rights and the financial sector for the OECD Working Party on Responsible Business Conduct has found many financial institutions to be 'at the early stages of understanding the implications for their institutions'.[53] Indeed, progress on the surface looks good, the recent study by the Sustainable Finance Advisory found that 90 per cent of respondents had a human rights policy in place, with 50 per cent of these having been in place for over five years, and 60 per cent of its recent survey respondents from the financial institutes were 'aware' of the Guiding Principles.[54] In turn, a report from KPMG in 2004 confirmed human rights policies and statements for eight of the major global banks.[55] Meanwhile, many financial institutions are signatories of the United Nations Global Compact, which emphasizes human rights promotion as one of its ten areas of focus within its annual 'Communication of Progress'.

---

[50] F&C Asset Management and KPMG LLP UK, see n. 23, p. 8.

[51] The Sustainable Finance Advisory report takes pains to point out that the 2011 update to the OECD Guidelines were confirmed as applicable to all sectors including the financial sector. See Sustainable Finance Advisory, *Environment and Social Risk Due Diligence in the Financial Sector* (Report commissioned by the Netherlands in support of the Proactive Agenda of the OECD Working Party on Responsible Business Conduct Amsterdam, 2013), p. 6.

[52] Ibid., p. 7.

[53] Ibid., p. 7.

[54] Ibid., p. 45.

[55] F&C Asset Management and KPMG LLP UK, see n. 23. Aviva counted among those issuing its first human rights policy at that time.

In light of the above, it must be noted that some commentators have suggested that the finance sector's efforts to integrate human rights concerns into its core business practices have been too slow.[56] In this respect Dowell-Jones has highlighted that 'financial institutions have largely failed to get to grips with an understanding of how their operations may directly impact on human rights enjoyment'.[57] She has further argued that 'efforts have largely related to a few keys areas where environmental and some human rights impacts are the most visible and directly attributed to corporate activity'.[58] Others have stated that 'what constitutes integration of social issues into the financial sector is still not fully developed or agreed upon'.[59] Meanwhile, the Sustainability Finance Advisory committee found from their study that:

> [D]ifferent business models of financial institutes and the specific mix of financial products and services they provide drive different environment and social due diligence approaches (...) Unless such standards are directly relevant to the financial sector and provide a framework which assists financial institutions in assessing underlying environmental and social risks, their uptake by the sector is low.[60]

For some, the limited progress can be attributed to confusion with how human rights operates philosophically alongside the fiduciary responsibility – the foundational pillar of trust and a legal construct within the financial services. The fiduciary duty for asset managers is, at its simplest, 'the duty to act loyally'[61] and to follow the investment mandate. The UNEP-FI and UNPRI platforms have gone to great lengths to persuade asset managers and pension fund trustees that ESG considerations do not interfere with the fiduciary responsibility and, if anything, can enhance it. Margaret Hodge, former Minister of State for Industry and Regions in the United Kingdom, has contributed to the debate by echoing an increasingly shared view since the 'massive financial crisis and acute loss of confidence'[62] of recent years:

> [T]here was a time when business success in the interests of shareholders was thought to be in conflict with society's aspirations for people … for the long

---

[56] Mary Dowell-Jones, 'Financial Institutions and Human Rights', *Human Rights Law Review*, (2013), 13(3): 423–468, p. 444.

[57] Ibid., p. 423.

[58] Mary Dowell-Jones and D. Kinley, 'The Monster Under the Bed: Financial Services and the Ruggie Framework', in Radu Mares (ed.), *The UN Guiding Principles on Business and Human Rights: Foundations and Implementation* (Brill, 2011) 193–216, p. 197.

[59] Roca and Manta, *Values Added*, see n. 49, p. 25.

[60] Sustainable Finance Advisory, *Environment and Social Risk Due Diligence in the Financial Sector* (Report commissioned by the Netherlands in support of the Proactive Agenda of the OECD Working Party on Responsible Business Conduct Amsterdam, 2013, pp. 8 and 26).

[61] UNEPFI, *Fiduciary Responsibility: Legal and Practical Aspects of Integrating Environmental, Social and Governance Issues into Institutional Investment* (Geneva: UN Environment Programme, July 2009), http://www.unepfi.org/fileadmin/documents/fiduciaryII.pdf, accessed 8 March 2014, p. 27.

[62] Ibid., p. 25.

term well-being of the community and protection of the environment. The law is now based on a new approach. Pursuing the interest of shareholders and embracing wider responsibilities are complementary purposes, not contradictory ones.[63]

Some thus argue that, traditionally, fiduciary responsibility has been too narrowly interpreted when making financial decisions on behalf of others, a factor that has led to an investment culture that excludes human rights considerations.[64] Dowell-Jones argues that the size of assets under the management of the signatories of the UN Principles of Responsible Investment, whilst an impressive number, 'is still a very small fraction of financial markets, which are worth in excess of US$ 1000 trillion and are made up of complex, interlocking layers of financial activity'.[65]

Some of the criticism relating to the sector's limited progress is further attributed to a disinterest or lack of leadership from the sector, or even wilful neglect.[66] Controversial or not, this criticism must be considered in light of observations put forward by Barry Herman, an economist, who suggested to the Office of the High Commissioner for Human Rights that, 'whether or not falling within the explicit human rights framework, the financial activities to be discussed here [in the paper] are, at least, clear injustices, morally offensive and not often enough illegal.'[67] Examples from Herman include the Spanish *cajas de ahorros* (savings bank), which he argues, with hindsight, '[to] have been abusive practices … they heavily lent during the housing bubble, when funds to lend were easy to obtain and market opportunities were apparently irresistible. Many people have lost homes and savings as a result.'[68] Other examples include 'institutions [that] have taken on risks that exceed their mandate, for which they have paid with insolvency. This includes the bankruptcies of "Fannie Mae" (Federal National Mortgage Association) and "Freddie Mac" (Federal Home Loan Mortgage Corporation) in the United States.'[69]

The Thun Group of Banks – which was established in 2011 to consider the potential implications of the UN Guiding Principles on the banking sector – stated in its latest report that, for banks 'most human rights impact areas arise via the actions of their clients and are addressed through influence, leverage and dialogue rather than through the direct action from the banks themselves'.[70]

[63] Ibid., p. 23.
[64] Dowell-Jones, 'Financial Institutions and Human Rights', see n. 56, p. 444.
[65] Dowell-Jones and Kinley, 'The Monster Under the Bed', see n. 58, p. 197.
[66] Responses to the challenges faced by survey respondents on human rights due diligence and the UNGP in the Sustainable Finance Advisory (2013) report consistently cite 'lack of definitions, tools and lack of clarity', pp. 46–47. The tone implies that when this is provided financial institutions may act upon it.
[67] Barry Herman, *Regulating Financial Sectors for Development and Social Justice. Note for the expert group meeting organized by The Office of the High Commission for Human Rights United Nations* (New York, 24 April 2013), http://www.ohchr.org/Documents/Issues/Development/RightsCrisis/BarryHerman.pdf, accessed 8 March 2014, p. 1.
[68] Ibid., p. 6.
[69] Ibid., p. 6.
[70] The Thun Group of Banks is made up of Barclays, BBVA, Credit Suisse, ING Bank, RBS Group, UBS AG, UniCredit. The Thun Group of Banks, *UN Guiding Principles on Business and Human Rights*, see n. 21, p. 20.

The Thun Group of Banks has emphasized that:

> The degree to which it is feasible for banks to exert influence on their clients' behaviour is a matter of complexity. Governments are, as the Guiding Principles, reiterate, the primary duty-bearers of rights. Commercial organisations, including banks, cannot be expected to become human rights 'regulators' as a surrogate for government.[71]

The question of the balance between States' and financial institutions' responsibilities is a fair challenge. However, the global financial crisis of recent years has prompted experts to counter that there is only an indirect link between human rights abuses and violations and the financial sector.[72] This renders the statement of the financial services regulatory bodies interesting to note. For example, the UK's Financial Conduct Authority stated in 2013 that,

> Financial services design (structures and processes) and management (including culture and incentives) have been developed over time in ways that allow firms to profit from the systematic consumer short-comings and market failures. These characteristics have been the root of poor conduct outcomes in the past.[73]

Whether the regulatory bodies associate poor conduct with human rights abuses is not known. However, an assessment of the broad systemic and macro levels of harm that the finance sector can cause in aggregate terms to human rights worldwide, has led some to argue that:

> The globalisation of financial services has far outstripped the capacity of international human rights law to oversee its effects, as the latest financial crisis has so amply demonstrated. The integration of human rights principles into the day-to-day operations and management of the international financial sector has so far been geared towards a few key target issues where the negative impact of financial activity is highly visible, and where the causative financial act can be most directly traced to a given financial institution, largely by human rights and corporate social responsibility (CSR) advocates without expertise in the more technical corners of the financial system.[74]

This critique centres on the premise that, 'although many of the linkages are not yet well understood, it is plainly inconceivable that a system of the size and influence of modern finance, that is so deeply integrated into the socio-economic fabric of the world and that can cause such enormous damage, raises no direct human

---

[71]   Ibid., p. 5.
[72]   Dowell-Jones and Kinley, 'The Monster Under the Bed', see n. 58, p. 194.
[73]   Financial Conduct Authority, *FCA Risk Outlook 2013* (2013), http://www.fca.org.uk/static/fca/documents/fca-risk-outlook-2013.pdf, accessed 8 March 2014, p. 18.
[74]   Dowell-Jones and Kinley, 'The Monster Under the Bed', see n. 58, p. 195.

rights issues of its own'.[75] Looking across the divergent viewpoints, it becomes evident that there is a disconnect between the way in which multinational financial institutes have embraced the language of the global business and human rights agenda and the way it is being interpreted in some academic and civil-society circles. It appears that the source of this discrepancy turns principally on the interpretation of Guiding Principle 13, which is framed in the following terms:

> The responsibility to respect human rights requires that business enterprises avoid causing or contributing to adverse human rights impacts through their own activities, and address such impacts when they occur; seek to prevent or mitigate adverse human rights impacts that are directly linked to their operation, products and services by their business relationships, even if they have not contributed to those impacts.

Financial services organizations consider this provision as the most challenging component of the Guiding Principles. Further debate as to its scope, along with shifting views on the neutrality of capital, will help shape the course of additional progress in integrating human rights standards into the practice of financial services. As different lines are drawn between where and how financial services organizations are complicit (or not) in causing or contributing to human rights abuse, constructive dialogue will help determine key areas of focus for the future. In this light, Dowell-Jones challenges 'those tasked with operationalisation to think more extensively and more technically about the relationship between human rights and financial services'.[76] As highlighted by the Institute for Human Rights and Business in its 2014 Top Ten Business and Human Rights Issues list,[77] this specifically requires that the financial sector adopts additional tools and approaches in order to more effectively address human rights risk as a priority.

As the industry moves forward, it may need to embrace more searching questions about its role in society, its philosophy of profit-making and its ethical decision-making frameworks to ensure that human rights considerations are central to its business. The best way to track this dialogue is through open disclosure.

Disclosing progress

Human rights is playing an increasing role in the communication and dialogue of the finance sector, as multiple references to related standards emerge in the annual statements and corporate responsibility reports of global financial services companies, as well as in the statements of industry leaders, such as the Thun Group of Banks.[78] This highlights that human rights are increasingly perceived as a material issue for the industry. Various National Action Plans on Business and

---

[75] Dowell-Jones, 'Financial Institutions and Human Rights', see n. 56, p. 436.

[76] Dowell-Jones and Kinley, 'The Monster Under the Bed', see n. 58, p. 195.

[77] See http://www.ihrb.org/top10/business_human_rights_issues/2014.html, accessed 8 March 2014.

[78] The Thun Group of Banks, *UN Guiding Principles on Business and Human Rights*, see, n. 21.

Table 10.1 Sample study of major Southeast Asia financial services organizations' public disclosure on human rights as per the Guiding Principles

Financial institution	Human rights statement?	Human rights policy?	Human rights update or due diligence reference?
Banks			
Major Singapore bank	No	No	No
Major Thai bank	Yes	Unclear	Yes
Major Indonesian bank	No	No	No
Insurance			
Major Philippines insurer	No	No	No
Major Singapore insurer	No	No	No
Major Pan-Asia insurer	No	No	No
Asset management			
Major Pan-Asia	No	No	No

Human Rights are also actively encouraging official disclosure on human rights risks and issues.[79]

In view of these initial steps, it is worth examining additional progress in the communications of financial institutes across Southeast Asia. This assessment has been conducted in accordance with Guiding Principle 16, which underscores that part of the responsibility to respect human rights requires the public and internal issuance of a human rights policy. It is also conducted in accordance with Guiding Principle 21, which calls upon business enterprises to 'be prepared to communicate externally on how they are addressing their human rights impact through the due diligence process'. The analysis is based on a limited sample study of the major Asian financial institutions, and is restricted to information that is publicly available (see Table 10.1).[80]

The research suggests a prevailing lack of consistency of formal reporting and statements relating to human rights. Within the regional sample of leading finance institutions, it is striking that only one major Southeast Asian bank has issued a clear human rights statement. It is unclear whether the Thai bank's statement constitutes a policy, as it is not presented in the format prescribed by the Guiding Principles.

The data further highlights the extent to which Southeast Asian financial institutions are lagging behind other parts of the world, where human rights policies are more likely to be available and communicated to the public. The regional sample suggests that human rights are not seen as material to the sector, a factor that represents a key challenge to embedding human rights in financial institutions.[81]

---

[79] For instance, this is the case for the National Action Plans of the United Kingdom and Denmark.

[80] This study was completed on publicly disclosed information on the company corporate websites during November 2013. The details of the institutions have remained confidential as this is a quick sample of the top financial institutions. Naming the institutions would require a more considered and in-depth study to have been made, which was outside the scope of this chapter. The author welcomes more extensive research in this space.

[81] Roca and Manta, *Values Added*, see n. 49, p. 4.

Furthermore, it emerges that of the 12,000 or more UN Global Compact participants across the world,[82] less than 5 per cent (409) are classified as financial institutions. Of these, only six originate from an ASEAN Member State (one from Malaysia, one from Vietnam and four from Singapore). To put these figures into perspective, Panama, a South American country of just 3.8 million people,[83] in contrast to Southeast Asia's half a billion, has nine financial services companies listed on the latest UNGC participant list.[84] Experts confirm that, 'information on human rights performance by corporations (in Asia) is not widely available'.[85] Shortcomings in compliance further extend to noticeably limited human rights due diligence reporting across the region.

Despite limited progress in disclosure, recognition of the efforts to improve environmental, social and corporate governance disclosure is beginning to gain momentum in the region. Civil-society groups in the region are calling for more action from corporations to 'ensure access to information, participation and consultation' in order to ensure greater corporate accountability, especially with the introduction of the ASEAN Economic Community (AEC).[86] Furthermore, the Singapore Stock Exchange (the Exchange), located in the region's largest and most influential financial service centre, provided recent sustainability reporting guidance for listed companies in Singapore in 2012. It did so, acknowledging very candidly that:

> The interaction with the communities in which the company operates, and its environment and social interactions within such communities affect long-term organizational success. The company's relationship with its stakeholders drives the company to conduct business responsibly. The Exchange notes that corporate transparency on responsible business practices, particularly the environment and social aspects, may not be perceived as necessary or important in the company's reporting to stakeholders. To address the information gap, the Exchange encourages listed companies to communicate with their stakeholders on their corporate footprint in the environmental and social realms.[87]

---

[82] See statement issued by Bindu Sharma, http://www.unglobalcompact.org/Participants AndStakeholders/index.html, accessed 8 March 2014.

[83] See http://data.worldbank.org/country/panama, accessed 8 March 2014.

[84] See http://www.unglobalcompact.org/participants/search?utf8=%E2%9C%93andcommit=Se archandkeyword=andcountry%5B%5D=154andjoined_after=andjoined_before=andbusiness_ type=2andsector_id=58andlisting_status_id=allandcop_status=allandorganization_type_ id=andcommit=Search, accessed 8 March 2014.

[85] Bindu Sharma, *Contextualising CSR in Asia: Corporate Social Responsibility in Asian Economies and the Drivers that Influence Its Practice* (Singapore: Lien Centre for Social Innovation, 2013), p. 43.

[86] Forum Asia, 'Corporate Human Rights abuses in ASEAN: Civil Society Calls for Corporate Accountability and Compliance with International Human Rights Law', (Asian Forum for Human Rights and Development), http://www.forum-asia.org/uploads/press-release/2013/October/Press-Release_Civil-Society-Launch-A-Corporate-Accountability-in-ASEAN.pdf, accessed 26 March 2014

[87] SGX Singapore Exchange, *Guide to Sustainability Reporting for Listed Companies: Policy Statement*, (2012), p. 3.

This issue was recently revisited by the Exchange's Chief Executive Officer, Mr Magnus Bocker, during the course of the Responsible Business Forum on Sustainable Development in 2013. During the forum, he affirmed the Exchange's commitment to 'take the lead' as custodians of corporate responsibility and called upon all Singapore-listed companies 'to review how they can better disclose and report their environmental, social and governance footprints'.[88]

In reality, however, the insight gained from the brief regional overview suggests that human rights are unlikely to form a core policy or due diligence consideration of most financial services organizations across Southeast Asia. As such, nascent efforts in the region remain largely focused on the extractive and manufacturing industries. It is a consideration that the broader integration of the key sustainability indices and frameworks in Asia will nonetheless strengthen the Southeast Asian finance sector's performance in relation to human rights disclosure.

Going forward

The development of the finance sector is something that directly or indirectly impacts everyone. Financial institutions thus have a key a role to play in protecting and promoting human rights. As aptly noted by Dowell-Jones, 'the fact that many areas of finance have not yet been examined in detail from a human rights perspective does not mean that there is nothing to find from a responsibility to respect point of view – it just means there is a lot of work to do to fully flesh this out'.[89] As a result, suitably accounting for the different focuses in different types of financial products stands out as an area in need of particular attention. As elaborated by Roca and Manta:

> Actors and assets such as hedge funds, brokerage houses, insurance, derivatives, private equity and variable income investments have proved difficult to include in the present analysis. Hedge funds involve a great deal of short-term products, and the actors and the assets are not compatible with long-term only thinking. Structured finance, built on a series of complex intermediate operations linking one asset to multiple others, to future dividends, or to funds of funds, makes it difficult to create a feasible methodology that includes social concerns, considered not to be significant to valuation. The high frequency of transactions and the volatility of these assets also make long-term thinking irrelevant.[90]

[88] Jessica Cheam, 'SGX Chief: "We Need Tougher Regulations and Efficient Capital Markets"', *Eco-Business*, 27 November 2013, http://www.eco-business.com/news/sgx-chief-we-need-tougher-regulations-and-efficient-capital-markets, accessed 8 March 2014.
[89] Dowell-Jones, 'Financial Institutions and Human Rights', see n. 56, p. 465.
[90] Roca and Manta, *Values Added*, see n. 49, p. 19.

The Thun Group has likewise concluded that distinct forms of due diligence are required for different types of banking.[91] This is a recommendation that has been recalled in a number of other guidance documents, including those from the UNEP-FI human rights working group.[92] Unpacking what these distinct forms of due diligence will consist of will be crucial to the effective mainstreaming of the respect for human rights into industry practice. To achieve this in relation to the more complex areas of finance will prove especially challenging, as experts point to 'the majority of financial sector actors hav[ing] weak in-house capacity to integrate human rights information into their decision making'.[93] Whether or not this is true is something to be tested, and greater disclosure will enable this to be monitored.

Ultimately, the active engagement of each financial services actor in its own human rights impacts is critical for this work to be relevant for the individuals and communities across Southeast Asia and beyond. It is imperative that financial institutions in the region join the dialogue and begin their journey towards bridging business and human rights, in acceptance that their actions are not neutral. This is likely to be best served by a collaborative effort, similar to that of the Thun Group of Banks. It is therefore critical to encourage leadership within the sector across the region – either through an existing mechanism such as the UNEP-FI or through the Global Compact, using the Guiding Principles as a starting point. The risks of a sector being left behind in a critical growth region such as Southeast Asia are too grave to ignore. The region's peace and prosperity depends on economic sustainability. The financial sector's leadership in respecting human rights can play an important role in contributing to this end.

---

[91] The Thun Group of Banks, *UN Guiding Principles on Business and Human Rights*, see n. 21, accessed 8 March 2014, p. 9.

[92] Sullivan and Birtwell, *CEO Briefing: Human Rights*, see n. 44.

[93] Roca and Manta, *Values Added*, see n. 49, p. 4.

Part IV

11 Rule-making for rights protection in the Philippines

The judiciary's new powers for environmental regulation and access to remedy for business-related rights abuses

Bobbie Sta. Maria[1]

Introduction

In the seminal case of *Oposa* v. *Factoran*,[2] the Supreme Court of the Philippines cancelled existing timber licence agreements issued by the Department of Environment and Natural Resources, and prohibited the Department from issuing new ones. It cited the petitioners' right to *a balanced and healthful ecology*,[3] ruling that this right is linked to the constitutional right to health, and is 'fundamental', 'constitutionalized', 'self-executing' and 'judicially enforceable'.[4] The petitioners, several minors represented by their parents, were granted legal standing on the basis of *intergenerational responsibility*,[5] as they claimed that they represented others

---

[1] The views expressed in this chapter are the author's alone and do not represent the views of her employer, the Business and Human Rights Resource Centre.

[2] *Minors Oposa* v. *Factoran* (1993), G.R. No. 101083 (Philippine Supreme Court).

[3] 'While the right to a balanced and healthful ecology is to be found under the Declaration of Principles and State Policies and not under the Bill of Rights, it does not follow that it is less important than any of the civil and political rights enumerated in the latter. Such a right belongs to a different category of rights altogether for it concerns nothing less than self-preservation and self-perpetuation – aptly and fittingly stressed by the petitioners – the advancement of which may even be said to predate all governments and constitutions. As a matter of fact, these basic rights need not even be written in the Constitution for they are assumed to exist from the inception of humankind. If they are now explicitly mentioned in the fundamental charter, it is because of the well-founded fear of its framers that unless the rights to a balanced and healthful ecology and to health are mandated as state policies by the Constitution itself, thereby highlighting their continuing importance and imposing upon the state a solemn obligation to preserve the first and protect and advance the second, the day would not be too far when all else would be lost not only for the present generation, but also for those to come – generations which stand to inherit nothing but parched earth incapable of sustaining life.' *Oposa* v. *Factoran*, see n. 2.

[4] *Oposa* v. *Factoran*, see n. 2.

[5] 'This case, however, has a special and novel element. Petitioners minors assert that they represent their generation as well as generations yet unborn. We find no difficulty in ruling that they can, for themselves, for others of their generation and for the succeeding generations, file a class suit. Their personality to sue in behalf of the succeeding generations can only be based on the concept of intergenerational responsibility insofar as the right to a balanced and healthful ecology is

of their generation as well as generations yet unborn. This decision marks a progressive evolution of the judiciary's role in protecting legal rights, especially when executive or legislative means are unavailable or lacking. It is a departure from the known reluctance of the Supreme Court to provide a similar kind of recognition to certain rights under the 1987 Constitution.[6] In the earlier case of *Basco* v. *Philippine Amusements and Gaming Corporation*, the Court held that several provisions in the Constitution, particularly on Social Justice and Human Rights, Education, Science and Technology, and Arts, Culture and Sports, 'are merely statements of principles and policies. As such, they are basically not self-executing, meaning a law should be passed by Congress to clearly define and effectuate such principles.'[7]

Prior to the *Oposa* decision, most environmental lawsuits related to damage suits and licensing or regulatory disputes that rarely (if ever) targeted entire industries, and that presented burdens that were difficult to overcome by litigants with limited resources. One example is the difficulty of presenting evidence to prove causality between certain acts and the resulting damage. With their limited scope, these individual cases hardly made as big an impact as the *Oposa* case, especially on decision-makers, including business groups. While advancing new doctrines in judicial standing and rights enforceability, the *Oposa* decision also provided environmental and rights groups with the impetus to pressure implementers of the law into using their political power to act in favour of the environment and affected communities – even if this meant going against business interests.[8]

The latest judicial innovation in the area of rights and environmental protection comes in the form of the Rules of Procedure for Environmental Cases (Rules),[9] which were promulgated by the Supreme Court in April 2010. These Rules have enabled claimants to pursue new and creative legal avenues beyond those that were available in the *Oposa* case. The 2010 Rules have increasingly become a popular form of recourse for claimants who have been adversely affected by socially and environmentally harmful business activities, and can be viewed as an innovation not just in environmental law, but also in domestic business and human rights law. They demonstrate how Philippine courts have assumed a remarkably broader role in the realization of the widely recognized United Nations *Protect, Respect and Remedy* Framework.

As this chapter will show, the Rules effectively grant persons adversely affected by environmentally harmful business activities unprecedented access to formal judicial systems, and they also provide substantive forms of relief and remedy, such

---

concerned. Such a right, as hereinafter expounded, considers the 'rhythm and harmony of nature'. *Oposa* v. *Factoran*, see n. 2.

[6] D. A. Desierto, 'Justiciability of Socio-Economic Rights: Comparative Powers, Roles and Practices in the Philippines and South Africa', *Asian-Pacific Law and Policy Journal*, (2009), 11(1).

[7] *Basco* v. *Phil. Amusements and Gaming Corporation* (1991), G.R No. 91649 (Philippine Supreme Court).

[8] O. A. Houck, *Taking Back Eden: Eight Environmental Cases that Changed the World* (Washington, DC: Center for Resource Economics, 2010), pp. 54–55.

[9] Rules of Procedure for Environmental Cases 2010, A.M. No. 09–6-8-SC (Philippine Supreme Court).

as environmental protection orders, and orders to protect, preserve or rehabilitate the environment. This cutting-edge remedial framework enables the courts to investigate and, to a certain extent, penalize, prevent and redress abuses by private actors, thereby advancing the State duty to protect human rights. In time, the framework may pave the way for companies to adequately address and mitigate the adverse impacts in which they are involved or even to prevent these abuses from occurring, thereby promoting the corporate responsibility to respect human rights. In sum, the Rules provide for, or have the potential to provide for, all three pillars of the United Nations Framework for Business and Human Rights.

Environmental and human rights groups have hailed the Rules as a triumph for legal advocacy,[10] and have been eager to use them to address the community impacts of various projects. In addition to providing options for new independent judicial actions, the Rules also support the implementation of existing environmental laws and regulatory rules, while adding a recourse to environmental protection orders. They are the first of their kind in Southeast Asia, where most of the innovations related to business and human rights have been focused on promoting 'softer' options – such as better reporting and 'corporate social responsibility' – as opposed to access to judicial recourse.[11] However, it remains to be seen whether these Rules will indeed be effective in altering the conduct of government and business. While the 2010 Rules contain ground-breaking features that could potentially pave the way for environmental and social justice, they do not address certain practical challenges that the judiciary has continually faced. These include the varying levels of capacity of different courts to implement such Rules; the inconsistency in decisions by and between these courts – including the Supreme Court – on similar issues; and the fact that enforcement of judicial decisions remains in the hands of government agencies or units that may not act in accordance with the same progressive judge-made environmental policies.[12]

This chapter will discuss the rule-making power of Philippine courts and the extent to which this power has changed environmental litigation as embodied in the 2010 Rules. It will further provide examples of how these Rules have been invoked against business (including the challenges in doing so). Finally, it will also analyse the impact the Rules have had on environmental and social issues involving communities and businesses, as well as their role in the advancement of the *Protect, Respect and Remedy* Framework in business and human rights.

---

[10] *See* Alternative Law Groups, 'Alternative Law Groups (ALG) Commends the Supreme Court for Issuing the New Rules of Procedure for Environmental Cases', (PIPLinks, 3 May 2010), http://www.piplinks.org/Alternative+Law+Groups+(ALG), accessed 21 January 2014; Kalikasan PNE, 'Environmentalists Praise Philippine's New Rules for Environmental Cases', (Mines and Communities, 24 April 2010), http://www.minesandcommunities.org/article.php?a=10060, accessed 21 January 2014.

[11] *See* Human Rights Resource Centre, *Business and Human Rights in ASEAN: A Baseline Study* (Jakarta: Human Rights Resource Centre, 2013).

[12] E. B. Ristroph, 'The Role of Philippine Courts in Establishing the Environmental Rule of Law', (2012), *Environmental Law Reporter*, 42, ELR 10866.

How the judiciary found its place in environmental and social issues

The power of the Supreme Court to promulgate these 2010 Rules emanates from the Constitution, which both guarantees 'the right of the people to a balanced and healthful ecology'[13] and grants the Supreme Court the power to promulgate rules concerning the protection and enforcement of constitutional rights.[14] While almost legislative in nature, it is widely held that the rule-making power that the Court has taken upon itself is well supported in the Constitution. It has been said that the framers intended this expansion of powers to redirect the courts away from the more passive doctrines applied under the earlier Constitution, and which were invoked to avoid judicial review of certain issues – particularly the former dictator Ferdinand Marcos's acts.[15]

The application of this expanded power to cases involving environmental and social issues coincides with a growing international recognition of the role of judges in sustainable development, embodied in the Johannesburg Principles on the Role of Law and Sustainable Development,[16] which states that 'an independent Judiciary and judicial process is vital for the implementation, development and enforcement of environmental law, and that members of the Judiciary, as well as those contributing to the judicial process at the national, regional and global levels, are crucial partners for promoting compliance with and the implementation and enforcement of, international and national environmental law'.[17] As judges take a more active role in sustainable development by advancing progressive environmental rules, they allow themselves to speak through their decisions and become helpful in trying to strike the careful balance between the environmental, social and economic dimensions of development – this balance being a crucial component in the determination and achievement of sustainable development goals.[18]

Even prior to the 2010 Rules, the Philippine Supreme Court had begun to etch its role in rights protection by introducing innovative doctrines in its decisions. In the *Oposa* case mentioned above, it introduced the concept of intergenerational responsibility to 'preserve the rhythm and harmony for the full enjoyment of a

---

[13] The 1987 Constitution of the Republic of the Philippines, Art. II Sec. 16.

[14] Phil. Constitution, Art. 8 Sec. 5(5). According to the *Oposa* v. *Factoran* (see n. 2) case, 'While the right to a balanced and healthful ecology is to be found under the Declaration of Principles and State Policies and not under the Bill of Rights, it does not follow that it is less important than any of the civil and political rights enumerated in the latter. Such a right belongs to a different category of rights altogether for it concerns nothing less than self-preservation and self-perpetuation ... the advancement of which may even be said to predate all governments and constitutions. As a matter of fact, these basic rights need not even be written in the Constitution for they are assumed to exist from the inception of humankind.'

[15] Desierto, 'Justiciability of Socio-Economic Rights', see n. 6.

[16] Johannesburg Principles on the Role of Law and Sustainable Development (adopted August 2002); *See* Ristroph, 'The Role of Philippine Courts', see n. 12.

[17] Johannesburg Principles, see n. 16.

[18] United Nations Environment Programme [UNEP], *Embedding the Environment in Sustainable Development Goals – UNEP Post-2015 Discussion Paper*. UNEP (2013).

balanced and healthful ecology … for the generations to come'.[19] It also classi-fied the right to a balanced and healthful ecology as self-executing and judicially enforceable.[20] The Court took this further in its 1997 decision in the case of *Manila Prince Hotel* v. *Government Service Insurance System*,[21] where it ruled that 'unless it is expressly provided that a legislative act is necessary to enforce a constitutional mandate, the presumption now is that all provisions of the constitution are self-executing'.[22] In other words, the Court created the presumption that rights under the Constitution are actionable and therefore subject to judicial review, unless it is expressly stated that legislation is needed.

In another case, the Supreme Court ordered twelve national government agen-cies to perform their duty to clean up Manila Bay, and introduced the doctrine of the writ of continuing mandamus as it ordered quarterly progressive reporting of the activities undertaken in accordance with the decision. It did so by citing the objective of ensuring that its decision would not be nullified by administrative inaction or indifference.[23] This doctrine, which makes court orders effective until full satisfaction of judgment, has found its place in the 2010 Rules,[24] and may be read to apply to government duties pertaining to the regulation or control of busi-ness activities as they affect the environment.

Resort to citizen suits for failure of government agencies and public officials to implement the law is also codified in the 1999 Clean Air Act[25] and 2001 Solid Waste Management Law[26] – both applicable to business entities as potential sources of air pollution and solid waste and both imposing penalties that include fines, suspension and closure. These statutes demonstrate that the separate role and powers of the judiciary in addressing and enforcing environmental and social rights is expressly recognized by the legislature.[27]

Key features of the 2010 Rules

The Rules of Procedure on Environmental Cases govern the procedure in civil, criminal and special civil actions in courts involving enforcement or violations of environmental and other related laws, rules and regulations.[28] As will be illustrated in examples in succeeding sections, the procedural innovations have

---

[19] *Oposa* v. *Factoran*, see n. 2.

[20] Ibid.

[21] *Manila Prince Hotel* v. *Government Service Insurance System [GSIS]* (1997), G.R. No. 122156 (Philippine Supreme Court).

[22] Ibid.

[23] *Metro Manila Development Authority (MMDA), et. al.* v. *Concerned Residents of Manila Bay* (2008), G.R. Nos. 171947–48 (Philippine Supreme Court).

[24] Rules of Procedure for Environmental Cases, Rule 8.

[25] Philippine Clean Air Act of 1999, Republic Act No. 8749.

[26] Ecological Solid Waste Management Act of 2000, Republic Act No. 9003.

[27] *See* Policy Studies Organization, 'The Power of Law to Advance Intergenerational Equity: A Conversation with Environmentalist Antonio A. Oposa Jr.', (2011), *Asian Policy and Politics*, 3(2): 285–294.

[28] Rules of Procedure for Environmental Cases, Rule 1 Sec. 2.

provided new remedies to communities affected by the environmental and social impacts of businesses, especially those in the extractive sectors. The frequency with which the 2010 Rules have been invoked since their passage shows how they have served the purpose of encouraging citizens to enforce their rights by way of lawsuits. These innovations include the following: relaxed court requirements and expedited processes;[29] provisions for citizens' suits; temporary environmental protection orders;[30] protection against disingenuous countersuits;[31] adoption of the precautionary principle;[32] and, most notably, the special civil actions relating to the writ of *kalikasan*[33] and the writ of continuing mandamus.[34]

Relaxed court requirements and expedited processes

In a system known for expensive and protracted litigation, as well as delayed decisions, the 2010 Rules provide some concrete measures that help address the usual hurdles faced by seekers of justice. For instance, under the 2010 Rules, the payment of filing and other legal fees is deferred until after judgment.[35] This presents one less obstacle for affected communities, whose corporate opponents are capable of guarding their business interests with almost inexhaustible litigation budgets. Furthermore, to expedite proceedings, the 2010 Rules prohibit certain pleadings that could be a source of unnecessary delays, such as the motions to dismiss and for a bill of particulars.[36] They also disallow seeking time extensions for filing pleadings,[37] and spell out clear time lines for the various steps in litigation: pre-trial should be held not later than one month from filing of the last pleading;[38] pre-trial conferences should be held within a period of two months from the first conference;[39] and continuous trials should be held not exceeding two months from the issuance of the pre-trial order.[40] Witnesses also have to be fully examined in one day, with affidavits being admitted in lieu of direct examination.[41] All these guard against the usual dilatory tactics that are designed to exhaust litigants, especially those with limited resources for legal representation and support, and who have very limited capacity for court-related travel or flexibility to miss work.

---

[29] Rules of Procedure for Environmental Cases, Rule 1 Sec. 2, Rule 2 Sec. 2, Rule 3 Sec. 1 and 6(m), Rule 4 Sec. 1–3, Rule 7 Sec. 9, Rule 16 Sec. 1, Rule 17 Sec. 1–2.
[30] Rules of Procedure for Environmental Cases, Rule 2 Sec. 8, Rule 13 Sec. 2.
[31] Rules of Procedure for Environmental Cases, Rule 6.
[32] Rules of Procedure for Environmental Cases, Rule 20 Sec. 1.
[33] Rules of Procedure for Environmental Cases Rule 7.
[34] Rules of Procedure for Environmental Cases Rule 8.
[35] Rules of Procedure for Environmental Cases, Rule 1 Sec. 2.
[36] Rules of Procedure for Environmental Cases, Rule 2 Sec. 2, Rule 7 Sec. 9.
[37] See n. 35.
[38] Rules of Procedure for Environmental Cases, Rule 3 Sec. 1, Rule 16 Sec. 1.
[39] See n. 35.
[40] Rules of Procedure for Environmental Cases, Rule 4 Sec. 1, Rule 17 Sec. 1.
[41] Rules of Procedure for Environmental Cases, Rule 3 Sec. 6(m), Rule 4 Sec. 2–3, Rule 17 Sec. 2.

Provisions for citizens' suits

As a general rule, any party with an interest in the proceedings, whether private or public, may file a civil action. Meanwhile, any offended party or public law enforcer may file a criminal complaint under the 2010 Rules.[42] The Rules also provide for citizens' suits, allowing all citizens in representation of others (including minors or generations yet unborn) to file an action to enforce rights or obligations under environmental laws[43] – a codification of the doctrine espoused in the *Oposa*[44] case. Relief available for citizens' suits includes protection, preservation or rehabilitation of the environment and the payment of litigation expenses. The courts may also require the violator to submit a programme of rehabilitation or restoration of the environment.[45]

Temporary environmental protection orders

The Rules allow for the issuance of temporary environmental protection orders (TEPO) when the matter is of extreme urgency and the applicant will suffer grave injustice and irreparable injury if not granted such an order.[46] Within the TEPO's 72-hour time period, the court conducts a summary hearing to determine whether the order may be extended until the termination of the case.[47] Unlike regular injunctive orders available outside of the environmental rules, the payment of a bond or security for costs is not required for the issuance of a TEPO.[48] This removes a major hurdle for communities affected by environmentally harmful activities and that cannot afford to post a bond – which can amount to a significant financial sum in the case of regular injunctions. The TEPO offers a swift remedy, especially for urgent environmental concerns, and allows courts to provide immediate relief to communities, who are now, in effect, on more of an even playing field opposite corporate defendants with greater legal and financial resources at their disposal.

Protection against disingenuous countersuits

There are known cases of companies suing or counter-suing individuals or groups for exposing rights abuses in which these companies are alleged to be involved.[49] By

---

[42] Rules of Procedure for Environmental Cases, Rule 2 Sec. 4, Rule 9 Sec. 1.
[43] Rules of Procedure for Environmental Cases, Rule 2 Sec. 5.
[44] *Oposa* v. *Factoran*, see n. 2.
[45] Rules of Procedure for Environmental Cases, Rule 5 Sec. 1.
[46] Rules of Procedure for Environmental Cases, Rule 2 Sec. 8, Rule 13 Sec. 2.
[47] See n. 45.
[48] Ibid.
[49] For examples, see Chevron's racketeering lawsuit against Ecuadorian villagers' lawyers and representative in US federal court: Business and Human Rights Resource Centre, 'Case Profile: Texaco/Chevron Lawsuits (re Ecuador)', http://business-humanrights.org/Categories/Lawlawsuits/Lawsuitsregulatoryaction/LawsuitsSelectedcases/TexacoChevronlawsuitsreEcuador, accessed 21 January 2014; and Natural Fruit's defamation cases against Andy Hall: Business and Human Rights Resource Centre, 'Reports and Statements on 3 Lawsuits Filed by Natural Fruit Against

putting concerned individuals or groups on the defensive, these lawsuits may cause a chilling effect on valid legal actions. The Rules prevent potential legal bullying by companies who may use countersuits as a form of distraction rather than to address the substantive arguments in the main case. The Rules further encourage the resort to courts in situations of environmental and human rights abuse by protecting litigants from these harassment lawsuits. In the event that a countersuit is filed as a response to a litigant's invocation of environmental rules, the defendant in the countersuit is now entitled to argue that the latter case was unmeritorious and designed to harass.[50] As a result, the countersuit may be resolved immediately, with the party filing the countersuit being left with the burden to prove that the counter-action is a valid claim and is not simply meant to harass.[51]

Special civil actions relating to the writ of **kalikasan** *and the writ of continuing mandamus*

The 2010 Rules introduce two unique special civil actions that provide both individuals and communities with more effective and expeditious means of addressing violations of the constitutional right to a balanced and healthful ecology. The special civil action relating to the writ of *kalikasan* can be filed to seek indefinite injunctive relief when an unlawful act or omission involves environmental damage that prejudices the life, health or the property of inhabitants in two or more cities or provinces.[52] Relief under this writ includes permanently ceasing and desisting from committing the acts that cause the alleged environmental damage; directing the respondent to protect, preserve, rehabilitate or restore the environment; or directing the respondent to make periodic reports on the execution of the judgment.[53] The writ may also be used by environmental litigants in order to compel the disclosure of information necessary for the support of their case. This becomes especially important in the Philippines, where there is no freedom of information law. This is also particularly significant in Southeast Asia, where transparency in big development and extractive projects remains a problem. Various discovery measures available under the special civil action relating to the writ of *kalikasan* include ocular inspection and production or inspection of documents or material when necessary to establish the magnitude of the violation or the threat to life, health or property of inhabitants in two or more cities or provinces.[54]

The special civil action relating to the writ of continuing mandamus echoes the Supreme Court ruling in the *Manila Bay* case.[55] In this case, people residing near Manila Bay filed a case against several government agencies for alleged neglect in

---

Researcher and Activist Andy Hall for Alleged Defamation', http://www.business-humanrights. org/Documents/Natural-Fruit-lawsuits-against-Andy-Hall, accessed 21 January 2014.
[50]   Rules of Procedure for Environmental Cases, Rule 6.
[51]   Ibid.
[52]   Rules of Procedure for Environmental Cases, Rule 7 Sec. 1.
[53]   Rules of Procedure for Environmental Cases, Rule 7 Sec. 15.
[54]   Rules of Procedure for Environmental Cases, Rule 7 Sec. 12.
[55]   *MMDA et al. v. Concerned Residents of Manila Bay*, see n. 23.

abating the pollution of the bay, thereby constituting a violation of rights, local statute and international law.[56] The Court introduced the doctrine of continuing mandamus and ordered the respondent agencies to implement the judgment until it was fully satisfied. The writ of continuing mandamus under the 2010 Rules applies to agencies or instrumentalities of the government who are found to be negligent in the performance of their duties in connection with the enforcement or violation of an environmental law.[57] Relief under this writ includes a number of requirements: for the respondent agency or instrumentality to perform an act or series of acts until the judgment is fully satisfied; for periodic reports detailing the progress and execution of the judgment; and for evaluating and monitoring compliance. It can also provide for monetary damages resulting from an agency's malicious negligence.[58] In both special civil actions, no docket and filing fees are required upon filing the complaint or petition, and the case is set for hearing immediately.[59]

Applied in the context of the UN Framework and Guiding Principles for business and human rights, these special civil actions could serve as useful tools for prompting the State to provide redress for business-related human rights harm within its jurisdiction.

Recognition of the precautionary principle

While the 2010 Rules clearly make judicial remedies more accessible to potential litigants, there remains an evidentiary challenge in showing the causal relationship between an act and the resulting environmental harm, especially when that harm concerns human health. This is addressed in the 2010 Rules through the recognition of the precautionary principle. The relevant rule states that, '[w]hen there is a lack of full scientific certainty in establishing a causal link between human activity and environmental effect, the court shall apply the precautionary principle in resolving the case before it. The constitutional right of the people to a balanced and healthful ecology shall be given the benefit of the doubt.'[60] The Rules recognize the following factors in applying the precautionary principle: (1) threats to human life or health; (2) inequity to present or future generations; and (3) prejudice to the environment without legal consideration of the environmental rights of those affected.[61] Proper application of this new principle will require fresh judicial training for judges and justices who are accustomed to applying strict evidentiary rules in courts. The cases discussed below illustrate the seeming inconsistency in the application of this principle.

---

56 Ibid.
57 Rules of Procedure for Environmental Cases, Rule 8 Sec. 1.
58 Rules of Procedure for Environmental Cases, Rule 8 Sec. 7.
59 Rules of Procedure for Environmental Cases, Rule 7 Sec. 4 and 11, Rule 8 Sec. 3 and 5.
60 Rules of Procedure for Environmental Cases, Rule 20 Sec. 1.
61 Rules of Procedure for Environmental Cases, Rule 20 Sec. 2.

Testing the rules

The Redondo Peninsula Energy case

The special civil action relating to the writ of *kalikasan* filed by militant organizations against Redondo Peninsula Energy for its 600MW coal-fired power plant project in Subic Bay in Zambales Province is considered to be the first writ of *kalikasan* case against a power project, and therefore was deemed to set an important precedent for similar cases in the future.[62] A February 2013 decision by the Court of Appeals (upheld in a May 2013 resolution after motions for reconsideration were filed) denying the writ was reportedly seen by a power industry insider as 'a relief for proponents of other planned power projects that were being threatened with similar cases'.[63]

Petitioners filed the case before the Supreme Court, claiming that the planned construction of the power plant posed health risks to residents of the provinces of Zambales and Bataan, and would cause environmental damage in these areas. The Supreme Court issued the writ of *kalikasan*[64] and remanded the case to the Court of Appeals for trial. The Court of Appeals denied the petition, saying that the petitioners had failed to prove that their right to a balanced and healthful ecology was violated or threatened with violation and that any damage would affect the lives of locals in two or more cities or provinces.[65] The Court of Appeals emphasized that the burden of proof in the case lay with the petitioners and that they had been unable to discharge this burden. It said that there was no proof presented that the challenged 'circulating fluidized bed technology' would cause environmental damage.[66] The Court of Appeals also denied the petitioner's application for an environmental protection order for failing to show that the matter was of extreme urgency and that petitioners would suffer grave injustice and irreparable injury.[67] The Court, however, invalidated the Environmental Compliance Certificate issued to the company (as proof of its compliance with environmental requirements such as an environmental impact assessment) on the basis of a legal procedural technicality, i.e. that the Statement of Accountability lacked a vital signature.[68]

The *Redondo* case highlights a possible challenge that could be faced by litigants when filing a case under the Rules. It shows that while the Supreme Court

---

[62] *Subic Bay News*, 'CA Junks Writ of Kalikasan Case vs. RP Energy', (8 February 2013), http://subicbaynews.net/?p=4001, accessed 21 January 2013.

[63] Ibid.

[64] *Philippine Daily Inquirer*, 'Writ of Kalikasan Issued to Stop Subic Coal Plant', (3 August 2012), http://business.inquirer.net/74781/writ-of-kalikasan-issued-to-stop-subic-coal-plant, accessed 21 January 2014.

[65] A. R. Remo, 'CA Junks Environment Case vs. Subic Coal-Fired Power Plant Project', *Philippine Daily Inquirer*, 7 February 2013, http://business.inquirer.net/106495/ca-junks-environment-case-vs-subic-coal-fired-power-plant-project, accessed 21 January 2014.

[66] *Subic Bay News*, see n. 62.

[67] Remo, see n. 65.

[68] I. Reformina, 'CA Stands Pat on Denial of Writ of Kalikasan for Subic Plant', *ABS-CBN News*, 28 May 2013, http://www.abs-cbnnews.com/business/05/28/13/ca-stands-pat-denial-writ-kalikasan-subic-plant, accessed 21 May 2013.

could issue a writ of *kalikasan* based on these progressive Rules, the case would still be remanded to a lower court for trial. Once a case is before trial courts, it will be ruled on by judges with varying degrees of appreciation for the nuances of environmental policy and procedure, and with different levels of expertise on environmental law – particularly the precautionary principle, which apparently was not applied in the *Redondo* case. By saying that the petitioners were not able to discharge the burden of proof required to prove the health and environmental impacts of a planned coal-fired power plant, one could question whether the precautionary principle recognized under the 2010 Rules was indeed applied. After all, the Rules say that, '[w]hen there is a lack of full scientific certainty in establishing a causal link between human activity and environmental effect, the court shall apply the precautionary principle in resolving the case before it. The constitutional right of the people to a balanced and healthful ecology shall be given the benefit of the doubt.' The *Redondo* decision highlights the importance of invoking and highlighting the precautionary principle before the courts, and of ensuring that lower courts have the knowledge, expertise and acumen to apply it properly and purposively.

The LNL Archipelago Minerals, Inc. case

15th Congress AGHAM Party List Representative Angelo B. Palmones filed a petition for a writ of *kalikasan* to stop the damage allegedly being caused by LNL Archipelago Minerals, Inc. (LAMI) on a mountain in Sta. Cruz, Zambales, for its metallic ore mining.[69] At stake in this case were the rights of the people to be consulted in mining projects within their surroundings, and their rights to life, health and property that were at risk as the damage caused by the mining activity allegedly increased the chances of disasters brought about by typhoons and flooding. This petition was initially denied by the Court of Appeals in November 2012, but this decision was reversed in September 2013 upon reconsideration – after Rep. Palmones expounded on how the levelling of the mountain by LAMI had not been sanctioned by the Department of Environment and Natural Resources (DENR), how the mining activities had been done without public consultation, and how the levelling of the mountain caused great damage to the environment.[70]

In its September 2013 decision, the Court of Appeals ordered LAMI to 'permanently cease and desist from scraping off the land formation in question or from performing any activity in violation of environmental laws resulting in

[69] Agham Party List, 'Court Grants Petition for Writ of Kalikasan for Zambales Mountain', (19 September 2013), http://agham.org.ph/court-grants-petition-writ-kalikasan-for-zambales-mountain/, accessed 22 January 2013.

[70] J. R. San Juan, 'CA Permanently Stops Chinese Miner from Levelling a Mountain in Zambales', *Business Mirror*, 22 September 2013, http://www.businessmirror.com.ph/index.php/en/news/economy/19751-ca-permanently-stops-chinese-miner-from-leveling-a-mountain-in-zambales, accessed 22 January 2013.

environmental destruction or damage'.[71] The Court also directed LAMI and the DENR Secretary 'to protect, preserve, rehabilitate and restore the subject land formation including the plants and trees therein'; and the DENR Secretary 'to monitor strict compliance with Orders of the Court and make periodic reports on a monthly basis on the execution of the final judgment'.[72] Remarkably, the Court cited the precautionary principle in its decision, stating that 'when human activities may lead to threats of serious and irreversible damage to the environment that is scientifically plausible but uncertain, actions shall be taken to avoid or diminish that threat'.[73] The Court further highlighted that, '[w]e know it costs more to repair the environment than to prevent it. If we err in our decisions affecting the future of our children and our planet, let us err on the side of caution.'[74] This presents a marked and welcome departure from the judicial approach in the *Redondo* case, also decided by the Court of Appeals, where petitioners were denied the writ for failing to prove that their right to a balanced and healthful ecology was violated or threatened to be violated. The rulings in the *Redondo* and the *LAMI* cases suggest that the 2010 Rules could be applied according to varying standards and illustrate the need to employ uniform standards of application among courts by promoting greater understanding of the Rules and their underlying environmental and constitutional principles. The Supreme Court, should, at the earliest opportunity, make this clarification.

Earlier cases

In July 2010, three months after the issuance of the Rules, petroleum leaked from a pipeline running from the Province of Batangas to the Shell and Chevron oil depot in Manila. The leak consequently affected the health and safety of residents in Barangay (or 'village') Bangkal in Makati City.[75] Affected residents of West Tower Condominium in Makati took to the courts, and by November of the same year, were granted a writ of *kalikasan*, stopping the First Philippine Industrial Corporation from operating the pipeline until its integrity was ensured.[76] While the granting of the writ by no means concluded the legal proceedings with finality, the speed with which it (and the related relief) was attained by community litigants against a big Filipino corporation was remarkable and unusual. Indeed,

---

[71] *Philippine Star*, 'Court Issues Writ of Kalikasan vs Zambales Mining Firm', (23 September 2013), http://www.philstar.com/nation/2013/09/23/1237275/court-issues-writ-kalikasan-vs-zambales-mining-firm, accessed 22 January 2013.

[72] Ibid.

[73] Agham Party List, see n. 69.

[74] Ibid.

[75] *Philippine Daily Inquirer*, 'What Went Before: FPIC Pipeline Oil Leak', (10 January 2013), http://newsinfo.inquirer.net/338613/what-went-before-fpic-pipeline-oil-leak, accessed 22 January 2013.

[76] ABS-CBN News, 'SC Issues Writ of Kalikasan, Shuts down FPIC Pipeline', (19 November 2010), http://www.abs-cbnnews.com/nation/11/19/10/sc-issues-writ-kalikasan-shuts-down-fpic-pipeline, accessed 22 January 2014.

it was an early indication of the viability of the judicial options available under the Rules.

Meanwhile, in March 2011, the Supreme Court issued a writ of *kalikasan* in favour of residents of Marinduque Province[77] affected by the 1996 tailings disaster in a mine then operated by Placer Dome (now Barrick Gold). This constituted one of the worst mining disasters in Philippine history,[78] having had a severe impact on the health of residents – especially children – with health studies showing elevated lead and mercury content in residents' blood streams. The writ granted by the Court directed the company to restore and rehabilitate the environment,[79] a remedy that residents had been seeking for fifteen years. While a similar lawsuit between Marinduque and Barrick Gold is still pending before a Nevada court in the USA, with Barrick Gold reportedly offering to settle,[80] this ruling from the Philippine Court in the *Placer Dome* case was unprecedented and highlights the value of the new Rules in seeking to hold corporations accountable for their gross negligence and other misconduct.

Conclusion

Advancing the UN Framework for Business and Human Rights requires the interplay of many components, and the Philippine example shows how stated national policies could be made to evolve into improved laws and more effective mechanisms to implement these laws – all leading to a better means of upholding the framework. This is evident from various environmental laws that were passed after the 1987 Constitution, related executive rules to implement these laws, and the introduction of new doctrines in Supreme Court decisions such as in the *Oposa* and *Manila Bay* cases. Their continued invocation by litigants helped increase awareness and understanding among implementers, and allowed challenges – most notably procedural ones – to become better understood and addressed.

The right to a balanced and healthful ecology embodied in the Constitution has inspired the three branches of government to develop more progressive rules, laws and decisions that protect human rights and the environment. This development

---

[77] *Eliza M. Hernandez, et al. v. Placer Dome, Inc.* (2011), G.R. No. 195482 (Philippine Supreme Court).

[78] *See* University of Michigan, 'Environmental Justice Case Study – Marcopper in the Philippines', http://www.umich.edu/~snre492/Jones/marcopper.htm, accessed 22 January 2014; and NGO Forum on ADB, 'Development Debacles: The Worst Mining Disaster in the Philippines', http://developmentdebacles.blogspot.co.uk/2008/02/marinduque-mining-project-worst-mining.html, accessed 22 January 2014.

[79] I. Reformina, 'SC issues writ vs Placer Dome for Marcopper disaster', (ABS-CBN News, 9 March 2011), http://www.abs-cbnnews.com/nation/regions/03/08/11/sc-issues-writ-vs-placer-dome-marcopper-disaster, accessed 22 January 2014.

[80] *See* K. Adraneda, 'Marinduque Includes US Company in Nevada Lawsuit', *Philippine Star*, (23 July 2006), http://www.philstar.com/nation/348869/marinduque-includes-us-company-nevada-lawsuit, accessed 22 January 2014; and M. Cinco, 'Firm Offers Marinduque $20M for PH's Worst Mining Disaster', *Philippine Daily Inquirer*, (17 September 2013), http://newsinfo.inquirer.net/489741/firm-offers-marinduque-20m-for-phs-worst-mining-disaster, accessed 22 January 2014.

should be applauded. After all, as the court held in *Oposa*, 'the advancement of (this right) may even be said to predate all governments and constitutions'.[81]

The 2010 Rules are a product of various factors, including the continued effort of rights-holders to make existing policies, laws, rules and procedures work for the protection of their rights through efforts that are persistent, sustained, and often-times creative. It has been said that legal doctrines and procedural innovations such as intergenerational responsibility and the writ of continuing mandamus have the potential to 'hang out there on the legal horizon like a distant star … terribly attractive, but everything else is meanwhile'.[82] The court decisions analysed in this chapter point to a stark need to improve the capacity of all courts to apply the Rules in a uniform and consistent fashion, and to strengthen the grasp of the underlying principles among all court officers that argue for and decide on these cases. In other words, there is a need to apply the Rules properly and in a way that will result in tangible environmental protection. While some communities have successfully relied on the Rules in order to bring their grievances against big companies to court, remaining challenges point to a gap between legal and constitutional doctrine and community experience. The issuance of these Rules presents a real milestone, but their application presents another story – one that deserves a closer look if their intended objectives are to be met. Filing more cases with a view to strengthening jurisprudence will help promote a better understanding of the principles and procedures under the Rules, a better understanding that will not only benefit judges and lawyers, but also the litigants themselves.

The Chamber of Mines of the Philippines claims that laws such as the Philippine Mining Act and other environmental laws provide sufficient safeguards against environmental degradation, and that allegations of environmental abuse are best handled by the executive branch.[83] However, a Chamber of Mines representative admitted that, even when a writ is denied, companies still suffer damage to their image as a result of cases filed under the Rules.[84] This candid response from the business sector shows that, despite a noticeable inconsistency in judicial application, the Rules have indeed made an impact, if only to shed greater light on alleged abuses and highlight their importance in public consciousness and debate. With improved application by capable lawyers, judges and justices, the true impact of these ground-breaking rules on the environmental and human rights issues can be better assessed.

---

[81] *Oposa* v. *Factoran*, see n. 2.
[82] *See* Policy Studies Organization, see n. 27.
[83] L. Dalangin-Fernandez, 'Writ of Kalikasan: Just in Time?', *Interaksyon*, (31 October 2012), http://www.interaksyon.com/article/46924/writ-of-kalikasan-just-in-time, accessed 22 January 2014.
[84] Ibid.

12 The reality of remedy in mining and community relations

An anonymous case-study from Southeast Asia

Deanna Kemp and John R. Owen

Introduction: mining and human rights in Southeast Asia

In the past decade, the Association of Southeast Asian Nations (ASEAN) has sought to bolster its mining and extractives sector on the basis that its rich mineral endowment is yet to realize its full economic potential.[1] Development of mineral resources is now considered essential to growing the region's economy. With the explicit aim of increasing the contribution of mining and extractive industries to national and regional economies, ASEAN has endorsed a series of ministerially agreed action plans to enhance mining-related trade and investment, promote responsible practices, and optimize mineral resource revenues.[2] And, while many foreign investors have for the past decade turned their attention towards China and India, a shift of focus back to Southeast Asia is gaining momentum, which is likely to support growth in the region, despite a general market downturn.[3]

Many mine-affected communities in Southeast Asia have claimed that their human rights have been infringed upon by mining activities. Claims typically relate to impacts on traditional culture, effects on the natural environment, and disruption to livelihoods.[4] The acquisition, use and management of natural resources remain contentious issues throughout the region. Often brought to the attention of the international community by human rights defenders or non-government

---

[1] See remarks in 2005 by Secretary-General of ASEAN at the Sixth Asia Pacific Mining Conference and Exhibition, Makati City, Philippines, http://www.asean.org/resources/2012–02–10–08–47–56/speeches-statements-of-the-former-secretaries-general-of-asean/item/asean-perspective-on-the-region-s-mining-industry-remarks-by-he-ong-keng-yong, accessed 12 January 2014. According to the statement, in 2003, non-energy minerals and base metals productions accounted for less than 1 per cent of total ASEAN GDP.

[2] For example, the cooperation action plan for 2011–2015 was entered into in November 2013 at the Fourth ASEAN Ministerial Meeting on Minerals, http://www.asean.org/news/asean-statement-communiques/item/joint-press-statement-the-fourth-asean-ministerial-meeting-on-minerals, accessed 12 January 2014.

[3] Price Waterhouse Coopers, 'South East Asia Investment Opportunities Report: Tax and Other Incentives', (September 2012), http://www.pwc.com.au/asia-practice/south-east/assets/publications/South-East-Asia-Investment-2012.pdf, accessed 20 December 2013.

[4] C. Ballard and G. Banks, 'Resource Wars: The Anthropology of Mining', (2003), *Annual Review of Anthropology*, 32: 287–313.

organizations (NGOs), claims have been made by some of the poorest people on the planet. Emblematic cases from ASEAN include PT Freeport Indonesia's Grasberg mine,[5] and the Marcopper tailings disaster on the island of Marinduque in the Philippines.[6] Also included is Newmont's now closed Minahasa Raya mine in the North Sulawesi Province of Indonesia, which in its final year of operation became deeply embroiled in a multi-party conflict over allegations of impacting the health of local villagers living in the nearby Buyat Bay.[7]

Most global mining companies have interests in the region. Rio Tinto, Barrick Gold, BHP Billiton, MMG, Glencore Xstrata, Goldfields, Newmont, Newcrest, Anglo American and Vale are each actively exploring or operating in the region. Foreign and domestic mid-tier companies and a range of exploration and junior companies are also active. Artisanal and small-scale mining (ASM) is prevalent throughout the region, due in large part to the accessibility of alluvial gold and shallow coal deposits.[8] In many mining locations, the human rights risks associated with the interaction between large- and small-scale mining is not always accounted for by regulators.[9] Across Southeast Asia, there are a range of complex human rights-related issues associated with resource extraction, including regulatory architecture, institutional capacity, corruption, political freedoms, use of security forces, resettlement and land acquisition. Additional implications arise as a result of rapid socio-economic transformation, such as in the case of Myanmar.[10] The geopolitics associated with foreign direct investment, including China's interest in Southeast Asia's mineral wealth, also points to an ever-evolving business and human rights landscape. At this stage, little is known about the degree to which

---

[5] P. A. Rifai-Hasan, 'Development, Power and the Mining Industry in Papua: A Study of Freeport Indonesia', *Journal of Business Ethics*, (2009), 89 (2), 129–143; C. Ballard and G. Banks, 'Between a Rock and a Hard Place: Corporate Strategy At the Freeport Mine in Papua, 2001–2006', in B.P. Resosudarmo and F. Jotzo (eds), *Working with Nature Against Poverty*, (ISEAS: Singapore, 2009), pp. 147–177.

[6] I. Macdonald and K. Southall, 'Mining Ombudsman Case Report: Marinduque Island', (2005), Oxfam Australia, http://oxfam.org.au/explore/mining, accessed 20 December 2013.

[7] D. Kemp, R. Evans, J. Plavina and B. Sharp, 'Newmont Community Relationships Review – Organisational Learnings from the Minahasa Case Study', (2008), http://www.beyondthemine.com/pdf/Minahasa_Newmont_CRR_report.pdf, accessed 20 December 2013.

[8] K. Lahiri-Dutt, 'Informality in Mineral Resource Management in Asia: Raising Questions Relating to Communities Economies and Sustainable Development', (2004), *Natural Resources Forum*, 28: 123–132. Lahiri-Dutt also calls attention to the gendered aspects of mining in Asia. See, for example: K. Lahiri-Dutt, 'Globalization and Women's Work in the Mine Pits in East Kalimantan, Indonesia', in K. Lahiri-Dutt and M. Macintyre (eds), *Women Miners in Developing Countries: Pit Women and Others* (England: Ashgate Publishing, 2006), pp. 349–369.

[9] G. Hilson and J. McQuilken, 'Four Decades of Support for Artisanal and Small-Scale Mining in Sub-Saharan Africa: A Critical Review', forthcoming, *Extractive Industries and Society*; S. Spiegel, 'Governance, Institutions, Resource Rights Regimes and the Informal Mining Sector: Regulatory Complexities in Indonesia', 2011, doi:10.1016/j.worlddev.2011.05.015.

[10] For example, T. O'Callaghan, 'Patience Is a Virtue: Problems of Regulatory Governance in the Indonesian Mining Sector', (2010), *Resources Policy*, 35(3): 218–225; D. Smith and K. Naito, 'Asian Mining Legislation: Policy Issues and Recent Developments', (2012), *Resources Policy*, 24(2): 125–132.

these and other human rights considerations are being integrated into human rights due diligence processes, or whether, in fact, human rights due diligence is part of doing business in the region.[11]

There is no doubt that mining is an inherently conflictual practice involving disruption to land, livelihoods and patterns of everyday life. Resource companies form unique relational structures with host communities who, alongside various social and environmental impacts, shape the dynamics of engagement between these actors. This chapter focuses on company–community conflict and grievance, recognizing that such grievances can serve as a proxy for grievances against the State.[12] The general character of company–community grievances can be discerned through scholarly research, international campaigns and contemporary media sources. While information may appear readily accessible, surprisingly little insight is offered about grievance-handling practice. Beyond the standard public responses issued by legal counsel or media representatives about specific claims, case-studies in glossy company-produced reports, or abstract corporate social responsibility (CSR) policies, the gap in knowledge about how community grievances are handled is significant.[13] Little is known about the internal patterns of response, defensive organizational routines, and the role of company personnel in bringing human rights to the fore in grievance-resolution processes and outcomes.[14] This gap reflects CSR practice more generally, and business and human rights in particular. Given the sensitivity of information, the option of legal privilege, and the level of expertise required, organizational aspects of grievance handling is, by and large, a privatized body of knowledge.[15]

This chapter seeks to open up the space for building knowledge on grievance-handling practices in the mining industry by providing grounded insights on the intersection between CSR and human rights in the context of a foreign-owned mine in Southeast Asia. Nonetheless, there are limitations to disclosure, in part due to the vulnerability of some interviewees, and, because of this, the case-study has been anonymized. The chapter describes and analyses grievance-handling processes at the mine and compares this against contemporary international

---

[11] See D. Kemp and F. Vanclay, 'Impact Assessment and Human Rights: Making the Connection', (2013), *Impact Assessment and Project Appraisal*, 31(2): 86–96 for an exploration of the challenges of building knowledge in this area.

[12] L. Zandvliet and M. Anderson, *Getting It Right: Making Corporate Community Relations Work*, (Sheffield, England: Greenleaf Publishing 2009).

[13] G. Whiteman and K. Mamen, 'Examining Justice and Conflict Between Mining Companies and Indigenous Peoples: Cerro Colorado and the Ngabe-Bugle in Panama', (2002), *Journal of Business and Management*, 8(3): 293–329.

[14] c.f. in the South African context, L. Farrell, R. Hamann and E. Akres, 'A Clash of Cultures (and Lawyers): Anglo Platinum and Mine-Affected Communities in Limpopo Province, South Africa', (2012), *Resources Policy*, 37(2): 194–204. For an analysis of six mining-related project-level grievance mechanisms globally, see D. Kemp, J. R. Owen, N. Gotzmann and C. Bond, 'Just Relations and Company-Community Conflict in Mining', (2010), *Journal of Business Ethics*, 101(1): 93–109.

[15] Kemp and Vanclay, see n. 11.

standards.[16] The chapter proceeds by providing a brief overview of the operating context and the methods of data collection. Findings are presented, and implications for mining, CSR and human rights considered. The chapter concludes by suggesting that mining companies cannot claim neutrality in contexts where single-party States exercise high levels of authority. Neither can they claim a 'social licence' by virtue of an absence of community dissent.[17] Companies must take an active role in understanding the socio-political context, the character of the grievance landscape, and their role in influencing that context.[18] Without this knowledge, companies cannot claim to discharge their responsibility to respect

[16] The standards used as a benchmark include the International Finance Corporation (IFC) Performance Standards 1 – Assessment and Management of Environmental and Social Risks and Impacts and Performance Standard 5 – Land Acquisition and Involuntary Resettlement; the IFC Compliance Adviser Ombudsman Guide to Designing and Implementing Grievance Mechanisms for Development Projects; the International Council on Mining and Metals (ICMM) Guidance Note on Local Level Complaints and Grievance Handling; and the UN Guiding Principles (GPs) on Business and Human Rights.

[17] For an overview of the 'social licence' concept, see I. Thomson and R. Boutilier, 'The Social Licence to Operate', in P. Darling (ed.), *SME Mining Engineering Handbook*, 3rd edn (Colorado, USA: Society for Mining, Metallurgy, and Exploration, 2011). For a more critical perspective relating to the minerals sector, see J. Owen and D. Kemp, 'Social Licence in Mining: a Critical Perspective', (2012), *Resources Policy*, 38(1): 29–35.

[18] There is a plethora of standards that require mining companies to understand their social context and manage risk. The IFC's Social and Environmental Performance Standards are mandatory for clients, and have become an industry benchmark for social performance. See 'IFC Sustainability Framework', (2012), http://www.ifc.org/wps/wcm/connect/topics_ext_content/ifc_external_corporate_site/ifc+sustainability/sustainability+framework/sustainability+framework+-+2012/framework_2012, accessed 10 January 2014. International industry-endorsed standards include, for example, the International Council of Mining and Metals (ICMM) Sustainable Development Framework and the Voluntary Principles on Security and Human Rights. See 'Sustainable Development Framework', (2014), http://www.icmm.com/our-work/sustainable-development-framework, accessed 10 January 2014; 'Voluntary Principles on Security and Human Rights', (2013), http://www.voluntaryprinciples.org/wp-content/uploads/2013/03/voluntary_principles_english.pdf, accessed 12 January 2014. National industry bodies such as the Minerals Council of Australia (MCA) and the Mining Association of Canada (MAC) have a similar set of standards that apply to members operating domestically and offshore. Examples of standards that are endorsed by multinational organizations include the Organisation for Economic Co-operation and Development (OECD) Guidelines for Multinational Enterprises, and the International Organization for Standardization (ISO) 2600 Guidance on Social Responsibility. For further explanation see 'OECD Guidelines for Multinational Enterprises', (2011), http://www.oecd.org/daf/inv/mne/48004323.pdf, accessed 12 January 2014; 'Discovering ISO 26000', (2010), http://www.iso.org/iso/discovering_iso_26000.pdf, accessed 15 January 2014. Some researchers have observed an increasing set of requirements at national and sub-national level, representing a shift beyond 'voluntary' industry standards. See K. McNab, J. Keenan, D. Brereton, J. Kim, R. Kunanayagam and T. Blathwayt, 'Beyond Voluntarism: The Changing Role of Corporate Social Investment in the Extractives Sector', (2012), https://www.csrm.uq.edu.au/publications/beyond-voluntarism-the-changing-role-of-corporate-social-investment-in-the-extractive-resources-sector, accessed 15 January 2014, for an explanation of emerging 'social legislation' in the context of mining. There are also a number of guidance notes produced by a broad range of organizations from NGOs (e.g. Oxfam Australia) to international financial institutions.

human rights under the United Nations (UN) Framework and Guiding Principles on Business and Human Rights (Guiding Principles).

Access to remedy in the operating context

'Access to remedy' represents the third pillar of the UN *Protect, Respect and Remedy* Framework, which recognizes that even the most concerted efforts cannot prevent all human rights abuse.[19] A range of judicial and non-judicial remedies and associated principles are canvassed in the UN Guiding Principles, including non-State-based, operational-level grievance mechanisms.[20] Largely as a result of international pressure to address human rights risk and impact, the global mining industry has made a range of significant public commitments to these newly agreed international standards through corporate policies, industry organizations and stand-alone agreements with indigenous peoples and other mine-affected groups.[21]

The country context for our case-study represents one of a small number of single-party States, with a history of post-colonial conflict and a protracted high-profile war. The country is not a conflict zone. Since the early 1990s, it has received significant foreign investment from the 'West', and in recent years has witnessed an upsurge in investment from Chinese and other East Asian nations. The rapid development of the country over the past twenty years has brought with it a heightened level of international interest in its commitment and hand-ling of governance, corruption and human rights issues. Major natural resource and infrastructure projects have contributed to the country's substantial economic growth over the last decade. The regulation of these sectors has proven challenging for the government, as evidenced by the spike in complaints and grievances related to land concession projects gaining national media coverage.

[19] United Nations, 'Promotion and protection of all human rights, civil, political, economic, social and cultural rights, including the right to development – protect, respect and remedy: A framework for business and human rights. Report of the special representative of the secretary-general on the issue of human rights and transnational corporations and other business enterprises', United Nations Human Rights Council, Eighth Session, Agenda item 3, 7 April 2008, UN Doc, A/HRC/8/5, http://daccess-dds-ny.un.org/doc/UNDOC/GEN/G08/128/61/PDF/G0812861.pdf?OpenElement, accessed 20 December 2013.

[20] United Nations, 'Report of the special representative of the secretary-general on the issue of human rights and transnational corporations and other business enterprises, Guiding Principles on Business and Human Rights: Implementing the United Nations "Protect, Respect and Remedy" Framework', United Nations Human Rights Council, Seventeenth Session, Agenda item 3, 21 March 2011, UN Doc, A/HRC/17/31, http://daccess-dds-ny.un.org/doc/UNDOC/GEN/G11/121/90/PDF/G1112190.pdf?OpenElement, accessed 20 December 2013.

[21] Many companies are also members of a range of other human rights-related frameworks, including the Voluntary Principles on Security and Human Rights, the UN Global Compact, both of which are aligned with the UNGPs, but do not expound on the concept of grievance mechanisms. See 'Voluntary Principles on Security and Human Rights', see n. 18; 'UN Global Compact Brochure', (2014), http://www.unglobalcompact.org/docs/news_events/8.1/GC_brochure_FINAL.pdf, accessed 12 January 2014.

Similar to many single-party States, the country that is the focus of our case-study does not have a strong track record of supporting the political rights of its citizens or in its handling of public dissent. While the country has officially ratified a range of core human rights treaties, the political apparatus, in conjunction with a fledgling and partisan judicial system, has created stark inconsistencies between ratification and the reality as implemented on the ground. Avenues for seeking legal and political redress are generally considered to be either risky or ineffective due to the corruptibility of officials throughout the 'formal' process.[22] Mechanisms for registering complaints will often draw on informal sets of relationships where complainants feel less exposed. Alternatively, complainants may utilize protest methods, which do not require individuals to formally or directly disclose their complaint – but where the source and the nature of the grievance are nonetheless well understood by all parties.[23] The presence of foreign-owned mining companies, with explicit international requirements and expectations relating to grievance handling, represents a notable challenge for all parties.

Since commencement of operations over a decade ago, the mine's geographic footprint has continued to spread, thereby increasing the level of ground-disturbance activity, land acquisition, sedimentation, waste generation and water use. Historically, the approach to land acquisition has been spatially and temporally incremental, but is now cumulatively significant.[24] This represents a high-impact context for near-mine communities, many of whom live well below the national poverty level and rely to a large extent on foraged goods to meet their livelihood needs. In addition to a significant poverty context, the mine operates in a multi-ethnic and multi-linguistic community in which many of the mine's neighbours do not have proficiency in the national language and find it difficult to navigate the administrative systems of both the mine and government authorities. Given the unique political context in which the project operates, the level of open conflict and disruption has been low relative to mines of a similar size and nature in other parts of the world.

The lease area of the mine does not have the benefit of a formal land tenure system – with land users having a vast array of formal and informal land entitlements. The company's system for mapping, analysing and tracking land tenure is best described as rudimentary. Impact to land and livelihood characterizes the majority of community–company engagement. Contestation over impacts has

---

[22] The issue of corruption in legal and political processes has been identified as a severe problem within many Southeast Asian countries. See K. Kis-Katos and G. Schulze, 'Corruption in Southeast Asia: A Survey of Recent Research', (2013), *Asian-Pacific Economic Literature*, 27(1): 79–109. The issue, however, is by no means unique to Southeast Asia.

[23] This pattern of raising grievances against powerful individuals or entities is well established. For examples see: M. Adas, '"Moral Economy" or "Contest State"?: Elite Demands and the Origins of Peasant Protest in South East Asia', (1980), *Journal of Social History*, 13(4): 521–546; J. C. Scott, *Weapons of the Weak: Everyday Forms of Peasant Resistance* (Yale University Press, 1985).

[24] See G. Banks, 'Little by Little, Inch by Inch: Project Expansion Assessment in the Papua New Guinea Mining Industry', (2013), *Resources Policy*, 38(4): 688–695 for an overview of the effects of incremental expansion in Papua New Guinea.

resulted in a more intense emphasis on compensation as a means of mediating the community–company relationship in recent years. Local and international standards vary considerably on the question of rates: the former favouring developers, the latter favouring affected communities. This comes at a point in time when the mine continues its expansion trajectory.

Like the rest of the industry, the company is operating within a cost-constrained environment and is subject to significant cost-reduction pressure. In turn, mine management is under intense production pressure. The corporate entity has incorporated international commitments into corporate requirements, which includes ensuring human rights-compatible grievance mechanisms are in place for each of its project sites. The operation has a dedicated complaints unit consisting of five staff located on site and within the community relations department. The unit was established informally three years ago and formalized more recently. While a dedicated 'point of contact' for grievance handling is common practice for leading non-judicial, project-level mechanisms, recent research suggests 'shared responsibility' for grievance handling as an important indicator of effectiveness.[25] This issue is explored in the analysis below. In addition to the complaints unit, the community relations department also has units for land access, cultural heritage, community development, local government relations and stakeholder engagement.

Methods and sample

In developing this chapter, the authors draw on their multiple engagements in mining and Southeast Asia, prior studies at the site, and a more recent study of the effectiveness of the grievance mechanism itself. Much of this work was undertaken with the support of a bilingual, bi-cultural research assistant.[26] For the purposes of the grievance study, the research team requested a list of background documents to build an understanding of the site's grievance mechanism and associated processes. Documents that were provided to the team included a range of the site's procedures, including community complaints and grievance resolution, the community relations department's social management plan, organizational charts, job descriptions for personnel charged with grievance-handling responsibilities, grievance reports and complaints data. These documents were reviewed for the purposes of understanding how the department is structured and resourced, and how responsibilities are allocated for grievance handling. Public reports and scholarly literature were also reviewed and analysed for the purposes of understanding the grievance landscape.

---

[25] For an overview of lessons learned about applying the UNGP's remedy principles for effective company–stakeholder grievance mechanisms, see C. Rees, 'Piloting Principles for Effective Company-Stakeholder Grievance Mechanisms: A Report of Lessons Learned', (2011), Harvard Kennedy School, Harvard University, http://www.business-humanrights.org/SpecialRepPortal/Home/Materialsbytopic/Grievancemechanismsnon-judicial, accessed 12 January 2014.

[26] Our collaborator has chosen not to be named in this instance, as this would compromise anonymity.

During the grievance study, thirty detailed field interviews were conducted involving approximately fifty people. Interviewees were identified in consultation with the community relations department and included discussions with company representatives (managers, superintendents and other personnel) from a range of departments, including community relations, exploration, mining, environment and the regional head office. Government representatives were also interviewed, as were local community representatives, committees and village groups in the 'near-mine' area (i.e. communities with a high rate of grievances relative to those who live further away from the mine). The researchers applied a semi-structured interview protocol, adapted to the cultural context. A range of informal, unstructured interviews was also conducted. All interviews were oriented towards understanding the grievance context, procedures, practices, issues, cases and responses, over time. It was considered inappropriate to audio record discussions or type into a computer while in the field, so handwritten notes were taken and typed up post-interview. These notes have been analysed to identify patterns, themes and exceptional cases.

The research process was subject to full university ethics-approval processes and all interviewees provided informed consent following a series of prior notices given by the authors and the community relations unit. Although the study was funded by the company, it was agreed from the outset that all interview data would remain confidential to the research team.

The mechanism: procedure, pathways and pressure

On a desktop reading of the site's standard operating procedure, the operational-level grievance mechanism appears stable, relatively straightforward, and aligned with key requirements of contemporary international standards. The procedure explains the role of the operation's complaints unit as the central coordinating point for grievance resolution. Responsibilities of complaints unit staff, the community relations department manager and the general manager are stipulated. There are multiple lodgement points; defined processes for screening, recording and assessing complaints against agreed criteria; and specified timeframes for response and close out. There are no limitations imposed on complainants in accessing the judicial system (although in reality, litigation is out of reach for most local people). The procedure also encourages the participation of complainants in key processes. Nonetheless, there are a number of areas of non-alignment with international standards.

There is no clear process for investigating community-related grievances outlined in either the procedure or evident in practice. An investigative process could not be described by any of the interviewees. At best, the process described was an initial joint inspection. Where a technical investigation had been conducted by other departments, the process for involving complainants was not clear either. The operation had, in fact, fallen into the habit of paying compensation without a formal investigation process. One superintendent observed: '*You see, there has been a pattern of compensating small issues over a number of years, but this does not mean that the issue is finished. They come back and it is a bigger issue because it was not resolved in the first place.'* For some time, the approach to resolving grievances has come to rely on compensation in order to maintain land access and avoid disruption. This pattern of using short-term measures to shore up land access has been observed repeatedly in other contexts.[27]

There is no provision for confidential lodgement of complaints in the procedure. Nor is there an explanation as to how the procedure accommodates the needs of minority ethnic groups, who are present in the lease area. Furthermore, the procedure does not reference, recommend or require any third-party involvement. Parties involved in the mechanism are those with interests; that is, company, government and complainant. One villager said: *'The local government will not back us. The direction from the central government is to develop, and enable mining.'* Local authorities confirmed that the project is part of the government's strategy of nation building, and that going against the project is seen as contradicting the national policies. In this context, the local government's ability to advocate for local people is constrained.

The procedure does not provide clarity regarding escalation or appeals processes for grievances that cannot be resolved directly with the company. Processes for joint 'inspection', 'investigation' and 'mediation' involving complainants, village committees, government representatives and the company are mentioned, but there is no outline or description of the process or methodologies involved, or the roles and responsibilities of named parties. In practice, the company defers to the government to resolve intractable grievances and protracted land negotiations. Complainants who seek to elevate their grievance beyond the complaints unit are subject to a series of 'discussion cycles' with various joint committees or government agencies.

If a complainant does not accept or agree, the issue elevates to higher levels of the government. 'Resolution' relies on one of three processes: devolution to the same committee that was unable to resolve the issue originally; application of administrative pressure by the State; and acquiescence by the complainant. This pressure starts at the local level of government, and moves upwards within the State apparatus. The aim is to provide information and persuade complainants (or landowners in the case of land access) to understand and accept the situation (i.e. not pursue things further) or terms of the negotiation (e.g. levels of compensation or mitigation measures). If complainants cannot be persuaded through the application of gentle pressure, interviewees claim that this pressure will increase, that they will be held or face arbitrary detention by the State. The location and period of detention is not made known to the detainee or their family.

At the time of the research, one village group said that a number of households had been in negotiations with the company over a land-acquisition process for a

[27] Owen and Kemp, see n. 17; N. Bainton and M. Macintyre, 'My Land, My Work: Business Development and Large-Scale Mining in Papua New Guinea', in F. McCormack and K. Barclay (eds), *Engaging Capitalism: Cases from Oceania: Research in Economic Anthropology 33*, (UK: Emerald, 2013), pp. 139–165.

significant period of time. They explained that they had been subject to government 'counselling' whereby they were given information about the importance of the project and the generosity of the company's offer. There was no process of seeking to build mutual understanding of issues and their underlying or root causes. When they refused, they understood that their issue had been elevated further and they were reconciled that they or members of their family would be arbitrarily detained. A village group representative said: *'We are at the end of the line … on the edge of a cliff. There is no more discussion. We are outside the company process. It has been elevated to government. We are expecting it [detention].'* Other than acquiescence, the process has few points of exit.

Senior company representatives are generally aware of the political process, some more so than others. One senior manager explained: *'If the deal is not agreed, we can move into a political process where the government applies some pressure.'* Several senior staff interviewed for this study did not accept the proposition that villagers are mistreated by mere provision of information, or are subject to cruel treatment by the State 'on behalf of' the project. During interviews, senior managers were either unwilling to discuss their engagement with the State in any detail, or were under the impression that other senior company representatives were engaged at the highest levels of government about what is 'acceptable practice' in their engagements with local people. They also indicated that claims of pressure being applied by the State to near-mine villages are grossly exaggerated. Whether the risk of arbitrary detention is real or perceived, villagers do not understand how the company can condone the government's approach, let alone benefit from it. One village elder said: *'The company has the ability to change what is done here, not us. But they don't. They turn their back.'* A grievance mechanism that relies on the government to pressurize communities in this way is neither defensible nor aligned with international standards and guidance materials. As the procedure does not require the identification of systemic issues, or regular evaluation of the mechanism, there are few opportunities for the company to surface issues, discuss the complexities and determine an appropriate response.

Not all of the pathways described above fall within the remit of the company's grievance mechanism, but they nonetheless form an integral part of how grievances are handled in practice. That the procedure does not acknowledge the presence of State-directed processes heightens the unpredictable nature of the system and precludes transparency. These 'hidden' processes also exclude the company's complaints unit, which is supposed to serve as the central coordinating point for complainants themselves. Their exclusion increases the risk that cases simply 'go nowhere'. There was a view among several senior company personnel that the informal dimensions of the mechanism merely reflect the cultural norms of the country. There is, of course, a careful balance to be struck in terms of how a company integrates established processes with new requirements for resolving grievances. Nonetheless, reliance on political processes which cannot be openly discussed – and which senior company representatives do not consider to be of concern, but that have direct bearing on the functionality of the mechanism – renders the formal procedure partial, misleading, and suggests human rights incompatibility.

Experiences of the mechanism in use

This section provides further insight into the grievance mechanism in use by drawing on perceptions data from internal and external interviews about cases and their management. The cumulative effect of these more mundane managerial processes reveal how, other than for relatively straightforward issues, the mechanism defers to the existing socio-political order and fails to account for international human rights standards. Findings are grouped under four key themes: (i) committees and structures; (ii) operational systems and processes; (iii) capacity and resources; and (iv) communication and relationships.

Committees and structures

The study revealed that, in practice, there is no one person, department or committee with a clear sense of how the grievance mechanism works in practice. The various internal, external and joint committees (i.e. company, community and government) that form part of the broader grievance-handling process give the impression of an intentional and well-ordered administrative structure. In practice, however, there is a general lack of clarity about roles and responsibilities. External stakeholders and complainants understand little of the internal company process, and company representatives indicate that they are not always clear about how the various external committee structures and government processes are supposed to work, or actually work.

Site management has limited knowledge of the role played by the company's regional office, which is responsible for managing political affairs. While it is not documented in the procedure, representatives from the regional office often 'step in' to assist with protracted grievances and land negotiations. Site management has limited knowledge about the discussions had by regional representatives with government authorities, or the status of cases that escalate out of the local area's immediate control. Similarly, representatives from the regional office could not describe key aspects of the site-level procedure or the status of cases where they had some involvement. When different parts of a business do not understand each other's respective roles in a grievance-handling process, accountability is weak. Weak accountability is linked to a lack of transparency, which, in the case of this particular mine, mirrors the lack of transparency embedded in the political system.

One key area of misunderstanding relates to the role of village committees. The company and the local government agree that company-related community-level complaints should involve the government-mandated village committees that were established to deal with intra-community complaints. The company and the local government provided information to villagers about the role and responsibility of village committees in the event of a company–community complaint or grievance. Some villagers describe committees as a *'channel'* through which grievances need to travel to reach the company. Others describe the committee as a *'witness'*, or a group that is available to *'support'* complainants. At other times it is described as helping to *'resolve'* issues. These descriptions are not mutually exclusive. At times, villagers described all three roles as being held concurrently. Staff from the complaints unit have an expectation that committees will undertake investigations, or at least be involved in the grievance-resolution process. There is not a consistent understanding amongst villagers.

In practice, internal ownership of the grievance mechanism is limited to the community relations function. Staff from other departments regard themselves as users (rather than owners) of the system and readily explained the frustrations of having to work with a mechanism that was not able to service their needs. They did not tend to make a direct link between their own actions, or those of their department, and the rate/intensity of community complaints and claims for compensation. There is a sense amongst some community relations staff that the grievances are increasing in number and intensity as a *'punishment'* for the negative impacts the mine has brought, as it is customary to apply a fine for doing something taboo within the local culture. Several managers outside of the community relations department disagree and believe that communities are simply becoming savvier about claiming compensation and *'working the system to get as much as they can out of the company'*. The risk of holding this view too tightly is that the company begins to see every case as an example of opportunism on the part of the community, instead of an opportunity for the company to manage (and indeed limit) the extent of its impact on the local community.

Within the community relations department itself, other units are often reluctant to involve themselves in the grievance-handling processes. The procedure indicates that *any* company representative can receive a complaint or a grievance, and refer it to the complaints unit. During the field visit, villagers described numerous instances where they had tried to lodge a complaint with a regular member of staff who had refused to take the complaint, suggesting that the villager lodge their complaint with the complaints unit directly, or write to the department rather than making a verbal complaint. The procedure indicates that both written and verbal complaints are accepted. However, in practice, there is a strong preference for written complaints, which are considered to be more valid than those lodged verbally. Given low levels of literacy amongst villagers, particularly women and ethnic minority groups, it is important that both verbal and written lodgement remain equally valid.

There are a number of structural and cultural factors that inhibit the effectiveness of the grievance mechanism and the complaints unit. Current organizational arrangements require complaints unit staff to communicate across disciplines, engage upwards into the hierarchy of the business and influence across cultural and linguistic boundaries. The procedure indicates that other departments must have input into issues where they may be the root cause, or have contributed to the issue, in order to find potential resolution pathways. National community relations department staff indicated that they often have to rely on expatriate managers and superintendents within the department to *'force'* other departments to engage with them. The main excuse other departments give to complaints unit staff for their lack of response is that they are simply too busy. Fundamentally, the mechanism relies on complaints unit staff to push other departments, rather than other departments readily working with the complaints unit to resolve issues.[28]

The mechanism's primary pathways for resolution are largely external; the focus is on forums and committees external to the company. Internal points of escalation are minimal. Within the business, the community relations manager and the general manager are the only internal points of elevation from the complaints unit. If a matter cannot be resolved through this process, it immediately reverts to the joint committee system and the government process. A recently agreed requirement for other departments to nominate a 'complaints representative' is not yet embedded in the procedure, and not all departments have responded to this request. Leading practice indicates that internal, multi-disciplinary and cross-departmental forums help to ensure that other departments become meaningfully engaged in grievance resolution.[29]

Operational systems and processes

During the course of the review, it became clear that there are a number of business systems that are a recurrent source of grievance. These include the land access process, compensation, and monitoring and evaluation, each of which are discussed below.

Land access-related grievances are typically generated as a result of the land access protocol itself. In terms of the process, staff from the mining and exploration departments explained that disagreement with landowners is common upon the commencement of land-disturbance work, even after a land access request has been approved. Specific examples were given about landowners coming forward at the commencement of disturbance activities to claim additional compensation. Staff from the land access unit explained that they are under immense pressure to secure access, and are not always given the time to consult properly. Staff explained: *'Other departments get very frustrated that we are slow and don't give them a clear timeframe for access.'* Land access staff also indicated that internal understanding about the degree of difficulty in their work has improved in recent times. Nonetheless, other departments do not always give sufficient lead times and still apply pressure, which means that consultation and approvals processes often remain inadequate in terms of reaching genuine agreement (or understanding, for that matter).

Technically, if a community-related complaint arises after a request for access is granted, the complaints unit has responsibility for resolution. However, it is the land access unit that has undertaken the negotiation, knows the parties and understands the terms of the (dis)agreement. In terms of overarching responsibility, it is not clear where negotiation ends and grievance handling commences. There

[28] This type of dismissive attitude to community relations personnel has been documented elsewhere: D. Kemp and J. R. Owen, 'Community Relations in Mining: Core to Business but not "Core Business"', (2013), *Resources Policy*, 38 (2): 523–531.

[29] Rees, see n. 25; C. Rees, D. Kemp and R. Davis, 'Corporate Culture and Conflict Management in Extractive Industries', (2012), Harvard Kennedy School, Harvard University, http://www.hks.harvard.edu/m-rcbg/CSRI/CSRI_report_50_Rees_Kemp_Davis.pdf, accessed 14 January 2014.

is confusion between the respective responsibilities of the land access and complaints units. The land access unit believes that they are all too often pulled onto grievance cases that are not their responsibility, and the complaints unit believes that the land access unit does not always follow due process. Both units are under significant pressure to either gain access to land or resolve grievances. Some staff believe that the two units should be merged (as they were in the past) to avoid the 'handball effect', where issues bounce around between the two units. Where merging the units would enhance the potential for cooperation on land matters, this solution would not hold for non-land-related complaints and grievances. While there are ongoing issues, staff in both units are aware of the issues and have made some efforts to improve communication and coordination.

Another source of grievance relates to the timing of compensation payments and land-disturbance work. There are cases where the company has commenced ground-disturbance work before payments have been received by landowners. One village elder indicated that this had occurred in his village recently. He raised the issue with community relations unit staff verbally but has not heard back. He explained that the company had instructed villagers to establish bank accounts as payments could no longer be made in cash. Villagers had done this but had still not received payment. When the Chief raised the issue with the local-level government, they told him that it was up to the company to address the issue.

More broadly, the grievance mechanism does not provide a useful forum for raising grievances relating to compensation rates. Compensation rates are set by the government and the company currently adheres as closely as possible to the official schedule of rates. There is widespread contention over the classification of land and associated rates. One example relates to 'generational land' where, upon sale, there is an expectation that compensation is divided amongst members of a family with interests in the land. Family members who occupy or work the land receive a small share, which is not enough to replace livelihoods. Families believe that official rates should reflect the communal nature of ownership in this area and the number of claimants with established customary rights over the land.

Another compensation-related issue is the classification of productive agricultural land. One farmer explained that compensation rates are similar for newly established fields as they are for mature fields. This is not considered fair for farmers and families who have spent several years working a particular productive agricultural land. When complainants do not agree with the compensation amount, villagers say that neither the company nor the local-level government enter into discussions with the claimant. They explain that the land compensation committee repeats the same information and makes the same calculations. If farmers elect to take the issue further, they are often counselled by government representatives until they agree.

Capacity and resources

The issue of capacity and resourcing of the community relations department was raised by interviewees across the sample. The complaints unit superintendent explained that, in recent times, and despite the increasing number and intensity of grievances owing to complex land negotiations, his team had been reduced. There has also been staff movement within the department. Two of the team members are new to the complaints unit area, with comparatively less knowledge in complaints and grievances, but with other skills and experience that are considered complementary. Currently, there is no unit plan, or indeed a departmental-level plan, for building capacity in conflict handling and grievance mechanisms. While there have been some *ad hoc* capacity-building activities during the past three years, staff expressed concern about any future expansion and their capacity to cope with what may follow in terms of complaints and grievances.

There was a strong sense that staff were working to minimize their workload, rather than ensuring that all grievances were captured in the system. This has resulted in several major concerns not being recorded. For example, several villages said that there had been a marked decline of non-timber forest products on village foraging land. One village committee representative explained that they used to collect a particular plant species that is important in traditional diets, but that it was no longer abundant on their land and she attributed that to encroachment of the mine. She explained that they had been raising the issue since the commencement of operations, including with consultants during environmental impact assessments, as well as in other forums such as the community consultative committee, but had never made a formal complaint to the complaints unit. The issue was not logged in the system. Grievances that are raised in forums such as community consultative meetings, impact assessment studies and other consultations are not clearly connected to the grievance mechanism.

The complaints unit team's lack of capacity, knowledge and experience was noted by a number of external stakeholders. Village and local government interviewees believe that local staff tend to avoid confrontation, including the issue of not taking issues forward to managers of other departments. One villager reiterated: '*This means community relations staff make judgments about our issues. We need staff with experience who are prepared to represent us to management so that they can hear our issues.*'

Concern was also expressed about the quality and availability of resources available at the local government level. Several interviewees, including the mine management and staff, indicated that local-level government officials operate on the basis of personal networks of patronage, reciprocity and obligation. They believe that this inhibits the ability of the grievance-resolution process to operate in an open, transparent and '*professional*' manner. While there was some criticism of this characteristic of the local context, no one within the company provided an explanation of how the issue was being engaged or addressed.

Community relations department staff reported that limited access to vehicles and drivers constrain proactive engagement and timely responses to villages when they raise issues or lodge grievances. Currently, the community relations department has one light vehicle for every ten villages covering approximately 150 square kilometres of land. The complaints unit itself does not have a dedicated vehicle. This restricts the unit's ability to respond to complainants in a timely manner, follow up, provide information and updates and visit communities to complete a timely follow-up of issues or close out cases.

Communication and relationships

Interviewees discussed a range of communication issues that provide a source of complaint, exacerbate existing grievances and inhibit resolution. Local government representatives indicated, for example, that they would appreciate more detailed and timely information about the company's plans in order to more readily mobilize their limited resources for communication, community engagement and planning. Representatives indicated that the company did not appreciate the time and effort that community-level work requires. They emphasized that clearer and earlier communication would help to avoid misunderstandings and grievances.

An example of poor communication by the company is demonstrated in the following case. A farmer in one of the mine-affected villages requested information from the community relations department about why the company had not released water into a canal that fed her productive agricultural land. As there was no clear response, she asked an environment department representative during a routine water monitoring exercise. She was told that they had to 'check' the water before it could be released. She asked the community relations department a second time, and still did not receive a clear response. She raised a complaint at a formal consultative meeting with the company and yet does not know what happened to her complaint. Her growing assumption is that the company is purposely withholding information because there is a pollution issue.

Another example relates to casual employment. At the time of the fieldwork, there was an emerging concern within near-mine villages about casual work for vegetation cutting, although a formal grievance had not been lodged. In a cost-cutting initiative, the company had made a decision to use permanent junior front-line officers rather than casual labour. Villagers from affected communities who relied on this income had not been informed about why they were no longer able to work. The company indicated that village leaders had indeed been informed, but it was clear during interviews that this information had not been shared with many of the cutters themselves. In the context of increasing pressure on land and livelihoods, these jobs provided an important impact-mitigation measure for near-mine communities. Notably, one senior manager reported that there was no discussion about the impact on company–community relations when the decision was taken to stop employing casual cutters; instead the focus was on cost-benefit analysis of using the Level 1 staff.

Several interviewees raised issues about community relations unit staff. Several villagers feel that staff do not always serve as an effective conduit of information between company and community, as they often block information that expatriate management will either not understand or respond negatively towards. One example related to a sacrifice to the spirits under the community's belief system. After an incident relating to a land access issue, one village requested that the company compensate them for the cost of sacrificing a buffalo to the spirits. However, community relations unit staff said that they would not take the request forward because expatriates would not understand the issue or accept the proposal. One village elder said: *'It's not up to the local staff to decide not to tell them. They are foreign guests and they should know our ways. They need to acknowledge our beliefs.'* The perceived failure of staff to represent these issues internally and communicate to expatriate managers is an issue in some villages.

Villagers were asked to reflect on their relationship with the company since the beginning of the mine. Without exception, they indicated that the company's emphasis on relationship building had diminished. One village elder said: *'They used to visit the village … come and see us. They don't take the time anymore.'* Another elder said: *'Before, they had regular visits to us. Now they have what they want, they don't come. If they need help, they come. If not, they do not come.'* Yet another said: *'Community relations managers of a generation ago were different. None of them work on site anymore. Before, senior people used to come out here. Now the junior people ask us to go to see them in the local government.'* Leaders said that this puts the onus on them to represent village issues and communicate back. Some explained that when company representatives visit the village, it enables others to access information by witnessing discussions. Women and youth may not actively participate, but direct observation provides an important source of information. Elders remarked that company decision-makers no longer understand the reality of village life because they do not visit as often as they used to.

Discussion and conclusion

This concluding section presents a summary of key themes and issues emerging from our case-study. This chapter highlights the challenge of negotiating meta-level frameworks and principles in a context in which the State adopts internationally agreed norms while, at the same time, seeking to preserve domestic standards. The entry of foreign mining companies with their international commitments and obligations presents unique sets of opportunities and risks, which companies are not always aware of (or active in preventing or harnessing). Company-introduced grievance mechanisms, for instance, open up new pathways for engaging the question of human rights, and companies need to be fully conscious of how their processes interact with local systems, in addition to understanding the outcomes that can, and may, follow as a result. Mining companies are not neutral parties, particularly in contexts where single-party States exercise high levels of political authority. The argument that companies should adopt a seemingly neutral position in order to adhere to national law is difficult to defend when a company becomes, or is perceived to become, a direct beneficiary of government oppression, which would suggest corporate complicity in State-sponsored human rights violations.

Under these circumstances, foreign-owned mining companies in Southeast Asia face the very real risk of failing the complicity test. Even if companies are able to demonstrate that they have not directly contributed to negative impacts on human rights, companies 'sitting on their hands' or claiming that an issue is outside of their authority represents an equally important human rights risk as direct and outright abuse. In order to avoid these sorts of risks, companies need to take an active role in understanding the local context and, importantly, their role and influence within that context. In this sense, context may be crucial.[30] However, characterizing that context is essential in the face a community's own experience of social and political history, and the cast of mind that this history creates for the reading of future events. This foundational knowledge and a commitment to engage and report on cases where rights may be compromised are powerful determinants of the corporate responsibility to respect human rights, by undertaking a meaningful human rights due diligence process. Understanding the remedy landscape is central to this:

> The remedy landscape is important in any given development context, and impact assessment has an important role to play in understanding the effectiveness of existing mechanisms, in addition to highlighting the need for additional grievance mechanisms to fill an identified remedy gap.[31]

Developing a working knowledge of the operating context goes beyond understanding the impacts of the mine on the community – it includes history as a reference point for relationships, social order, community and political norms, as well as a key consideration behind many of the socio-economic factors that the mine will need to characterize. In this light, there is a need to carefully differentiate between 'grievance', as often having deep cultural and psychological elements, and the administrative dimensions of the 'mechanism'. This distinction is not mere word play, but in fact represents a pressing need for companies to develop more rigorous and relational systems of engagement among the communities in which they operate. In single-party systems, and indeed in systems that are slowly emerging from such arrangements, mining companies can easily wander into a false sense of comfort in terms of reading the status of their so-called 'social licence'. The absence of direct opposition, protest or 'shut down' scenarios may provide a positive reading of a social licence, however, the underlying factors that stir the waters of discontent suggest that such readings are likely to be illusory.

What becomes important in the context of operating in single-party States, or in fact any State that is yet to develop frameworks to protect human rights, is the extent to which human rights risks become submerged by a company's interest in its own social licence, rather than a prima facie test of its respect for human rights under the UN Guiding Principles and overall contribution to human development. In socio-political contexts whereby citizens' rights to protest are curtailed by the State or where avenues for redress are clouded in the potential for harm to the claimant, there is an undeniable obligation on the part of responsible companies to take additional steps to ensure they are acting in accordance with internationally agreed standards.

---

[30] Evans and Kemp, 'Community Issues', in P. Darling (ed.), see n. 17, at pp. 1767–1777.
[31] Kemp and Vanclay, see n. 11.

International standards and emerging norms require companies to exercise human rights due diligence to identify and manage human rights risk and impacts that stem from corporate conduct. This must include understanding the grievance landscape and the mechanism in its full social and historical context. This must also include knowledge of the full range of available judicial and non-judicial processes and institutions, and the extent to which the company and its activities interact with that landscape and existing mechanisms. For social scientists, the term 'institution' includes culture, history, households, land tenure, and many other constructs that contribute meaning, understanding and order. A comprehensive due diligence process must help a company to understand and judge the extent to which the company's grievance mechanism and broader process of handling grievances are 'rights compatible' in both process and outcome. Without understanding the character of a context and how human rights risks interact with local systems of authority, belief and entitlement, a company has no basis for establishing 'defensible practice' in relation to grievance-handling and other processes.

13 Right to development

A path to securing more effective remedies?

Cynthia Morel[1]

Introduction

As the effects of globalization have intensified over the past decades, allegations of human rights violations by transnational corporations (TNCs) have steadily increased. However, while the activities of TNCs have significantly expanded, the ability to seek redress for business practices that negatively impact on human rights has not kept pace. The emphasis of the UN Guiding Principles on Business and Human Rights on the duty of both states and corporations to provide access to remedies is an important step towards addressing this imbalance.[2] The present chapter nonetheless contends that focus must extend beyond the mere availability and accessibility of remedial processes. The debate must equally consider how remedies can more effectively respond to the needs of those seeking reparations.

This chapter will draw attention to the scale and complexity of the governance gaps posed by globalization, and the extent to which the acts and omissions of State and non-State actors are interrelated in their effects. While the primary responsibility for implementing human rights falls upon the State, the chapter contends that the ability to secure effective remedies is dependent on holistic solutions that reflect the interdependence between all relevant actors.

The right to development (RTD), 'with its focus on global structural obstacles to the realisation of human rights, duties of international cooperation, the need for an enabling environment at all levels, and rights-focused development processes and outcomes', has been hailed as a 'highly relevant juridical framework to address the challenges of the 21st century'.[3] This, as it will be argued, includes

[1] The author wishes to thank Sumi Dhanarajan and colleagues at Natural Justice for their review and comments of this chapter, as well as Lisa Ho for her research assistance. The author also wishes to thank Estelle Askew-Renaut and Margot Salomon for their suggestions of valuable resources. Any errors contained in this chapter are the sole responsibility of the author.

[2] UN OHCHR, *Guiding Principles on Business and Human Rights: Implementing the United Nations 'Protect, Respect and Remedy' Framework*, (2011), http://www.ohchr.org/Documents/Publications/GuidingPrinciplesBusinessHR_EN.pdf, accessed 5 December 2013.

[3] Margot Salomon, 'Towards a Just Institutional Order: a Commentary on the First Session of the UN Task Force on the Right to Development', (2005) *NQHR*,23(3), p. 416. See also Sakiko Fukuda-Parr, 'The Right to Development: Reframing a New Discourse for the Twenty-First Century', (2012) *Social Research: An International Quarterly*, 79(4): 839–864.

challenges related to securing remedies that are sustainable for communities and businesses alike, and thus beneficial to both.

Finally, the linkages drawn between the access to an effective remedy and the right to development will be examined in the context of the latter's inclusion into the normative scope of the recently adopted ASEAN Human Rights Declaration (2012).[4] The relevance of its formal codification cannot be overstated in light of the region's rapid economic growth, where competing interests between states, corporations and interests intensify.

Right to development

The Declaration on the Right to Development (DRD) was adopted by the UN General Assembly in 1986.[5] It has been reaffirmed as an inalienable human right in the Vienna Declaration and Programme of Action,[6] as well as in various international meetings, including the Earth Summit in Rio de Janeiro,[7] the International Conference on Social Development in Copenhagen[8] and the UN Millennium Declaration.[9] At a regional level, it has been codified as Article 22 of the African Charter on Human and Peoples Rights. The inclusion of RTD in the ASEAN Human Rights Declaration serves as a further indication of the strengthening consensus around its place in, and inherent value to, the regional and international frameworks governing the protection of human rights.[10]

Despite these advances, the right to development has proven highly contentious over the past decades. Debates over the nature and scope of State obligations in relation to this right have been particularly divisive.[11] Consequently, since the late 1990s, various UN mandates have been created in order to clarify the norms in the DRD. These included the appointment of an Independent Expert and a Working Group on the right to development.[12] A High-Level Task Force was

---

[4] ASEAN Human Rights Declaration (adopted 18 November 2012). Referred to hereafter as AHRD.

[5] UN Declaration on the Right to Development (adopted 4 December 1986) UNGA Resolution 41/128 (DRD).

[6] Vienna Declaration and Programme of Action (adopted 12 July 1993) A/CONF.157/23, paragraph 10.

[7] Rio Declaration on Environment and Development (adopted 14 June 1992) A/CONF.151/26 Vol. I, Principle 3.

[8] Copenhagen Declaration and Programme of Action (adopted 12 March 1995) A/CONF.166/9, paragraph 26 (j).

[9] UN Millennium Declaration (adopted 8 September 2000) UN Doc. A/Res/55/2, paragraphs 11 and 24.

[10] AHRD, see n. 4, Arts. 35–37.

[11] For a brief overview of controversies regarding the right to development, see Arjun K. Sengupta, 'Conceptualizing the Right to Development for the Twenty-First Century', in *Realizing the Right to Development: Essays in Commemoration of 25 Years of the United Nations Declaration on the Right to Development* (UN, 2013), p. 73.

[12] The Independent Expert, Arjun Sengupta, produced six reports on the right to development between 1999 and 2004. The core elements of these reports are reflected in the publication cited in n. 11. In turn, the open-ended working group on the right to development was established

also established in order to assist the Working Group in defining the criteria and operational sub-criteria required to measure RTD's effective implementation.[13] Progress towards this end has been complemented by the findings of the African Commission on Human and Peoples' Rights in the *Endorois* case, which, in 2010, constituted the first ruling globally to adjudicate on the right to development.[14]

In terms of normative scope, the DRD describes RTD as 'an inalienable human right by virtue of which every human person and all peoples are entitled to participate in, contribute to, and enjoy economic, social, cultural and political development'.[15] This includes the right to effective participation in all aspects of development and at all stages of decision-making processes; the right to equal opportunity and access to resources; the right to fair distribution of the benefits of development; and the right to an international environment in which all human rights and fundamental freedoms can be fully realized.[16] The DRD thus places the human person as the 'central subject of development', while underscoring the importance of placing individuals, groups and peoples as active participants and beneficiaries of RTD.[17] Accordingly, development is framed as a comprehensive economic, social, cultural and political process, which 'aim[s] at the constant improvement of the well-being of the entire population and of all individuals on the basis of their active, free and meaningful participation in development and in the fair distribution of benefits resulting therefrom'.[18]

Remedies under international law

The right to a remedy is comprised of procedural and substantive components that are guaranteed in both international and regional human rights instruments. Procedurally, the provision of remedies must be impartial, protected from corruption and free from political or other attempts to influence the outcome.[19] The substantive element, in turn, affords relief to successful claimants.[20] Under international law, states responsible for an internationally wrongful act are

through Commission on Human Rights Resolution 1998/72 (adopted 22 April 1998) UN Doc. E/CN.4/1998/72 (1998).

[13] See 'Report of the High-Level Task Force on the Implementation of the Right to Development on Its Sixth Session', Addendum, Right to development criteria and operational sub-criteria (8 March 2010) A/HRC/15/WG.2/TF/2/Add.2.

[14] *CEMIRIDE and Minority Rights Group International (on Behalf of the Endorois Community)* v. *Kenya*, Communication 276/2003, African Commission on Human and Peoples' Rights (2010). Cited hereafter as 'the *Endorois* case'.

[15] DRD, see n. 5, Art.1 (1).

[16] *Realizing the Right to Development*, see n. 11, p. 59. See also A. Sengupta, 'First Report of the Independent Export on the Right To Development', (1999) UN Doc. E/CN.4/1999/WG.18/2, paragraph 47.

[17] DRD, see n. 5, Art. 2 (1).

[18] Ibid., Art. 2(3).

[19] UN GPs, see n. 2. Commentary on GP 25. The commentary goes on to detail the form and content of these procedural and substantive components.

[20] Dinah Shelton, *Remedies in International Human Rights Law*, 2nd edn (Oxford University Press, Oxford, 2005), p. 9.

typically under an obligation to: (a) cease the act, if it is continuing; (b) offer appropriate assurances and guarantees of non-repetition, if circumstances so require; and (c) make full reparation for the injury (whether material or moral) caused by the act.[21]

International law further establishes that efforts towards full reparation 'must, as far as possible, wipe out all the consequences of the illegal act and reestablish the situation which would, in all probability, have existed if that act had not been committed'.[22] Additional forms of reparation may include financial compensation, public apologies and the erection of monuments, as well as punitive sanctions.[23] Ultimately, the suitability and scope of remedial measures will be as varied as each set of circumstances that are relevant to a given case. Factoring among these are the socio-economic and political contexts in which a harmful impact is being addressed.

As the 'third pillar' of the *Protect, Respect and Remedy* Framework and its related Guiding Principles (GPs), the access to remedy focuses attention on the importance of ensuring the effectiveness of both judicial and non-judicial grievance mechanisms. In both cases, the GPs emphasize that these mechanisms must be: (a) legitimate; (b) accessible; (c) predictable; (d) equitable; (e) transparent; (f) rights compatible; and (g) a source of continuous learning.[24] The GPs further stress that operational-level mechanisms administered specifically by businesses should also be based on engagement and dialogue: consulting the stakeholder groups for whose use they are intended on their design and performance, and focusing on dialogue as the means to address and resolve grievances.[25]

The shared State and corporate responsibility to provide access to effective remedies partly stems from the crucial preventative role that they can and must play in the interrelated and dynamic system of accountability. However, as noted by UN Secretary-General Ban Ki-moon, perhaps the greatest value that can be attributed to reparations is that '[they] are arguably the most victim-centered justice mechanism available and the most significant means of making a difference in the lives of victims'.[26] In post-conflict societies in particular, UN experience demonstrates

---

[21] International Law Commission, 'Draft Articles on the Responsibility of States for Internationally Wrongful Acts', (2001) UN Doc A/56/10 (2001), Arts. 30, 31 and 34., http://legal.un.org/ilc/texts/instruments/english/draft%20articles/9_6_2001.pdf, accessed 10 January 2014.

[22] *Case Concerning the Factory at Chorzów* (*Germany* v. *Poland*) (Merits) PCIJ Rep Series A No 17, at 47.

[23] For a more comprehensive overview, see Shelton, see n. 20, and Thomas M. Antkowiak, 'Remedial Approaches to Human Rights Violations: The Inter-American Court of Human Rights and Beyond', (2008) *CJTL*, 46(2). The Inter-American Court constitutes the only international human rights body with binding powers that has consistently ordered equitable remedies in conjunction with compensation. The Court's unique reparative approach is consistent with many of the RTD-related arguments set forth in this chapter.

[24] UN Guiding Principles, see n. 2. Each of these criteria are described in greater detail under GP 31 and its related commentary.

[25] Ibid.

[26] Report of the Secretary–General to the Security Council, 'The Rule of Law and Transitional Justice in Conflict and Post-Conflict Societies', (2011) S/2011/634, paragraph 26.

that by facilitating reconciliation and confidence in the State, reparations play an important role in laying the foundation for more stable and durable peace.[27] It follows that greater confidence gained through accessible and legitimate remedial processes can equally contribute to the stability and, in turn, the prosperity of the communities and businesses that engage with them.

Evolving context: opportunities and challenges in the quest to secure effective remedies

While certain industries or circumstances may pose greater risks than others, the potential impact of business practices on virtually all internationally recognized human rights has prompted the international community to mobilize towards greater accountability for victims of corporate abuses.[28] Considerable momentum has been gained towards this end, with the adoption of several new standards in recent years. For instance, since the adoption of the GPs by the UN Human Rights Council in 2011, its principles have been reflected in the updated Guidelines for Multinational Enterprises of the Organisation for Economic Co-operation and Development (OECD), as well as in the human rights chapter of the Guidance on Social Responsibility from the International Organization for Standardization (ISO 26000). The GPs have also informed the revised Sustainability Framework and Performance Standards of the International Finance Corporation, which forms part of the World Bank Group. A reference to the GPs was further incorporated into the European Commission's renewed strategy for corporate social responsibility (2011–14).[29] States were consequently invited to develop national plans for the implementation of these principles by the end of 2012.[30] The ASEAN Intergovernmental Commission on Human Rights (AICHR), for its part, has chosen corporate social responsibility as the topic of its first thematic study. AICHR has stated that the aim has been to produce 'an ASEAN Guideline that is fully compliant with the UN frameworks, especially the Protect, Respect and

---

[27] Ibid.

[28] UN Guiding Principles, see n. 2, GP 12.

[29] European Commission (EC) 'Communication from the Commission to the European Parliament, the Council, the European Economic and Social Committee and the Committee of Regions: A renewed EU strategy 2011–14 for Corporate Social Responsibility', (25 October 2011) COM(2011) 681 final., http://eur-lex.europa.eu/LexUriServ/LexUriServ.do?uri=COM:2011:0681:FIN:EN:P DF, accessed 15 January 2014.

[30] See, for instance, the United Kingdom's National Action Plan (2013–15), which sets out a series of 20 commitments by the Government, organized around the themes of (a) open data – radically opening up government data for greater accountability, public service improvement and economic growth; (b) government integrity – fighting corruption and strengthening democracy through transparent government; (c) fiscal transparency – helping citizens to follow the money; (d) empowering citizens – transforming the relationship between citizens and governments; (e) natural resource transparency – ensuring natural resources and extractive revenues are used for public benefit, http://www.opengovernment.org.uk/national-action-plan, accessed 14 December 2013. Denmark's National Action Plan is also available at http://www.humanrightsbusiness.org/files/News/ICAR-DIHR%20National%20Action%20Plans%20Project%20Summary.pdf, accessed 14 December 2013.

Remedy Framework for Business and Human Rights and the Guiding Principles for Business and Human Rights which were endorsed by the UN Human Rights Council'.[31]

The momentum gained as a result of these developments is indicative of a global convergence around the standards set out in the GPs and, most notably, of the distinct yet complementary roles and capabilities of states and companies regarding human rights. In this regard, companies are expected to uphold their independent human rights responsibilities, irrespective of whether a state is able or willing to fulfil their own.[32] Thus, where government is weak, companies need to enhance their due diligence procedures and commitment to providing effective remedies. However, the extent of the relief that these emerging standards are capable of offering to victims of corporate abuses remains limited by virtue of their status as soft law; a factor that limits their justiciability, whatever the level of governance at hand.

Unfortunately, the scope for securing binding legal remedies through formal judicial procedures presents its own set of challenges, as the costs associated with such processes (among other factors) impede the access of many to such recourses.[33] Holding TNCs accountable through formal legal channels is often further complicated by the doctrine of *forum non conveniens*, which provides a court with the right to refuse to take jurisdiction over matters in instances where it considers another forum to be more appropriate to adjudicate over the case at hand.[34] And, perhaps most crucially, the US-based Alien Tort Claims Act (ATCA) – which had been invoked by a growing number of human rights victims since the 1980s – was significantly narrowed in scope as a result of the recent US Supreme Court ruling of *Kiobel v. Royal Dutch Petroleum, Co. (Shell)*.[35] Following a 2010 US Court of Appeals ruling that ATCA could not be used to hold corporations liable for violations of customary international law,[36] the Supreme Court relied on the doctrinal

---

[31] Remarks by Rafendi Djamin, Indonesian Representative to the ASEAN Intergovernmental Commission on Human Rights, at the Asia Pacific Forum of National Human Rights Institutions Regional Conference on Business and Human Rights, October 11–13, 2011, Seoul, South Korea.

[32] UN GPs, see n. 2, GP 11.

[33] For instance, Commentary on GP 31 indicates that additional barriers to access may include a lack of awareness of the mechanism, language, literacy and physical location, and fears of reprisal.

[34] For further insight on this issue, see Erin Smith, 'Right to Remedies and the Inconvenience of *Forum Non Conveniens*: Opening US Courts to Victims of Corporate Human Rights Abuses', (2010) 44 *Colum. J.L. and Soc. Probs.* 145.

[35] The ATCA was passed by the first Congress of the United States in 1789. It was seldom relied upon until 1980 in the case of *Filartiga v. Peña-Irala*. In this ruling, the US Court of Appeals (Second Circuit) reaffirmed that the statute provided jurisdiction over (i) tort actions, (i) brought by aliens (only), (iii) for violations of the law of nations (also known as 'customary international law'). This included war crimes and crimes against humanity as well as crimes in which the perpetrator could be deemed *hostis humani generis* – i.e. 'an enemy of all mankind'. See *Filartiga v. Peña-Irala*, 630 F.2d 876, 890 (2d Cir. 1980).

[36] *Kiobel v. Royal Dutch Petroleum*, 621 F.3d 111 (2d Cir. 2010), p. 43. The Court had reached its decision on the basis that: '[I]mposing liability on corporations for violations of customary international law has not attained a discernible, much less universal, acceptance among nations of the world in their relations inter se. Because corporate liability is not recognized as a "specific, universal, and

principle of 'presumption against extraterritoriality' as the basis for limiting the statute's application concerning violations committed outside the United States.[37] ATCA had long been regarded as the most sophisticated avenue of redress for victims of corporate abuses that have been left unpunished in other jurisdictions, so with this narrowing of scope, the imperative for viable alternatives could not be greater.

Gaps in world governance

Difficulties in securing effective remedies are further exacerbated by what the former Special Representative John Ruggie describes as 'the fundamental institutional misalignment ... between the scope and impact of economic forces and actors, on the one hand, and the capacity of societies to manage their adverse consequences, on the other'.[38] This misalignment has been said to 'create the permissive environment within which blameworthy acts by corporations may occur without adequate sanctioning or reparation'.[39]

The extent of the increase in corporations' wealth, power, influence and responsibility over the last few decades is evidenced by the fact that more than half of the top economies in the world are corporations rather than states.[40] In turn, while the rights of companies and investors have significantly expanded over the past generation, governments have proven less capable than ever to protect against harmful corporate impacts through legislation or regulation.[41] This is particularly so in developing countries, where competition for international investment often results in a 'race to the bottom', as those with the least amount of regulation are likely to attract the most investment.[42]

---

obligatory" norm ... it is not a rule of customary international law that we may apply under the ATS. Accordingly, insofar as plaintiffs in this action seek to hold only corporations liable for their conduct in Nigeria (as opposed to individuals within those corporations), and only under the ATS, their claims must be dismissed for lack of subject matter jurisdiction.'

37 *Kiobel* v. *Royal Dutch Petroleum Co*, 133 S.Ct. 1659 (2013).

38 Special Representative of the UN Secretary-General, 'Report of the Special Representative of the Secretary-General on the Issue of Human Rights and Transnational Corporations and Other Business Enterprises: Business and Human Rights: Mapping International Standards of Responsibility and Accountability for Corporate Acts', (2007) UN Doc. A/HRC/4/35, paragraph 3.

39 Ibid.

40 Sarah Anderson and John Cavanagh, 'Top 200: The Rise of Global Corporate Power', (Global Policy Forum, 2000), http://www.globalpolicy.org/component/content/article/221/47211.html, accessed 28 November 2013. See also Mary Robinson, 'Second Global Ethic Lecture by Mary Robinson, UN High Commissioner for Human Rights', (Global Ethic Foundation, 2002) http://classic.weltethos.org/dat-english/00-lecture_2-robinson.htm, accessed 28 November 2013.

41 Carlos López Hurtado, 'Business and Human Rights: Toward the Development of an International Law Framework' in *Business and Human Rights: A Complex Relationship* (Magazine of the Due Process of Law Foundation, 4 September 2011), p. 8.

42 E. E. Daschbach, 'Where There's a Will, There's a Way: The Cause for a Cure and Remedial Prescriptions for *Forum Non Conveniens* as Applied in Latin American Plaintiffs' Actions Against U.S. Multinationals', (2007) 13 *Law & Bus. Rev. Am*, 11: 27.

The effects of these gaps in world governance are reflected in, for example, the proliferation of large-scale land acquisitions by foreign interests for food production, which often results in the forced eviction of small-scale farmers with little or no compensation.[43] Many of these individuals become agricultural workers on large-scale plantations, where they are often paid lower than subsistence wages and left without social or legal protection.[44] Meanwhile, approximately 500 million of those who do continue to depend on small-scale agriculture are reported to suffer from hunger as a result of the diminishing prices that their crops can command.[45] The inability to compete is further aggravated by the disparity in resources available to larger production units to secure arable land and reliable means of irrigation.[46] What is more, experts warn that, 'the future is sure to invite (even) greater competition as a growing population and diminishing natural resources foster an ethic premised on survival of the (global) fittest'.[47]

In Southeast Asia, analogous trends include moves to convert 1–2 million hectares of rainforest and small-scale farming plots to an export-led crop and agrofuel plantation in the Meruake region of Indonesia, a move that could affect the food security of 50,000 people.[48] Likewise, approximately 3,000 hectares of so-called 'idle' land has been converted to sugar cane for agrofuel production in the Isabela region of the Philippines, with a further 8,000 hectares due to be added, meaning a major land transformation and uncertain impacts for the municipality's 45,000 inhabitants.[49] In such contexts, communities that had been self-sufficient prior to investment often become reliant on assistance following disenfranchisement, creating a burden on the State where none existed previously. In investigating these cases, the UN Special Rapporteur on the right to food and the UN Special Rapporteur on the rights of indigenous peoples questioned land lease and compensation arrangements in Isabela, while raising concerns over allegations of signing away land rights under coercion in Meruake. Both mandate holders subsequently urged the respective Southeast Asian governments 'to align – as a matter of urgency – their biofuels and investment policies with the need to respect

[43] Olivier De Schutter, 'Report of the Special Rapporteur on the Right to Food', (11 August 2010) UN Doc A/65/281, paragraphs 6–9.
[44] Ibid., paragraph 1.
[45] Ibid., paragraph 1.
[46] Ibid., paragraph 1.
[47] Margot Salomon, 'The Ethics of Foreign Investment: Agricultural land in Africa', *The Majalla: The Leading Arab Magazine*, (4 August 2010), http://www.majalla.com/eng/2010/08/article5594948, accessed 23 October 2013.
[48] 'South-East Asia / Agrofuel: UN Rights Experts Raise Alarm on Land Development Mega-Projects', (23 May 2012), http://www.srfood.org/images/stories/pdf/press_releases/20120523_southeastasia_en.pdf, accessed 25 November 2013. See also Forest Peoples Programme, 'Request for Further Consideration of the Situation of the Indigenous Peoples of Merauke, Papua Province, Indonesia, under the Committee on the Elimination of Racial Discrimination's Urgent Action and Early Warning Procedures', (25 July 2013), pp. 5–14, http://www.forestpeoples.org/sites/fpp/files/publication/2013/08/cerduamifeejuly2013english.pdf, accessed 20 December 2013.
[49] Ibid.

land users' rights'.[50] The need for greater alignment can be further illustrated by the fact that the drive to boost food production through foreign investment continues, despite hunger and malnutrition in many countries having more to do with poverty and inequality impeding *access* to food, than with the *availability* of food in sufficient quantities.[51]

The World Bank equally draws attention to amplifying pressures on arable land as a result of the global search for energy and food supplies, and emphasizes the severity of the problem in developing countries, especially where institutions are weak.[52] It warns that the increasing level of commercial leases and purchases by foreign governments or foreign-backed enterprises can lead to tensions when such external pressures conflict with communal land claims.[53] In Madagascar, the effects of overriding commercial interests over a large land-leasing deal – compounded by other long-standing tensions – contributed to resentment and unrest that led to the eventual overthrow of the government in early 2009.[54] While tensions deriving from a failure to exercise due diligence and provide effective remedies will seldom lead to such extreme outcomes, the scale and complexity of the governance gaps posed by globalization showcase the extent to which the acts and omissions of State and non-State actors are interrelated in their effects.

Inadequate responses to these challenges have already proven to be most costly to businesses and governments, as well as to society at large. For instance, strained community relations due to lack of engagement on core grievances have often led to demonstrations, road blockages and other acts by those adversely affected.[55] In many cases, initial threats to the viability of investments have culminated in the suspension of projects, as has been the case with Vedanta's planned bauxite mine project in Odisha, India, and the China Power Investment Corporation's Myitsone hydroelectric dam in Myanmar.[56] Meanwhile, the struggle for control over natural resources has been central to a number of long-running armed conflicts across

---

[50] Ibid.

[51] Salomon, see n. 47.

[52] See World Bank, *World Development Report: Conflict Security and Development* (2011), pp. 230–231. See also J. W. Bruce, 'USAID Issues Brief: Land and Conflict: Land Disputes and Land Conflicts, Property Rights and Resource Governance', *Briefing Paper No. 12*, (April 2011) and USAID's briefing paper on land scarcity, insecurity of tenure, and the lure of valuable of resources as core causes of conflict. The report also highlights the pitfalls of 'normative dissonance' – i.e. how poorly harmonized bodies of law are used as tools by different actors in conflict over land.

[53] Ibid.

[54] Ibid.

[55] See, for example, Rachel Davis and Daniel Franks, *Costs of Company–Community Conflict in the Extractive Sector*, Corporate Social Responsibility Initiative Report No. 66. Cambridge, MA: Harvard Kennedy School, 2014.

[56] Corinne Lennox, 'Corporate Responsibility to Respect the Rights of Minorities and Indigenous Peoples', in *State of the World's Minorities and Indigenous Peoples: Focus on Land Rights and Natural Resources* (Minority Rights Group International, 2012), p. 48. For further references to the challenges posed by the failure to act in conformity with principles of due diligence and broader international norms, see also Salil Tripathi, 'Getting Land Acquisition Right', *IHRB*, (18 November 2009), http://www.institutehrb.org/blogs/staff/getting_land_acquisition_right.html, accessed 4 December 2013.

Southeast Asia, as evidenced in Mindanao (Philippines), Indonesia's Papua, and in ethnic minority regions of Myanmar.[57] Unfortunately, the potential for violence remains significant even in the absence of armed conflict, as the relocation of communities to new areas increases demands on resources that may already be in limited supply.

Together, these factors point to failed policies and practices that require the urgent attention of governments and leading corporate actors alike. They equally underscore the urgency with which holistic approaches are required to address the breadth of the impacts that may be disproportionately felt by vulnerable communities.

RTD and the pursuit of effective remedies in ASEAN

While the newly adopted ASEAN Human Rights Declaration (AHRD) has been subjected to widespread criticism for falling below international standards,[58] the inclusion of RTD within its provisions must nonetheless be regarded as both innovative and a reflection of the region's potential for creative approaches to existing challenges.[59] This is evidenced by the shared commitment of Member States to realize the right so as to 'meet equitably the developmental and environmental needs of present and future generations'.[60] It is further revealed through the emphasis placed on 'the creation of conditions including the protection and sustainability of the environment for the peoples of ASEAN to enjoy all human rights … on an equitable basis, and the progressive narrowing of the development gap within ASEAN'.[61] The recognition of the need for effective development policies at the national level, as well as equitable economic relations and international cooperation in order to secure implementation of the right additionally underscores the regional understanding of the multidimensional aspects of RTD.[62]

---

[57] Nicole Girard, 'South East Asia' in *State of the World's Minority and Indigenous Peoples: Focus on Land Rights and Natural Resources* (Minority Rights Group International 2012), p. 143.

[58] Criticism was chiefly drawn from local, regional and international human rights organizations, as well as the UN Office of the High Commissioner for Human Rights. Concerns focused in part on the extent to which the GPs of the Declaration subject the realization of human rights to regional and national contexts, and brandish broad and all-encompassing limitations on rights in the Declaration, including rights deemed non-derogable under international law. Concerns have also been expressed about the Declaration's failure to include several key basic rights and fundamental freedoms, including the right to freedom of association and the right to be free from enforced disappearance. Criticism further extended to lack of civil-society involvement throughout the drafting process. For a more detailed account of relevant concerns, see http://www.hrw.org/news/2012/11/19/civil-society-denounces-adoption-flawed-asean-human-rights-declaration, accessed 28 November 2013.

[59] The right to development is not formally codified into the European or Inter-American systems.

[60] AHRD, see n. 4, Art. 35.

[61] Ibid., Art. 36.

[62] Ibid., Art. 37.

More broadly, the AHRD's call to 'mainstream the right to development into the relevant areas of ASEAN community building and beyond' echoes the underlying principles of the Roadmap for an ASEAN Community 2009–2015, which sets out the direction that ASEAN is committed to pursue in order to ensure that the benefits of regional integration are fully realized.[63] It further reflects the purposes and principles espoused by the ASEAN Charter, which are binding upon Member States.[64] The interrelationship between these normative frameworks arguably lends promise to the effective implementation of these standards over time. Until that juncture, the RTD provisions' emphasis in the AHRD on 'the need for Member States to work with the international community to promote equitable and sustainable development, fair trade practices and effective international cooperation'[65] calls attention to the key role that business and civil society must play alongside these actors in order to improve the availability of effective remedies and, ultimately, the attainment of sustainable solutions in the face of contemporary challenges. The imperative for such leadership from the private sector across Southeast Asia is particularly significant in view of the influence it wields as a driving force behind the region's rapid economic growth. It is also crucial in light of the protection gaps that exist as a result of the varying degrees to which the rule of law is upheld across ASEAN, a gap that is likely to persist in the absence of a regional mechanism capable of adjudicating human rights complaints.[66]

In view of such limitations, the following sections seek to examine how principles related to RTD may assist in bridging prevailing governance gaps and help secure more effective remedies for victims of corporate abuses.

Increase in choice and capabilities

The realization of the right to development is measured in terms of increased capabilities and also by the extent to which the range of choice has ameliorated for the beneficiary.[67] Within this framework, development is therefore conceptualized as a 'right to a process that expands the capabilities or freedom of individuals to improve their well-being and to realize what *they* value'.[68] Key to any satisfactory

[63] ASEAN, 'Roadmap for an ASEAN Community 2009–2015', (Jakarta: ASEAC, 2009), p. 5. This is equally in line with the pledge of ASEAN leaders to 'resolve and commit to promote ASEAN peoples to participate in and benefit fully from the process of ASEAN integration and community building', (ibid., p. 5.).

[64] While the Declaration itself is not binding, it constitutes the first step towards its potential adoption as a binding Convention in the future.

[65] AHRD, see n. 4, Art. 37.

[66] For a detailed overview of the state of the rule of law across ASEAN, see: Human Rights Resource Centre, 'Rule of Law for Human Rights in the ASEAN Region: A Base-line Study', (2011), http://hrrca.org/system/files/Rule_of_Law_for_Human_Rights_in_the_ASEAN_Region.pdf, accessed 31 October 2013.

[67] Amartya Sen, *Development as Freedom* (Oxford University Press, 2000).

[68] Arjun Sengupta, 'Third Report of the Independent Expert on the Right to Development', (2 January 2001) UN Doc E/CN.4/2001/WG.18/2. Additionally, in its 2000 Human Development Report,

form of compensation is thus the freedom for victims to make an *informed* choice about what may be most suitable, and that this choice include the possibility for hybrid compensatory measures that are commensurate with the specific circumstances of each individual case. Freedom of choice, in this respect, extends to information being disseminated in relation to all available mechanisms for redress, as prescribed by the GPs.[69] The RTD's emphasis on choice additionally dovetails with the GP requirement that those seeking reparations be enabled to participate in decisions on how to proceed.[70] Crucially, however, the underlying tenets of the RTD make the distinction between active and passive forms of participation. While the passive form is may amount to little more than a superficial attempt to engage with affected parties, the active form involves *empowerment*.[71] In this regard, active participation depends on awareness-raising and organization-building.[72] Other relevant factors in assessing participatory processes include the representativeness and accountability of decision-making bodies. Effectiveness must also be assessed from a subjective perspective, based on the opinions and attitudes of those concerned – especially with respect to their belief in the ability to affect decisions.[73] Furthermore, UN mandate holders have emphasized that,

> free, prior and informed consent is essential for the human rights of [vulnerable communities] in relation to major development projects, and this should involve ensuring mutually acceptable benefit-sharing, and mutually acceptable independent mechanisms for resolving disputes between the parties involved, including the private sector.[74]

If considered within the scope of remedial processes, RTD's emphasis on increasing choice and capabilities thus serves to build on the criteria set out in the

---

the UNDP articulated an understanding of development based on choice and capacity: 'Human Development, in turn, is a process of enhancing human capabilities – to expand choices and opportunities.' United Nations Development Programme, *Human Development Report* (2000), p. 2.

[69] UN GPs, see n. 2. See, in particular, GP 31(c) relating to predictability; GP 31(d) equitable access to sources of information; and GP 31(e) transparency.

[70] Ibid., GP 31(h)

[71] Report of the Global Consultation on the Right to Development as a Human Right, 'The Challenge of Implementing the Right to Development in the 1990s', in *Realizing the Right to Development: Essays in Commemoration of 25 Years of the United Nations Declaration on the Right to Development* (UN, 2013), p. 55.

[72] Ibid., p. 55.

[73] Ibid., p. 62.

[74] Rodolfo Stavenhagen, 'Report of the Special Rapporteur on the Situation of Human Rights and Fundamental Freedoms of Indigenous People', (21 January 2003) UN Doc E/CN.4/2003/90, paragraph 66. The original reference to 'indigenous peoples' has been expanded to 'vulnerable communities' in order to reflect developments in international jurisprudence that extend such protection to communities (such as tribal communities) who can demonstrate '*a profound and all-encompassing relationship to their ancestral lands* that [is] centered, not on the individual, but rather on the community as a whole'. Such protection further depends on evidence of distinct social, cultural and economic characteristics, along with the extent to which the disputed land is required to guarantee the physical and cultural survival of the community. See *Samaraka People* v. *Suriname*, Inter-American

GPs, by strengthening the scope to secure remedies that are more relevant – and thus more adequate – to those seeking reparations. This, in turn, can be argued to maximize the effectiveness and sustainability of remedies awarded as they more aptly reflect the needs of those adversely affected by the impacts of business practices. In the *Endorois* case, for example, counsel for the applicants argued that the right to development raised an obligation to protect the resources essential for the survival and well-being of the community. The African Commission accepted the argument, highlighting that due to the inextricable link between these resources and the Endorois' traditional land use systems, mere *access* to the ancestral lands would not constitute an effective remedy.[75] Accordingly, the African Commission held that 'if international law were to grant access only, indigenous peoples would remain vulnerable to further violations/dispossession by the State or third parties'.[76] The community was thus granted rights of ownership on the basis that it would enable it to 'engage with the State and third parties as active stakeholders rather than as passive beneficiaries'.[77] It further held that the right to obtain fair compensation translated into a right of the members of a community to 'reasonably share in the benefits made as a result of a restriction or deprivation of their right to the use and enjoyment of their traditional lands and of those natural resources necessary for their survival'.[78]

In keeping with this ruling, the UN Special Rapporteur on the rights of indigenous peoples has emphasized that 'under a corporate approach based on respect for indigenous rights, benefit-sharing must be regarded as a means of complying with a right, and not as a charitable award or favour granted by the company in order to secure social support for the project or minimize potential conflicts'.[79] To this end, it is important that companies create structures to provide ongoing income

---

Court of Human Rights, Judgment of November 28, 2007, Series C No. 172, paragraphs 85 and 86. See also *Moiwana Community* v. *Suriname,* Inter-American Court of Human Rights, Judgment of June 15, 2005, Series C No. 124, paragraphs 132–133. (Emphasis added)

[75]   *Endorois* case, see n. 14, paragraphs 203–06.

[76]   Ibid., paragraphs 204–205.

[77]   Ibid., paragraphs 204–205. While the African Commission's ruling on the community's rights of ownership fell under its consideration of Article 14 of the African Charter on Human and Peoples' Rights (the right to property), its findings in relation to the leverage and capacity necessary to secure adequate access and benefit-sharing highlighted the interconnection between property rights and RTD under the Charter. See paragraphs 275, 280–283, and in particular, 294.

[78]   Ibid., paragraphs 295–96. These findings echo the (former) Special Rapporteur on indigenous peoples' emphasis on benefit-sharing responding in part to the concept of fair compensation for deprivation or limitation of the rights of the communities concerned, particularly with regards to their right of communal ownership of lands, territories and natural resources. He thus urges companies to ensure that benefit-sharing mechanisms genuinely fulfil that purpose, and that they are appropriate to the specific context of indigenous peoples. See Rodolfo Stavenhagen, see n. 74, at paragraph 91.

[79]   James Anaya, 'Report of the Special Rapporteur on the Situation of Human Rights and Fundamental Freedoms of Indigenous People', (19 July 2010), UN Doc A/HRC/15/37A/HRC/15/37, paragraph 79. The UN Special Rapporteur on the right to food has raised similar concerns, leading to the drafting of core principles and measures that aim to assist States and investors to ensure that land deals are compatible with human rights and sustainability requirements. These include procedural requirements that aim to ensure informed participation of local communities as well as adequate benefit-sharing. See Report of the Special Rapporteur on the right to food, 'Large-

streams for communities as a means of strengthening the sustainability of those adversely affected. However, states and businesses alike are warned that, 'benefit-sharing must go beyond restrictive approaches based solely on financial payments which, depending on the specific circumstances, may not be adequate for the communities receiving them'.[80] Parties involved in the remediation of adverse impacts are therefore invited to adopt mechanisms that genuinely strengthen the capacity of indigenous and other vulnerable communities 'to establish and follow up their development priorities and which help to make their own decision-making mechanisms and institutions more effective'.[81] The right to development thus expands on the GPs by regarding communities as more than mere recipients of compensation. Processes and outcomes are instead viewed as a means of enfranchising and, in turn, empowering those affected by economic investments to 'collectively determine their needs and priorities and ensure the protection and advancement of their rights and interests'.[82] The aspect of choice therefore turns not only on the availability of suitable remedial processes, but also on the quality and sustainability of outcomes for expanded capabilities.

Equality of opportunity and growth with equity

Reports of the former Independent Expert on the right to development have emphasized that RTD as a whole must be realized in a rights-based manner that is transparent, accountable and participatory, as well as equitable and just. Equal emphasis has been placed on the importance of realizing the right in a manner that is non-discriminatory.[83] As an overarching theme in the right to development, equity (or diminishing disparities) with respect to economic growth further requires 'equality of opportunity for all in their access to basic resources, education, health services, food, housing, employment and the fair distribution of income'.[84] Experts point to this having several implications, chief among which:

> [T]he search for growth, or any economic or social reforms, must not violate any human right; it must target people or groups with unequal opportunity

scale Land Acquisitions and Leases: a Set of Core Principles and Measures to Address the Human Rights Challenge', (11 June 2009), pp. 13–15. Others have cautioned that: 'In instances where a venture will affect both indigenous and non-indigenous communities, it may be in a company's best interests to secure buy-in from both constituencies, even if greater legal responsibility is due to the former. This option has been deemed particularly appropriate where non-indigenous groups are especially vulnerable for various historical reasons.' See Amy Lehr and Gare Smith, *Implementing a Corporate Free, Prior, and Informed Consent Policy: Benefits and Challenges* (Foley Hoag eBook, May 2010), p. 61.

80 Anaya, see n. 79, paragraph 80. Suitable benefit-sharing mechanisms are likewise discussed in: Permanent Forum on Indigenous Issues, 'Report of the International Expert Group Meeting on Extractive Industries, Indigenous Peoples' Rights and Corporate Social Responsibility', (4 May 2009) UN Doc. E/C.19/2009/CRP. 8, paragraphs 14–22.

81 Ibid., paragraph 80.

82 Report of the Global Consultation on RTD, see n. 71, p. 59.

83 Arjun Sengupta, 'Second Report of the Independent Expert on the Right to Development', (11 September 2000), UN Doc. E/CN.4/2000/WG.18/CPR.1, paragraph 24.

84 DRD, see n. 5, Art. 8(1).

to access the minimum essential level of rights, for example the poor, minorities, indigenous peoples, children, women, people in rural areas; and it must have as its objective the elimination of injustices characterized by unfulfilled human rights.[85]

This is said to 'imply a change in the structure of production and distribution in the economy to ensure growth and equity'.[86] As previously outlined, it further implies 'providing for equality of opportunity ... which could translate to equitable distribution of income or amount of benefits accruing from the exercise of the rights'.[87] While this raises obligations in relation to substantive improvement in well-being, it remains that economic growth alone does not fully realize the right to development.[88] In keeping with this, former Independent Expert Sengupta has underscored that '[f]or economic growth to be included as an element of the claims representing the right to development, it must satisfy the basic condition of facilitating the realization of all other rights ... In other words, policies adopted to increase economic growth must be consistent with human rights standards'.[89]

RTD's emphasis on growth with equity further rejects the narrow understanding of development as being purely limited to 'increased national income based on the "trickle down approach" and aggregate benefit, with inadequate attention being given to concurrent increases in intra-State inequality and regional disparities or to exploitive conditions of employment'.[90] As signalled by Salomon, '[a]n increase in GDP tells us nothing about the human and environmental sacrifices made in realising growth or whether benefits have been fairly distributed'.[91] This reasoning is particularly relevant when seeking to determine the extent to which remedies secured by communities adversely affected by the extractive industries, hydroelectric projects or other economic activities correspond or contrast with wider sustainable development strategies, including the fulfilment of the Millennium Development Goals. It is arguably in response to such challenges that the Working Group on the right to development has underscored the need to build synergies between growth-oriented development strategies and human rights.[92] To this end, the Working Group has emphasized RTD's value as 'a guide in setting priorities and resolving trade-offs in resource allocations and policy

---

[85] Margot E. Salomon, *Global Responsibility for Human Rights: World Poverty and the Development of International Law* (Oxford University Press, 2007), p. 131.

[86] Arjun Sengupta, 'Development Cooperation and the Right to Development', Francois-Xavier Bagnoud Center Working Paper, (2000), http://www.tanzaniagateway.org/docs/Development_cooperation_and_the_Right_to_Development.pdf, accessed 30 October 2013.

[87] Ibid.

[88] DRD, see n. 5. Art. 2(3) stipulates that peoples shall experience 'constant improvement of the well-being of the entire population and of all individuals'.

[89] Arjun Sengupta, 'Fifth Report of the Independent Expert on the Right to Development', (18 September 2002) UN Doc. E/CN.4/2002/WG.18/6 (2002).

[90] Salomon (2005), see n. 3, p. 428.

[91] Salomon (2010), see n. 47.

[92] See 'Report of the Working Group on the Right to Development', (1 August 2010), UN Doc. A/66/216, paragraph 15.

frameworks'.[93] As highlighted by Salomon, '[t]hat rights taken together reflect more than the sum of their parts can be an important policy tool, serving to emphasise the value of norm coherence and increasing sensitivity to legitimate means of determining any trade-offs in rights that may come as a result of resource constraints.'[94]

RTD's value in negotiating critical compromises is perhaps most evident in relation to the practice of large-scale land acquisitions. The acceleration of land-grabbing since the beginning of the 2008 global food crisis – which has exacerbated the ability of many of the most vulnerable to meet their basic dietary needs – serves as a particularly striking example of the need for greater synergies between all relevant actors, and thus the pertinence of remedial approaches premised on the right to development.[95] In this respect, while states must act both individually and collectively to prevent destabilizing price speculation, ensure adequate food production and take necessary actions to slow climate change,[96] it is imperative that corporate actors involved in the agribusiness industry and other forms of large-scale land acquisitions be guided by sustainable policies. The Special Rapporteur on the right to food has indicated that this 'call[s] for leases or purchases to be fully transparent and participatory and the revenues to be used for the benefit of the local population, as provided for by both the Declaration on Permanent Sovereignty over Natural Resources and the Declaration on the Right to Development'.[97]

Equality of opportunity and growth with equity also crucially depend on companies making realistic assessments of the amount of land required for their commercial purposes, and ensuring that land being considered for acquisition meets a genuine need. The practice of acquiring large plots in adjacent areas should be avoided if the project does not require it, particularly as land that remains idle over several years increases the risk of conflict. That said, exceptions to the practice of 'land banks' may arise in instances where legitimate safety or security considerations make such an arrangement necessary. Ideally, the legitimacy of such exceptions should be assessed by bodies that are not only independent but also perceived to be so by the individual or community stakeholders.[98] Non-judicial

---

[93] Ibid., paragraph 15.

[94] Salomon (2005), see n. 3, p. 412.

[95] Report of the Special Rapporteur on the right to food (Addendum), 'Large-Scale Land Acquisitions and Leases: A Set of Minimum Principles and Measures to Address the Human Rights Challenge', (28 December 2009) UN Doc. A/HRC/13/33/Add.2, paragraph 2. The Special Rapporteur discusses land grabbing as a result of land being leased at very low prices, sold below market prices, or given away in exchange for promises of employment creation or transfer of technology (paragraph 31).

[96] Susan Randolph and Maria Green, 'Theory into Practice: a New Framework and Proposed Assessment Criteria', in *Realizing the Right to Development: Essays in Commemoration of 25 Years of the United Nations Declaration on the Right to Development* (UN, 2013), pp. 412–413.

[97] Report of the Special Rapporteur on the right to food, see n. 95, paragraph 32.

[98] See generally, Institute for Human Rights and Business, 'Preventing Conflicts over Land: Exploring the Role of Business and the Value of Human Rights Approaches', (November 2009). See also, Klaus Deininger et al., *Using the Land Governance Assessment Framework (LGAF): Lessons and Next Steps* (World Bank, 2009).

grievance mechanisms may play a key role in this respect, particularly if they operate in accordance with the effectiveness criteria set out in the GPs. However, while
the quality of the mechanism itself is critically important, equality of opportunity
and growth with equity further depend on both the quantitative and qualitative
adequacy of the remedies secured through these processes.[99] The RTD framework
is valuable in this regard, as guarantees of the availability of abundant food sources
following displacement would be of limited value if the food in question were nutri-
tionally poor or culturally inappropriate.[100] In the case of small-scale farmers, the
adequacy of remedies would thus heavily depend on their relocation to plots of
equal size and agricultural quality so that they can meet their dietary requirements.
In instances where this is not feasible, an RTD-compatible strategy for delivering effective remedies would involve companies working in conjunction with local
authorities to establish appropriate institutional frameworks to ensure benefit to
all relevant parties.[101] Participation, which has been identified as key to ensuring
long-term sustainability and success of investments, must also be central to the
reparations process.[102] For those unable to sustain their traditional livelihoods due
to relocation, the adequacy and effectiveness of remedies would further depend
on their compatibility relative to the prices of – and accessibility to – productive
resources such as water, financial capital, training and technology.[103] In sum, by
placing equal value on 'quality as well as quantity', on the 'individual as well as the
social dimension of human needs', in addition to 'material, intellectual and cultural
needs',[104] the operative criteria for measuring progress in the realization of RTD
provide a holistic framework that is optimal for calibrating remedies more precisely
to the situation and requisites of those adversely impacted by business practices.

[99] The World Commission on Dams (WCD) highlights the perils of resettlement programmes focused
predominantly on the process of physical relocation rather than on the economic and social development of the displaced. It states that such an approach has resulted in the impoverishment of
a majority of those resettled from most dam projects throughout the world. It provides examples
of resettlement sites selected without consideration of the availability of livelihood opportunities
or the preferences of the displaced persons themselves. Often, they have been forced to resettle in
resource-depleted and environmentally degraded areas, where such lands have rapidly lost their
capacity to support the resettled population. The WCD indicates that such instances have been
recorded from Hoa Binh in Vietnam, Sirindhorn in Thailand, Batang Ai in Sarawak Malaysia,
and other rice-growing East Asian countries with large rural populations. Statistics outlined by the
WCD further emphasize the devastating consequences of ineffective remedies – e.g. 72 per cent of
the 32,000 displaced people from the Kedung Ombo dam in Indonesia were found to be worse off
after resettlement. See World Commission on Dams, 'Dams and Development: A New Framework
For Decision-Making', (November 2000), pp. 103–108.

[100] Report of the Global Consultation on RTD, see n. 71, p. 62.

[101] Nicolaas Schrijver, 'Self-Determination of Peoples and Sovereignty Over Natural Wealth and
Resources', in *Realizing the Right to Development: Essays in Commemoration of 25 Years of the United Nations
Declaration on the Right to Development* (UN, 2013), p. 100. See also Lorenzo Cotula, Sonja Vermeulen,
Rebeca Leonard and James Keeley, *Land Grab or Development Opportunity? Agricultural Investments and
International Land Deals in Africa* (FAO, IIED and IFAD, 2009) p. 104.

[102] Ibid., p. 100.

[103] Report of the Global Consultation on RTD, see n. 71, p. 62. See also Report of the High-Level
Task Force, see n. 13, with particular emphasis on criteria 1(a), 1(f), 1(g) and 1(h).

[104] Ibid., p. 62.

Differential impacts

The GPs point to the effectiveness of grievance mechanisms partly depending on accessibility – a factor that requires the dissemination of information to all stakeholder groups, as well the provision of adequate assistance for those who may face particular barriers to access.[105] Additional criteria highlight the importance of ensuring that affected communities are able to engage with these mechanisms on equitable terms – i.e. that they be provided with the necessary advice, expertise and resources to engage on fair, informed and respectful terms.[106] However, the ability to secure remedies that are adequate and thus sustainable in their effects additionally requires that suitable attention be drawn to the differential impacts that business practices may have on various segments of a given community. The experience of women in the context of large-scale land acquisitions is particularly noteworthy. Business practices at greatest risk of negatively affecting women are those driven by 'gender-blind' policies that do not differentiate between men and women, and thus compromise the gender neutrality of their impacts on respective roles in a given society.[107]

Against this backdrop, effective remedies must be particularly mindful of the extent to which women are denied ownership rights to property in many countries, often as a result of the cultural norms in place.[108] This extends to the obstacles faced by countless women with regard to the right to inherit property from a family member or spouse. As a result of such challenges, statistics indicate that while women produce between 60 and 80 per cent of the food in most developing countries and are responsible for half of the world's food production, fewer than 10 per cent own the land upon which they toil.[109] The differential impacts experienced by men and women in this respect are acutely felt in relation to matters of compensation, which heavily depend on the recognition of formal ownership status. Companies should therefore seek ways to ensure that compensation is equitably distributed – irrespective of such status (e.g. through policies of equal payments to spouses) – and further ascertain that female-headed households, widows and single females are also duly incorporated into compensation strategies. The effectiveness of remedies will also depend on the extent to which they are capable of addressing the significant increase in the burden of work that women may experience due to greater difficulties in accessing clean water, fuel and traditional food sources. Conversely, due regard must be given to means of mitigating

---

[105] UN Guiding Principles, see n. 2, GP 31(b).

[106] Ibid., GP 31(d).

[107] Kathryn Dovey, *Business and Land Acquisition: Integrating a Gender Perspective*, (IHRB, 2010).

[108] See, for instance, Elisa Scalise, 'Indigenous Women's Land Rights: Case Studies from Africa' in *State of the World's Minorities and Indigenous Peoples: Focus on Land Rights and Natural Resources* (Minority Rights Group International, 2012), pp. 52–59. See also Bina Agarwal, 'Gender and Land Rights Revisited: Exploring New Prospects via the State, Family and Market', (2003) *Journal of Agrarian Change*, 3(1–2): 184–224.

[109] SDdimension, 'Women and Sustainable Food Security', Sustainable Development Department, Food and Agriculture Organization of the United Nations (FAO), http://www.fao.org/sd/fsdirect/fbdirect/fsp001.htm, accessed 11 May 2014.

the need for men's migration for employment once traditional occupations are no longer viable.[110]

More broadly speaking, in the context of natural resource development, it is important to recognize that dominant priorities espoused by governments and corporations can override alternative priorities and conceptions of progress that may be held by indigenous and tribal peoples as well as minorities.[111] Accordingly, the marginalization of these communities not only heightens the risk of them being disproportionately affected by the exploitation of these resources, but also increases the likelihood of remedies being ill-equipped to effectively address the specific ways in which their property and other rights may have been infringed upon. Evidence of disproportionate impact has been widely acknowledged, starting with the World Bank's 1994 *Bank-wide Review of Projects Involving Involuntary Resettlement*, which highlighted that those resettled as a result of dam projects – and arguably other forms of development – were generally from the poorest and most vulnerable sections of society.[112] Examples abound in this respect, as illustrated by the case of the Philippines, where nearly all of the larger dam projects that have been initiated or proposed have been located on the land of the country's 6–7 million indigenous peoples.[113] Meanwhile, in India, 40–50 per cent of those displaced by development projects have been reported to be tribal peoples, despite these groups only accounting for 8 per cent of the country's population.[114] Similarly, reports suggest that ethnic minorities in Vietnam have been denied fair and full compensation following the construction of the Yali Falls dam, in contrast to the resettled ethnic majority group.[115] In other instances, the same community may be repeatedly subjected to displacements over time, as has been the case for the Temuan people, who have traditionally lived along the banks of the Selangor River in Malaysia.[116]

---

[110] Lennox, see, n. 56, p. 14.

[111] Ibid., p. 14. The importance of including minorities and indigenous peoples for achieving sustainable development and preventing conflict is persuasively argued in *The Millennium Development Goals: Helping or Harming Minorities*, Working Paper by Minority Rights Group International to the 11th session of the UN Working Group on Minorities (19 April 2005) UN Doc. E/CN.4/Sub.2/ AC.5/2005/WP.4.

[112] World Bank, 'Resettlement and Development, Report of the Task Force for the Bank-Wide Review of Involuntary Resettlement 1986–1993', (1994).

[113] World Commission on Dams, see n. 99, p. 110.

[114] Ibid., p. 110. See also, Forum-Asia, 'Corporate Accountability in ASEAN: A Human Rights-Based Approach', (2013). The publication provides a comprehensive overview of the nature of development in ASEAN as well as the impact of business on human rights in the region. See specifically, 'Contradictions of Corporate Social Responsibility in ASEAN: Policy and Practice', pp. 61–63.

[115] Those particularly hard-hit included ethnic minority communities such as the Jarai, Bahnar and Ro Nhao peoples, who did not receive land and were given less compensation than ethnic Kinh Vietnamese. For many, the only way to survive is by walking for days to clear new fields deep in the forests, by entering into low-wage employment, or by scavenging at the local dumpsite. See International Rivers Network, 'Damming the Sesan River: Impacts in Cambodia and Vietnam', (Briefing Paper 4, October 2002), http://www.internationalrivers.org/files/attached-files/04. sesan.pdf, accessed 4 February 2014.

[116] The Temuan people count as one of the Orang Asli, or the 'Original People' of Malaysia. In early 2010, 75 Temuan families living on the banks of the Selangor River in Malaysia were informed that their land was at risk of being submerged by the construction of a dam. The Selangor River

Additional challenges arise as a result of the disregard for customary tenure across various jurisdictions. As compensation schemes often only extend to those with formal legal title, many indigenous or tribal peoples and ethnic minorities are considered ineligible for resettlement. Such was the case for the Karen ethnic group in Thailand, who comprised one-fifth of those physically displaced for the construction of the Kao Laem dam.[117] Even where legal provisions for the recognition of collective title exist, such as in Cambodia, few communities succeed in securing land.[118]

Furthermore, the disregard for customary tenure may not only prejudice the treatment of these communities as legitimate rights-holders to compensation, but may also lead to remedies that are inconsistent with the collective forms of ownership that underpin their traditional livelihoods. Consequently, even when some form of reparation is granted, it must be mindful of the inextricable link that exists between indigenous and tribal peoples' access to ancestral lands and their socio-economic and cultural survival.[119] Scholars point to traditional practices and knowledge not being readily transferable to new spaces.[120] Moreover, in the absence of due diligence and effective remedies, ample evidence points to the destruction of traditional lands, resources and livelihoods often leading to 'cultural erosion', which can threaten the very existence of affected communities.[121] It is in light of this crucial relationship that international law only permits displacement of indigenous and tribal peoples as an 'exceptional measure'.[122]

dam would be the fifth affecting them, and already more are being planned. One of the original impacts adversely affecting the community dates back to 1883, when a much smaller dam across the Selangor River burst and destroyed the entire village. See Zuzanna Olszewska, 'Thoughts on the Selangor River Dam: Orang Asli and the Politics of Indigenousness in Malaysia', (April 2010), http://www.culturalsurvival.org/publications/cultural-survival-quarterly/233-fall-1999-going-under-struggle-against-large-dams, accessed 4 February 2014.

[117] World Commission on Dams, see n. 99, p. 105.

[118] As of August 2013, only eight collective titles had been officially issued to indigenous communities (two in Ratanakiri, five in Mondulkiri), despite the existence of laws recognizing that indigenous communities are allowed to acquire collective title (2001 Land Law, Sub-decree on Procedures of Registration of Land of Indigenous Communities). Meanwhile, according to the 2012 Report of the Special Rapporteur on the situation of human rights in Cambodia, at least 98 concessions have been granted on indigenous peoples' land. Moreover, Directive 001 (part of a national titling campaign) has had the effect of de-prioritizing indigenous land titling programmes. See 'Role and Achievements of the Office of the United Nations High Commissioner for Human Rights in Assisting the Government and People of Cambodia in the Promotion and Protection of Human Rights', (19 September 2013) UN Doc A/HRC/24/32, paragraph 17.

[119] The essence of this inextricable link has perhaps been best described by Erica-Irene Daes as (former) Special Rapporteur for the prevention of discrimination and protection of indigenous peoples: 'Limitations, if any, on the right to indigenous peoples to their natural resources must flow only from the most urgent and compelling interest of the State. Few, if any, limitations on indigenous resource rights are appropriate, because the indigenous ownership of the resources is associated with the most important and fundamental human rights, including the right to life, food, the right to self-determination, to shelter, and the right to exist as a people.' Erica-Irene Daes, 'Indigenous Peoples' Right to Land and Natural Resources', in Nazila Ghanea and Alexandra Xanthaki (eds), *Minorities, Peoples and Self-Determination* (Martinus Nijhoff, 2005).

[120] Lennox, see n. 56, p. 14.

[121] Ibid., p. 14.

[122] See, for example, Art. 16(2) of ILO Convention 169 on Indigenous and Tribal Peoples (1989). More generally, the UN Committee on Economic Social and Cultural Rights likewise stipulates

While standards relating to rights over land, territories and natural resources are not explicit in relation to minorities, it remains that they may also require some form of collective reparation in order to sustain their particular way of life.[123] For instance, in some cases, development-based evictions may disrupt the availability of education or access to core services in their language, factors that may threaten both the linguistic and cultural integrity of such communities. In other instances, as previously discussed, relocation schemes may threaten the food security of affected populations. This, particularly, has been apparent in cases where minority groups dependent on farming have been resettled into villages or plots too small to sustain traditional farming practices.[124] For example in Vietnam, the construction of the Son La hydropower plant led to the resettlement of 91,000 people belonging to ethnic minorities – the largest resettlement programme in the country's history.[125] The Vietnam Union of Science and Technology Associations subsequently reported that, 'relocation [was] breaking down existing social structures and community relationships and creating trauma for minority groups … Most [have been] left without any agricultural land.'[126]

In response to such challenges, the right to development should be regarded as a valuable means of securing the remedial frameworks necessary to mitigate the differential impacts felt by indigenous and tribal peoples, as well as minorities. As a group right, its capacity to address affected communities as an integrated whole allows for remedial frameworks that more aptly respond to the tangible and subtle impacts of natural resource development upon them. In contrast, remedies that solely focus on the sum of their parts risk fragmenting the tenets upon which the viability and sustainability of such collectivities depend.

Mutually beneficial outcomes

It has become widely agreed that equality facilitates growth and promotes other aspects of human well-being at the national level.[127] Conversely, there is also a growing consensus on the interplay between inequality and global financial instability.[128] Within the context of reparations, the adoption of inappropriate

---

that: 'instances of forced eviction are *prima facie* incompatible with the requirements of the Covenant and can only be justified in the *most exceptional circumstances*, and in accordance with the relevant principles of international law', CESCR, 'General Comment 4 on the Right to Adequate Housing', (1991) UN Doc. HRI/GEN/1/Rev.6, paragraph 18, emphasis added.

[123] For more comprehensive detail on the rights of minorities in this regard, see Lennox, n. 56, pp. 16–18.

[124] Gay McDougall, 'Report of the Independent Expert on Minority Issues: Mission to Viet Nam', (24 January 2011), UN Doc. A/HRC/16/45/Add.2, paragraphs 31–36.

[125] Ibid., paragraph 35. Of the ten different groups affected, the majority were ethnic Thai.

[126] Ibid., paragraph 36.

[127] Randolph and Green, see n. 96, p. 407. See also P. Aghion, Eve Caroli, and Cecilia Garcia-Penalosa, 'Inequality and Economic Growth: the Perspective of New Growth Theories', (1999) *Journal of Economic Literature*, 37(4): pp. 1615–1660.

[128] See, for example, Phillip Aldrich, 'Davos WEF 2011: Wealth Inequality Is the "Most Serious Challenge for the World"', *The Telegraph* (London, 26 January 2011).

or destructive processes and outcomes that are governed by purely financial considerations can further exacerbate inequalities of power and control of resources among groups, and thus increase the scope for social tensions and conflict.[129] The human and financial costs of such tensions to all segments of society cannot be ignored.

The multiple economic, financial, social and ecological dimensions of the challenges that communities, businesses and states collectively face highlight the urgency to reconsider the means by which private and public sectors engage in economic development. The fact that the World Economic Forum has singled out 'inequality' as one of the underlying causes of the financial crisis and subsequent recession suggests that global business leaders are increasingly mindful of the pivotal role that the corporate sector can and must play to help redress some of these imbalances.[130] Insofar as this extends to improving the effectiveness of remedies, Professor Ruggie has nonetheless stressed from the outset of his mandate that, while the GPs constitute a vital starting point for improving the effectiveness of non-judicial grievance mechanisms, the business and human rights debate 'need[ed] to expand beyond establishing individual corporate liability for wrongdoings'.[131] In his view, 'an individual liability model alone [could not] fix larger imbalances in the system of global governance'.[132] This underscores the need to reassess the dynamics governing the relationships between all relevant actors. The task at hand further calls for a holistic approach that extends beyond the narrow focus of existing remedial processes, if the fallouts of harmful impacts and systemic inequities are to be successfully addressed.

In requiring that development be pursued in respect of all internationally recognized human rights, RTD's added value for addressing existing gaps stems from its 'categorical rejection of one of the most prominent narratives about the nature of development and growth, that "you cannot make an omelet without breaking a few eggs"'.[133] It further stems from its rejection of the traditionally narrow focus on aggregate growth, which is predicated on 'accept[ing] too readily a system of winners and losers'.[134] Instead, by seeking to empower individuals and communities, RTD's participative approach can serve as a valuable tool for optimizing remedial processes and outcomes, as strengthening the capacity of those affected by corporate and State development projects enables them to meaningfully engage with those processes. Moreover, its emphasis on the treatment of individuals and communities as active stakeholders rather than passive beneficiaries helps broaden the focus beyond the narrow mitigation of loss or impact, in favour of partnerships.

---

[129] Report of the Global Consultation on RTD, see n. 71, p. 61. See also 'Independent Expert Mission to Viet Nam', see n. 124, paragraph 36.

[130] The issue of inequality continues to feature prominently in World Economic Forum meetings. See World Economic Forum, *Insight Report: Global Risks*, (9th edn, 2014).

[131] John Ruggie, 'Business and Human Rights: The Evolving International Agenda', (2007) *AJIL*, 101: 839.

[132] Ibid.

[133] Salomon (2007), see n. 85, p. 130.

[134] Ibid., pp. 129–130.

While companies initially may resist drawing upon the RTD framework on account of real or perceived short-term costs, its potential for generating mutually beneficial outcomes suggests that it should be welcomed more justly as a means of generating significant opportunities. Numerous examples serve to showcase its potential in this regard. This includes case-studies published by Oxfam Australia's former mining ombudsman, which confirmed that redress for communities has been achieved in tandem with measurable financial benefit to companies. Among the various success factors and challenges involved towards this end, Oxfam noted the importance of defining and communicating the roles and responsibilities of the respective parties, establishing systems to monitor project implementation and progress, establishing a communication mechanism, understanding the distinct cultural aspects of the communities and involving a wide range of stakeholders.[135] In accordance with these principles, a project undertaken by Hamersley Iron Pty Limited actively engaged Aboriginal groups in developing an iron ore mine and railway in the Pilbara region of Australia to ensure minimal adverse impact to them. The project commenced only after the affected communities' informed consent was obtained. Negotiations between Hamersley and the Aboriginal communities resulted in the Yandicoogina Land Use Agreement, which provided the basis for a long-term collaborative framework between the parties. Hamersley, in turn, reduced permitting time, completed construction under budget by US$100 million, and commenced production six months early.[136]

Meanwhile, the Malampaya Deep Water Gas-to-Power Project – which involves the extraction and transport of natural gas to a refinery plant on Luzon island in the Philippines – further showcases the scope for mutual benefits across other industries.[137] In the course of its operations, Shell deliberately engaged community stakeholders prior to and throughout the project's lifetime, enabling it to successfully address the concerns of the affected communities. This involved monthly meetings with community representatives, which served to provide updates on project operations and impacts, and to allow the community to raise concerns and grievances. Sustainable development programmes in each affected province were also established. These provided services requested by the communities, such

[135] Oxfam Australia, *Community–Company Grievance Resolution: a Guide for the Australian Mining Industry* (2010), pp. 15–16. Four years on from the date of publication, questions have been raised as to the sustainability of the benefits cited in relation to the Tolukuma Water Supply project in Papua New Guinea. However, the Tintaya Dialogue Table in Peru continues to be regarded as a successful outcome. See also Caroline Rees, *Access to Remedies for Corporate Human Rights Impacts: Improving Non-Judicial Mechanisms*, Report of a Multi-Stakeholder Workshop (20–21 November 2008), Corporate Social Responsibility Initiative, Harvard Kennedy School, Report No. 32, p. 6.

[136] See 'Engaging Communities in Extractive and Infrastructure Projects', (2009), http://pdf.wri.org/breaking_ground_engaging_communities.pdf, accessed 7 December 2013.

[137] The Malampaya Deep Water Gas-to-Power Project is a joint venture between the Shell subsidiary Shell Philippines Exploration, Chevron Texaco, and the Philippine National Oil Company. For additional information, see Steven Herz, Antonio la Vina and Jonathan Sohn, in Jonathan Sohn (ed.), *Development Without Conflict: The Business Case for Community Consent* (World Resources Institute, 2007), http://www.wri.org/publication/development-without-conflict, accessed 5 December 2013.

as job training, livelihood workshops, employment link-ups, scholarships, microfinance, health and safety workshops, and conservation activities. Teams composed of local government representatives, NGOs, community leaders, and provincial and community environmental officers were also established to monitor the environmental and social impacts of the project during its implementation. Shell has estimated that the incremental costs of avoiding and mitigating adverse impacts and securing community consent during planning and implementation amounted to little more than 0.13 per cent of total project costs, and produced significant quantifiable benefits since it did not encounter any delays caused by community opposition. In aggregate, avoiding these anticipated delays saved the project US$50–$72 million, producing a 'return on investment' on its community consent efforts of as much as 1,200 per cent.

Furthermore, in the context of environmental protection, studies have shown that the designation of 'indigenous areas' (in contrast to strictly protected areas, such as national parks) has been highly effective at reducing tropical deforestation – an outcome that again benefits a wide range of actors.[138] Likewise, indigenous medicinal knowledge has often proven to save medical researchers valuable time and resources as plant samples identified and genetically manipulated by indigenous peoples are used to develop new pharmaceutical products.[139] Indigenous knowledge has also played an important role in developing more viable agricultural practices. For instance, in Asia and elsewhere, agricultural companies have realized enormous benefit from their access to disease-resistant seeds – again identified and genetically manipulated by indigenous peoples.[140] Unfortunately, many of these gains have been made at the expense of indigenous peoples, in what has been termed 'biopiracy'. The increasing resistance of these communities to engage with or support these scientific advances is entirely understandable in the absence of robust benefit-sharing schemes and mechanisms to protect their interests. Public health, food security and the protection of biodiversity – on which all of us depend – can thus only benefit from a more equitable partnership with the guardians of this ancestral knowledge.

Together, these examples serve to illustrate that equitable and sustainable outcomes are not only necessary, but possible. This not only requires grievance mechanisms that are compliant with the effectiveness criteria set out in the GPs, but also a marked shift in dynamics, where states and businesses engage with affected

---

[138] For instance, recent findings indicate that policies safeguarding local populations' sustainable use of the forest reserves were not only effective but, on average, even more so than strictly protected areas that focused exclusively on conservation. The findings further indicated that most effective of all were indigenous areas, which were estimated to reduce deforestation by approximately 16 percentage points over the period of 2000–2008. See World Bank, 'New Study Finds Indigenous Areas Highly Effective at Reducing Tropical Deforestation', (16 August 2011). The study compared indigenous areas with strictly protected areas, such as national parks. The report is available at: http://www.plosone.org/article/info%3Adoi%2F10.1371%2Fjournal.pone.0022722, accessed 2 February 2014.

[139] Michael Bengwayan, *Intellectual and Cultural Property Rights of Indigenous and Tribal Peoples in Asia* (Minority Rights Group International, 2003), p. 20.

[140] Ibid., p. 20.

communities as viable partners. As eloquently stated by a leading practitioner, 'the development of natural resources need not be harmful or unjust. The future of natural resource development is our *common* future, and [vulnerable communities] have a right not only to benefit in this, but also to help determine its path'.[141]

Conclusion

Overall, the effectiveness of remedies depends on the extent to which they are relevant to those affected and sustainable in their outcome. The right to development serves as a valuable tool in enriching strategies towards this end, as it determines not only the equitable processes by which development and economic activities should be undertaken, but also the quality of the remedies available through meaningful engagement with those adversely affected by their impacts. The leverage gained by communities as active stakeholders rather than passive beneficiaries is of particular relevance in the context of the imbalances resulting from existing governance gaps, as it creates a space for dominant priorities for development and large-scale investment to be challenged and adapted to accommodate – however modestly – alternative perspectives. The RTD framework thus encourages thinking beyond mere reparations by paving the way for viable partnerships, where a 'third way' may be explored as the foundation for a future that is more equitable for present and future generations. Its added value in negotiating trade-offs cannot be overstated as competing interests intensify over diminishing resources, threatening not only the sustainable management of these resources but also the viability of the communities, businesses and states that depend on them.

---

[141] Lennox, see n. 56, p. 21.

Conclusion and afterword

Makarim Wibisono

In recalling the 61st session of the UN Commission on Human Rights, since reconstituted as the UN Human Rights Council, I realize how far we have come in so short a time. It was this session in 2005, which I chaired, that led to the appointment of Professor John Ruggie as the Special Representative to the UN Secretary-General on human rights and transnational corporations and other business enterprises. The session resolved that the Special Representative should identify and clarify standards of corporate responsibility and accountability for transnational corporations and other business enterprises with regard to human rights. This was ultimately to lead to the development of the United Nations Guiding Principles on Business and Human Rights, which were unanimously endorsed by the United Nations Human Rights Council on 16 June 2011.

When serving as the chairperson for the second annual UN Forum on Business and Human Rights in Geneva last December, I was heartened to see that all regions were represented, with registered delegates from over 115 individual countries. As the former Executive Director of the ASEAN Foundation, I believe that Southeast Asia is particularly well suited to playing a major role in the field of business and human rights, for the region has come a long way since 2005. I am pleased to say that this book chronicles those advances and provides a comprehensive overview – both in theory and in practice – of how they pertain to business and human rights. In so doing, it provides an invaluable insight into the challenges and opportunities that exist in trying to put the Guiding Principles into practice.

To address the challenges that the book highlights in a meaningful fashion, it is imperative that we not only study its detailed analysis, but respond to the recommendations made, and provide sufficient regulatory legislation to support these efforts. Yet even with all the will in the world, this cannot be achieved by any single group, but rather demands concerted efforts from multiple stakeholders working in harmony to progress down the road towards the common goal of ameliorating the adverse impacts business activities can have on human rights. This search for greater accountability and transparency does not just involve individual businesses and governments, but requires the shared commitment of inter-governmental human rights institutions within ASEAN, as well as academia, trade unions, civil society, donor agencies and the relevant United Nations agencies operating in the Southeast Asian region.

I fully agree with the editors of this book that we have reached an inflexion point in Southeast Asia. ASEAN is poised for what the editors term a 'regulatory turn', as the regional bloc's member nations become an integrated economic community based on the rule of law.

This comes at a time when the need to develop innovative tools for guidance and capacity-building could not be greater. ASEAN States and corporations operating within their borders can no longer blame a lack of capacity as the reason for failing to ensure that strong corporate, environmental and human rights practices are the norm rather than the exception.

Yet a single flourish cannot cure all ills, for adherence to the Guiding Principles can pose different problems depending on the circumstances. Policy-makers and international scholars would do well to heed this fact and can learn much from the data that the book's authors have collected and analysed in such diverse sectors as the extractive industry, agriculture, energy, information technology, finance, and accounting.

Guided by empirical research, the book also examines the experiences of those communities in Southeast Asia whose human rights have neither been adequately protected nor respected, and asks how international law, ASEAN instruments and national legislation can better serve the interests of such affected communities.

The book's scholarly analysis and practical recommendations reflect the paradigm shift that is embodied in the Guiding Principles in regard to business accountability for human rights impacts. I commend the editors and authors, and am confident that this will prove a useful treatise for policy-makers, academics and students not only in Southeast Asia but around the world.

Makarim Wibisono
United Nations Special Procedure
Chairperson, United Nations Annual Forum on Business & Human Rights (2013)
Executive Director, ASEAN Foundation (2011–2014)

Index

State, the: debates over role in right
to development 258–9; discretion
to derogate from business impact
protections in Myanmar 43; duty
in relation to female human rights
protection 66–8; duty to incorporate
human rights in business 121–2;
framework for Asian businesses
operating in Myanmar 186–9; need
for cooperation to support adoption of
business human rights 130–2; need for
respect of human rights in Myanmar
172–85; obligations in relation to
business practice and child rights
81–5; upholding duty of to protect from
business excess in Philippines 46
stock exchanges: role in promoting
CSR 18–20
structures, socio-political: impact on
grievance resolution 249–51
supply, business: use of MIHRSC to audit
management of 200
sustainable development goals 123
sustainability, business: characteristics as
principled pragmatism 121–2; impact of
international standards 124–5; significance
of challenges facing 122–5; *see also* factors
supporting *e.g.* rights, human; *see also*
particular *e.g.* palm oil; *see also* particular
challenges *e.g.* pollution, air
systems, operating: impact on grievance
resolution 251–2

technologies, information *see* information
and communications technology
Thailand: development of environmentally
responsible investment 113–16;
discrimination on grounds of ethnicity
and gender 64; impact of financing of
river dams by banks of 100–3; impact
of human rights on female migrant
workers 69–70; investigation on impact
of Mekong River dams 104–6; linking
financial integration with investment
118–19; participation and opportunity
according to gender 59; process of
financial cooperation and integration
in 116–18; response to private sector
policy involvement 86; signatory to UN

Women's Empowerment Principles 65;
significance of Myanmar for business
and investment 168; *see also* specific
projects of *e.g.* Xayaburi dam
trade *see* business and businesses
tradition: impact on Indonesian
business 32–3
transnational human rights litigation
(THRL): case study of in Koh
Kong province 156–7; significance
for corporate responsibility 134–6;
significance of usage in
ASEAN 134–8

UN Framework for Business and Human
Rights 227, 233, 237, 258, 263
UN Global Compact 14, 20, 22, 27, 51,
65–6, 79, 95, 123–4, 129, 131, 132, 213,
220, 222
UN Principles for Responsible Investment
124, 126, 210, 211, 213, 215
Universal Declaration on Human Rights
(UN) 13, 61

Vietnam: changes, challenges and
obligations for mining industries 144,
152–6; environmental and social
implications of Xayaburi dam 99,
100–1, 102–3; investigation on impact
of Mekong River dams 104, 105; land
ownership structures 60; participation
and opportunity according to gender
58, 59; role of global compact local
networks 20–1
violence, gender-based: essentiality of
business to remedy 74–5

workers *see* employment and workers

Xayaburi dam: impact of Thai bank
decision to finance 100–3; regional
and local concerns about issue of
104–6; responsibility of Thai banks
for financing 110–12; *see also* factors
affecting *e.g.* environment; society

youth: use of MIHRSC to audit use as
labour 198
Youth 21 Agenda 81